Springer Series: *FOCUS ON WOMEN*

Violet Franks, Ph.D., Series Editor

Confronting the major psychological, medical, and social issues of today and tomorrow. *Focus on Women* provides a wide range of books on the changing concerns of women.

Ruth Formanek, Ph.D., is Professor of Education at Hofstra University, Chief Psychologist at Jewish Community Services of Long Island, Adjunct Clinical Associate Professor and Supervisor at Adelphi University Post-Doctoral Program in Child and Adolescent Psychotherapy, and a therapist in private practice. She has published many articles and books and is presently writing a book on the menopause. She was the first President of the Section on Women and Psychoanalysis of APA Division 39. Dr. Formanek received her Masters Degree from City University of New York, her Doctoral Degree from University of Vienna, and her Post-Doctoral Certification in Psychoanalysis from Adelphi University.

Anita Gurian, Ph.D., is Coordinator of the Child Development/Learning Diagnostic Program at Schneider Children's Hospital of the Long Island Jewish Medical Center, Adjunct Associate Professor at Hofstra University and in private practice. She has produced films on child development and has authored several books for parents. In addition, she has conducted numerous workshops on parent and child relationships. Dr. Gurian received Masters Degrees from Adelphi University and St. John's University and her Doctoral Degree from Hofstra University.

Women and Depression
A Lifespan Perspective

Ruth Formanek, Ph.D.
Anita Gurian, Ph.D.

Editors

Springer Publishing Company
New York

Springer Publishing Company, Inc.
536 Broadway
New York, NY 10012

87 88 89 90 91 / 5 4 3 2 1

Library of Congress Cataloging-in-Publication Data

Women and depression.

    (Springer series, focus on women; v. 11)
    Bibliography: p.
    Includes index.
    1. Depression, Mental.   2. Women—Mental health.
I. Formanek, Ruth.   II. Gurian, Anita.   III. Series.
RC537.W66   1987   616.85′27′088042   87-16684
ISBN 0-8261-5140-X

Printed in the United States of America

Contents

■   **TWO**
Depression in Childhood and Adolescence

■   **THREE**
Depression in Adult Women

■ **FOUR**
Depression and the Aging Woman

Contributors

Jan Charone-Sossin, Ph.D., private practice, New Hyde Park, New York

Barbara Fibel Marcus, Ph.D., Assistant Professor of Psychology and Psychiatry, Cornell University Medical College; Assistant Attending Psychologist, New York Hospital, Cornell Medical Center, Westchester Division

Suzette Finkelstein, Ph.D., Adjunct faculty, Case Western Reserve University School of Medicine; Consultant, Jewish Family Association, private practice; Cleveland, Ohio

Ruth Formanek, Ph.D., Professor of Education, Hofstra University; Chief Psychologist, Jewish Community Services of Long Island; Adjunct Clinical Associate Professor and Supervisor, Adelphi University Postdoctoral Program in Child and Adolescent Psychotherapy

Lisa Greenberg, Ph.D., Senior Psychologist, Psychological Services, Fairleigh Dickinson University, private practice; Hackensack, New Jersey

Anita Gurian, Ph.D., Coordinator and Senior Psychologist, Child Development/Learning Diagnostic Center, Schneider Children's Hospital, Long Island Jewish Medical Center, New Hyde Park, New York

Helena Harris, Ph.D., Adjunct Associate Professor, Columbia University; private practice; New York

Dana Jack, Ed.D., M.S.W., Fairhaven College, Western Washington University, Bellingham, Washington

Susan Joseph, Ph.D., Training Director, Atlanta Center for Cognitive Therapy; private practice, Atlanta, Georgia

Gerald Klerman, M.D., Professor of Psychiatry, Harvard University Medical School; Director, Stanley Cobb Research Laboratories, Department of Psychiatry, Massachusetts General Hospital, Boston, Massachusetts

Cheryl Kurash, Ph.D., Coordinator of Training, University Counseling Center, State University of New York at Stony Brook

Harriet Goldhor Lerner, Ph.D., Staff Psychologist, The Menninger Foundation, Topeka, Kansas

Helen Block Lewis, Ph.D., °Professor Emerita, Yale University, New Haven, Connecticut

Marilyn Maxwell, M.A., Hewlett Schools, Hewlett, New York

Randy Milden, Ph.D., Assistant Professor, Dept. of Psychiatry and Reproductive Biology, Case Western Reserve University School of Medicine, Cleveland, Ohio

Ruth Nemtzow, C.S.W., Jewish Community Services of Long Island

Charles Neuringer, Ph.D., University of Kansas

Jonathan F. Schaul, Department of Family Medicine, Southside Hospital; State University of New York at Stony Brook

K. Mark Sossin, Ph.D., Supervising and Research Psychologist, Center for Parents and Children, Child Development Research, Sands Point, New York; private practice

Myrna M. Weissman, Ph.D., Professor of Psychiatry and Epidemiology, Department of Psychiatry, Depression Research Unit, Yale University School of Medicine, New Haven, Connecticut

°deceased, January 1987

Acknowledgments

This book grew out of our conviction that depression is a major mental health problem at this time, not only for women, but for children and families as well. We are grateful to patients, students, friends, and relatives who shared their experiences with us. We express our gratitude to our editor, Barbara Watkins, for her supportive and astute critical assistance. In addition, we thank those who critically read our manuscripts: Elsa Blum, Claude Brunell, Miriam Formanek-Brunell, Jean Franco, Irene Hassett, Helen Silver, and Carol Smith. Special thanks are due as always to Bernard Gurian. Margot and Athan Karras gave us the benefit of their special knowledge of the relevant literature as well as their editorial expertise. A Hofstra University Faculty Development Grant aided Ruth Formanek in the preparation of her chapters. The librarians at Hillside Hospital, Long Island Jewish Medical Center, and Hofstra University were, as usual, indefatigable in their efforts. We are indebted to Irene McQuillan, who patiently and efficiently typed neat copies of our chaotic notes.

A few days after we received Helen Block Lewis's final draft of her chapter, we learned that she was very ill. She died shortly thereafter. Helen was a good friend, a valued colleague, thoroughly committed to the cause of women and their need for egalitarian treatment—in psychotherapy as well as in society. Our present understanding of the role of shame and guilt in the development of the individual and its relation to gender differences is due primarily to her work.

Introduction

Sad mood and depressed feelings have been part of the human condition in all cultures and all periods of history, although descriptions and conceptualizations have varied with time and place. As we use the term "depression" in this volume, it encompasses the many varieties of mood on a continuum from feeling blue at one extreme, to being overwhelmed and suffering from hopelessness, helplessness, feelings of guilt, self-recrimination, and low self-esteem, at the other. Whether or not there is a unitary dimension to such affective states is currently uncertain.

Researchers have categorized depression in a number of ways—according to cause, symptom, severity, chronicity, risk factors, time of onset, and others. In this book we explore, without such categorization, the relationship between depression and gender at different stages of the lifespan. We hope that this emphasis on the interaction between gender and depression will add to our knowledge and raise some questions as to the reasons for the preponderance of depressed women as compared to depressed men.

We focus on the complexities of psychological, socioeconomic and cultural factors influencing women's lives—their social and occupational roles, their interpersonal relationships, their physiological functioning. We examine societal perceptions of women as well as women's perceptions of their own lives. In particular, we call attention to the ways in which socialization practices heighten women's vulnerability to depression. We have not emphasized physiological, neurochemical, and hereditary factors, undoubtedly all capable of contributing to depression. While insufficient empirical verification exists at this time, it is unlikely that depression will ever be found to be due solely to one factor. Rather, we view each individual depression as multiply caused and comprehensible only through exploration of a woman's life history.

While an individual woman's depression is best viewed in the context of her life history, the development of depression as a concept can only be studied as part of social history as highlighted in the following account. Although the history of depression has been documented by Jackson (1986), a historical account of its pertinence to women has yet to be written.

Depression was known in antiquity as "melancholia." The ancient Greeks believed melancholia was due to a defilement of the blood with gall, bile, and slime. It was viewed as a chronic form of madness affecting men and women alike; they became sad, misanthropic, tired of life, and sometimes subject to delusions and gastrointestinal symptoms. Aristotle, alluding to cyclothymic disorders, believed that black bile, which is cold by nature, can produce paralysis, depression, or anxiety states. However, when warmed, the black bile could evoke gaiety, singing and ecstasy. The suspicion of a relationship between depression and physiological functioning continues in present-day psychiatry, although gall, bile, and slime have now been ruled out in favor of neurotransmitters.

In the second century A.D., the church used the term "acedia" to designate undesirable feelings and behavior, including sorrow, dejection, and despair. With the rediscovery of Aristotelian thought during the Renaissance, sorrow–dejection–despair became associated with classical notions of melancholia.

Depression was tied to being female by Burton (1621) who also speculated on the influence of poverty and loneliness on depression: "These infirmities are generally most eminent in old women and in such as are poor and solitary." Moreover, he stated that "melancholia gives old women the extraordinary powers of witches, such as riding in the air, flying out of the chimney top, transforming themselves into cats and other animals, meeting on the heath, etc."

Underlying such pejorative perceptions of women as not only depressed but as malevolent and insane are ancient fears of menstruation. It was believed that menstrual blood predisposed women to insanity, in that an abnormality of the flow might affect the brain. During the nineteenth century, "suppressed" menstruation was greatly feared, and it was believed that in many women, the menopause would be accompanied by "involutional melancholia."

In contrast to outdated medical and popular expectations that women's depressions were linked to their physiological functioning, historians have delineated the contributions of social-historical factors. Smith-Rosenberg (1985) has described one contribution—conflicts in role expectations. Nineteenth-century America valued the "True Woman," which mandated girls to be socialized as emotional, dependent, and gentle—followers rather than leaders. However, the "Ideal Mother," another valued nineteenth-century model, was expected to be strong, self-reliant, efficient—the manager of her family. The discontinuity between the socialization for the True Woman and the demands of the Ideal Mother may have caused many young women conflict and uneasiness when they confronted their role change with marriage and the birth of children. Such role changes may have been a time of crisis for women who were ill-equipped to cope with either major changes or adversity and who may have become depressed.

In recent years, epidemiologists have identified social origins of depression in women. British researchers Brown and Harris (1978) found that the combination of low socioeconomic status, the presence in the home of three or more children under 14 years of age, the lack of a supportive, confiding relationship with a partner, the loss of the mother before age 11, and/or the lack of a job all increase the likelihood of a woman becoming depressed.

In this book we view women's depressions in a lifespan perspective. While some accounts of lifespan development have been based solely on the experience of men and extended to include women, the following account is gender-neutral.

Three sets of factors influence development (Baltes, Reese & Lipsitt, 1980): (1) factors that are similar for most people of a given culture, such as health, family life, education and occupation; (2) factors specific for a given time period, such as epidemics, wars, political or economic upheavals; and (3) life events that exert a major influence, such as accidents, divorce, unemployment, illness, or the death of significant others. For women, life events also include pregnancy, childbirth, etc. The joint impact of these three sets of factors on the individual represents "lifespan development" and accounts for both similarities and differences between the sexes and among individuals.

The manifestations of depression furthermore vary with culture, are expressed in somatic symptoms in some cultures, in psychological ones in others, and even lack recognition as a disorder in others.

Overview of Chapter Contents

Our book begins with an orientation by Weissman and Klerman who provide an orientation to the problem of depression among women, summarizing data from different fields. Evidence from epidemiologic, family, and clinical studies shows that the rates of major depression are about two-fold higher among women than men, although no gender differences exist in bipolar depression. Many explanations—artifactual, psychosocial, genetic, endocrine—have been offered to account for these findings, and each is discussed by the authors. The evidence suggests that the prevalence findings are not due to an artifactual difference, but that gender differences in reporting or seeking help are real. There are no definitive psychosocial explanations. At least two studies suggest that genetic transmission *per se* cannot account for the sex difference. Weissman and Klerman conclude that it is highly unlikely that any one explanation will solely account for the prevalence of depression among women or that all types of depression will be associated with the same risk factors.

While this book as a whole follows the course of depression in women from infancy to old age, individual chapters use the lifespan perspective to a greater or lesser extent. Some chapters carve out a time-limited era, such as childhood or the postpartum period, while others examine a particular issue across a larger span, such as suicide, shame, or vulnerability to loss.

Part I presents four contributions representing major theoretical frameworks: classical psychoanalysis and self-psychology (Harris); object relations (Fibel Marcus); self-in-relation theory (Jack), and cognitive theory (Joseph). Although theories of depression in the past have not specifically addressed issues of gender, each author discusses those aspects of theory that contribute to the ways in which depression among women may be conceptualized.

Modern theorizing about depression began with Freud's *Mourning and Melancholia*. Harris, in Chapter 1, surveys his work as well as that of subsequent psychoanalytic theorists. While theorists in classical psychoanalytic or self-psychological frameworks omit gender distinctions in regard to depression, some psychoanalytic developmentalists have maintained, with Freud, that the young girl grows up with a sense of anatomical inferiority, predisposing her to depressive feelings.

In Chapter 2, Fibel Marcus discusses object loss as precipitating depression and emphasizes the significance of internalized object relations. She distinguishes two types of depressions ("anaclitic" and "introjective") and their relevance to women. The preponderance of women among "anaclitic" depressives may be a consequence of their prolonged attachment phase and their less decisive separation from their mothers. However, girls who separate early, as boys do, may then suffer a more fragile sense of self and guilt deriving from aggression inherent in separations. Thus, some women may also become vulnerable to "introjective" types of depression. In short, women are in double jeopardy.

Jack (Chapter 3) also focuses on the importance of object loss in depression. She bases her account on self-in-relation theory, which stresses social intimacy as the organizer of female experience. It is not essential to separate from others in order to develop one's self, as some theorists have held in the past, and "dependency" need not be equated with immaturity and neurosis. On the contrary, self-in-relation theory views women's development within a social context, in which relationships are essential to their sense of well-being.

Joseph, in Chapter 4, summarizes Beck's cognitive theory, with its emphasis on a distortion of thought process and content, a dysfunctional processing of information leading to negative evaluations of the self, the world, and the future. She examines gender-related differences in cognitive processing, which may lead to an increase in negative cognitions among women. Beck differentiates between personality modes that may have gender implications: the active/autonomous personality mode, typical of males, is characterized by *doing* and the passive/socially dependent personality mode, typical of females, is characterized by *receiving*. Being passive and receiving suggests a proneness to depression.

Some of the other chapters in this book represent different theoretical formulations. In addition to dynamic psychoanalysis, object relations, cognitive, and self-in-relation theory, some authors have included systems theory, sociocultural or sociohistorical approaches. Thus, the various chapters reflect important contemporary approaches to the study of women's depression. Moreover, many authors have collected empirical evidence in efforts to validate particular theories.

The chapters in Parts II through IV, as they follow the lifespan, make explicit the ideas underlying present-day conceptualizations, research, and treatment of depression.

Chapter 5 begins the developmental sequence. Gurian examines depression among girls in the early and middle childhood years, focusing on prevalence studies; theories of childhood depression; family, school, and other socialization influences, as well as manifestations of depression at different developmental stages. Although it has been assumed that adolescence is the turning point at which girl depressives outnumber boy depressives, precursors may be identified at earlier ages. Gurian raises questions about future prevalence rates of depression in infants and young girls who are likely to be affected by maternal depression, which is affecting women at increasingly younger ages, i.e., during their childbearing years.

Kurash and Schaul, in Chapter 6, combine an object relations and systems perspective in their exploration of depression among adolescent girls. They examine the particular stresses of adolescence and manifestations of depression in relation to the individual's defensive repertoire and internalized object representations. Female adolescent depression is viewed as an interactive process that is invariably linked to the girl's relationships with her parents and the culture within which she is maturing. The parent's, particularly the mother's, own degree of individuation is a critical variable. The degree to which the mother has come to terms with her own adolescence, and is capable of separating her needs from her daughter's and can tolerate and respect differences, affects her daughter's ability to establish a mature, affirmative, and cohesive identity without undue depression. Both parents and daughter undergo a fundamental reorganization of self and object representations that corresponds more accurately to the adolescent's new level of development, cognitive capacities, identity, and relational capabilities.

Eating disorders, increasingly common in adolescent girls and young adult women, are discussed in Chapter 7 by Finkelstein, who asks: Why women? And why now? Finkelstein summarizes epidemiological and historical aspects, the clinical features of anorexia and bulimia, the characteristics of women with eating disorders, family patterns, and some of the explanatory theories as they relate to depression. She discusses biochemical, family dynamics, psychodynamics, social psychological, and sociocultural models. Women who develop anorexia and/or bulimia are those in whom developmental deficits and intrapsychic conflicts are particularly troubling. It is these young women who face the greatest difficulties posed by their coming into womanhood at this particular time and place.

Part III examines depression and adult women. In Chapter 8, Milden discusses those disturbances of mood, such as premenstrual syndrome, which in the past have been labeled "endogenous" depressions and in which a biological basis has been suspected. She comments on the dramatic gains of biological psychiatry in treating such depressions, but raises questions as to its efficacy in treatment of the nonendogenous depressed patient. Milden comments on how psychobiological perspectives on depressive illness affect a patient's sense of herself and suggests that the meaning of the biologically defined disease becomes interwoven with the meaning of being female.

Chapter 9 (by Nemtzow) and 10 (by Charone-Sossin and Sossin), explore depressions occurring after childbirth. Nemtzow led New Mothers Groups, in which significant numbers of women reported anxiety states, role conflict, and mild to moderate depressed mood, suggestive of postpartum depression. She discusses the range of depressive states developing after childbirth and their potential effects on mother, child, and family functioning. Major psychosocial stressors are associated with postpartum depression and interact with individual personality styles, interpersonal relationships, and stressful life events.

Charone-Sossin and Sossin discuss depression reactive to the birth of an impaired child and its effect on the earliest relationship between mother and infant. Parents of impaired infants mourn the loss of the wished-for child while simultaneously adapting to a love relationship with the impaired child. Such parents cannot merely mourn but will experience depression, since the self is entwined with the ideal object representation of the child that is experienced as lost. The authors discuss the role played by depression and denial in facilitating the mother's attunement to her child, underscoring the importance of recognizing that a protracted state of depression, in the face of the grim reality of an impaired infant, may be a necessary, albeit high-risk, period of accommodation to the child.

In Chapter 11, Jack explores how cultural forces interact with women's adult development and their experience of self to create a vulnerability to depression. Jack's findings from an in-depth longitudinal study of twelve clinically depressed women provide the basis for her observations. Her theoretical framework is that of "self-in-relation," i.e., a woman's self is organized and developed through practice in close relationships rather than by means of goals focusing on separation and autonomy. Such relationships, and their inner representations, are essential for a woman's sense of well-being. Depression, according to Jack, reveals the vulnerabilities of a relational sense of self within a culture that values individual achievements and places little value on relationships.

Lewis, in Chapter 12, discusses the role of shame in women's depression. Attention to the existence of shame, beginning with childhood, helps us to understand why adult women are more prone to depression than men. Lewis describes the phenomenology of shame, distinguishes it from guilt, and summarizes empirical studies on shame. Traditionally androcentric and pejorative attitudes toward attachment and shame are still found among psychotherapists almost 100 years after Freud treated Dora. In his formulations of that case, Freud neglected to recognize Dora's shame, which had derived from both sexual abuse and a sense of personal betrayal which resulted in the failed analysis.

In Chapter 13, Lerner discusses self-sacrifice and self-betrayal in women's relationships to men. She addresses women's depression as it relates to a particular aspect of loss that occurs as women betray or sacrifice the self in order to preserve harmony in a relationship. In a case excerpt, Lerner demonstrates how female depression is inextricably interwoven with the sacrifice of self to relationship as a consequence of the fear of object loss. The culture has mandated that men are the makers and shapers of culture in the world outside the home, and women are not free to define the terms of their own lives. Thus, it must be recognized that individual and family dysfunction are inseparable from the dysfunction caused by patriarchal culture.

Maxwell, in Chapter 14, elaborates on the influence of culture by drawing on portrayals of depressed women in two novels and one play. Her analyses suggest that, despite their different historical contexts, socio-economic levels, and ages, the three protagonists face the same fundamental conflicts inherent in being female in a patriarchal environment. Each woman, states Maxwell, is shown as living in a society that marshals institutions that socialize women into conforming to the feminine stereotype of dependency, submissiveness, passivity, and silence.

Neuringer, in Chapter 15, reviews the empirical literature on suicide in women. Even though fewer women than men commit suicide, the prevalence of other types of self-destructive behavior is disturbingly high. Suicidal women are found to differ from suicidal men in "dichotomous thinking," a tendency toward organizing their value systems in bipolar opposites. People, activities, and ideas are viewed as either "very good" or "very bad" with little moderation between these two poles. Thus, women, and some men, who think dichotomously demand perfection from themselves and others, have inordinately high levels of aspiration, and respond to disappointment with a sense of complete failure. Such thinking jeopardizes one's capacity to live in the world where compromises and the acceptance of alternatives are essential. In suicidal women, dichotomous thinking combines with intense negative emotions and orientations toward others. The suicidal woman is caught in a negative affect web in which relief is never experienced.

The three chapters in Part IV examine depression in older women. Formanek, in Chapter 16, discusses the socially constructed link between menopause and depression. She examines the historical forging of this link, which held that women were vulnerable to "involutional melancholia," or a first-onset depression concomitant with menopause. Early medical, and later psychoanalytical views, clinical and population surveys, and historical and cross-cultural differences in attitudes toward the menopause are surveyed. Pejorative attitudes toward the menopause throughout the nineteenth and part of the twentieth century were consistent with negative views of women's functioning in general, instilling fears of insanity or depression in women approaching this normal developmental phase.

In Chapter 17, Formanek discusses depression and the older woman. She compares older women to other groups, such as older men and younger women, in regard to the prevalence of depression and discusses the effects of retirement and widowhood. Investigators have maintained their distance from older people in general, and studies usually focus on concrete and superficial issues, such as income, number of relatives or friends visited, marital status, etc. Internal, psychological states have been neglected. To fully understand gender differences in depression, socio-cultural attitudes toward aging and women's self-perceptions, as shaped by a socialization to be maternal and intimate, must be explored. On the other hand, women's zest and ascendancy with age, noted cross-culturally, militate against a first-onset depression late in life.

Greenberg, in Chapter 18 reports the results of a retrospective investigation on the subjective experiences of older women. She contrasts one group of women who retired from a job with women who spent their adult lives as homemakers. What contributes to a sense of contentment, rather than depression, in Greenberg's sample of women in their seventies, was the transition in focus from external sources of gratification to an increase in amount of gratification derived from themselves. Greenberg explores individual differences. Although most subjects reported themselves as equally satisfied throughout their lives, they now viewed themselves as less active, less powerful, and less good than at earlier ages. Retired women were somewhat more satisfied than homemakers. Greenberg concludes that the determinants of genuine life satisfaction include the valuing of one's own choices. These are not to be found in one's environment, but are internal.

REFERENCES

Baltes, P.B., Reese, H.W., & Lipsitt, L.P. (1980). *Annual review of psychology*. Palo Alto, CA: Annual Reviews, Inc.

Brown, G., & Harris, T. (1978). *The social origins of depression: a study of psychiatric disorders in women*. London: Tavistock Publications

Burton, R. (1801). *Melancholy, as it proceeds from the disposition and habit, the passion of love and the influence of religion*. London: Vernor and Hood

Jackson, S.W. (1986). *Melancholia and depression*. New Haven: Yale University Press.

Jackson, S.W. (1985). Acedia the sin and its relationship to sorrow and melancholia. In A. Kleinman and B. Good (Eds.), *Culture and depression*. Beverly Hills, CA: University of California Press.

Smith-Rosenberg, C. (1985). *Disorderly conduct*. New York: Oxford University Press.

Sontag, S. (1972). The double standard of aging. *Saturday Review of Literature, 54*, (September 23), 29–38.

ORIENTATION

Gender and Depression

**MYRNA M. WEISSMAN, Ph.D. and
GERALD L. KLERMAN, M.D.**

Epidemiologic and clinical studies of affective disorders have found that the rates of depression are higher in women than men (Weissman & Klerman, 1977). A sex difference in the frequency of any disease is an epidemiologic finding that attracts attention and stimulates explanations. Recent investigations suggest that the finding is true for some, but not all, types of affective disorders. Moreover, there is evidence that rules out some explanations for the sex difference.

AFFECTIVE DISORDERS

Affective disorders are a group of psychiatric conditions in which the disturbance of mood predominates. While there is disagreement over which affects to include and how much significance should be attached to symptom patterns, precipitants, severity, or chronology with other disorders, there is consensus that clinical states of depression and elation constitute the major affective disorders.

Over the last decade there has been improvement in research on specification of diagnostic criteria with the resultant increase in the

This research was supported in part by Alcohol, Drug Abuse and Mental Health Administration grant #MH7607624-5 from the National Institute of Mental Health (NIMH) Clinical Research Branch (CRB) Collaborative Program on the Psychobiology of Depression, Department of Health and Human Services, Washington D.C. and by the Network on Risk and Protective Factors in the Major Mental Disorders, funded by the John D. and Catherine T. MacArthur Foundation. Appreciation is also expressed to the George Harrington Trust, Boston, Massachusetts for support of Dr. Klerman and the George Harrington Program.

reliability of psychiatric diagnoses. This research culminated in the publication in 1980 of the American Psychiatric Association's *Diagnostic and Statistical Manual of Mental Disorders* (DSM-III) (1980). The DSM-III built on a decade of research in psychopathology. Diagnostic reliability was improved by specifying symptom, duration, and exclusion criteria for psychiatric diagnoses and by developing methods for systematically collecting this information required to make a diagnosis. These new diagnostic methods have been incorporated into research conducted on psychiatric disorders and on the problem of sex differences in depression.

The DSM-III has several categories of affective disorders, but the Major Affective Disorders include major depression and bipolar disorder (i.e., major depression plus mania occurring at some time in the person's life). Most of the relevant research on sex differences has been conducted on these two disorders. Because of the recency of publication of the DSM-III, many of the studies examining sex differences in depression had been based on the use of older diagnostic schemes. In this review, where possible, the available data have been reinterpreted in light of the DSM-III classification.

SEX DIFFERENCES IN RATES OF DEPRESSION

In 1977, prior to the publication of the DSM-III, we reviewed the evidence for the predominance of females among depressives (Weissman & Klerman, 1977). Forty studies from 30 countries found few exceptions to the predominance of women, with a two- to threefold increase in the rates of depression.

In 1981, the studies of depression were reassessed and the DSM-III criteria of affective disorder were applied to studies using other diagnostic systems (Boyd & Weissman, 1981). It was possible to reorder the data using the DSM-III criteria, particularly separating bipolar from other affective disorder. This diagnostic separation provided new insights into the sex ratios in types of depression. The sex ratios of bipolar disorder, a disorder that is relatively less common, were about equal. The rates in those depressions that were not bipolar (it was not always possible to determine if they also met criteria for DSM-III major depression) were considerably higher in women than in men.

NEW EVIDENCE ON SEX RATIOS

Since 1981, there have been several large epidemiologic and family studies conducted in the United States that have applied the DSM-III diagnostic classifications, or their equivalents, and that confirm most of the earlier findings. Included are the Epidemiologic Catchment Area Study (ECA), which surveyed over 15,000 subjects selected from probability samples of five urban areas in the United States (Myers, Weissman, Tischler, Holzer, Leaf, Orvaschel, Anthony, Boyd, Burke, Kramer, & Stoltzman, 1984; Robins, Helzer, Weissman, Orvaschel, Gruenberg, Burke, & Regier, 1984), and three large family studies of the first-degree relatives of patients with affective disorders. The family studies include (1) the National Institute of Mental Health (NIMH) Collaborative Program on the Psychobiology of Depression, involving 2,400 first-degree relatives of over 600 probands with affective disorders from five University Centers in the United States (Rice, Reich, Andreasen, Lavori, Endicott, Clayton, Keller, Hirschfield, & Klerman, 1984); (2) the Yale–NIMH Collaborative Family Study of the relatives of affectively ill probands involving over 2,000 first-degree relatives of probands with bipolar and major depression from two centers in the United States (Weissman, Gershon, Kidd, Prusoff, Leckman, Dibble, Hamovit, Thompson, Pauls, & Guroff, 1984); and (3) the Iowa 500 Study involving over 3,000 first-degree relatives of approximately 400 psychiatrically ill probands (Winokur, Tsuang, & Crowe, 1982).

These studies, comprising combined samples of more than 20,000 persons from different parts of the United States, report identical findings: increased rates of major depression in women and equal sex ratios for bipolar disorder.

The ECA is the most informative study, as its data are obtained from probability samples of different United States communities in independently conducted surveys using similar diagnostic methodology. Family studies of depressives, while useful for determining sex differences, report overall higher rates of disorders than community surveys because of the familial aggregation of depression.

Figures 1 and 2 show the nearly twofold increase in females over males in six-month prevalence rates for major depression in three of the five ECA sites from which data are currently available, and the equal sex ratios for six-month prevalence rates/100 for bipolar disorder. The similarity in sex ratios for all three sites is striking. These findings support the importance of separating bipolar disorder from major depression; these two disorders have different prevalence rates and epidemiology.

Similar findings for major depression were reported in 1982 by Hagnell, Lanke, Rorsman, and Ojesjo from a cohort of inhabitants of Lundby, Sweden, studied since 1947 and followed up between 1957 and 1972. Even though the Lundby study used different diagnostic methods from those in the United States studies, it was possible to reevaluate their findings using DSM-III criteria for major depression.

The Lundby study, as one of the few longitudinal studies, provided a

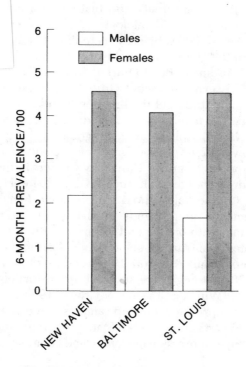

FIGURE 1. Major Depression: DSM III.
Data derived from Myers et al. (1984).

more complete picture of secular changes. The results of this follow-up study suggest that the rates in younger men may be increasing and that the sex differences in rates may be diminishing. However, at all time periods, the rates were higher for women than for men.

POSSIBLE EXPLANATIONS FOR THE SEX DIFFERENCES IN RATES OF DEPRESSION

On the basis of available evidence, it can be concluded that the sex differences are real and not an artifact. A number of possible explanations for the differences in sex ratios have been proposed, as outlined in Table 1 and as previously discussed in detail (Weissman & Klerman, 1977).

Women and men have different help-seeking patterns. However, increased female utilization of health care could not account for the preponderance of depressed women in community surveys, since most survey "cases" were not in psychiatric treatment either at the time of the inter-

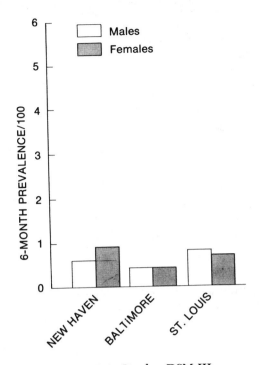

FIGURE 2. Bipolar: DSM III.
Data derived from Myers et al. (1984).

view or in the past. Epidemiologic studies have not found that women have more stressful life events or that they judge life events as more stressful. Although women reported the presence of symptoms and affective distress more frequently than men, this did not seem to be because they felt less stigma or because they wished to win approval.

More males than females have alcohol abuse problems, so that some unknown proportion of depressed men are not identified as depressed and appear in the alcoholism rates. Moreover, recent studies of familial transmission (Merikangas, Weissman, & Pauls, 1985) show that while depression and alcohol may occur together in individuals, familially they are independent disorders. Alcoholism in males is not the equivalent of depression in females.

Similar considerations apply to the possibility that the depressed men are to be found in the law enforcement system. Pending future research to test this possibility, it remains an interesting, but unproved, hypothesis that alcoholism and antisocial behavior are the equivalents of depression in men. Taking into account these alternative explanations, we conclude that

TABLE 1 Explanations for the Increased Rates of Depression in Women

A. *Artifact*

    Differences in reporting stress and distress
- Women are under more stress
- Women weigh events as more stressful
- Women are more willing to acknowledge symptoms
- Women seek help more often

    Men use more alcohol

    Men are more often into legal difficulties

B. *Real*

    Psychosocial
- Disadvantage of women's social status
- Learned helplessness
- Demographic changes

    Genetic Transmission

    Female endocrine physiology

---

the female preponderance is not an artifact. Possible explanations for the real differences include psychosocial, demographic, genetic, or endocrine explanations.

Psychosocial Explanations

Until recently, psychosocial explanations for the sex differences have received the most attention. The conventional wisdom is that the long-standing disadvantaged social status of women has psychological consequences that are depressing, and the historical persistence of these social status discriminations is proposed to explain the female predominance in depression.

Two main hypotheses have been proposed specifying the pathways whereby women's disadvantaged status might contribute to clinical depression.

The *social status hypothesis* is widely proposed in the recent discussions on social discrimination against women. Presumably, women find their situation depressing since the real social discriminations make it difficult for them to achieve mastery by direct action and self-assertion. It is hypothesized that these inequities lead to legal and economic helplessness, dependency on others, chronically low self-esteem, low aspirations, and, ultimately, clinical depression.

The *learned helplessness hypothesis* proposes that socially conditioned, stereotypical images of men and women produce in women a cognitive set against assertion and independence, which is reinforced by societal expectations. In this hypothesis, the classic femininity values are redefined as a variant of learned helplessness, characteristic of depression.

The most interesting evidence supporting the hypothesis that social role plays an important role in the vulnerability of women to depression had been the previous reports suggesting that marriage has a protective effect for men but a detrimental effect for women. This finding was used to support the hypothesis that elements of the traditional female role may contribute to higher rates of depression among women. However, recent epidemiologic studies using DSM-III criteria did not support this hypothesis. Marriage is protective against major depression in both sexes.

Understanding of social stress and its interactions with the traditional female role remains an area of research that would need to take into account intervening variables such as women's employment, the quality of the marriage, and recent demographic changes.

Demographic Explanations: Birth Cohort Trends

Recent demographic research has identified a number of changes in the population since 1900 that may have differential impact on men and women and that may have psychiatric consequences.

In the society at large, there has been an overall increase in population, increased longevity—especially for females—and increased urbanization. Although the sex ratio at birth has not changed, the ratio of males to females in the adult population has fluctuated with an excess of women in recent decades (Guttentag & Second, 1983).

Recent decades have also witnessed increased numbers of women entering the labor force. The consequences of the baby boom involve delay of entrance into labor force and later age of marriage for both sexes and decreased fertility (Easterlin, 1980). The psychiatric significance of these changes is suggested by recent increases in rates of suicide death and suicide attempts and sharp increases in alcohol and drug abuse problems.

The possible importance of these demographic forces is highlighted by new evidence for birth cohort trends in depression. A number of investigators have observed indications of increase in rates of depression since World War II, particularly among young females (Hagnell et al., 1982; Klerman, 1976; Klerman, 1978; Klerman, 1979; Klerman, Lavori, Rice, Reich, Endicott, Andreasen, Keller, & Hirschfield, 1985; Weissman, Leaf, Holzer, Myers, & Tischler, 1984).

Verification of these hypotheses is now possible because of the existence of large data sets on population samples and from family studies. Application of newer diagnostic methods and of multivariate statistics has provided evidence of increased rates of depression and earlier age of onset in birth cohorts born since 1950. In all birth cohorts, females predominate, although the magnitude of the male–female ratio does fluctuate over time.

The cohorts, both male and female, who came to maturity after World War II are experiencing increased rates of major depression and earlier onset. This pattern has been observed in an epidemiological survey conducted in 1975 in New Haven, Connecticut (Weissman & Myers, 1978), in the 1980 ECA study conducted independently in New Haven, St. Louis and Baltimore (Robins et al., 1984), and in a 25-year longitudinal survey from Lundby, Sweden (Hagnell et al., 1982).

The same patterns have been shown in two large family studies of the first-degree relatives of affectively ill probands (Klerman et al., 1985; Weissman et al., 1984), previously noted. The magnitude is greater among the relatives of patients with affective illness, consistent with previous findings of increased familial aggregation of depression.

These cohort trends suggest that there are environmental forces operating to increase the rates of depression. The environmental risk factors could be biological, or there could be factors that accelerate the age of onset of the disorder but do not change the overall incidence (i.e., vulnerable individuals are affected earlier, and the disorder is expressed in more of them). Alternatively, the effects may be only for certain, as yet unidentified, subgroups of major depression. These cohort trends need to be considered in future understanding of sex differences.

Familial Aggregation and Genetic Transmission

In support of genetic transmission as an explanation for the sex differences, there is reasonable evidence from twin and family studies that genetic factors are operating in the genesis of affective disorders. The specific mode of genetic inheritance is not established.

One possible genetic explanation is x-linkage; that is, the position of the relevant locus on the x chromosome. If the gene for depression is located in the x chromoxome and the trait is dominant, females, who have two x chromosomes, will be more often affected than males, who have only one x chromosome. If the trait is recessive, males will be more often affected than females. However, different types of depression (e.g., bipolars and unipolars) complicate the testing of the x-linkage hypothesis, and the results of family studies of affective disorders investigating x-linkage have been conflicting and inconclusive. Moreover, findings of progressive increases in the rate of depression, earlier age of onset, and shifts in the male–female ratio cannot be explained by a single-factor theory of genetic predisposition. The recent demonstration of birth-cohort trends (Klerman et al., 1985) does not rule out genetic contributions to the vulnerability of depression. But environmental factors often must operate to make manifest a genetic vulnerability, similar to that demonstrated for diabetes and other genetic disorders.

Another possible explanation of the different incidences in the two sexes is a differential interaction of genotype and environment depending on sex. It has been shown that a sex effect can be treated as a differential threshold, with the less commonly affected sex having a higher threshold (Weissman & Klerman, 1977). The underlying liability is determined by a combination of genetic and environmental factors. Two types of inheritance have been considered: a polygenic model and a single major autosomal locus. Many of the commonly observed aspects of the sex effect could be explained by these models.

In 1977, when the evidence was first reviewed, the samples studied were small, and family data on major depression were not available. The evidence from genetic studies, it was concluded, was insufficient to draw conclusions about the mode of transmission or to explain the sex differences.

Recently, several large family studies with samples of both bipolar and major depressive disorders, using modern diagnostic criteria, have been completed. These studies confirm the high familial aggregation of both bipolar and major depression in the first-degree relatives of bipolar probands and the high familial aggregation of major depression in the first-degree relatives of patients with major depression (Angst, Frey, Lohmeyer, & Zerbin-Rudin, 1980; Gershon, 1983; Rice et al., 1984; Weissman, Gershon et al., 1984; Winokur et al., 1982).

Possible genetic transmission as an explanation of the increased risk of major depression in women has been investigated by Merikangas et al., (1985). If the sex difference is related to the genetic transmission of a disorder, in family studies, relatives of the less prevalent sex of the proband will have higher rates of the disorder. Thus, if the sex difference in major depression were related to genetic factors, it would be expected that relatives of male probands would have higher rates of depression than relatives of female probands. This principle has been demonstrated for several other complex human disorders with a genetic component and an increased prevalence of one sex, such as stuttering and Tourette's syndrome (Merikangas, 1985).

If rates do not differ among relatives of male and female probands, one can conclude that the sex difference in prevalence of the trait is not due to genetic transmission of that trait. This explanation is true for the majority of multifactorial genetic models that have been applied to complex human disorders.

Examining data on over 1,000 first degree-relatives of 133 probands with major depression and 82 matched normal controls, Merikangas and associates (1985) found that the sex of the proband was not involved in the transmission of depression; relatives of male and female probands had equal rates of depression. The results suggested that the increased prevalence of depression in women cannot be attributed to genetic factors responsible for the transmission of depression. Sex of the proband was not associated with different risks for relatives.

The sex difference can therefore be attributed to nontransmissible factors. Major depression, however, is probably heterogeneous as to etiology. These results may not apply to all subtypes of the disorder. Furthermore, genetic factors may be involved in other factors (e.g., endocrine), which may be related to the penetrance of the disorder.

Rice et al. (1984) reached similar conclusions. In a study of 523 families of affectively ill probands, they found equal sex ratios of bipolar disorder in relatives and increased rates of major depression in females, which persisted when relatives were classified by a variety of subtypes of major depression. There was a maternal effect, which applied equally to both sisters and brothers of probands. These findings on sex differences are compatible with a cultural or a nongenetic biological mechanism in transmission. While the findings suggest that genetic factors cannot explain the preponderance of women in rates of depression, genetic factors are likely to be important in the transmission of some form of major depression for both sexes.

Endocrine Physiology

Interest in the possible relationship between female gender hormones and affective states derives from clinical observations that clinical depressions often occur in association with events in the female reproductive cycle, such as premenstrually, with the use of contraceptive drugs, in the postpartum period, and during the menopause.

The relationship of endocrine status to clinical states is inconsistent. In the 1977 review (Weissman & Klerman), there was good evidence that premenstrual tension and use of oral contraceptives may increase rates but that these effects were probably small. There was excellent evidence that the postpartum period did induce an increase in depression. Contrary to widely held views, there was good evidence that the menopause has no effect to increase rates of depression (Weissman, 1979).

There is little evidence to relate these mood changes and clinical states to altered endocrine balance or to specific hormones or their metabolites. No study has been reported that correlated clinical state with the female endocrine status, utilizing modern endocrinological methods or sensitive quantitative hormonal assays. While some portion of the sex differences in depression, probably during the childbearing years, may be explained endocrinologically, this factor did not seem sufficient to account for the large differences.

New endocrine data reviewed by Hamilton and Hirschfeld (1984) suggest that female endocrine physiology may be a fruitful area of research. Gonadal steroids have a profound effect on certain neurotransmitter-related enzymes and receptors in the brain, including receptors that are hypothesized to be the site of antidepressant drug action. Moreover, a sex-related difference in the behavioral effect of a monoamine oxidase inhibiting drug has been reported in animals. There may be sex–age (ovarian states) interactions in the time course on responsivity to antidepressants and in the side effects. Hamilton and Hirschfeld (1984) noted that these differences may be obscured in current research since biological studies of depression often do not include data by age and sex.

Since neuroendocrine and neurotransmitter systems change with age in both sexes, important information may be obscured unless sex distributions of the variable under study within each decade of life are presented.

In a small study of sex differences in response to clorgyline and *D*-amphetamine drugs known to predict antidepressant response, sex differences in self-perceptual processing were found, which could be linked to differences in encoding or consolidating information about experiences for late recall and could obscure neuroendocrine studies in humans (Hamilton & Hirschfeld, 1984).

The relation of endocrine physiological research to normal mood and clinical depressions remains a potentially fruitful area of investigation. No reported research has simultaneously applied newer diagnostic and clinical assessment methods and advanced biochemical and immunological assays of hormones to the same sample.

THE FUTURE

The evidence in support of the increased risk for major depression in women comes from studies of Western industrialized societies. Studies in non-Western countries, particularly in Africa and Asia, are necessary before any conclusions can be drawn as to the universality of this differential rate.

Future biological research on sex differences in depression needs to consider at least two phenomena: the birth cohort effect and the diagnostic heterogeneity of the affective disorders. The best evidence for heterogeneity is the separation of bipolar from major depressive disorder.

Moreover, the major depressions are also heterogeneous. The recent family studies suggest that the delusional, or psychotic form, of major depression, major depression with an onset earlier than age 30, or major depression with accompanying panic disorder are separate homogeneous subtypes of depression. These subtypes are associated with increased familial transmission and suggestion for specificity of transmission, although the evidence is still preliminary. Epidemiologic studies have not examined the sex ratios in these subtypes of major depression. While major depression and bipolar disorder are the two major affective disorders, there are more chronic forms, identified in the DSM-III as cyclothymia and dysthymia, which have been less intensely studied.

It is highly unlikely that any of the explanations already described will be the sole factor accounting for the phenomena, or that all types of depression will be associated with the same risk factors. The explanations cross such a wide variety of disciplines that rarely are all interactions entertained by any one group of investigators. There has been an unfortunate tendency for fragmentation, such that the investigators in genetics, demography, social psychology, or endocrinology are not specifically aware of attempts by their scientific colleagues to deal with similar phenomena. Nevertheless, there is little doubt that the sex differences found in depression are a promising lead that requires considerable broader-based inquiry.

REFERENCES

American Psychiatric Association (1980). *Diagnostic and Statistical Manual of Mental Disorders, Third Edition (DSM-III)*. Washington, DC: American Psychiatric Association.

Angst, J., Frey, K., Lohmeyer, B., & Zerbin-Rudin, E. (1980). Bipolar manic-depressive psychosis: Results of a genetic investigation. *Human Genetics, 55*, 237–254.

Boyd, J.H., & Weissman, M.M. (1981). Epidemiology of affective disorders: A re-examination and future direction. *Archives of General Psychiatry, 38*, 1039–1046.

Easterlin, R.A. (1980). *Birth and fortune*. New York: Basic Books.

Gershon, E.S. (1983). The genetics of affective disorders. In L. Grinspoon (Ed.), *Psychiatry update, Vol. 2*. Washington, DC: American Psychiatric Press, (pp. 434–456).

Guttentag, M., & Second, P.L. (1983). *Too many women?* Beverly Hills, CA: Sage Publications.

Hagnell, O., Lanke, J., Rorsman, B., & Ojesjo, L. (1982). Are we entering an age of melancholy? Depressive illnesses in a prospective epidemiological study over 25 years: The Lundby Study, Sweden. *Psychological Medicine, 12*, 279–289.

Hamilton, J.A., & Hirschfeld, R.M.A. (1984). Letter to the Editor: An additional recommendation on reporting depression. *American Journal of Psychiatry, 141*, 1134–1135.

Klerman, G.L. (1976). Age and clinical depression: Today's youth in the twenty-first century. *Journal of Gerontology, 31*, 318–323.

Klerman, G.L. (1979). The age of melancholy. *Psychology Today, 12*, 36–42.

Klerman, G.L., Lavori, P.W., Rice, J., Reich, T., Endicott, J., Andreasen, N.C., Keller, M.B., & Hirschfeld, R.M.A. (1985). Birth cohort trends in rates of major depressive disorder among relatives of patients with affective illness. *Archives of General Psychiatry, 421*, 689–693.

Merikangas, K.R., Weissman, M.M., & Pauls, D.L. (1985). Genetic factors in the sex ratio of major depression. *Psychological Medicine. 15*, 63–69.

Myers, J.K., Weissman, M.M., Tischler, G.L., Holzer, C.E., Leaf, P.J., Orvaschel, H., Anthony, J.C., Boyd, J.H., Burke, J.D., Kramer, M., & Stoltzman, R. (1984). Six-month prevalence of psychiatric disorders in three communities. *Archives of General Psychiatry, 41*, 959–970.

Rice, J., Reich, T., Andreasen, N.C., Lavori, P.W., Endicott, J., Clayton, P.J., Keller, M.B., Hirschfeld, R.M.A., & Klerman, G.L. (1984). Sex-related differences in depression: Familial evidence. *Journal of Affective Disorders, 7*, 199–210.

Robins, L.N., Helzer, J.E., Weissman, M.M., Orvaschel, H., Gruenberg, E., Burke, J.D., & Regier, D.A. (1984). Lifetime prevalence of specific psychiatric disorders in three sites. *Archives of General Psychiatry, 41*, 949–958.

Weissman, M.M. (1979). The myth of involutional melancholia. *Journal of the American Medical Association, 242*, 742–744.

Weissman, M.M., Gershon, E.S., Kidd, K.K., Prusoff, B.A., Leckman, J.F., Dibble, E., Hamovit, J., Thompson, W.D., Pauls, D.L., & Guroff, J.J. (1984). Psychiatric disorder in relatives of probands with affective disorders: The Yale-NIMH collaborative family study. *Archives of General Psychiatry, 41*, 13–21.

Weissman, M.M., & Klerman, G.L. (1977). Sex differences and the epidemiology of depression. *Archives of General Psychiatry, 34*, 98–111.

Weissman, M.M., & Myers, J.K. (1978). Affective disorders in a U.S. urban community. *Archives of General Psychiatry, 35*, 1304–1311.

Weissman, M.M., Leaf, P.J., Holzer, C.E., Myers, J.K., & Tischler, G.L. (1984). The epidemiology of depression: An update on sex differences in rates. *Journal of Affective Disorders, 7*, 179–188.

Winokur, G., Tsuang, M.T., & Crowe, R.R. (1982). The Iowa 500: Affective disorders in relatives of manic-depressed patients. *American Journal of Psychiatry, 139*, 209–212.

■ One
THEORETICAL FRAMEWORKS FOR DEPRESSION IN WOMEN

■ 1
Psychoanalytic Theory and Depression

HELENA HARRIS, Ph.D.

What does psychoanalytic theory indicate about gender in regard to depression among adults, either explicitly or implicitly?

In order to answer this question, a review of several theoretical models will be presented: the traditional psychoanalytic (Freudian); ego psychology; self psychology. The traditional psychoanalytic model includes a dynamic theory and a developmental theory, two approaches which will be contrasted. After a discussion of the theoretical explanations of depression by the leading writers in each group, we will return to the question of gender differences. The next chapter will deal with object relations theory and its contributions to the understanding of women's depression.

TRADITIONAL PSYCHOANALYTIC MODEL

The traditional psychoanalytic view on depression is expressed in Freud's paper, "Mourning and Melancholia" (1917), in which loss is identified as the cause of both conditions. Loss refers to the loss of an object (a loved person) or some abstraction that has taken the place of a person. Mourning is the normal reaction to a loss of this kind, while melancholia, or depression, which resembles mourning in many respects, is pathological.

Freud differentiated between the two conditions primarily by the profound change in self-concept characteristic of melancholia but not of mourning. Melancholia, in fact, is defined by a drastic decline in self-esteem. Otherwise, the observable aspects of the two conditions are the same: "profoundly painful dejection, cessation of interest in the outside world, loss of capacity to love, inhibition of all activity" (p. 244).

Freud described the dynamics of melancholia in terms of its departure from the normal mourning process in which there is a gradual withdrawal of feelings of attachment to the lost person. While this is occurring, it is very clear what is being mourned—the lost person. By contrast, it is not clear *what* has been lost in melancholia.

Although it is evident that an absorbing inner process like that of mourning is occurring in melancholia, the consequent loss of interest in the outside world is puzzling. A clue as to how the inner process might differ from that of mourning is provided by the verbal self-abasement so characteristic of melancholia. The self-reproaches are really reproaches against another person—a person experienced as lost, and the identity of that person has been assimilated by the patient into his/her own ego. This indicates that the gradual withdrawal of feeling from the lost person, which occurs in mourning, is not taking place. Instead, an identification of the ego with the lost person is established. Freud views this identification as regressive insofar as it is characterized by ambivalence. The ensuing love–hate conflict is directed against both the ego and the lost person.

Furthermore, the "lost" person, Freud notes, is often someone with whom the patient is living in close contact. But this person is experienced as having abandoned the patient or as having been abandoned by the patient. Therefore, all of the self-reproaches are really descriptive of that person, as well as being mingled with feelings about the self because of the identification that has been formed. Finally, it should be noted, that mourning, the normal process, may turn into melancholia, becoming pathological, to the degree that the individual has ambivalent love–hate feelings for the lost person.

Other contributions to Freud's view of depression include the following: The issue of orality was emphasized by Abraham (1927) who felt that certain individuals became fixated at the oral level and were therefore prone to depression because of excessive oral needs. Rado (1928) extended the concept of orality to include all of the infant's pleasurable sensations in the nursing situation such as security and warmth. Fenichel (1968) emphasized the dependency of orally fixated characters and their need to be loved and nurtured by their love objects.

EGO PSYCHOLOGY MODEL

Bibring (1968), in contrast to his predecessors, emphasized the importance of "a state of the ego" in the pathology of depression. His thinking, therefore, represents a shift away from emphasis on instinctual drives such as oral fixations to the position known as ego psychology. Depression, according to Bibring, involves a conflict within the ego, experienced in feelings of helplessness and powerlessness. The conflict is induced by the discrepancy between one's *goals* and one's perceived inability to achieve those goals. The conflict is so acute that it may result in a collapse of the person's self-esteem.

Bibring identified three sets of goals that play a crucial role in depression: (1) the wish to be worthy, loved, and appreciated; (2) the wish to be strong, superior, and secure; (3) the wish to be good and loving. Depression is the result of tension between these highly charged aspirations and an acute awareness about failure to achieve them. Thus, although goals and aspirations may vary and may co-exist in any combination, the basic mechanism resulting in depression is the same.

Although Bibring took issue with the idea of a predisposition to depression based on oral fixations, he did concede that "the orally dependent type" represents the most frequent type of predisposition to depression. In accounting for the development of this outcome, he explicitly rejected explanations based on instinctual drives. Instead his explanation focuses on real situations—specifically the situation of frequent frustration of oral needs. If this situation continues, it may mobilize anxiety and anger at first, and be replaced later by feelings of helplessness and depression. The infant's shock-like reaction and feeling of helplessness, rather than the drive-related oral fixation, produces the vulnerability to later depression. These early traumatic experiences establish a predisposition to the state of helplessness that is reactivated in later life whenever situations occur that resemble the primary shock condition. It is here that one notes a convergence between "learned helplessness" and ego psychological views of depression.

Depression, in Bibring's terms, is primarily an ego phenomenon, i.e., essentially independent of both oral and aggressive drives. Because self-reproaches and self-accusations are so characteristic of depressive illness, every depression was incorrectly viewed as resulting from the turning of aggression against the self, according to Bibring. The turning of aggression against the self is secondary to the breakdown of self-esteem, Bibring maintains. And this breakdown occurs in the context of conflictual wishes about goals and aspirations.

The role of people (objects) in the development of depression emerges clearly in Jacobson's account of her treatment of severely depressed individuals. In the course of treatment, Jacobson (1968) writes, the analyst becomes a central love object, indicating the extent to which objects figure in the development of the illness. Infantile pathogenic patterns result in an impairment of the ability to love. Consequently, depressives in the treatment situation tend to try to regain their own lost ability to love through the magic love they feel for and from their love object/analyst.

Jacobson (1975) elaborates on the role of self-esteem regulation in vulnerability to depressive illness. Pathological self-esteem regulation, she states, results from early caretaker relationships that prevented the child from developing a stable, positive image of the self vis-à-vis other people. Ambivalence plays a crucial role in the self-esteem regulation of these "narcissistically vulnerable" individuals. In the most severe cases of depression, unusually unloving and punitive parents set harsh, unrealistic standards for the small child. Intense hostility toward such parents develops along with the normal childlike love. This hostility prevents a positive identification with the parent—the kind of identification necessary for the development of a positive self-image. The resulting vulnerability to narcissistic injuries in adulthood leads to feelings of shame and inferiority, which, in turn, interfere with the stable maintenance of self-esteem.

Bowlby (1968) also views the vulnerability to depressive illness as stemming from real-life influences originating in early life. Bowlby's position is not a "pure" psychoanalytic one, representing as it does an interface between psychoanalytic theory and ethology. His extensive work on attachment and loss (1969, 1973, 1980) makes a direct and significant contribution to the understanding of depression.

According to Bowlby, loss during the first year of life predisposes the child to depression in later life. It is the experience of loss "provoked . . . in such a degree, over such length of time, or with such frequency, that a disposition is established to respond to all subsequent losses in a similar way" (p. 264). He regards the mourning responses to object loss as both universal and normal, and he bases his understanding of depressive illness on his study of this normal process.

Stated briefly, Bowlby views the normal mourning process as consisting of three phases, identified as protest; despair; detachment. He defines the subjective states characteristic of each phase. The first phase, protest, elicits the "instinctual response systems"—attachment systems that bind an individual to the lost loved person; it consists of repeated disappointments, persistent separation anxiety, grief, and angry efforts to recover the lost person. Despair consists of disorganization accompanied by pain and despair. The third phase, detachment, consists of reorganization partly in connection with a new person or persons.

Depressive illness, the pathological response, is the subjective aspect of a state of disorganization. Disorganization of behavior is the key concept of Bowlby's formulation of depression. He states, "The depressed individual of any age and species is the one whose behavior is no longer organized and self-sustaining (and, as a result) interaction between himself and his world has ceased" (p. 310). It is this situation that explains the loss of self-esteem so characteristic of depression.

Finally, Bowlby describes the relationship between a normal and pathological reaction. The depressive phase of mourning is regarded as a special case of the depression that arises as a result of the disorganization of behavior patterns—a disorganization that is a consequence of loss of a significant object or goal in the external world.

SELF PSYCHOLOGY MODEL

Kohut (1977) introduces the concept of "empty" depression in his discussion of self pathology. Like self pathology itself, the concept of empty depression differs considerably from formulations so far discussed. Empty depression is descriptive of nonpsychotic episodes in which guilt feelings and self-accusations play no significant role. Kohut reports the presence of this syndrome in a fairly broad range of pathology—from severe to mild.

In severe self pathology, the empty depression is related to what Kohut terms the fragmented, depleted self. He views this pathology as an outcome of early life experience in which the necessary empathic response from caretakers was lacking. The empty depression of the depleted self suggests a developmental deficit that results in an inner world devoid of ambitions and ideals and, therefore, of goals.

Kohut also writes, however, that despite the absence of neurotic conflict some people are "not protected against succumbing to the agony of the hopelessness and lethargy of pervasive empty depression" (p. 242). He finds this kind of depression more likely to appear in later middle life among people who are beset with a feeling of the meaninglessness of their existence.

Basch (1975), another analyst of the Kohut Self Psychology group, in contrast to all other theorists so far discussed, seeks a "satisfactory causal explanatory theory of depression" (p. 530). He believes that a theory of brain function is a prerequisite for a model of that kind. Basch presents a conception of depression as a system disturbance in the goal-seeking aspect of brain function. Using a general systems theory framework, depression is viewed as a systemic disturbance, indicating that the brain's operation is converting from an open, transactional state to a closed, reactive state.

Depression, defined as a system dysfunction rather than a unitary disease entity, requires the assumption of brain function as an open system in contrast to the closed system implied in the traditional Freudian "mental apparatus" model. Living systems are open systems that influence their environment by selective interaction and actively participate in shaping their own future. The brain's ordering activity, which consists of message-processing and pattern-matching, is necessary for the maintenance of the open system. Above all, the brain's ordering activity is goal-setting and goal-seeking. Interference with this ordering activity results in the symptoms of apathy and regression characteristic of depression.

ling to Basch, the dysfunction called "depression" signifies some-
...g different at different levels of maturity. The symptoms of depression
observed in maternally deprived infants, for example, are not indicative of
the same kind of brain dysfunction that occurs in adult depression. Based
on the work of Piaget and others, symbolic message-processing does not
begin until about 1½ or 2 years of age. Before that age the brain's ordering
activity consists primarily of the pattern matching of sensorimotor schemas. The feedback necessary to restore the ordering function of the infant's brain does not consist of symbolic input, but the physical intervention of the caretaker. Because the goal-setting activity of the infant's brain
is, as noted, pattern-matching of sensorimotor schemas, the feedback loop
is completed when the infant is soothed and comforted.

In contrast, the central issue in adult depression is a highly symbolic
one—the concept of self. Self is "the reflection on one's own reflections . . . objectified as 'I'" (p. 523). In adult depression, Basch writes, the
ordering activity of the brain is impaired to the point where the self-
concept cannot be maintained. Because the resultant depression is due to
symbolic loss, supportive attempts at reversal are often of no avail. The
symbolic concept of the self has been impaired, and it is only when
"restitution or alterations have been made in the concept of self" (p. 526)
that the patient is able to respond to the efforts made by others in his/
her behalf.

GENDER DIFFERENCES AND DEVELOPMENTAL THEORY

We return to the question: What does psychoanalytic theory indicate
about gender differences in regard to depression among adults, either explicitly or implicitly?

At the outset it is apparent that no explicit gender difference was indicated in the dynamic explanations of depression we have discussed. In
order to cite an explicit gender difference, some theorist would have had
to argue as follows: that women are more likely than men to experience
greater goal tension about the wish to be loved and appreciated and are
therefore more prone to depression (Bibring, 1968). No theorist, as we
have seen, has made such a claim. In contrast to other aspects of psychoanalytic theory, the dynamic mechanism of depression described by all
theorists, including the traditional Freudian model, is gender neutral.

However, the traditional Freudian model includes a developmental
theory as well as a dynamic theory. In contrast to any other model discussed, the Freudian model contains a strong implicit suggestion that
women would be more prone to depression than men. The early psychosexual development of girls, as compared to boys, suggests impaired

self-esteem as a result of genital differences. According to Freud (1925), the little girl's discovery of her lack of a penis, which she considers a superior organ, constitutes a major wound to her narcissism, resulting in a sense of inferiority and humiliation. Because Freudian theory maintains that this aspect of the little girl's development is central to female personality formation, a vulnerability to depression in later life could reasonably be derived from it.

Roiphe and Galenson (1981) suggest that the discovery of the anatomical difference occurs earlier than Freud believed, usually between the 16th and 21st month, and that this discovery results in depressed mood. Roiphe and Galenson noted mood changes in many young girls occurring concurrently with castration reactions. The girls who suffered the most intense castration reactions also suffered a constriction of their fantasy life. Their imaginative play became sparse and stereotyped, their intellectual curiosity restricted: "their exploration of the world around them became definitely narrower in scope" (p. 258).

Mahler, Pine, and Bergman (1975) believe that, in both boys and girls, the basic depressive mood develops at about 2 years of age. It is said to result not only from the discovery by girls of the anatomical difference but from the "intrapsychic working through of that unavoidable, predetermined growing away from the previous state of 'oneness' with the mother . . . .This loss . . . implies the gradual giving up of the more or less delusional fantasy of symbiotic omnipotence" (p. 157). But "it seems quite plausible that the proclivity to a basic depressive mood is greater in girls than in boys . . . " (p. 216). "Our data indicate that the girl is more prone to depressed mood than the boy. The realization of separateness is compounded in the case of the girl by a lesser degree of motor-mindedness and by her awareness of her anatomical 'shortcoming'" (p. 214).

CONCLUSION

A consideration of less obvious, implicit suggestions of gender differences would involve departing entirely from psychoanalytic theory. Since the issue of self-esteem and self-concept emerges clearly from all theoretical positions discussed, one might argue that women are more vulnerable than men in this area. However, any argument based on the negative effects of women's secondary social status on their self-concept would be beyond psychoanalytic theory. Similarly, any argument based on the possible effect constitutional gender differences, for example, might have on the attachment tendencies described by Bowlby, would be outside the framework of psychoanalysis.

It must be concluded, therefore, that psychoanalytic dynamic theory, ego psychology, or self psychology provide no explicit basis for assuming a gender difference in the incidence of depressive illness in adults. However, gender differences are explicit in Freud's developmental theory.

In the next chapter, we turn to object relations theory and its contribution to the understanding of depression in women.

REFERENCES

Abraham, K. (1927). Notes on the psychoanalytical investigation and treatment of manic-depressive insanity and allied conditions. In *Selected papers*, pp. 137–156. London: Hogarth Press.

Basch, M.F. (1975). Toward a theory that encompasses depression: A revision of existing causal hypotheses in psychoanalysis. In E.J. Anthony and T. Benedek (Eds.), *Depression and human existence* (pp. 485–534). Boston: Little, Brown.

Bibring, E. (1968). The mechanism of depression. In W. Gaylin (Ed.), *The meaning of despair* (pp. 154–181). New York: Science House.

Bowlby, J. (1968). Process of mourning. In W. Gaylin (Ed.), *The meaning of despair* (pp. 263–320). New York: Science House.

Bowlby, J. (1969). *Attachment*. Volume one of *Attachment and Loss*. New York: Basic Books.

Bowlby, J. (1973). *Separation: Anxiety and anger*. Volume two of *Attachment and Loss*. New York: Basic Books.

Bowlby, J. (1980). *Loss: Sadness and depression*. Volume three of *Attachment and Loss*. New York: Basic Books.

Fenichel, O. (1968). Depression and Mania. In W. Gaylin, (Ed.), *The meaning of despair* (pp. 108–153). New York: Science House.

Freud, S. (1917). Mourning and melancholia. In *Standard edition*, Vol. 14 (pp. 243–260). London: Hogarth Press.

Freud, S. (1925). Some psychical consequences of the anatomical distinction between the sexes. *Standard edition*, Vol. 19 (pp. 248–258). London: Hogarth Press.

Greenberg, J.R., & Mitchell, S.A. (1983). *Object relations and psychoanalytic theory*, Cambridge, MA: Harvard University Press.

Jacobson, E. (1968). Transference problems in the psychoanalytic treatment of severely depressive patients. In W. Gaylin (Ed.), *The meaning of despair* (pp. 338–352). New York: Science House.

Kohut, H. (1977). *The restoration of the self.* New York: International Universities Press.

Mahler, M., Pine, F., & Bergman, A. (1975). *The psychological birth of the human infant.* New York: Basic Books.

Rado, S. (1928). The problems of melancholia. *International Journal of Psychoanalysis, 9*, 420–438.

Roiphe, H., & Galenson, E. (1981). *Infantile origins of sexual identity.* New York: International Universities Press.

■ 2
Object Relations Theory

BARBARA FIBEL MARCUS, Ph.D.

The present chapter will develop an object relations model of depression in women and will demonstrate the centrality of object loss as the prototype for depressive reactions.

An object relations theory of depression shifts the emphasis from the external precipitant (e.g., actual loss) to its psychological significance vis-à-vis internalized object relations. Blatt's (Blatt, 1974; Blatt & Shichman, 1983) formulations on the etiology of depression provide the matrix for the current formulation. His assertion that women are relatively more vulnerable than men to *anaclitic* psychopathology, that is, to disorders organized around interpersonal relatedness, links the study of depression to female developmental issues.

The theoretical basis for women's vulnerability to anaclitic depression is explored and its empirical support reviewed. Crucial to this discussion are the gender-based differences in the separation-individuation process in the stereotypical matricentric family. For females, early primary caretaking by a same-sex parent implies a less decisive, more protracted separation process. Ordinarily, this constellation leads to enhanced capacities for attachment, relationship, and commitment at the expense of an autonomous self. When development is compromised, these capacities are also impaired. The implication of this aspect of separation and individuation is discussed in relation to the prevalence and types of depression in women.

The author wishes to acknowledge the help of Drs. Sidney Blatt and Richard Munich in the conceptualization of this chapter. Thanks also to Don Greif for research assistance and Nina Huza for her secretarial assistance.

DEVELOPMENT OF AN OBJECT RELATIONS MODEL OF DEPRESSION

The current review will focus on approaches that have special relevance for an object relations model and that bear on the psychological development of women. It will demonstrate (1) the centrality of object loss as a prototypical precipitant of depression; (2) the etiological significance of *untoward* object losses (i.e., object losses that are age/phase inappropriate, severe, protracted, complicated, or multiple) for depression, and conversely, the role of age/phase *appropriate* object loss (separation) in inuring one to depression by facilitating the normal management of loss. Normal developmental experiences of object loss help establish a sufficiently differentiated, articulated, integrated, and thus stable and positive self-representation, which aids the handling of subsequent losses. Untoward losses disturb the establishment of adequately developed self-representations and thus impair the capacity for weathering loss and for consolidating one's autonomy. This overview will also show the convergence of such a model of the origins of depression with so-called normal female psychological development as described by psychoanalytic theory. Women, owing to the retention of the primary object of identification, establish less differentiated self-representation and thus have an enhanced capacity for relatedness and attachment ("self-in-relation"), but are thereby also more vulnerable to loss/separation and thus to depression. This model also helps understand some of the sex differences in the manifestations of depression and its precipitants.

From the outset, object loss and depression have been intimately linked in psychoanalytic theory. For a brief overview of psychoanalytic models of depression, see H. Harris (*this volume*).

The concept of identification was first formulated by Freud in an effort to understand the disruption to self esteem engendered by real or fantasied object love in melancholia (Freud 1917/1957). In this way he attempted to account for the oftentimes lacerating self-hatred unleashed by such loss, viewing it as an expression of ambivalence toward the lost object. These ideas were elaborated on and modified by others (Benedek, 1975; Fenichel, 1945; Jacobson, 1971; Rado, 1928; Zetzel, 1953). Klein (1934) was the first psychoanalyst to place primary emphasis on the role of the internalized object world in the etiology of depression. Depression derived from a failure to resolve the normative depressive position, the second of two developmental stages. In the first stage, the "paranoid-schizoid position," the infant ego struggles to keep the persecutory object from overwhelming the ideal object. The child endeavors to introject the good and to project the bad. This defensive "splitting" of good and bad aspects of the object into distinct entities orders experience and sets the stage for later reintegration. The successful management of the anxieties of the paranoid-schizoid position paves the way for the "depressive position."

The "depressive position" is heralded by the infant's recognition of and relation to the whole object. The infant begins to realize that the "good mother" whom she/he loves and the "bad mother" whom she/he hates is the same person.

Of crucial significance is Klein's (1934) assertion that the integrated infant can remember and retain love for the good object even while hating it. This is the basis for mourning the lost object, for feelings of concern and guilt, and for reparative efforts, which first make their appearance in the depressive phase.

The work of Blatt and his colleagues (Blatt, 1974; Blatt & Ritzler, 1974; Blatt & Shichman, 1983; Blatt & Wild, 1975) extended and elaborated Klein's ideas while integrating recent empirical findings and ego analytic theories.

Blatt (1974) refined an understanding of the development of object representation and its implications for depression. He postulated that object representations initially grow out of repeated experiences of frustration and gratification with a consistent and need-gratifying object. Gradually, representations become more accurate, complex, differentiated, integrated, and stable as parent–child interactions become more differentiated. Thus, object representations and their progression through the developmental sequence depend upon the nature of object relationships. Thus, Blatt preserved the importance of the affective and interactional components in his schema of the development of the concept of the object.

In using this schema to understand depression, Blatt identified two types of depression, *anaclitic* and *introjective*. He argued that not only is the predisposition to depression determined by a failure to establish adequate levels of object representation, but also that the level at which the object is represented is related to the type of depression.

In *anaclitic* depression, the object is represented at a sensorimotor level, that is, requiring direct, physical, sensory-gratifying contact to maintain the representation. Since the object is then cathected almost entirely in relation to its need-gratifying function and is synonymous with need-gratifying activities, its loss threatens physical annihilation and stimulates a search for a direct and immediate replacement. In the absence of a substitute or the reappearance of the object, the need to deny the loss is potent. The clinical manifestation of such a depression may be recognized in the desperate object-seeking and/or efforts to induce states of oblivion via drugs or alcohol of some depressed patients.

By contrast, the *introjectively* depressed individual represents the object at the perceptual and iconic levels. While this level is developmentally more advanced than the sensorimotor level, it consists of fragmented, isolated, static, and ambivalent representations without resolution of the contraindications between separate images or part properties. It is not the loss of the object per se that is feared, but rather the loss of love, acceptance, and approval offered by the object. In anticipation of the loss, the individual strives for perfection and outstanding achievement to forestall it. Blatt viewed the constant self-criticism, guilt, and overstated representations of part properties of the object as efforts to sustain contact with the object.

According to Blatt, the capacity to resolve object loss without prolonged or severe depression requires a conceptual level of representation within which an integration of contradictory and ambivalently perceived part properties and attributes has been attained. The representations, based as they are on abstract and enduring inner form and structure of the object, have stability and continuity. In Blatt's words, "they transcend time and are independent of the physical properties or presence of the object" (p. 150). In the object's absence, the capacity for its symbolic representation is retained.

In a later paper, Blatt and Shichman (1983) revised this formulation and extended the application of the development of the concept of the object to psychopathology more broadly, to other types of psychopathology, and to other spheres of ego functioning. They argue for two primary configurations of psychopathology: one anaclitic, the other introjective, each with its own developmental line. The anaclitic line of development normatively leads to the establishment of satisfying, intimate interpersonal relationships. The introjective line of development leads to a stable, realistic, and largely positive identity. Although Blatt and Shichman suggest that these two lines evolve in a complex, dialectical relationship to one another, psychopathological distortions may arise from exaggerations of the tasks of either or both developmental lines. Anaclitic psychopathologies reflect exaggerated or distorted attempts to maintain satisfying interpersonal experiences; introjective psychopathologies reflect exaggerated or distorted attempts to establish a firm, positive sense of self.

Blatt and Shichman observed that disorders of an introjective configuration occur more commonly in men, whereas disorders of an anaclitic type occur more commonly in women. They point out, and Freud (1896/1962) observed, a greater frequency of obsessional neurosis in men as compared to women. Although it was never commented on by Freud, of course, cases of hysteria were uniformly female. Chevron, Quinlan, and Blatt (1978) found empirically that, in men, symptoms often reflect struggles to consolidate a self-concept, whereas in women, symptoms express primary struggles vis-à-vis interpersonal relatedness. In an effort to explain this apparent sex difference, Blatt and Shichman (1983) state,

> In development, both males and females begin with a primary attachment to the mother. Males have to shift from the mother to the father in order to find a primary object for identification while they maintain continuity with the primary object of affection. Conversely in females there is continuity in the primary figure of identification, but in development they must switch the primary figure for affection. . . . It may be the demand for women to switch from the primary relationship with mother in order to find an appropriate object for affection, and for men to change from the primary relationship with mother in order to find an appropriate figure for identification, that creates differential vulnerability to disturbances in the anaclitic or the introjective configuration. (pp. 247–248)

It is now possible to explore the relationship between Blatt's models of depression and observations of the nature of female development. This discussion will show the powerful convergence between the developmental struggles of normative female development and vulnerability to depression. The cogency of Blatt's formulation and the related work of Chodorow (1978) and others will also be discussed.

DEPRESSION AND FEMALE DEVELOPMENT

The dynamic processes central in depression and their outcome for personality development are strikingly parallel to stereotypical female development. Aggression turned inward (Deutsch, 1944), guilt (e.g., Deutsch, 1944), ambivalence toward the maternal object (e.g., Chodorow, 1978), low self-esteem (e.g., Freud, 1925/1961, 1931/1961), a sense of helplessness (e.g., Zetzel, 1965), passivity (e.g., Freud, 1925/1961, 1931/1961; Bibring, 1953; Jacobson, 1971; Zetzel, 1965), and dependency (e.g., Stoller, 1974) are attributes associated with stereotypical femininity within psychoanalytic theory.

Kaplan (1984), observing the convergence of core depressive features and aspects of female development, posited that depression is the consequence of the thwarting or devaluation of women's central, organizing principle of self, that is, the active capacity to facilitate and enhance connectedness with others or, "self-in-relation." Similarly, Herman (1983) asserted that "depression is an exaggeration of normal feminine socialization" (p. 504).

Examining this hypothesis, then, from the perspective of an object relations theory of depression, the prevalence of depression, particularly of an anaclitic type, must reflect impairments in the conceptual level of object representation associated with female development. Yet a model for understanding sex differences in the separation-individuation process and its impact on the nature of object representation has not been well elaborated. Blatt and Shichman have provided a starting point from which to elaborate such a model. The further articulation of such a model together with some empirical support follows.

A human infant is born without the adaptive capacities necessary for independent survival. Thus, dependence on caretakers and reactions to this feeling of helplessness is a universal experience of infancy (Fairbairn, 1952).

The infant's needs are met by what is experienced as omnipotent action on the part of the self. Differentiations between good (pleasurable) and bad (unpleasurable) experience begin to accrue. Gradually, through sensory and perceptual maturation of the first month of life, the infant's autistic shell is broken, and the perception of a dual unity between mother and infant sharpens. Progress from this symbiotic phase toward separation and individuation occurs in four subphases: (1) differentiation, (2) practicing, (3) rapprochement, and (4) the consolidation of individuality and the beginnings of emotional object constancy (Mahler, Pine, & Bergman, 1975).

In the differentiation subphase, the infant begins to extricate herself/himself from the symbiotic tie to mother via locomotion and the expanding sensory and perceptual capacities. The infant's explorations away from mother are accompanied by a variety of mechanisms designed to reassure the infant of a successful return to mother, who has progressively become recognized as a separate being and as a uniquely special caretaker.

Elements of the practicing phase begin to make their appearance between seven and ten months of age and fully assert themselves by the age of one year. The infant ventures further away from mother, a corollary of the capacity to stand upright and walk. As a result, there is a quantum leap in the child's knowledge and mastery of the other-than-mother world and, concomitantly, her/his narcissistic investment in her/his own faculties. Checking back periodically with mother, emotionally "refueling," reassures the child of mother's continued availability.

Rapprochement, the third subphase, occasions a restimulation of the child's interest in and concern for mother's whereabouts along with an enhanced sense of separateness. During this period, from 18 to 21 months to the third year of life, the need for closeness and the fear of reabsorption into symbiosis oscillate.

Mahler, Pine, and Bergman (1975) observed the first indications of depressive moods in children during the rapprochement phase in response to mother's absence. The mood was often accompanied by an inability to engage in play for some length of time. Occasionally children would seek a substitute to join in with them in a regressive symbiotic union. Mahler et al. noted, too, that during rapprochement a new constellation of responses that involve activity and restlessness may arise in response to missing mother. They suggested that these behaviors may constitute early strategies to defend against sadness. As the subphase progresses, the toddler generally finds more active coping strategies including turning to the other-than-mother world of nearby adults and to symbolic play. Serious difficulty in resolving the rapprochement crisis is signalled by escalating separation anxiety, impulse-laden darting away, excessive "shadowing," and sleep disturbances. Mahler et al.'s observations clearly suggest that later ability to manage depressive affect is dependent upon the establishment of object constancy and thus upon the successful negotiation of the rapprochement subphase.

DEVELOPMENTAL MODEL OF DEPRESSION IN WOMEN

A model of differential vulnerability to depression must begin, then, with an effort to identify possible differences between male and female children of the pre-oedipal era.

Chodorow (1978) summarized extensive clinical material supporting the idea that the pre-oedipal period is more protracted in women. Studies of gender differences in early childhood provide some additional support for this contention. Galenson (1974–1976), Galenson and Roiphe (1971), and McDevitt (1979) found that girls have greater difficulty resolving the rapprochement crisis than boys. Goldberg and Lewis (1969) reported that, when placed in a strange room with their mothers, girls, as compared to boys, stayed closer to their mothers, ran back to them more frequently, maintained more eye contact, and showed greater frustration and less initiative when a barrier was placed between them and their mothers. Similarly, in a study of 2- and 3-year olds placed in a nursery school setting with mothers present, Olesker (1984) reported that girls showed more intense involvement with mothers, engaged in less peer play than boys, had lowered mood and level of play, and were less directly aggressive, but more controlling, in their play with peers. Abelin (1975) noted that by 18 months of age gender identity emerges more readily for boys, while, for girls, generational identity emerges more readily. In other words, boys make a categorical distinction; girls establish the self on a continuum derived from dual identification as mother—as her mother's baby and as one who will become a mother.

Chodorow (1978) considered both sides of the mother–daughter relationship and made a similar point.

The more prolonged and conflictual nature of a girl's separation from mother, while it may enhance the capacity for relatedness, clearly also poses risks for the continuation of more regressive wishes for the early, need-gratifying relationship with the pre-oedipal mother. Thus, the girl is more vulnerable to the restimulation of these desires either in the face of separation and loss, or, defensively, in relation to competitive, oedipal issues. In Blatt's terms, women are especially vulnerable to disorders of the anaclitic (object relations) line by virtue of their primary parent being a female like themselves.

Several lines of research support the contention of a greater vulnerability of women to anaclitic type depressions. Chevron et al. (1978) found more anaclitic depression among women and more introjective depression among men. Hammen and Padesky (1977) administered the Beck Depression Inventory to a large group of male and female college students. Sex differences in symptom patterns among depressed subjects were found, with male subjects reporting more introjective type symptoms (e.g., sense of failure, loss of interest in other people), whereas women reported symptoms associated with an anaclitic depression (e.g., indecisiveness). Similarly, Herman (1979) found that when women were depressed, the precipitant was more likely to be an interpersonal event and that they were more likely to seek out other people. Conversely depressed men were more likely to withdraw from others. It has been well established that men are two to three times more likely to complete suicide, whereas women are more likely to attempt suicide in this same proportion (Hankoff, 1982). Although speculative, this has been interpreted as a reflection of differential motives; for women, suicide attempts may be a misguided effort to gain attention and help, whereas for men suicide is seen as a final solution and the ultimate withdrawal from others (Herman, 1983).

Blatt and Shichman (1983) noted that in men who are confronting issues of sexual identity confusion, psychopathology seems to be configured along anaclitic lines (LoPiccolo & Blatt, 1972), suggesting that sex-role identification rather than biological sex is most significant. Indeed, research in the area of sex-role identification has revealed that traditionally feminine women tend to have poorer ego strength (Gump, 1972) and more "involutional" depression (Bart, 1971). Good psychological adjustment has been shown to be related to androgyny (Bardwick, 1971; Block, 1973; Gump, 1972; Mednick & Weissman, 1975). Golding and Singer (1983) found that psychological sex role was a better predictor of the style of emotional responding in depression than was biological sex. Findings were consistent with an association between psychological femininity and an anaclitic style, and between psychological masculinity and an introjective style.

Considerable theoretical and empirical support then is available for the idea that women are more subject to depression in general and, in particular, to anaclitic type depression as a consequence of the stereotypical configuration of matricentric primary care-giving as well as the attendent difficulties for the girl's negotiation of the rapprochement phase of the separation-individuation process. The significantly greater prevalence of depression in women as compared to men, however, suggests that women are also vulnerable to depressions having an introjective source. Although little has been written from an object relations perspective on the roots of introjective depressions, extrapolating from Blatt's work, one can argue that these depressions result from premature, abrupt, or traumatic separations. Such separations stimulate or are stimulated by aggression and produce a fragile sense of self. This fragility must therefore be defended against intrusions as the self is vulnerable to excessive stimulation of guilt over aggressive wishes.

In contrast to the female's prolonged attachment to mother, males are generally pushed toward early separation and exploration of the other-than-mother world (Bergman, 1982; Chodorow, 1978). Many studies have found, at least in the past, that boys are more aggressive, impulsive, and fight more often than girls (e.g., Bardwick, 1971; Cohen, 1966; Hartup & Zook, 1960; Maccoby, 1966; Santrock, 1970; Scott, 1958; Sears, 1961; Sears, Maccoby, & Levin, 1957; Terman & Tyler, 1954). Bardwick (1971) pointed out that sex-role expectations are more stringent for boys than for girls. Parental demands for autonomy in little boys begins early on in development, manifesting itself in the previously noted sex differences in the rapprochement subphase.

However, girls, too, may prematurely withdraw form the early, symbiotic tie to mother or be driven from it. Cole (1983) and Kestenbaum (1984) observed that depressed mothers often precipitate premature separation of their daughters who may then feel disloyal and guilty.

Even in the usual circumstances, the girl's shift from a pre-oedipal attachment to mother to the oedipal attachment to father is complicated by ambivalent feelings. Orthodox psychoanalytic theory contends that the girl turns toward the father out of anger and disdain for the "castrated" mother. Others (Balint, 1939; Brunswick, 1940; Chasseguet-Smirgel, 1964; Chodorow, 1978; Lampl-de Groot, 1927, 1952; Rubin, 1975) have accounted for this spurning of mother as a consequence of the girl's recognition that her mother prefers her father, a man, to her. She then rejects her mother in kind by becoming her (ambivalent) competitor for the father.

The oedipal situation for the girl indeed propels her away from the mother and thereby aids in her separation, but, as Chodorow observed, this must always be bittersweet, tainted by the vengeance of unrequited love.

Moreover, as Blatt and Shichman pointed out, the lines of self and object development are intimately intertwined so that lags or deficits in one sphere reverberate in the other. Thus, the little girl's difficulties in separation may be expected to impede the parallel development of a stable, differentiated sense of self apart from mother. These difficulties may be less apparent in the girl until adolescence and adulthood begin to make greater demands on autonomous thinking and action.

Although the love for the father may provide some compensation for her unrequited love for mother, he cannot serve easily as an object of identification for her, as he can for her male counterpart. She must instead turn back to the mother, now her rival as well as her nurturer, to establish a sense of self as a female. This presents complexity not inherent in the boy's efforts to establish a masculine identity. Of couse, the boy is also faced with the regressive pull toward the mother owing to his attachment to her and his early immersion in a feminine environment as well as the relative unavailability of the father with whom he must identify. In contrast to the girl, the boy lacks the double identification with the mother. The girl can identify with the mother—both as the young girl her mother once was and as a future mother. The awareness of his anatomical similarity to father enhances his identification with him as well. In regard to establishing a firm, positive sense of self, then, the little girl is potentially disadvantaged.

Developmental research supports this contention. For example, studies indicate that girls are more fearful of success and experience anxiety over competitive behavior (Bardwick, 1971; Kagan & Moss, 1962; Komorovsky, 1946; Maccoby, 1966; Stienmann & Fox, 1966; Veroff, 1969). Girls have been found to lack confidence in their ability to attain goals and are less willing than boys to try new or difficult tasks (Bardwick, 1971; Coleman, 1961; Crandall, 1969; Crandall & Rabson, 1960; Douvan, 1960; Douvan & Adelson, 1966; Kagan, 1964; Kagan & Moss, 1962; Komorovsky, 1946; Maccoby, 1966; Murphy, 1962; Veroff, 1969; Winterbottom, 1953).

Although the Women's Movement has produced some changes, by and large opportunities for achievement and self-enhancement are relatively less available to women than to men, even when women work outside the home and establish careers (Weissman & Klerman, 1979). Indeed, the gap between heightened expectations for achievement and opportunities that have not kept pace with such expectations may make women today even more prone to depression, particularly the introjective type. The rising rates of depression, especially in young women (Secunda & the staff of the NIMH Clinical Research Branch, 1973), and the corresponding increase in suicide attempt rates in young women (Weissman, 1974) provide an empirical marker for this kind of cultural impact.

In summary, women appear to have developmental sources for introjective depression as well as a special vulnerability to anaclitic depression. From an object relations perspective, the preponderance of women among depressives can be viewed as a consequence of the generally longer attachment phase and more complicated, less decisive separation from mother owing to the interlocking same-sex identifications between mother and daughter. Further, in the face of multiple sources of ambivalence toward the mother on the part of her daughter, a daughter must retain a positive attachment for identificatory purposes while feeling spurned by her mother's attachment to the father and, similarly, seek a relationship with the father, her competitor for mother's affection. Alternatively, girls may, like boys, separate early, but then suffer a more fragile sense of self and guilt attendant to the aggression inherent in separations. These latter dynamics make her vulnerable to introjective disorders, which may be triggered later in life by curtailed opportunities for self-expression in the realm of personal achievement. In short, women are in double jeopardy. Of interest for the future will be studies of nontraditional family structures and their impact on the development of women's sense of an autonomous self, on the anaclitic versus introjective configurations of psychopathology in men and women, the effect on psychological sex role, and, finally, on the incidence of depression in women.

REFERENCES

Abelin, E.L. (1975). Some further observations and comments upon the earliest role of the father. *International Journal of Psychoanalysis, 56,* 293–302.

Balint, A. (1939). Love for the mother and mother-love. In M. Balint (Ed.), *Primary love and psycho-analytic technique.* New York: Liveright Publishing.

Bardwick, J. (1971). *The psychology of women: A study of biocultural conflicts.* New York: Harper & Row.

Bart, P. (1971). Depression in middle-aged women. In V. Gornick & B. Moran (Eds.), *Woman in sexist society.* New York: Basic.

Bergman, A. (1982). Considerations about the development of the girl during the separation-individuation process. In D. Mendell (Ed.), *Female development: Current psychoanalytic views.* New York: Medical and Scientific Books.

Bibring, E. (1953). Mechanism of depression. In P. Greenacre (Ed.), *Affective disorders.* New York: International Universities Press.

Blatt, S.J. (1974). Levels of object representation in anaclitic and introjective depression. *Psychoanalytic Study of the Child, 29,* 107–157.

Blatt, S.J., & Ritzler, B.A. (1974). Thought disorder and boundary disturbance in psychosis. *Journal of Consulting and Clinical Psychology, 42,* 370–381.

Blatt, S.J., & Shichman, S. (1983). Two primary configurations of psychopathology. *Psychoanalysis and Contemporary Thought, 6,* 187–255.

Blatt, S.J., & Wild, C.M. (1975). *Schizophrenia: A developmental analysis.* New York: Academic Press.

Block, J.H. (1973). Conceptions of sex role: Some cross-cultural and longitudinal perspectives. *American Psychologist, 28,* 512–526.

Brunswick, R.M. (1940). The preoedipal phase of the libido development. In R. Fliess (Ed.), *The psychoanalytic reader: An anthology of essential papers with critical introductions.* New York: International Universities Press.

Chasseguet-Smirgel, J. (1964). Feminine guilt and the Oedipus complex. In J. Chasseguet-Smirgel (Ed.), *Female sexuality.* Ann Arbor: University of Michigan Press.

Chevron, E.S., Quinlan, D.M., & Blatt, S.J. (1978). Sex roles and gender differences in the experience of depression. *Journal of Abnormal Psychology, 87,* 680–683.

Chodorow, N. (1978). *The reproduction of mothering: Psychoanalysis and the sociology of gender.* Berkeley: University of California Press.

Cohen, S. (1966). Personal identity and sexual identity. *Psychiatry, 29,* 1–14.

Cole, K. (1983). Daughters' reactions to maternal depression. *American Journal of Psychoanalysis, 43,* 291–299.

Coleman, J. (1961). *The adolescent society.* New York: Free Press.

Crandall, V. (1969). Sex differences in expectancy of intellectual and academic reinforcement. In C. Smith (Ed.), *Achievement related to motives in children.* New York: Russell Sage Foundation.

Crandall, V., & Rabson, A. (1960). Children's repetition choices in an intellectual achievement situation following success and failure. *The Journal of Genetic Psychology, 97,* 161–168.

Deutsch, H. (1944). *Psychology of Women.* New York: Grune & Stratton.

Douvan, E. (1960). Sex differences in adolescent character processes. *Merrill-Palmer Quarterly, 6,* 203–211.

Douvan, E., & Adelson, J. (1966). *The adolescent experience.* New York: Wiley.

Fairbairn, W.R.D. (1952). *An object-relations theory of the personality.* New York: Basic.

Freud, S. (1896/1962). Further remarks on the neuro-psychoses of defense. In J. Strachey (Ed.), *The standard edition, 3.* London: Hogarth.

Freud, S. (1925/1961). Some physical consequences of the anatomical distinction between the sexes. In J. Strachey (Ed.), *The standard edition, 19.* London: Hogarth.

Freud, S. (1931/1961). Female sexuality. In J. Strachey (Ed.), *The standard edition, 21.* London: Hogarth.

Galenson, E. (1974). The emergence of genital awareness during the second year of life. In R.C. Friedman, R.M. Richert, & R.J. Van de Wiele (Eds.), *Sex differences in behavior.* New York: Wiley.

Galenson, E. (1976). Some suggested revisions concerning early female development. *Journal of the American Psychoanalytic Association, 24,* 29–57.

Galenson, E., & Roiphe, H. (1971). The impact of early sexual discovery on mood defensive organization and symbolization. *Psychoanalytic Study of the Child, 26,* 195–216.

Goldberg, S. & Lewis, M. (1969). Play behavior in the year-old infant: Early sex differences. *Child Development, 40,* 21–31.

Golding, J., & Singer, J.L. (1983). Patterns of inner experience: Day-dreaming styles, depressive moods, and sex roles. *Journal of Personality and Social Psychology, 45,* 663–675.

Gump, J. (1972). Sex-role attitudes and psychological well-being. *Journal of Social Issues, 28,* 79–92.

Hammen, C.L., & Padesky, C.A. (1977). Sex differences in the expression of depressive responses on the Beck Depression Inventory. *Journal of Abnormal Psychology, 86,* 609–614.

Hankoff, L.D. (1982). Suicide and attempted suicide. In E.S. Paykel (Ed.), *Handbook of affective disorders.* New York: Guilford Press.

Hartup, W., & Zook, E. (1960). Sex-role preferences in three- and four-year old children. *Journal of Consulting and Clinical Psychology, 24,* 420–426.

Herman, M.F. (1979). *Sex differences in depression.* Unpublished doctoral dissertation, University of Michigan, Ann Arbor.

Herman, M.F. (1983). Depression and women: Theories and research. *Journal of the American Academy of Psychoanalysis, 11,* 493–512.

Jacobson, E. (1971). *Depression.* New York: International Universities Press.

Kagan, J. (1964). Acquisition and significance of sex-typing and sex-role identity. In M. Hoffman and L. Hoffman (Eds.), *Review of child development research.* New York: Russell Sage Foundation.

Kagan, J., & Moss, H. (1962). *Birth to maturity.* New York: Wiley.

Kaplan, A. (1984). *The "self-in-relation": Implications for relationship to affective disorders in adult life.* Store Center Work in Progress Series, Working Papers No. 24.

Kestenbaum, C.T. (1984). Pathological attachments and their relationship to affective disorders in adult life. *American Journal of Psychoanalysis, 44,* 33–49.

Klein, M. (1934). *A contribution to the psychogenesis of manic-depressive states: Love, guilt, and separation and other works, 1921–1945.* New York: Delacorte.

Komorovsky, M. (1946). Cultural contradiction and sex roles. *American Journal of Sociology, 15,* 508–516.

Lampl-de-Groot, J. (1927). The evolution of the Oedipus Complex in women. In R. Fliess (Ed.), *The psychoanalytic reader: An anthology of essential papers with critical introductions.* New York: International Universities Press.

Lampl-de-Groot, J. (1952). Re-evaluation of the role of the Oedipus Complex. *International Journal of Psychoanalysis, 33,* 335–342.

LoPiccolo, J., & Blatt, S.J. (1972). Cognitive styles and sexual identity. *Journal of Clinical Psychology, 28,* 148–151.

Maccoby, E. (1966). *The development of sex differences.* Stanford: Stanford University Press.

Mahler, M.S., Pine, F., & Bergman, A. (1975). *The psychological birth of the human infant.* New York: Basic.

McDevitt, J.B. (1979). The role of the internalization process in the development of object relations during the separation-individuation phase. *Journal of the American Psychoanalytic Association, 27,* 327–343.

Mednick, M., & Weissman, H. (1975). The psychology of women. *Annual Review of Psychology, 26,* 1–18.

Murphy, L.B. (1962). *The widening world of childhood: Paths toward mastery.* New York: Basic Books.

Olesker, W. (1984). Sex differences in two and three-year-olds: mother-child relations, peer relations, and peer play. *Psychoanalytic Psychology, 1,* 269–287.

Rubin, G. (1975). The traffic in women: Notes on the "Political Economy" of sex. In R. Reiter (Ed.), *Toward a new anthropology of women.* New York: Monthly Review Press.

Santrock, J. (1970). Paternal absence, sex typing, and identification. *Developmental Psychology, 2,* 264–272.

Scott, J. (1958). *Aggression.* Chicago: University of Chicago Press.

Sears, R. (1961). Relations of early socialization experiences to aggression in middle childhood. *Journal of Abnormal and Social Psychology, 63,* 466–492.

Sears, R., Maccoby, E., & Levin, H. (1957). *Patterns of child rearing.* New York: Harper & Row.

Secunda, S.K., and the staff of the NIMH Clinical Research Branch. (1973). *The depressive disorders.* U.S. Department of Health, Education and Welfare, NIMH Clinical Research Branch, Division of Extramural Research Programs, Special Report.

Stienmann, A., & Fox, D. (1966). Male-female perceptions of the female role in the United States. *Journal of Psychology, 64,* 265–279.

Stoller, R.J. (1974). Facts and fancies: An examination of Freud's concept of bisexuality. In J. Strouse (Ed.), *Women and analysis.* New York: Viking.

Terman, L., & Tyler, L. (1954). Psychological sex differences. In L. Carmichael (Ed.), *Manual of child psychology.* New York: Wiley.

Veroff, J. (1969). Social comparison and development of achievement motivation. In C. Smith (Ed.), *Achievement-related motives in children.* New York: Russell Sage Foundation.

Weissman, M. (1974). The epidemiology of suicide attempts. *Archives of General Psychiatry, 30,* 737–746.

Weissman, M., & Klerman, G.L. (1979). Sex differences in the epidemiology of depression. In E. Gomberg & V. Franks (Eds.), *Gender and disordered behavior.* New York: Brunner/Mazel.

Winterbottom, M. (1953). *The relationship of childhood training in independence to achievement motivation.* Unpublished doctoral dissertation, University of Michigan, Ann Arbor.

Zetzel, E.R. (1965). Depression and the capacity to bear it. In M. Schur (Ed.), *Drives, affects, behavior, Vol. 2.* New York: International Universities Press.

■ 3
Self-In-Relation Theory

DANA JACK, M.S.W., Ed.D.

Classical theories describe normal personality development as a process of increasing separation from dependence in infancy on early objects to the relative autonomy and self-sufficiency of adulthood. It is now widely accepted that these theories have relied on men's lives to formulate ideas of health and maturity. Yet this perspective has obscured our comprehension of women's development, which consistently appears more oriented to relationships and more contextual in the sense of self, self-esteem, and morality. Since classical theories of normal development guide our perceptions of psychopathology, it becomes clear why women are commonly seen as more "dependent," as having problems with individuation and autonomy.

Dependence has been a central concept for psychodynamic formulations of depression (Arieti & Bemporad, 1978). Most commonly, interpersonal dependency is measured by the degree to which a person's self-esteem is maintained by the approval and support of other persons or their surrogates (Chodoff, 1972). The healthy person's self-esteem does not depend on external supplies, but derives from internal sources or from autonomous actions (Mendelson, 1974). Thus, clinicians consider that dependence predisposes women to low self-esteem and depression following loss.

Though loss is considered to be a core issue in depression, men and women appear to be disturbed by different kinds of losses. Women most frequently become depressed over disruption or conflict in close relationships, whereas men become depressed over the loss of an ideal or an achievement-related goal, or over performance issues (Arieti & Bemporad, 1978; Beck, Rush, Shaw, & Emery, 1979; Mendelson, 1974). Treatment interventions accept the premise of autonomy as health, and, for women, aim toward enabling them to separate and become less dependent on the relationship for a sense of self and self-esteem (Arieti & Bemporad, 1978; Beck, et al., 1979).

The conceptualization of women's vulnerability to depression as rooted in their unhealthy dependence on relationships requires rethinking. Recent research in women's psychology suggests that it is normal for a woman to experience herself as "relational" or "connected" rather than separate and autonomous (Chodorow, 1978; Gilligan, 1982; Miller, 1984). Self-in-relation theorists redefine a woman's orientation to her relationships as a central, positive, and crucial aspect of psychological development and functioning beyond her childhood. These theorists propose a new model of female development, influenced by those object relations theorists who see attachments as primary for growth (such as Bowlby, 1969, 1973, 1980; Fairbairn, 1952; Guntrip, 1961; Sullivan, 1962, 1964; Winnicott, 1965). Focusing on women specifically, the self-in-relation theorists consider that women and men have different ego capacities, strengths, and vulnerabilities resulting from the differing relational contexts and cultural norms that affect their development in characteristic ways.

According to Chodorow (1978), gender identification for girls does not require the same kind of separation from the primary caretaker as for boys. Daughters bring to adolescence and adulthood more aspects of the original, closely bonded mother–child relationship, whereas boys must relinquish the closeness of that relationship—which becomes entwined with sexual issues at adolescence—to form a gender identity based on differences from the mother. Because of an unbroken identification with a primary caretaker, girls come to experience themselves as "less separate" than boys, and have a stronger basis "for experiencing another's needs or feelings as one's own" (p. 167). Further, because girls do not repress nor give up completely their preoedipal and oedipal attachment to their mother, they "grow up with more ongoing preoccupations with both internalized object-relationships and with external relationships as well" (p. 168).

Cohler and Grunebaum's (1981) study of daughters, mothers, and grandmothers confirms that the concepts of autonomy and separation do not characterize women's adult lives. The daughter is usually socialized into an undifferentiated and interdependent relationship with her own mother that continues into adulthood. This mother–daughter relationship "becomes the model for the daughter's relational mode as an adult" (p. 331). The women's lives were organized around family and children, leading the researchers to view dependence as "normative," and to call for reconsideration of "the entire question of the significance for individual adjustment of this continuing affectional dependence across the life cycle" (p. 12).

Miller (1984) and Surrey (1985) agree that social intimacy is the profound organizer of female experience. They describe the "relational self" as the core self-structure in women, detailing how the self "is organized and developed through practice in relationships where the goal is the increasing development of mutually empathic relationships" (Surrey, 1985, p. 3). Such relationships are essential for a sense of well-being, and for continuing healthy development. Used in this sense, "relationships" denotes not only actual relationships, but also inner object relations, and inner constructions of the relational process (e.g., empathy, closeness).

Within this model, development occurs as a process of differentiation within ongoing relationships (Gilligan, 1982), leading to a more complex sense of self in more complex relationships to other selves (Miller, 1984). Aspects of self-development such as creativity, autonomy, competence, and self-esteem develop within the context of relationship. That is, one need not "separate" from relationships in order to develop one's own self. Developmental failure or arrest occurs not because of a failure to separate, but as a result of an inability to remain connected while forming and/or asserting a distinct sense of self (Gilligan, 1977).

Growing out of this relational sense of self is a different vision of the social world and morality. What Freud and Kohlberg describe as women's lesser developed morality, Gilligan (1982) reinterprets as a morality attuned to the specific contexts of people's lives, a morality that follows an ethic of care with the imperative not to hurt others. Within this framework, responsibility means an extension of self to protect another from hurt, whereas for the separate self, responsibility implies a restraint of aggression. Thus, what is seen from a traditional perspective as women's lack of ego boundaries, dependence, and weak superego, Gilligan reinterprets as a valuable strength, a reflection of a developmental context that values interdependency, empathy, and emotional closeness.

Women's orientation to relationships occurs within a social context which regards that orientation as a vulnerability and a sign of dependence or immaturity. As commonly used, "dependence" masks the important distinction between women's healthy, normal sense of self—as relational or connected—and a disturbed sense of self. Ego strength has come to be equated with a lack of reliance on others for emotional support or for reassurance of one's worth. Self-reliance is seen as mature, and reliance on others as immature. Thus women come to label their own relational modes and desires as "neurotic" and "dependent."

Social role and social values exert a powerful but contradictory influence on women's psychology. A woman is caught in a double bind: society still pushes her to define herself through her relationships and then invalidates her wish for connection by denigrating the importance of relationships. Observing that society places little value on relationships, women have difficulty affirming the high value they place on relationships and on the care-taking roles they occupy in adulthood. Achievements are judged to be more important than attachments, but if relationships falter or fail, the woman considers it her fault. In fact, a woman's striving for achievements can threaten her relationships (Miller, 1976). In my view, depression reveals the vulnerabilities of a relational sense of self within a culture that dangerously strains a woman's ability to meet basic needs for interpersonal relatedness, while maintaining a positive sense of self.

REFERENCES

Arieti, S., & Bemporad, J. (1978). *Severe and mild depression: The psychotherapeutic approach.* New York: Basic Books.

Beck, A.T., Rush, A., Shaw, B., & Emery, G. (1979). *Cognitive therapy of depression.* New York: Guilford Press.

Bowlby, J. (1969). *Attachment. (Vol. 1).* New York: Basic Books.

Bowlby, J. (1973). *Separation: Anxiety and anger (Vol. 2).* New York: Basic Books.

Bowlby, J. (1980). *Loss: Sadness and depression. (Vol. 3).* New York: Basic Books.

Chodoff, P. *(1972). The depressive personality. Archives of General Psychiatry,* 27, 666–672.

Chodorow, N. (1978). *The reproduction of mothering: Psychoanalysis and the sociology of gender.* Berkeley: University of California Press.

Cohler, B.J., & Grunebaum, H. (1981). *Mothers, grandmothers, and daughters: Personality and childcare in three-generation families.* New York: John Wiley and Sons.

Fairbairn, W.R.D. (1952). *An object relations theory of the personality.* New York: Basic Books.

Gilligan, C. (1977). In a different voice: Women's conception of the self and of morality. *Harvard Educational Review,* 47, 481–517.

Gilligan, C. (1982). *In a different voice: Psychology theory and women's development.* Cambridge: Harvard University Press.

Guntrip, H. (1961). *Psychoanalytic theory, therapy, and the self.* New York: Basic Books.

Mendelson, M. (1974). *Psychoanalytic concepts of depression* (2nd ed.). Flushing, N.Y.: Spectrum Publications.

Miller, J.B. (1976). *Toward a new psychology of women.* Boston: Beacon Press.

Miller, J.B. (1984). *The development of a feminine sense of self* (Work in progress; paper #12, available from The Stone Center for Developmental Services and Studies, Wellesley College, Wellesley, MA).

Sullivan, H.S. (1962). *Schizophrenia as a human process.* New York: Norton.

Sullivan, H.S. (1964). *The fusion of psychiatry and social science.* New York: Norton.

Surrey, J.L. (1985). *Self-in-relation: A theory of women's development* (Work in progress; paper #13, available from The Stone Center for Developmental Services and Studies, Wellesley College, Wellesley, MA).

Winnicott, D.W. (1965). *The maturational process and the facilitating environment.* New York: International Universities Press.

■ 4
Cognitive Theory

SUSAN JOSEPH, Ph.D.

Theories of depression have rarely addressed the issue of gender. Although psychoanalysis has emphasized gender differences, gender-neutral concepts, such as loss, have been used to explain depression. Few gender-related hypotheses exist in cognitive and behavior theory; concepts such as a reduction in the rate of reinforcement or an increase in negative thinking usually account for depression. Recently, however, there are indications that cognitive theorists have begun to take an interest in gender differences in depression.

While the absence of a gender-related theory of depression is surprising in view of the disproportionate representation of women in the depressed category, this absence appears to be typical of psychological theory and research in general, and cognitive and behavioral theories in particular. Critics of psychological research and theory development have noted several areas of omission:

1. Referring to developmental theory, Gilligan (1982) notes: "Traditional theories have adopted male life as the norm." Her observation applies to areas other than development as well. According to a recent study of papers in behavioral journals, little attention is paid to gender (Resnick, Calhoun, Rothblum, Dartnell, & Blechman, 1986). Resnick et al. (1986) point out that males are twice as likely to be the subjects of psychological research and that, when both sexes are used as subjects, fewer than half the articles analyze sex differences. When such differences are analyzed, 74% find statistically significant differences. Authors generalize to both genders when their subjects are males, but generalization is more restricted when the subjects are females. The failure to analyze for gender differences is a

serious one since the sex-role implications of cognitive and behavioral symptom patterns can be important in treatment (Resnick et al., 1986).

2. Traditional theorists fail to recognize the importance of the contribution of social and cultural context to an individual's identity and sense of self (Carmen, Russo, & Miller, 1984; Lerner, 1984).

3. Research bias negatively impacts on women because of the lack of study of the special concerns of women. Studies of the differential effects of divorce, widowhood, reproductive problems, or the impact of gender on diagnosis are uncommon (Hare-Mustin, 1983).

The absence of research on topics relevant to women and the general indifference to gender differences, are also found in cognitive and behavioral theorists. It may reflect a belief in the universality of the principles on which their work is based.

Certainly, the absence of gender-related theory has been seen by some as advantageous to women. Behavior theory and therapy, with which the various cognitive approaches are closely allied, are based on the belief that behavior principles are universal and thus need not be fitted to a particular group. Because behavior therapy entails the application of these principles (tailored to the individual patient), it has often been characterized as one of the least value-laden psychotherapeutic approaches (Collins & McNair, 1986). Lazarus (1974) expressed this position:

> Significant sex differences are by no means an integral part of social learning theory or behavior theory . . . there is nothing whatsoever in behavior theory that can lead to any sexist attitudes—no concepts like "penis envy" or "castration anxiety" . . . no credence is given to any other prejudicial sex-typed response patterns (p. 217).

While Lazarus (1974) recognizes that therapists, unlike theorists, do make value judgments, he contends that the value judgments of behavior therapy are of a type (e.g., in favor of assertive behavior) that makes this form of treatment a viable alternative for women. In behavior therapy, he says, "There are no double standards."

More recently, however, other behaviorists have begun to question this viewpoint (Blechman, 1984; Collins & McNair, 1986; Resnick et al., 1986). Behavioral theory is not in contention; rather, it is the cultural context in which therapy is conducted and the attitudes of the practitioners that is of concern.

Behaviorists believe that dysfunctional behavior is acquired and maintained by environmental contingencies. It is now being argued that these contingencies differ for men and women, that is, that different mechanisms of behavior operate in different social environments (Blechman, 1984; Resnick et al, 1986). "Differences in social environments may lead to differential characterizations of, and responses to, behavior problems and their treatment" (Collins & McNair, 1986). Other concerns include the focus on changing individual behaviors, the value systems of therapists who "typically hold the values of the larger society," and the failure to research the relationship among sex, race, class, and behavior therapy (Collins & McNair, 1986).

As is the case with behavior theory, there is little in cognitive theory that is overtly sexist; gender differences have rarely been addressed, and the principles upon which the therapy is based are assumed to be universal. The terms cognitive theory and cognitive therapy are both specific and general: more generally, the terms "cognitive therapy" or "cognitive behavior modification" refer to a variety of techniques based on numerous conceptual models all of which share an interest in the nature and modification of cognitions and use behavior therapy techniques for promoting change (Meichenbaum & Cameron, 1982). According to Meichenbaum and Cameron (1982), a common theme of the cognitive models consists of training clients to think and behave "like a scientist," the rationale being that an individual's affect and behavior are largely determined by the way in which he/she construes the world. Therapy is designed to help the client identify, reality-test, and correct maladaptive, distorted beliefs and perceptions. As used through the rest of this chapter, "cognitive therapy" specifically refers to the theory and treatment techniques developed by Aaron T. Beck.

Initially, Beck's model was developed to explain and treat depression (Beck, 1972) and was later applied to other emotional disorders (Beck, 1976; Beck & Emery, 1985).

Beck's cognitive theory postulates that a significant part of the depressive syndrome is distortion in thought process and content; this dysfunctional processing of information produces excessively negative evaluations of the self, the world, and the future (the depressive triad) (Beck & Epstein, 1982). While Beck does not believe that distorted cognitions alone cause the affective, motivational, and behavioral symptoms of depression (Beck, 1984; Beck & Epstein, 1982), he does see them as a major component of the depressive syndrome and, thus, an effective point of intervention.

Four types of cognitive phenomena are included in Beck's model. Least stable are the automatic thoughts that tend to be elicited by events or thoughts about events; these tend to be conscious, and their content is expected to be associated with particular affects and behaviors. Logical errors and schemas are more stable than automatic thoughts. Logical errors consist of systematic distortions in the appraisal of information; they reflect thinking style (Beck & Epstein, 1982). Beck (1972, 1976) has described five such errors: dichotomous thinking, overgeneralization, arbitrary inference, personalization, and selective abstraction. Schemas refer to underlying beliefs based on past experience; they often encapsulate an individual's view of the world and his/her relation to it in a brief phrase, e.g., "I'm an outsider." Schemas are believed to constitute a vulnerability to events. That is, schemas in interaction with stressful external events produce distorted automatic thoughts (Beck & Epstein, 1982).

Most stable of the cognitive phenomena defined by Beck are the personality modes (Beck, 1984). Two modes, autonomy and social dependence (or sociotropy), representing "central value systems or superordinate schemas" (Beck & Epstein, 1982) have been defined. Autonomy (or individuality) refers to an individual's investment in preserving and increasing his/her independence, mobility and personal rights, and freedom of choice; the autonomous person's well-being depends on preserving the integrity of his/her domain, directing his/her own activities, freedom from outside encroachment, restraint, or interference, and attaining meaningful goals. *Doing* is the theme of this cluster (Beck, 1984). Social dependence (or sociotropy) refers to an individual's investment in positive interchange with other people; the cluster includes wishes for acceptance, intimacy, understanding, support, appreciation, prestige, and validation of beliefs and behavior; the person is dependent on the social world for gratification, motivation, direction. *Receiving* is the theme of this cluster (Beck, 1984). While one or the other mode may predominate, they are not considered fixed: a person may have aspects of both modes and may shift from one mode to another (Beck, 1984; Beck & Epstein, 1982).

The personality modes are developmental in origin (Beck, Emery, Epstein, & Harrison, 1983) and may, in an adult, produce a heightened sensitivity to threats to attributes especially relevant to an individual's predominant personality mode. Thus, a particular personality mode may serve as a predisposing factor to specific types of disorders, e.g., sociotropy may predispose to agoraphobia, autonomy to claustrophobia. Beck (1984) believes that the personality modes may predispose individuals to a particular type of depression, a specific pattern of symptoms, and make them more likely to respond to specific therapeutic techniques.

Automatic thoughts, schemas, and logical errors are long-established aspects of Beck's theory. As they are currently defined, they do not appear to have any gender-related implications. While Beck (1976) has related specific types of cognitions to specific disorders, there is nothing in his writing to suggest that, within a nosological grouping, cognitions differ according to gender or that men and women distort in gender-related ways. (He has, however, noted that there may be gender-related precipitants for depression [Beck & Greenberg, 1974].) Instead, automatic thoughts, schemas, and logical errors are seen as universal components of the information processing system, the content of which will be defined by the interaction of the uniqueness of the person and the themes typical of the disorder.

Unlike automatic thoughts, logical errors, and schemas, personality modes do have gender implications. Beck (1984) asserts that the *autonomous*-type is likely to be more frequent in males, the *socially dependent* more frequent in females. Since Beck (1984) also states that there are "pure" cases of autonomy among women and "pure" cases of social dependence among men, and since most people are expected to have both qualities in ever-shifting proportions, there are theoretical and practical limits to Beck's gender categorizations. Despite such limits, Beck's typology represents an important step in acknowledging possible gender difference in cognitive theory and therapy, and as such it deserves serious consideration.

At first glance, the "active–passive" concepts embodied in the typology appear familiar, even stereotypical, as do the names of the personality clusters. Men have typically been identified as more active and autonomous, women as more passive and dependent (Archer & Lloyd, 1985). Yet, Beck does not restate commonly held stereotypes in his discussion of the personality modes. He notes, for example, that the learned helplessness syndrome (Seligman, 1977) often used as an analog for depression in women, is actually more common in the depressions of the autonomous type (Beck, 1984) even though he himself was one of the first to suggest that the syndrome might be relevant to women (Beck & Greenberg, 1974).

Nor does Beck appear to be discussing innate traits: to the contrary, personality modes are deemed to develop through the socialization process (Beck, Emery, Epstein, & Harrison, 1983). The values derived from this process, however, differ according to mode. Socially dependent individuals value relationships: their gratification derives from interpersonal interactions; they seek closeness to others. Autonomous individuals, on the other hand, value separation: their gratification comes from self-definition; they rely on distancing to facilitate goal achievement (Beck, 1984; Beck, Emery, Epstein, & Harrison, 1983).

There is a striking similarity in Beck's descriptions of the autonomous and sociotropic modes and Gilligan's (1982) descriptions of the differing "voices" of men and women. Although Beck is concerned with the impact of personality on pathology and Gilligan with moral development, both investigators focus on cognition. Thus, it is not surprising that their observations converge.

According to Gilligan (1982), separation and individuation are intimately related to gender identity for boys, who must separate from the mother to achieve masculine identity, but separation and individuation are less critical for girls and women since feminine identity depends neither on separation from the mother nor on progressively greater individuation.

Consequently, Gilligan believes that men and women experience attachment differently, each perceiving a danger of which the other is unaware: men in connection, women in separation. For the adult woman, then, the world is one of social interaction and personal relationships; for the adult male, it is one of separation:

> Women bring to the life cycle a different point of view and order human experience in terms of different priorities. . . . The mystery of women's development lies in its recognition of the continuing importance of attachment in the human life cycle. Woman's place in man's life cycle is to protect this recognition while the developmental litany intones the celebration of separation, autonomy, individuation, and natural rights. (Gilligan, 1982, p. 22–23)

These differing perspectives produce differences in self-image, relationships, and the construction of moral problems. Women define themselves in the context of relationships and judge themselves by their ability to care; for them, moral problems involve conflicting responsibilities not competing rights. Resolution of moral problems requires contextual thinking; for women, morality is centered on the understanding of relationships and responsibilities (Gilligan, 1982).

Both Beck and Gilligan, then, see men and women as operating from different cognitive modes or perspectives. Neither theorist assumes one mode to be superior to the other.

What is the nature of the empirical data? Beck's group has developed a series of scales designed to measure the various phenomena described in his theory. Although gender differences are rarely reported, there is some evidence to suggest that men and women differ on the Self-Concept Test and that, consistent with theory, the two personality modes are relatively independent, so that characteristics of both may exist in the same individual (Beck & Epstein, 1982; Beck, Emery, Epstein, & Harrison, 1983). There is also some evidence that there may be differential, gender-related responses to therapy. Comparing two matched groups, Coche, Cooper, and Peterman (1984) found that women gained more from an "interactive" form of group therapy, whereas men benefited from a "cognitive" problem-solving group.

Perhaps the most important research in this area so far are two studies by Clark and Teasdale (1985). Beck (1972, 1976), as noted above, has argued that the affective, motivational, and behavioral symptoms of depression are related to negative cognitions with certain kinds of content. Women, however, are more likely to become depressed (Weissman & Klerman, 1977) and remain depressed longer (Dunn & Skuse, 1981). Beck's theory, alone, does not explain these facts. Studying the effects of mood on the accessibility of pleasant and unpleasant words, Clark and Teasdale provide a partial explanation for women's greater vulnerability to depression as well as longer recovery times.

Using both Beck's theory and associated network models of the effects of mood on memory, which stress the importance of an individual's past emotional experience with particular cognitions, Clark and Teasdale (1985) found that women recalled significantly more mood congruent words. That is, in a pleasant mood, women recalled more pleasant words and in a dysphoric mood they recalled more unpleasant words. This suggests that mild depression in women may selectively induce the production of further negative cognitions. These, in turn, increase the depressed mood, creating a vicious cycle in which women move from a mild depression to a more severe one and, thus, take longer to recover. A previous episode of depression will increase a woman's risk of a future one, because it strengthens the association between the negative cognitions and the depressed mood (Clark & Teasdale, 1985; Teasdale, 1983).

Clark and Teasdale's work is important not only because it helps to explain women's vulnerability to depression in cognitive terms but also because it indicates that there may be gender-related differences in cognitive processing that could help explain women's disproportionate representation in other disorders (Archer & Lloyd, 1985). If such cognitive differences exist, it may be possible to devise specific therapeutic approaches to deal with them. Research on gender differences in cognition would seem then, on the basis of the current evidence, to be both a fruitful and clinically useful enterprise.

Further research is also needed on Beck's personality modes. Beck (1984) hypothesizes a continuity between premorbid personality, basic assumptions, specific vulnerabilities, the effect of premorbid personality on the patterning of depressive symptoms, the behavior of the patient in therapy, and differential effects of various cognitive techniques. Research thus far on the personality modes has been directed toward developing the Sociotropy Autonomy Scale. We need to know if the two modes are actually gender-related, whether the modes really predict type of depression and symptom patterns, and whether the two types do respond differentially to the therapeutic approaches suggested by Beck.

More generally, researchers need to include women in their studies, analyze data by gender, and discuss differences when they are found (Collins & McNair, 1986). Some of the differences found may be merely interesting observations, others may help us to refine our therapeutic techniques and develop new, more effective ones.

REFERENCES

Beck, A.T. (1972). *Depression: Causes and treatment*. Philadelphia: University of Pennsylvania Press.

Beck, A.T. (1976). *Cognitive therapy and the emotional disorders.* New York: International Universities Press.

Beck, A.T. (1984). Cognitive therapy of depression: New perspectives. In P. Clayton & J. Barrett (Eds.), *Treatment of depression* (pp. 265-291). New York: Raven Press.

Beck, A.T., & Emery, G. (1985), *Anxiety disorders and phobias.* New York: Basic Books.

Beck, A.T., Emery, G., Epstein, N., & Harrison, R. (1983). *Development of the sociotrophy-autonomy scale.* Unpublished manuscript. Center for Cognitive Therapy, University of Pennsylvania.

Beck, A.T., & Epstein, N. (1982, June). *Cognitions, attitudes and personality dimensions in depression.* Paper presented at meeting of the Society for Psychotherapy Research, Smugglers Notch, VT.

Beck, A.T., & Greenberg, R. (1974). Cognitive therapy with depressed women. In V. Franks & B. Vasanti (Eds.), *Women in therapy* (pp. 113-131). New York: Brunner-Mazel.

Blechman, E. (Ed.). (1984). *Behavior modification with women.* New York: Guilford.

Carmen, E., Russo, N., & Miller, J. (1984). Inequality in women's mental health. In P. Rieker & E. Carmen (Eds.), *The gender gap in psychotherapy* (pp. 17-38). New York: Plenum.

Clark, D., & Teasdale, J. (1985). Constraints in the effects of mood and memory. *Journal of Personality and Social Psychology, 48* (6), 1-13.

Coche, E., Cooper, J., & Peterman, K. (1984). Differential outcomes of cognitive and interactional group therapies. *Small Group Behavior, 15,* 497-509.

Collins, R., & McNair, L. (1986). Black women and behavior therapy. *The Behavior Therapist, 1,* 7-10.

Dunn, G. & Skuse, D. (1981). The natural history of depression in general practice. Stochastic models. *Psychological Medicine, 11,* 755-764.

Gilligan, C. (1982). *In a different voice.* Cambridge, MA: Harvard University Press.

Hare-Mustin, R. (1983). An appraisal of the relationship between women and psychotherapy. *The American Psychologist, 38,* 593-601.

Lazarus, A. (1974). Women in behavior therapy. In V. Franks & B. Vashanti (Eds.), *Women in therapy* (pp. 217-229). New York: Brunner-Mazel.

Lerner, H. (1984). Special issues for women in psychotherapy. In P. Rieker & E. Carmen (Eds.), *The gender gap in psychotherapy* (pp. 271-283). New York: Plenum.

Meichenbaum, D., & Cameron, R. (1982). Cognitive-behavior therapy. In G. Wilson & C. Franks (Eds.), *Contemporary behavior therapy* (pp. 310-338). New York: The Guilford Press.

Resnick, P., Calhoun, K., Rothblum, E., Dartnell, N., & Blechman, E. (1986). Sex bias in behavioral journals? *The Behavior Therapist, 2,* 27-29.

Seligman, M.E.P. (1975). *Helplessness: On depression, development, and death.* San Francisco: W.H. Freeman.

Teasdale, J. (1983). Negative thinking in depression: cause, effect or reciprocal relationship? *Advances in Behavior, Research and Therapy. 5,* 3-25.

Weissman, M.M., & Klerman, G.L. (1977). Sex differences in the epidemiology of depression. *Archives of General Psychiatry, 34,* 98-114.

■ Two
DEPRESSION IN CHILDHOOD AND ADOLESCENCE

■ 5
Depression and Young Girls: Early Sorrows and Depressive Disorders

ANITA GURIAN, Ph.D.

> *I cry all night;*
> *I know I'll always be a failure*
> Suzanne, aged 11

Sadness is a mood familiar to all of us, adults and children. For most children, sad moods are transitory, reactive to negative experiences—separation, failure, family conflict—and do not necessarily portend depression. Although the border between unhappiness and a psychiatric condition is blurred, there are some infants and young children who do suffer from depression.

In this chapter we focus on depression in girls—in their infancy, preschool, and school years. We will survey gender differences in (a) prevalence studies, (b) developmental manifestations, (c) theories of depression, (d) family factors such as the relationship to parental depression, (e) social factors such as cultural expectations and school effects, and finally, offer some speculations as to what research in the future will show and implications of the trends suggested by recent demographic data.

CHILDHOOD DEPRESSION—SOME QUESTIONS

Consideration of questions regarding childhood depression in general will provide a context for consideration of gender differences.

Is there such an entity as childhood depression? If there is, is it similar to or different from adult depression? Do depressed children become depressed adults? Although no definitive answers are forthcoming, there is general agreement that childhood depression with a set of symptoms constituting a clinical syndrome does exist.

However, there are several points of view as to its manifestations and diagnosis. Some investigators believe the basic signs and symptoms of depression to be quite similar from the age of six to old age and while they recognize that developmental variations occur, they consider such variations to be minor compared to the consistency of the symptomatology. These investigators apply the set of clinical signs specified for adult depression in the Diagnostic and Statistical Manual III (American Psychiatric Association, 1980), which include depressed affect, low self-esteem, feelings of self-reproach and guilt, social withdrawal, loss of pleasure in usual activities, loss of energy, psychomotor retardation or agitation, sleeping and eating disturbances, morbid ideation, diminished ability to concentrate and others.

Other researchers believe adult criteria are useful, but since manifestations of depression vary with age, developmental factors must be considered. According to this point of view, there are differences in the development of children's cognitive, linguistic, social, and emotional capacities, and therefore the experience and the manifestations of depression will differ according to age. If children are expected to show adult-type symptoms, many depressed children will be missed.

The concept of "masked depression" in children represents still another point of view. In the late 1960s and 1970s some researchers viewed behaviors such as enuresis, headache, school failure, truancy, acting out, etc. as "depressive equivalents" (Glaser, 1967; Lesse, 1974; Toolan, 1962). So many symptoms have been reported to be masking depression that the concept is of limited use. However, depressed mood in children does not occur in isolation, and depression has been found to co-exist with many of the conditions enumerated. In clinical samples, depressed children have been consistently found to exhibit aggressive behaviors, changes in school performance, conduct disorders, hyperactivity, and somatic complaints (Carlson & Cantwell, 1980; Jacobsen, Lahey, & Strauss, 1983; Weinberg, Rutman, Sullivan, Penick, & Deitz, 1973).

Research has proliferated during the past 10 years, but acceptance of childhood depression as a clinical entity has been slow. Depression scales for children have been constructed and numerous studies have expanded our knowledge, but there is no agreement as yet on criteria for diagnosis. There is agreement, however, that depression is multidimensional and includes emotional, cognitive, motor, neurochemical, and social components.

PREVALENCE OF CHILDHOOD DEPRESSION

It is not surprising, given the debate on diagnostic criteria, that reliable data are lacking on the prevalence of depression in childhood.

In addition to inconsistency of diagnostic criteria, studies have varied in age and sex of subjects and the assessment used. Therefore, as might be expected, reported incidence rates vary from 5 to 70% depending on the measures utilized. Cytryn, McKnew, and Bunney (1980), after reviewing studies of depression in children, conclude that 5 to 10% of children are depressed, similar to the proportion in the adult population. In families with a history of depression, the figure ranges from 30 to 50%. In psychiatric facilities, estimates of depressed children range between 12 and 60% of child outpatients (Pearce, 1977), a statistic so broad it underscores the inconsistency of diagnostic criteria.

Studies for the most part have dealt with school-age children who have received treatment. We still know little about depression in preschool children and in those school-age children who are not sufficiently depressed to be hospitalized or receive medication or psychotherapy or who do not come to clinical attention.

Until criteria are agreed upon, it is not possible to accurately state the prevalence of childhood depression. What is agreed upon by researchers, however, is that there are undoubtedly more depressed children than have been recognized.

STUDIES ON GENDER DIFFERENCES

Although it is well known that in adulthood more women than men become depressed, gender differences in childhood depression have been examined only incidentally. Researchers may have assumed that boys and girls have been equally affected, and that gender differences do not appear until adolescence. Some recent books on affective disorders in childhood even omit gender differences as an index entry—a marked contrast to the concern with gender differences in studies of depressed adults.

Despite the neglect of gender differences in childhood depression studies, such differences have been documented in other conditions of childhood. Males appear to be more vulnerable to a wide variety of ills. Although males are larger and stronger than females at most ages, they are more vulnerable to physical hazards. More male fetuses are stillborn, miscarried, born prematurely, or suffer from anoxia and birth defects. During infancy, 37% more boys than girls die, and throughout life more males are afflicted by the major diseases (Garai & Scheinfeld, 1968).

Eme (1979), in a review of the literature on psychopathology in childhood, finds a greater prevalence of boys in the following categories: adjustment reaction, antisocial disorders, attention deficit, gender identity disorders, learning problems, neurotic and psychotic disorders. While Eme does not consider depression as a separate category, it has been viewed as contributing to or co-existing with many of the above conditions. If this is the case, one might then assume that depression, similar to other psychopathology, is more often found in boys. This conclusion would be at variance with the adolescent and adult depressed population, in which females (with unipolar depression) outnumber males in a 2-to-one ratio (Weissman & Klerman, 1977).

Studies on depression in *prepubertal* children, which include some data on gender differences are summarized in Table 5.1. Although findings are inconclusive and in some cases contradictory, several studies raise the possibility that the female/male ratio typical of adult depression may be identified earlier than is generally believed.

DEVELOPMENTAL ASPECTS OF CHILDHOOD DEPRESSION

Although depressed children may in some respects resemble depressed adults, the clinical picture in childhood depression contains certain unique characteristics. Consider the following vignettes:

A nine-month old girl fails to thrive. Her 17-year-old mother has frequent crying spells and suicidal ideas. She has little time for her infant, who is unresponsive, difficult to arouse, looks withdrawn and distant, is undernourished, and her growth rate is slow.

Celia, a seven-year-old, refuses to go to school because of fear that she can't do the work and that the other children will tease her and make her cry. When Celia was two years old, her mother was depressed and had to be hospitalized for three months, during which time Celia was cared for by her grandmother. Celia now keeps asking if her mother will be home when she returns from school and if she can stay home.

Rhonda, 10 years old, daydreams in school and seldom completes her homework. When she gets home each afternoon, she watches television, eats all the cookies she can find, and goes to bed for the rest of the day.

Angela, 11 years old, gets excellent marks but feels she can never do anything right. She spends four hours each night on her homework, and the night before a test she cries and cannot sleep.

The symptoms, meaning, dynamics, and cognitive context for experiencing and understanding depressive feelings increase in complexity with age until adolescence.

A number of writers speculate that manifestations of depression are determined by parallel developments in psychic structure, cognitive level, and language (Anthony, 1975; Cicchetti & Schneider-Rosen, 1986; Rutter, 1986). Thus, the infant may fail to grow physically, the toddler may have prolonged tantrums, the nursery school child may be overly aggressive or withdrawn, the elementary school child may avoid school, the adolescent may refuse to eat. If manifestations of depression vary according to developmental level, a mere downward extension of the theories and concepts of adult depression may not be helpful. The recent trend in classifying children according to adult criteria focuses on the fact that some symptoms are common to both: low self-esteem, social withdrawal, fatigue, and suicidal ideation. However, this view does not take into account the fact that there may be specific features for different ages and developmental levels. Some symptoms of adult depression are not appropriate criteria for use with children and should be eliminated. Guilt and hopelessness, for example, require mature levels of cognitive functioning. On the other hand, aggression and somatic complaints which are not typical of adult depression express children's less mature coping strategies and inadequate defenses (Garber, 1984).

Developmental Stage Differences

Some investigators believe depression in infants does not exist whereas others support its existence (Poznanski & Zrull, 1970; Weiner, 1975). Since attachment to important figures begins early in life, lack or loss of a primary caregiver in infancy is likely to result in a developmental disturbance. Depressive symptoms such as listlessness, unresponsiveness, failure to thrive, and sleeping or eating disorders can exist at virtually any age (Weiner, 1975).

Three critical times in the lives of children are described by Rutter (1986): (1) the appearance of separation anxiety in the second half of the first year, (2) the lessening of this anxiety at about four or five years of age, and (3) the sharp rise in depressive feelings and depressive disorder after puberty, particularly among girls. Puig-Antich et al. (1978) finds a strong relationship between separation anxiety and major depressive disorder in prepubertal children.

The dependent preschool child is more vulnerable to loss or withdrawal of a parent than an older child. In children as young as three years, disturbances of appetite, failure to gain weight, lack of affection for others, and withdrawal have been observed (Poznanski & Zrull, 1970; Frommer, Mendelson, & Reid, 1972; Katz, 1979). Assessment of infants and preschoolers differs from other age groups in that it is based on observation and parental report rather than verbal expression or self-report. Whether depression in very young children is the same as depression in older children has not been established; nevertheless, at the very least, an observable manifestation of loss can occur.

TABLE 5.1 Studies of Depression in Preadolescent Children which Include Data on Gender Differences

Investigators	Year	Population	Ages	N	Criteria	Results
Rutter et al.	1970	General	10–15 years	2,000	Simplified psychiatric classification system	At age 10, 3 depressed children At age 15, 9 depressed & 25 mixed affective disorder; more frequent in girls
Weinberg, Rutman, Sullivan, Penick, & Deitz	1973	Children referred to an educational diagnostic center	6.6–12.8 years (mean age, 9.6 ± 1.4)	50 males, 22 females	Clinical criteria	42 of 72 met criteria. 12 girls; 30 boys depressed
Pearce	1978	Clinic	—	547	—	Prepubertal: 1 in 9 depressive symptoms twice as common in boys Postpubertal: 25% showed depressive symptoms twice as common in girls
Kuperman & Stewart	1979	Child psychiatry clinic, outpatients & inpatients screened	7.9 to 16.1 years	12 males, 10 females	Adult	Of 175 children admitted to clinic, 13% of girls and 0.5% of boys met criteria
Earls	1980	General population	35–42 months	100	Behavioral screening questionnaire	Girls more fearful. Twice as many girls as boys showed depressed mood
Leon, Kendall, & Garber	1980	Elementary grades 3–6	Mean age, 10.9 years	138: 65 females, 73 males	Personality Inventory for Children (PIC)[1]	21 children depressed Depressed boys higher on Inattentive, Impulse & Conduct Disorders

Study	Year	Setting	Age	Sample	Measures	Results
Lefkowitz & Tesiny	1981	Elementary grades 3–5	Mean age, 9.87 years	231 females, 205 males	Peer Nomination[4] Inventory for Depression (PNID)	5.2% overall depressed Underage 8.5 4.7% females 7% males depressed
Jacobson, Lahey, & Strauss	1983	Elementary grades 2–6	7–12 years	109: 50 males, 59 females	Children's Depression Inventory, Peer Nomination Inventory for Depression, Connors Teachers Rating Scale	No sex differences on mean depression scores, but different patterns of correlations. For males all 3 measures correlated with unpopularity & conduct disorders on TRS. For females all 3 measures intercorrelated adequately
Kovacs, Feinberg, Crouse-Novak, Paulauskas, & Finkelstein	1984	Outpatient psychiatric clinic, General pediatric clinic	8–13 years	65: 49 males, 16 females 49 comp. group outpatient psychiatric referrals	Interview[5] Schedule for Children, DSM III	More girls in depressed group than in psychiatric outpatient referral group ($\chi^2 = 7.01$, $p < 0.01$)

Children's Depression Inventory (CDI)[2] Connors Parent[3] Questionnaire (CPQ) Own Inventory

(continued)

TABLE 5.1 (continued)

Investigators	Year	Population	Ages	N	Criteria	Results
Lobovits & Handal	1984	Outpatient psychiatric centers	8–12 years	50: 37 males, 13 females	DSM III, PIC–D, CDI	22% depressed No gender differences
Blumberg & Izard	1985	General population	10–11 years	146: 82 males, 64 females	Children's Depression Inventory, Differential[6] Emotion Scale IV (DES IV), Children's Attributional[7] Style Questionnaire (CASQ)	16 met criteria for depression Girls higher on inner & outer directed hostility Boys higher on outer-directed hostility only; more likely to show conduct disturbance Girls profiles resembled adults more on sadness & hostility components, fear, & shyness
Finch, Saylor, & Edwards	1985	Grades 2–8	Mean age 11.03 years	1463: 705 males, 759 females	Children's Depression Inventory	Boys reported more depressive symptoms; magnitude and clinical significance small
Franko, Powers, Zuroff, & Moskowitz	1985	General population	6–11 years	32: 15 males, 17 females	Taped interviews	Girls reported higher proportions of sadness-inducing events. Higher sadness ratio among girls. Boys employed more cognitive coping strategies.

64

Author	Year	Setting	Age	Sample	Measure	Findings
Seligman & Peterson	1985	Elementary grades	8–11 years	96: 50 males, 46 females	Children's Depression Inventory, Children's Attributional Style (CASQ) Questionnaire (CASQ)	Girls reported more depressive symptoms Girls reported more depressive symptoms
Berenson	1987	Elementary/ grades	10–13 years	321: 157 males, 164 females	Children's Depression Inventory	8% depressed ($N = 25$) No gender differences
Blum, Gurian, & Hassett	1987	Outpatient diagnostic clinic for learning problems	6–11 years	106: 76 males, 30 females	Depression Scale, Child Behavior Checklist[8]	9% of learning-disabled boys in clinical range on Dep. Factor 28% of learning-disabled girls in clinical range on Dep. Factor

[1]Wirt, Lachar, Klinedienst & Seat, 1977
[2]Kovacs & Beck, 1977
[3]Connors, 1973
[4]Lefkowitz & Tesiny, 1981
[5]Kovacs, 1983
[6]Kotsch, Gerbing, & Schwartz, 1982
[7]Seligman & Peterson, 1985
[8]Achenbach, T, 1979

ıental differences in the symptoms of depression have been
by several studies (McConville, Boag, & Purohit, 1973; Ush-
h, 1972). The studies support the notion that symptoms of depression change with advancing age, with more diffuse symptoms found at
younger ages. The manner in which guilt feelings are manifested changes
with cognitive development. It is not until late childhood that the child
becomes able to engage in social comparison and to make more complex
causal attributions and thus to experience more enduring and more intense
guilt feelings (Hoffman, 1982).

Garber (1984), who examined the developmental progression of depression in girls, also found an increase in guilt feelings with age. She studied
137 girls referred because of academic, behavioral, or emotional problems,
aged 7 to 13 years, an age range chosen because it encompasses major
changes in cognitive and physical development.

As age increased, the frequency of individual depressive symptoms, such
as poor appetite, hypoactivity, school problems, depressed feelings,
pervasive loss of interest, hopelessness, irritability, and low self-esteem
increased. Consistent with previous studies, Garber found an increase in
feelings of guilt, hopelessness, and self-depreciation, all dependent on
maturing cognitive ability.

Developmental differences in other aspects of depression have also
been examined, as indicated by the following.

Expression of Sadness—Developmental and Gender Differences

Sadness is the key emotion in depression in both adults and children (Poznanski, 1982). Verbal expression of feelings of sadness increases with age
(Cytryn & McKnew, 1974; Garber, 1984; Glasberg & Aboud, 1981;
McConville et al., 1973; Wamboldt & Kaslow, 1984). Younger children do
not directly express feelings of sadness, but *appear* sad, bored, withdraw interest in previously enjoyable activities, or increase attention-seeking
behavior to communicate distress and obtain relief from painful negative
affect. If asked directly they may use words such as "rotten," "bad," "gross,"
etc., to describe their feelings (Bemporad, 1978; Cole & Kaslow, 1986;
Kovacs & Beck, 1977; Poznanski, 1982). By the fifth or sixth grade,
children can easily describe their feelings of sadness.

Do boys and girls cope differently with feelings of sadness? Franko,
Powers, Zuroff, and Moskowitz (1985) investigated (1) whether or not
children possess strategies for self-regulation of feelings of anger and
sadness, (2) how their strategies may vary with age, sex, or situation,
and (3) how the occurrence of negative emotions varies according to

age, sex or situation. The researchers asked 15 boys and 17 girls, aged six to eleven years, "Could you describe for me some times when you have felt good about something? Could you describe for me some times when you have felt bad about something?" After the children responded, the interviewer asked, "How did that make you feel? What did you do? What could a boy (girl) do to feel better if that happened? What did you do?"

They found that children were able to describe conscious strategies for dealing with negative affect, but found no sex or age differences. Both boys and girls expected to cope with sadness and anger in a variety of ways: (1) behavioral (I'll go tell my mother) rather than cognitive (I'll try to think of something), (2) nonverbalized rather than openly expressed, or (3) self-oriented (I'll watch television) rather than other-oriented (I'll look for a friend).

The most common strategy was to find a distracting activity—a behavioral, nonverbal, noninteractive strategy.

However, gender differences were found in the types of situations reported. Girls reported higher proportions of sadness-inducing events than did boys, especially in interactions with their mothers. In the older groups, boys employed more cognitive strategies in dealing with sadness than did the girls. Boys described more events that elicited anger than did the girls (boys, 53%; girls, 43%), suggesting that more girls might deny feeling angry. That more girls (50%) than boys (30%) reported sadness-inducing events raises the interesting possibility that there may be early precursors of adult sex differences in both depression and in modes of coping with depression. Franko et al. speculate that social learning factors seem to contribute to gender differences in sadness; i.e., sad behavior is differentially reinforced in boys and girls by mother, father, friends, etc., who may be less tolerant of sadness in boys. The finding that boys reported more anger than sadness is consistent with other research that shows that boys display more anger and aggression than girls. It remains unclear, however, whether children who express sadness have a greater or lesser propensity for depression later in life.

THEORIES OF DEPRESSION AND THEIR IMPLICATIONS FOR FEMALE DEVELOPMENT

Several concepts in psychoanalytic developmental and object relations theory apply to gender differences in childhood depression. A number of writers believe that girls psychological development renders them more prone to depression than boys (see H. Harris, *this volume;* B. Fibel, *this volume;* and D. Jack, *this volume.*)

Cognitive Theory of Depression

Cognitive models of depression include the cognitive distortion model proposed by Beck (1967) and Kovacs and Beck (1977), and the learned helplessness model based on the work of Seligman (1974) and Seligman, Peterson, Kaslow, Alloy, & Abramson (1978).

Cognitive Distortion Model. Beck proposes that three areas, referred to as the "cognitive triad," cause depression. These include one's view of self, the world, and the future. The depressed person is said to exaggerate or misinterpret events, view events out of context, and distort experience in such a way that it confirms his/her negative view of self, the world and the future. The result is a sense of worthlessness and self-rejection, defeatism, and hopelessness (see S. Joseph, *this volume*).

Cognitive style, according to Beck, evolves at an early age, as illustrated by the following letter written to a newspaper advice columnist and signed "Suzanne, Failure Forever at 11."

> I have a huge problem. Whatever I do, I seem to fail. At school, I got a D in social studies because of zeroes I didn't earn—because everyone copies my paper if they didn't do their homework, and the teacher thinks I copied or let them copy. When I talk to the kids, he marks me down for talking.
>
> When I got my report card, my father was really mad, so I ran away, but a day later he found me and was even madder and hurt. I talk to my parents, but they don't believe me about the zeroes. They think I just didn't do the work and think I talk all day.
>
> My brother and sister won't even listen to me. I cry all night. I'm really trying to change, but it's no use. I know I will always be a failure.

Learned Helplessness Model

The similarities between learned helplessness and depression are pointed out by Seligman (1974). Learned helplessness occurs when life experiences teach one to view problems as insurmountable, to perceive no connection between one's actions and the onset or termination of bad events. One expects failure to occur no matter what efforts one makes, and eventually depression results. However the *degree* of helpless feelings or depression depends on the "attributions" people make about the uncontrollable events—how people account for the causes of the events that trouble them.

Seligman et al. (1978) suggested that the following three dimensions are important: (1) *Internal attributions:* If bad events are attributed to characteristics *within* the individual, helplessness develops and self-esteem diminishes. (2) *Stable attributions:* Bad events are attributed to facts that persist over time; helplessness is expected to be permanent. (3) *Global attributions:* If bad events are attributed to causes that are present in a variety of situations, rather than in a specific situation, helplessness is predicted to be pervasive.

Learned Helplessness Theory and Children. Learned helplessness in children, as in adults, is marked by difficulties in problem-solving. When Seligman and Peterson (1985) asked 96 8- to 13-year-old children, with equal numbers of boys and girls, to complete block design and anagrams tasks and questionnaires on depression and attributional style, they found that those children who attributed failure to internal, stable, and global causes were more likely to report depressive symptoms than the children who attributed failure to external, unstable, and specific causes.

The children who showed the depressive attributional style were found to have depressive symptoms when retested six months later, which suggests that this attributional style may be a risk factor for depression.

Learned Helplessness and Girls. Girls are more likely than boys to show helpless patterns of attributions and are more likely than boys to make internal and stable attributions for their failures. Girls blame their own poor ability for failure, whereas boys persist despite their failure, blame bad luck, and place more emphasis on the role of their own effort. (Crandall, Katkovsky, & Crandall, 1965; Dweck & Licht, 1980; Dweck & Repucci, 1973; Nicholls, 1975).

When 10- and 11-year-old depressed children were studied by Blumberg and Izard (1985), girls were found to be more similar than boys to depressed adults in that they reported sadness, anger, self-directed hostility, and shame. More girls than boys explained negative events in terms of internal, stable, and global causes.

Socialization Effects

Learned helplessness in girls may be due to differing socialization experiences—two different tracks are established early in life. Boys are socialized to be independent, to persist in the face of failure, to develop internal standards for performance that render them less vulnerable to negative evaluation by others. Girls are socialized to remain more dependent on feedback from others in judging their own abilities or the adequacy of their performance (see D. Jack, *this volume*). They attribute failure to a lack in themselves, and when they do succeed, they attribute success to the ease of the task or luck, rather than to their own competence.

Gender differences in socialization exist even before a child is born. Expectant parents throughout the world, at least until recently, stated a preference for male children (Hoffman, 1977). Despite evidence to the contrary, girls are thought to be more delicate, and parents play rougher games with boys, encouraging them to move about and explore. Girls are kept physically close to the mother, more dependent, more confined to the physical limits of the home, whereas outdoor play is encouraged for boys. For girls, quiet behavior is expected and reinforced, but quiet behavior is seen as abnormal in boys. Aggressive behavior is not only tolerated in boys; it may even be encouraged.

Even children's literature reflects this pattern and until quite recently portrayed mothers as staying home, fathers actively exploring and interacting with the world. Bronfenbrenner (1979), describing the difference between boys' and girls' socialization notes that parents' socialization of sons seems to focus primarily on directing and constraining their impact on the environment. With daughters, parents aim to protect the girl from the impact of the environment. Thus, the boy is being prepared to actively mold his world, the girl to be passively molded by it. And throughout childhood, the media, schools, and other socializing agents reinforce this view. (For an object-relations point of view of girls' socialization, see B. Fibel, *this volume*).

Teacher/Boy/Girl Interaction.   The two different socialization tracks can be identified in school also. Teachers respond differentially to male and female students even at an early age. For example, preschool teachers are three times more likely to react to boys' behavior, positive or negative, and to ignore girls' behavior (Serbin & O'Leary, 1975). Girls, on the other hand, are rewarded for dependency behaviors and receive more attention while in close proximity to the teacher. In this way, boys learn that actions produce results, positive or negative, and that they have some control over rewards. Block (1975) has suggested that teachers see girls as needing help and protection.

Studies of type of teacher feedback and its relationship to female underachievement have found girls to be more sensitive to feedback from teachers than from their peers (Dweck & Bush, 1976; Dweck, Davidson, Nelson, & Enna, 1978; Goetz & Dweck, 1980). Elementary school teachers accompany corrections, suggestions and criticisms with attributions, such as "Robert, you can do it if you try harder with your long division problems" (Dweck & Licht, 1980). For boys, about 45% of the teachers' negative criticism focused on conduct or other *nonintellectual* aspects of their work, such as failure to obey the rules of form, lack of neatness or motivation. For girls, almost 90% of negative feedback related directly to the accuracy and *intellectual* quality of their work ("You just don't understand long division"). Thus, girls come to feel that an evaluation is indicative of their intellectual ability and attribute failure to a defect in themselves, which may cause them to feel they can't succeed. Boys, however, perceive the teacher's evaluations as unrelated to their intellectual ability and therefore are apt to attribute failure to motivational or external factors, such as the unfairness of the test, not having been taught the material, not trying hard enough, etc. Thus, for boys, negative feedback has little effect on the estimation of their own ability while for girls it results in lowered self-esteem.

Gender differences also exist in expectancies, as girls are less willing than boys to try new tasks and tend to rate tasks as more difficult than do boys (Dweck & Elliot, 1983).

Findings such as these suggest that such patterns of student/teacher interaction at a young age may contribute to women's perceptions of themselves as dependent on the opinions of others common among depressed women.

Depression and Learning Problems—Is There a Connection? Depression in children, difficult at best for mental health professionals to identify, can be unrecognized by teachers, who may be misdiagnosing depressed children as having learning problems (Colbert, Newman, Ney, & Young, 1982).

The relationship between school performance and depression is not clear. In some cases, depression may precede the learning problem, whereas in others, depression may be reactive to the learning problem. Some studies find no difference in achievement test scores between depressed and nondepressed children (Brumback, Dietz-Schmidt, & Weinberg, 1977), whereas others have found some aspects of cognitive functioning in depressed children to be impaired (Kaslow, Rehm, & Siegel, 1984; Kaslow, Tannenbaum, Abramson, Peterson, & Seligman, 1983; Lefkowitz & Tesiny, 1980; Tesiny, Lefkowitz, & Gordon 1980). Learning disabled children have been found to have higher rates of depression than would be expected (Brumback et al., 1977; Weinberg et al., 1973).

Depression and Learning Problems and Girls. Until recently the learning-disabled population contained five times as many boys as girls. There is evidence, however, that this ratio is changing as more girls are being identified. Differences have been found in behavior patterns, with learning-disabled girls characterized by withdrawal, boys by aggressive and acting-out behavior (Hassett & Gurian, 1984). When learning-disabled and nonlearning-disabled girls at different ages were compared by Epstein,

Cullinan, and Nieminen (1984), feelings of inferiority, anxiety, and social withdrawal were more prevalent among the learning-disabled girls. (They did not compare learning disabled girls and boys). Gender differences among learning-disabled children generally have not been examined.

Data collected by Formanek (1981) on ten 11- to 13-year-old girls referred for the diagnosis of learning problems showed that until the fifth grade, all had been obedient, good students who had worked hard, and acquired their basic skills. However they remained nonassertive, they asked few questions, clung to the safety of their families, and suffered from separation anxiety and low self-esteem. While obedience and conformity aid children in mastering the basic learning skills, these qualities may actually impede the academic work in the upper elementary and junior high schools, which demands greater cognitive autonomy. Students must learn to read critically, think about what they read, generalize, paraphrase, and at times take issue with the content. The girls withdrew from school work as the greater autonomy required conflicted with their wishes to remain dependent. Their academic functioning was impaired, they became more anxious with increasing age, and their learning problems might be viewed as contributing to depressed mood.

THE FAMILY AND DEPRESSION IN GIRLS

Twin, adoptee, and family studies suggest the operation of genetic factors in depression, and some genetic factors have been identified that may contribute to gender differences (see M. Weissman & G. Klerman, *this volume*).

The most important factor in the development of childhood depression is the presence of a depressed parent (McKnew & Cytryn, 1973; Orvaschel, Weissman, & Kidd, 1980). Parental depression can affect a child in several ways even if the predisposition is not genetically transmitted. Most children identify with their parents, and depressed affect may be modeled in this way. In addition, since the availability of an emotionally responsive caretaker is basic to healthy emotional development, it is obvious that a depressed parent may not be able to meet the needs of a child. Children of depressed parents represent a group at risk for deviations or delays in emotional development (Beardslee, Bemporad, Keller, & Klerman, 1983).

Mothers are generally the major caretakers, and maternal depression can affect even very young infants. In a recent critical review of the literature on postpartum depression, Hopkins, Marcus, and Campbell (1984) state that mild to moderate postpartum depression (similar to an untreated nonpostpartum clinical depression) affects as many as 20% of new mothers and, in turn, may be expected to exert its effects on infants.

Depressed affect in mothers may result in a pattern similar to a helplessness response in their infants. Infants as young as three months who are unable to evoke responsiveness or elicit changes in caregivers' affect may modify their own affective manifestations, i.e., avert their gaze or become wary (Cohn & Tronick, 1983).

The typical depressed patient today, according to Weissman and Klerman (1977), is apt to be a young woman in her reproductive years (i.e., between 25 and 44), often married, living at home, and rearing children. The illness has a serious impact on her capacity to enjoy life and on her capacity to be a good mother.

Weissman, Paykel, and Klerman (1972), who found depressed women to be impaired as parents due to their preoccupation with self, lack of energy, and irritability, identified four areas of impairment: (1) inability to be emotionally involved with their children, (2) inability to maintain communication, (3) inability to show affection for children, resulting in mothers' feelings of guilt and inadequacy, and (4) increased hostility directed toward the children. Many of the children withdrew, did not share feelings or problems, developed problems in school, with friends, or with the law, and some children became withdrawn and sad.

Maternal Depression—Differential Effects on Sons and Daughters

Depressed children are likely to have depressed mothers (Poznanski & Zrull, 1970; Schechtman, Gilpin, & Worland, 1976). Common sense suggests that a depressed mother's main influence would be on her younger and more dependent children. She would also influence those who spend more time with her and are more likely to imitate and identify with her. In most cases, these would be daughters rather than sons.

Two- and three-year-old girls are more intensely involved with their mothers than boys of the same age (Olesker, 1984). Toddler girls, due to their more rapid maturation, experience earlier awareness of separation. In Olesker's study, the girls engaged in less peer play than the boys, and their play differed in variety from that of the boys. Their predominant need was for closeness with, and control of their mothers. This need may have interfered with the development of greater independence and other ego capacities and hence for experiences that would stabilize the girls' sense of separateness.

Generally, girls' attachments to their mothers appear to last longer than do those of boys, according to Chodorow (1978). She states that because mothers and daughters are the same gender, mothers tend not to experience their daughters as separate from themselves, as they do their sons. Mothers' sense of oneness and continuity with daughters is stronger and lasts longer than with sons, contributing to the possibility of an ongoing undifferentiated dependent relationship with their mothers.

Children learn their attributional style (or depressive symptoms) from their mothers, and the depressions of mother and child may maintain each other. For example, in a family in which the depressed mother's relationship with her husband is a subservient one, the mother–daughter identification carries with it the message of a social position that fosters low self-esteem. In children of divorced families, the majority of whom live with their mothers, this effect would be heightened (Seligman, 1985).

Another factor to be considered in the prolonged mother–daughter closeness is that boys develop gross motor activities at an earlier age and thus physically move away from mother. In addition school and peer group activities become important for boys sooner than for girls (Wynne & Frader, 1979). Historically, the boy has been encouraged to leave the home as preparation for adulthood, whereas the girl's task has been to accept and cultivate passivity and dependence on the family, and then to transfer that dependence from parents to husband.

This pattern may be shifting somewhat at the present time. Although both boys and girls are vulnerable to depression when living with a depressed mother, the effects appear to be more negative for girls.

Amy Y.—A Depressed 10-Year-Old

The following case study, from a child development center, shows the effects of a divorce on a 10-year-old who continued to live with her mother. Divorce evokes many complex reactions, but in this account we focus on the interweaving of the effects of family break-up, environment, and maternal depression.

Ten-year-old Amy's mother, Mrs. Y., became depressed and was placed on an anti-depressant when her marriage of 15 years ended in divorce. Although she was a college graduate, she could obtain only a routine secretarial job, from which she was often absent because she could not get up on time. She worried a great deal about her appearance and her inability to buy new clothes. At the time of the divorce, Amy's brother, aged 12, went to live with their father in another city while Amy remained with their mother. When Amy was away from home, she would frequently telephone her mother to make sure she was all right.

Amy was brought to the child development center for evaluation at the age of 10 because she was failing in school. She was frequently ill with colds and sore throats and could not attend school regularly. During the initial interview, Amy sat close to her mother and reached out for her hand from time to time. Her downcast features mimicked those of her mother.

Amy, a tall, thin girl, carefully groomed, described herself as "not much to look at." Well-related and spontaneous in her conversation, she described herself as a victim of teachers who "don't care about me." Amy said she didn't try to do her work in school because she expected to fail. She scored in the above-average range of intelligence, except for a deficient fund of information, which was thought to be a function of her diminution of interest in the outside world. Her acquisition and recall of information was vague, and inaccurate, although her learning skills were adequate for grade-appropriate work. Projective tests suggested some reasons for Amy's poor school performance. An emotionally immature girl, she denied her neediness and dependence. Wishing her life to be conflict-free, Amy constructed a fantasy world in which she was happy. Amy denied unhappiness and projected blame onto others. Her chronic fatigue and illness suggested depressive feelings. She appeared to have given up on herself, withdrawing from responsibility. While Amy was interested in making friends, her relationships were clinging and lacked intimacy. Her aspirations about the future were vague and unrealistic. She was frightened of the future, unhappy and isolated, yet she maintained a facade of social appropriateness and interest.

In the Y. family, as in many families of divorce, the daughter, not the son, remained with the mother during her period of depression. Unable to express her own feelings of aggression and anger, she became overly identified with her mother's sadness, proneness to illness and fatigue, resistance to leaving the house, and concern with appearance and clothes.

IS ADOLESCENCE A TURNING POINT FOR DEPRESSION IN WOMEN?

According to a number of researchers, female depressives begin to outnumber males at adolescence (Kandel & Davies, 1982; Pearce, 1978; Rutter, 1970; Rutter, 1986; Rutter, Tizard, & Whitmore, 1981), and female gender is the strongest sociodemographic risk factor for depression in adolescence (Wells, Deykin, & Klerman, 1985).

A number of explanations have been offered as to why adolescence may be the critical period for girls to manifest overt depressive symptoms.

Rutter (1986) lists several possibilities for the change in gender ratio in depression, including (1) hormonal changes, (2) genetic factors, (3) the possibility that girls are more vulnerable to environmental stresses, (4) the possibility that girls experience disadvantages on reaching adolescence that were not operative during the childhood years, (5) the cognitive set associated with learned helplessness, and (6) developmental changes in children's concepts of emotions and in their ability to express them, to be aware of emotions in others, and to appreciate the emotional connotations of social situations. However, Rutter cautions that these explanations are speculative, and our understanding of the developmental mechanisms is incomplete.

Gove and Herb (1974), in a review of the literature on psychopathology in children, suggest that adolescence brings an increase of stress for girls and a decrease for boys. First, there is a sudden narrowing of the sex role; the girl is restricted from activities that are deemed masculine. This precipitous constriction of sex role is thought to induce conflict and anxiety. The prime example is that of the girl who was once rewarded for academic success but comes to believe in adolescence that she should not surpass men. As a result, she may avoid and/or fear success. During the adolescent and college years women are torn between the rewards of high academic and occupational success and the possible loss of relationships. In addition, as women are said to perceive their roles as depending on the actions of others, adolescents may experience more uncertainty about the future.

Physical changes may contribute to a more stressful adolescence for a girl. For some, menstruation is accompanied by feelings of tension, feelings of loss of control of their bodies, irritability, anxiety, and depression. Pubertal changes appear to cause more concern for girls, due in part to the fact that only the female has to face the possibility of unwanted pregnancy. Whereas the male only fears sexual failure, the female fears both failure and success.

In addition to citing endocrine factors as a possible cause for the apparent rise in female adolescent depression, Weissman and Klerman (1977) list other contributants: inferior social status resulting in passivity and dependency and higher reactivity to stress.

Females seem to respond to stress according to the sex stereotypical pattern of self-blame, regardless of situation, rather than externalizing blame. H.B. Lewis (*this volume*) comments on the vulnerability of women to feelings of shame and guilt, which may relate to depression in female adolescents. Lewis (1986) hypothesizes that when girls reach puberty they discover they are second-class citizens in a competitive world. Their guilt feelings, previously adaptive when experienced with a stably affectionate and appropriately judging mother, then become nonadaptive and contribute to depression.

The past two decades have seen substantial changes in the options for teenage girls, due to the influence of the Women's Movement and greater availability of education. These changes have brought a blurring of sex-role differences in adolescents, and for some adolescent girls, conflict about passivity and dependency on the one hand, and assertiveness on the other, has become a psychological issue (Wynne & Frader, 1979).

Is the adolescent turning-point a reality? Has depression in prepubertal girls been overlooked?

Numerous reasons have been offered—biological, familial, psychological, and societal—for the sharp increase in female depression apparent at adolescence. However, some data suggest that the precursors of depression in adult women may be present even before adolescence (Blumberg & Izard, 1985; Kovacs, 1983; Franko et al., 1985). It may be that depressed girls in the early and middle years go unrecognized, undiagnosed, and untreated. Parents and teachers view the docile or withdrawn girl as socially more appropriate than the docile or withdrawn boy. Thus, they may seek help sooner for the boy. In adolescence, symptoms typically associated with depression may emerge in more obvious form in girls, whereas boys' depressed mood may co-exist with and be overshadowed by more aggressive and self-destructive behaviors.

SUMMARY

This chapter focused on depression in girls, examining gender differences in prevalence studies, developmental manifestations, theories of depression as they relate to girls, and family and other socialization influences.

Despite the established 2:1 prevalence of depressed adult women to adult men, few attempts have been made to explore the antecedents of female adult depression. In addition to determining how the signs and symptoms of depression vary according to age, we need to know how they vary according to gender. In this respect, genetic processes, biological reorganizations, and individual differences in response to critical life events and to socialization practices, as well as their interactions, must be examined.

An emerging pattern that may affect the incidence of depression in young girls in the future demands consideration. Since evidence exists that depression is occurring in adult women at increasingly younger ages (M.M. Weissman and G. Klerman, *this volume*) it is likely to coincide with the period in their lives when they are bearing children and when their children are young. Young girls may be considered to be more vulnerable than boys to the effects of their mothers' depressions, since mother-daughter relationships are more intense, and their process of separation is more complex than that of boys. The groundwork for the separation/autonomy conflict that characterizes the lives of many adult depressed women, is established early in life. In addition, feelings of dependency, inhibition of anger, helplessness, lack of assertiveness, sense of powerlessness, and reliance on the opinions of others, all characteristics of female development, and predisposing to depression, are more common in pre-adolescent girls than boys. Critical questions regarding the mental health of women must include the following: How will the increase in depression in young adult women affect their daughters? Are the precursors of female adult depression discernible, and perhaps preventable, in young girls?

REFERENCES

Achenbach, T. (1979). The child behavior profile: an empirically based system for assessing children's behavioral problems and competencies. *International Journal of Mental Health, 7*, 24–42.

American Psychiatric Association. (1980). *Diagnostic and statistical manual of mental disorders* (3rd ed.), Washington, D.C.

Anthony, E.J. (1975). Childhood depression, In E. Anthony & T. Benedek (Eds.), *Depression and human existence*, (pp. 231–279). Boston: Little Brown and Co.

Beardslee, W., Bemporad, J., Keller, M., & Klerman, G. (1983). Children of parents with major affective disorder: a review. *American Journal of Psychiatry, 140*, 825–844.

Beck, A. (1967). *Depression: clinical, experimental and theoretical aspects*. New York: Harper and Row.

Bemporad, J. (1978). Manifest symptomatology of depression in children and adolescents. In S. Arieti & J. Bemporad (Eds.), *Severe and mild depressions: The psychotherapeutic approach*. New York: Basic Books.

Berenson, N. (1987). *Depressive correlates*. Unpublished doctoral dissertation, Hofstra University, Hempstead, NY.

Block, J. (1975). Another look at differentiation in the socialization behaviors of mothers and fathers. In F. Denmark & J. Sherman (Eds.), *Psychology of women: Future directions of research*. New York: Psychological Dimensions.

Blum, E., Gurian, A., & Hassett, I. (1987). Behavioral characteristics of learning-disabled children. (in preparation).

Blumberg, S., & Izard, C. (1985). Affective and cognitive characteristics of depression in 10- and 11-year-old children. *Journal of Personality and Social Psychology, 49*(1), 194–202.

Bronfenbrenner, U. (1979). *The ecology of human development*. Cambridge, MA: Harvard University Press.

Brumback, R., Dietz-Schmidt, S., & Weinberg, W. (1977). Depression in children referred to an educational diagnostic center. *Diseases of the Nervous System, 38*, 529–535.

Carlson, G., & Cantwell, D. (1980). Unmasking masked depression in children and adolescents. *American Journal of Psychiatry, 137*, 445–449.

Chodorow, N. (1978). *The reproduction of mothering. Psychoanalysis and the sociology of gender*. Berkeley: University of California Press.

Cicchetti, D., & Schneider-Rosen, K. (1986). An organizational approach to childhood depression. In M. Rutter, C. Izard, & P. Read (Eds.), *Depression in young people* (pp. 71–135). New York: Guilford Press.

Cohn, J., & Tronick, E. (1983). Three-month-old infants' reaction to simulated maternal deprivation. *Child Development, 54,* 185–193.

Colbert, P., Newman, B., Ney, P., & Young, J. (1982). Learning disabilities as a symptom of depression in children. *Journal of Learning Disabilities, 15,* 333–336.

Cole, P., & Kaslow, N. (1986). Interactional and cognitive strategies for affect regulation: a developmental perspective on childhood depression. In L.D. Alloy (Ed.), *Cognitive processes in depression.* New York: Guilford Press.

Connors, C. (1973). Rating scales for use in drug studies with children. *Psychopharmacology Bulletin, 41,* 24–31.

Crandall, V., Katkovsky, W., & Crandall, V. (1965). Children's beliefs in their own control of reinforcements in intellectual-academic achievement situations. *Child Development, 36,* 91–109.

Cytryn, L., & McKnew, D. (1974). Factors influencing the changing clinical expression of the depressive process in children. *American Journal of Psychiatry, 131*(8), 879–881.

Cytryn, L., McKnew, D., & Bunney, W. (1980). Diagnosis of depression in children: a reassessment, *American Journal of Psychiatry, 137*(1), 581–587.

Dweck, C., & Bush, E. (1976). Sex differences in learned helplessness: Differential debilitation with peers and adult evaluators. *Developmental Psychology, 12*(2), 147–156.

Dweck, C., Davidson, W., Nelson, S., & Enna, B. (1978). Sex differences in learned helplessness: II. The contingencies of evaluative feedback in the classroom and III. An experimental analysis. *Developmental Psychology, 14,* 268–276.

Dweck, D., & Elliott, E. (1983). Achievement motivation. In P. Mussen (Ed.), *Handbook of childhood psychopathology Vol. 4* (4th ed.), (pp. 643–691). New York: Wiley.

Dweck, C., & Licht, B. (1980). Learned helplessness and intellectual achievement. In J. Garber & M. Seligman (Eds.), *Human helplessness.* New York: Academic Press.

Dweck, C., & Repucci, N. (1973). Learned helplessness and reinforcement responsibility in children. *Journal of Personality and Social Psychology, 193*(25), 109–116.

Earls, F. (1980). Prevalence of behavior problems in 3-year-old children. *Archives of General Psychiatry, 37,* 1153–1157.

Eme, R. (1979). Sex differences in childhood psychopathology: A review. *Psychological Bulletin, 86,* 574–595.

Epstein, M., Cullinan, D., & Nieminen, G. (1984). Social behavior problems and learning disabled and normal girls. *Journal of Learning Disabilities, 17*(10), 609–611.

Finch, A., Saylor, C., & Edwards, G. (1985). Children's Depression Inventory: Sex and grade norms to normal children. *Journal of Consulting and Clinical Psychology, 53*(3), 424–425.

Formanek, R. (1981). Children and depression. Paper presented at meeting of American Association of Psychiatric Clinics for Children, San Francisco.

Franko, D., Powers, T., Zuroff, D., & Muskowitz, D. (1985). Children and affect: Strategies for self-regulation and sex differences in sadness. *American Journal of Orthopsychiatry, 55*(2), 210–219.

Froman, P. (1971). *The development of a depression scale for the Personality Inventory for Children (PIC)*. Unpublished manuscript, University of Minnesota.

Frommer, E., Mendelson, W., & Reid, M. (1972). Differential diagnosis of psychiatric disturbance in preschool children. *British Journal of Psychiatry, 121,* 71–74.

Garai, J., & Scheinfeld, A. (1968). Sex differences in behavioral traits. *Genetic Psychology Monographs, 77,* 169–299.

Garber, J. (1984). The developmental progression of depression in female children. In D. Cicchetti & K. Schneider-Rosen (Eds.), *Childhood depression: new directions for child development* (pp. 29–58). No. 26. San Francisco: Jossey-Bass.

Glasberg, R., & Aboud, F. (1981). A developmental perspective on the study of depression: Children's evaluative reactions to sadness. *Developmental Psychology, 17*(2), 195–202.

Glaser, K. (1967). Masked depression in children and adolescents, *Annual Progress in Child Psychiatry and Child Development, 1,* 345–355.

Goetz, T., & Dweck, C. (1980). Learned helplessness in social situations. *Journal of Personality and Social Psychology, 39,* 252–255.

Gove W., & Herb T. (1974). Stress and mental illness among the young: A comparison of the sexes. *Social Forces, 53,* 256–265.

Hassett, I., & Gurian, A. (1984). *The learning-disabled girl: a profile.* Paper delivered at the Second Interdisciplinary Congress on Women. University of Groningen, The Netherlands APA Meeting, Toronto.

Hoffman, L.W. (1977). Changes in family roles, socialization, and sex differences. *American Psychologist, 32,* 644–657.

Hoffman, M. (1982). Affect and moral development. In D. Cicchetti & P. Hesse (Eds.), *Emotional development.* San Francisco: Jossey-Bass.

Hopkins, J., Marcus, M., & Campbell, S. (1984). Postpartum depression: a critical review. *Psychological Bulletin, 95*(3), 498–515.

Jacobsen, R., Lahey, B., & Strauss, C. (1983). Correlates of depressed mood in normal children. *Journal of Abnormal Child Psychology, 11*(1), 29–40.

Kaslow, N., Rehm, L., & Siegel, L. (1984). Social and cognitive correlates of depression in children. *Journal of Abnormal Child Psychology, 12,* 605–620.

Kaslow, N., Tanenbaum, R., Abramson, L., Peterson, C., & Seligman, M. (1983). Problem-solving deficits and depressive symptoms among children. *Journal of Abnormal Child Psychology, 11,* 497–502.

Katz, J. (1979). Depression in the young child. In J. Nowells (Ed.), *Modern perspectives in the psychiatry of infancy* (pp. 435–449). New York: Brunner Mazel.

Kotsch, W., Geroing, D., & Schwartz, L. (1982). The construct validity of the Differential Emotions Scale adapted for children and adolescents. In C.

Izard (Ed.), *Measuring emotions in infants and children.* Cambridge, England: Cambridge University Press.

Kovacs, M. (1983). *Interview schedule for children.* Unpublished manuscript, University of Pittsburgh.

Kovacs, M., & Beck, A. (1977). An empirical-clinical approach towards a definition of childhood depression. In J. Schulterbrandt & A. Raskin (Eds.), *Depression in children* (pp. 1–25). New York: Raven Press.

Kovacs, M., Feinberg, T., Crouse-Novak, M., Paulauskas, S., & Finkelstein, R. (1984). Depressive disorders in childhood. *Archives of General Psychiatry, 41,* 229–237.

Kuperman, S., & Stewart, M. (1979). The diagnosis of depression in children. *Journal of Affective Disorders, 1,* 213–217.

Lefkowitz, M., & Tesiny, E. (1981). Assessment of childhood depression. *Journal of Clinical and Consulting Psychology, 48,* 43–50.

Leon, G., Kendall, P., & Garber, J. (1980). Depression in children: parent, teacher and child perspectives. *Journal of Abnormal Child Psychology, 8*(2), 221–235.

Lesse, S. (1974). Depression masked by acting-out behavior patterns. *American Journal of Psychotherapy, 28,* 352–361.

Lewis, H. (1986). The role of shame in depression. In M. Rutter, C. Izard & P. Read (Eds.), *Depression in Young People* (pp. 325–341). New York: Guilford Press.

Lobovits, D., & Handal, P. (1985). Childhood depression: prevalence using DSM III criteria and validity of parent and child depression scales. *Journal of Pediatric Psychology, 10,* 45–55.

McConville, B., Boag, L, & Purohit, A. (1973). Three types of childhood depression. *Journal of the Canadian Psychiatric Association, 18,* 133–139.

McKnew, D., & Cytryn, L. (1973). Historical background in children with affective disorders. *American Journal of Psychiatry, 130,* 1278.

Nicholls, F. (1975). Causal attributions and other achievement-related cognitions: effects of task outcome, attainment value, and sex. *Journal of Personality and Social Psychology, 31,* 379–389.

Olesker, W. (1984). Sex differences in two and three year olds: mother-child relations, peer relations, and peer play. *Psychoanalytic Psychology, 1*(4), 269–287.

Orvaschel, H., Weissman, M., & Kidd, K. (1980). Children and depression: the children of depressed parents. *Journal of Affective Disorders, 2,* 1–16.

Pearce, J.B. (1978). The recognition of depressive disorder in children. *Journal of the Royal Society of Medicine, 1,* 494–500.

Poznanski, E. (1982). The clinical phenomenology of childhood depression. *American Journal of Orthopsychiatry, 52,* 308–313.

Poznanski, E., & Zrull, J. (1970). Childhood depression: Clinical characteristics of overtly depressed children. *Archives of General Psychiatry, 23,* 8–15.

Puig-Antich, J., Blau, S., Marx, N. Greenhill, L., & Chambers, W. (1978). Prepubertal major depressive disorder: a pilot study. *Journal of the American Academy of Child Psychiatry, 17,* 695–707.

Rutter, M. (1970). Sex differences in children's responses to family stress. In E.

Anthony & C. Koupernik (Eds.), *The child in his family* (pp. 165–197). New York: Wiley.

Rutter, M. (1986). The developmental psychopathology of depression. In M. Rutter, C. Izard, & P. Read (Eds.), *Depression in young people* (pp. 3–33). New York: Guilford Press.

Rutter M., Tizard, J., & Whitmore, K. (1981). *Education, health, and behavior.* London: Longmans, 1970; Huntington, NY: Krieger.

Schechtman, J., Gilpin, D., & Worland, J. (1976). Symtomatic depression as seen in the clinic. In E. Anthony & D. Gilpin (Eds.), *Three clinical faces of childhood* (pp. 205–229). New York: Spectrum.

Seligman, M. (1974). Depression and learned helplessness. In F. Friedman and M. Katz (Eds.), *The psychology of depression.* Washington, DC: Winston.

Seligman, M., & Peterson, C. (1985). Depressive symptoms, attributional style, and helplessness deficits in children. In M. Rutter, C. Izard, and P. Read (Eds.), *Depression in young people* (pp. 223–251). New York: Guilford Press, 1986.

Seligman, M., Peterson, D., Kaslow, N., Alloy, L., & Abramson L. (1978). Attributional style and depressive symptoms among children. *Journal of Abnormal Psychology, 93,* 235–238.

Serbin, L., & O'Leary, D. (1975). How nursery school teaches girls to shut up. *Psychology Today,* December, 57–58.

Tesiny, E., & Lefkowitz, M. (1982). Childhood depression: a six-month follow-up study. *Journal of Consulting and Clinical Psychology, 50,* 778–780.

Tesiny, E., Lefkowitz, M., & Gordon, N. (1980). Childhood depression, locus of control and school achievement. *Journal of Educational Psychology, 72,* 506–510.

Toolan, J.M. (1962). Depression in children and adolescents. *American Journal of Orthopsychiatry, 32,* 404–414.

Ushakov, G., & Girich, Y . (1972). Special features of psychogenic depressions in children and adolescents. In A. Annell (Ed.), *Depressive states in childhood and adolescence.* Stockholm: Almquist and Wiksell.

Wamboldt, F., & Kaslow, N. (1984). Childhood depression: A biopsychosocial review. *Journal of Child Psychology and Psychiatry, 25,* 1–26.

Weinberg, W., Rutman, J., Sullivan, L., Penick, E., & Deitz, S. (1973). Depression in children referred to an educational diagnostic center. *Journal of Pediatrics, 83,* 1065–1072.

Weiner, I.B. (1975). Depression in adolescence. In F.F. Flach & S.C. Draghi (Eds.), *The nature and treatment of depression* (pp. 99–119). New York: John Wiley and Sons.

Weissman, M., & Klerman, G. (1977). Sex differences and the epidemiology of depression. *Archives of General Psychiatry, 34,* 98.

Weissman, M., Paykel, E., & Klerman, G. (1972). The depressed woman as mother. *Social Psychiatry, 7,* 98–108.

Wells, V., Deykin, E., & Klerman, G. (1985). Risk factors for depression in adolescence. *Psychiatric Developments, 3,* 83–108.

Wirt, R., Lachar, D., Klinedienst, R., & Seat, P. (1977). *Multidimensional description of child personality: A manual for the Personality Inventory for Children.* Los Angeles: Western Psychological Services.

Wynne, L., & Frader, L. (1979). Female adolescence and the family: a historical view. In M. Sugar (Ed.), *Female adolescent development* (pp. 63–82). New York: Brunner Mazel.

■ 6
Depression and Adolescent Girls

CHERYL L. KURASH, Ph.D. and
JONATHAN F. SCHAUL, Ph.D.

Given the recent interest in women's mental health, as well as renewed investigations into adolescence and adolescent depression and suicide, it is surprising that there is little that explores depression in adolescent girls. For the most part, clinical and developmental studies on depression have grouped men and women, boys and girls, together with underlying assumptions that development proceeds in identical manner for both sexes and that clinical syndromes share similar etiology and dynamic meaning for the two genders. Recent attention to women's development is beginning to redress past mistakes in this area. For while it is certain that there are a multitude of variables that interact in different ways for each individual, it is also clear that gender is a main organizing variable in any clinical syndrome.

Our approach to understanding depression in adolescent girls will bring together current knowledge about depression and the growing understanding of female development. In this endeavor, we will be guided by both an object relations and systems perspective. The interaction between the individual–family–culture is the broader framework from which any clinical syndrome develops; the linkage among these three systems must be reciprocally enriching for the adolescent to successfully traverse this developmental phase (Kaufman, 1979). It is our belief that the increase in adolescent depression, and particularly in female adolescent depression, is attributed primarily to dysjunction between these three systems. The well-noted instability of today's family system, our parenting/child-rearing practices, and the changing role of women in our society all have major impact on the adolescent girl's developing sense of self, her budding identity, and the regulation of her self-esteem. The focus of this chapter will be to explore female adolescent depression from this tripartite contextual framework and to elucidate particular considerations for today's adolescent girl.

DEPRESSION AND ADOLESCENCE

Epidemiologic studies consistently show that depression in the adolescent population has been increasing in frequency (Klerman & Weissman, 1980; Radloff & Rae, 1979) and that, beginning at age 13 to 14 years, there are higher rates of depression for females than for males (Kandel & Davies, 1982; Gove & Herb, 1974; Radloff & Rae, 1979; Teuting, Koslow, & Hirschfeld, 1981; Weissman and Klerman, 1981). The data on adolescent suicide attempts show that females attempt in far greater numbers (Petzel & Riddle, 1981). Weissman (1980) indicates that these sex differences are not artifacts of reporting or health care behavior, but real indicators of current psychiatric phenomena: females preponderate in rates of depression, even taking into account differences in judging stress, acknowledging symptoms, and help-seeking patterns.

Why the emergence of sex differences at puberty? Many different explanations have been offered, including genetic, endocrinological, psychological, and sociological. It is likely that the reasons are heterogeneous and involve the coincidence of multiple factors. Before exploring more fully some of the issues associated with depression in adolescent girls, we will define depression and discuss its application in adolescence.

Depression can be viewed along a continuum, ranging from a normal, inevitable mood, to a more persistent and pervasive symptom, to a functionally impairing clinical syndrome (Weissman, 1980). While explanations of depression vary, depending upon theoretical orientation and research methodology, it is generally accepted that depression is a reaction to loss of either a love object or a state of well-being, with feelings of diminished self-esteem and hopelessness (Toolan, 1971). The inhibition of anger and aggression (Freud, 1917; Kaplan, 1984) and the inhibition of action or assertiveness (Beck, 1972; Kaplan, 1984; Seligman, 1975; Spitzer, 1980) are frequently cited as characteristic signs of depression. In adolescence, developmental considerations have led to debate concerning the manifestation of depressive affect and the inevitability of depressive feelings during this life stage.

In the past, interest was devoted to the notions of "depressive equivalents" (Sperling, 1959; Toolan, 1962) and "masked depression" (Glaser, 1967; Lesse, 1974; Litman & Wold, 1974; Radloff & Rae, 1979). These terms describe situations in which actual depressive symptomatology was concealed behind various behavioral and somatic problems such as conduct disturbances, delinquency, school phobia (Glaser, 1967; Toolan, 1971); anorexia nervosa, obesity and hypochondriasis (Malmquist, 1972); and school problems and acting out (Bakwin, 1972). Underlying this notion is the belief that the experience and expression of depression depends upon an individual's stage of development and defensive repertoire, and that depression need not be defined solely by the conscious presence of despair or hopelessness.

Depression has many different faces and can be expressed and/or defended against in a wide variety of ways. Adolescence is a time when action, as a mode of expression and symbolization, and action discharge, as a way of managing emotional changes, become prototypical. Especially in early and midadolescence, action modes may replace ideational modes (Fibel, 1979; Greenspan, 1979; Schaul, 1983). Many so-called acting out behaviors turn out to co-exist with depressed mood, which may emerge more fully at later developmental levels. The manifestation and expression of depression depend, to a great extent, upon the nature of an individual's developmental level—his/her defensive repertoire and level of cognitive development—and upon the internal organization of object representations.

A second issue regarding adolescent depression concerns the inevitability of depressive feelings during adolescence. Many theorists and clinicians specializing in adolescence have highlighted the tumultuous nature of the adolescent passage. Anna Freud (1969) has described adolescence as the prototype of a "developmental disturbance." Others have indicated that the experience of depression in adolescence is ubiquitous, perhaps inevitable, given the necessary tasks of this period. In particular, the major psychosocial task of separation from parents involves a profound sense of loss, which has been described in the literature as leading to adolescent grief reactions (Bloom, 1980; Jacobson, 1966; Root, 1957), a mourning process (Blos, 1962; Root, 1957), and most commonly, adolescent depression (Blos, 1962; Jacobson, 1971).

Offer, Ostrov, and Howard (1981) provide an alternate perspective by suggesting that emotional turmoil is not necessarily inherent in adolescence. Their data, collected in an empirical longitudinal study of adolescents, shows a diversity of responses to the adolescent period. They conclude that the model American teenager is "confident, happy and self-satisfied" (p. 83), not beset by turmoil and dramatic mood swings. Likewise, Douvan and Adelson (1966) report little turbulence during this stage. While acknowledging the developmental challenges of this stage, they highlight successful coping mechanisms that facilitate growth and development. These research and clinical findings do not support the notion that turbulence and depression are inevitable in adolescence.

These controversial issues complicate any simple definition of depression in adolescence. The determination of depression depends upon the investigator's theoretical orientation, methodology, and subject sample. Our own perspective, based upon both research and clinical enterprise, is that the multitude of physiological changes, psychosocial, and interpersonal challenges in adolescence, taken in conjunction with the demands and nature of our society, does make this period of life particularly stressful, leading to increased lability in affect and heightened sensitivity/ proclivity to depression. We do not view depression as inevitable in adolescence, but rather as a likely occurrence, especially in girls, given the current societal expectations, familial patterns, and culturally-sanctioned behaviors. Thus, we see depressive mood as typical; depression as a symptom, frequent; and depression as a clinical syndrome increasing in frequency.

PRECURSORS OF ADOLESCENT DEPRESSION: THE INTERNAL CORRELATES OF FAMILY INSTABILITY

The ability to weather the physical and psychosocial stresses inherent in normative adolescence without prolonged depression depends upon both current circumstances and on past history. The nature of early parent–child relations and the concomitant development of an internal world are the bedrock upon which growth occurs. Without an adequate psychological base, the teenager will be vulnerable to the inevitable narcissistic injuries and interpersonal rejections that occur during adolescence and will be unprepared to deal with the vicissitudes of change and loss that accompany both separation-individuation and physical maturation without undue depression. Specifically, it is the structure and quality of self and object representations, with their cognitive and affective correlates, that play a crucial role in the determination of adolescent depression.

Object representations develop in close connection with the nuances of the parent–child interaction. Consistency of parenting and mutual empathic attunement between parent and child provide for the development of trust in oneself and in the world, a sense of reciprocity between oneself and others, and, on a more subtle level, a knowledge that change and growth are possible within the context of a loving relationship and need not entail major disappointment or loss. These aspects of parenting and family life are essential in facilitating the internalization of a stable and secure sense of self and others, reflected in the quality of object representations (Blatt, 1974; Jacobson, 1964). Object representations that manifest both stability and flexibility, and are predominately benevolent, provide a foundation not easily shaken by the multiplicity of changes that occur in adolescence (Schaul, 1983). On the other hand, object representations that are unstable, fragmented and/or rigid, and that reveal predominantly malevolent or aggressive affect leave the adolescent without internal resources upon which to rely.

The disruption or absence of consistent and stable parenting and mutual empathic attunement impedes the development of stable, consistent, integrated, and benevolent internalized self and object representations and is associated with adolescent depression (Feinstein, 1975; Fibel, 1979), and the incidence of adolescent suicidality (Cantor, 1976; Holinger, 1977; McAnarney, 1979; Miller, 1975; Peck, 1970; Petzel & Riddle, 1981; Sabbath, 1969, 1971; Schaul, 1983; Schrut, 1968; Stanley & Barter, 1970; Teicher, 1970; Toolan, 1971). Epidemiological studies (Crook & Raskin, 1975; Dorpat, Jackson, & Ripley, 1965; Sabbath, 1971; Schrut, 1968; Seiden, 1969; Teicher & Jacobs, 1966) indicate that from 50% to 80% of all suicidal cases in adolescence emerge from unstable family constellations, particularly divorce, desertion, or separation. The stability and quality of family life and its internal correlates emerge as the single most important variable contributing to or mitigating against adolescent depression.

The quality of object representations has a particular impact upon several important functions related to the experience of depression in adolescence, including the capacity to bear and manage object loss, the regulation of self-esteem, and the development of the sense of future. According to Blatt (1974), the importance of the structural organization of object representations in regard to depression centers around its mediating role in the capacity to bear object loss. Reviewing the literature on depression, he demonstrates how the capacity to bear and manage loss is developmentally acquired; he then goes on to illustrate the relationship between an individual's attempts to manage such an experience and the individual's underlying, predominant level of object representation. Those who have developed a higher level of object representation—object representations that are well-articulated, differentiated, integrated, stable and benevolent—have the capacity to resolve loss without prolonged or severe depression. On the other hand, those who maintain lower levels of object representation that vary in their degree of articulation, differentiation, integration, stability, and benevolence are less able to cope with loss and more prone to depression, especially action-oriented manifestations of depression (Blatt, 1974; Fibel, 1979; Schaul, 1983).

Related to the ability to tolerate object loss are the regulation of self-esteem and the developing sense of future. Impairments in object representations correspond to a diminished sense of future time (Blatt, 1974; Schaul, 1983) and make the adolescent more vulnerable to momentary events, which then assume a disproportionate influence on the adolescent's self-esteem. The first disappointing attempts to turn to new love objects may have a profound effect upon the adolescent's developing sense of self and subsequent relations with others (Jacobson, 1964). Frustration or gratification, success or failure, acceptance or rebuff, approval or criticism of the moment all have a major impact upon current feelings about the self because of a lack of a consolidated self-representation (Blatt, 1974). Without an internal sense of continuity and constancy over time provided by the achievement of higher level representations, there is little sense of a differentiated past and little sense of a potential future—the moment is often the extent of the temporal field. This situation exaggerates the adolescent's natural proclivity to be oriented in present time and short-circuits cognitive strides to problem-solve utilizing a broader time frame. Increased mobility in the dimensions of time and space are part and parcel of the development of formal operational thought (Greenspan, 1979; Inhelder & Piaget, 1958; Shapiro, 1963) and allow the adolescent to escape the concrete present and head toward the realm of the abstract and possible, and to view a situation in terms of multiple hypothetical possibilities. These advances are important and necessary tools in managing the adolescent period. Impairments in the development of formal operations result in "concretization" of thought (Blos, 1979; Sugarman, Bloom-Feshbach, & Bloom Feshbach, 1980), a diminished ability to take distance and reflect on perceptual-cognitive processes, and limited capacity to find viable solutions to problems (Neuringer, 1974)—a constellation of cognitive characteristics that render the adolescent more vulnerable to depression.

Family instability is a severe loss for any child or teenager, and empirical research confirms logic in establishing its relationship with depression and suicidality. Even when the family structure is intact, however, there are subtle influences that may contribute to depression in adolescent girls. Often these influences stem from cultural and/or familial internalizations that impede the normative psychosocial tasks of adolescence. Intergenerational transmission of negative societal attitudes toward women, contradictory societal messages about appropriate female identity, and current sex biases regarding allowed degrees of autonomy and individuation for girls compound the difficulties already inherent in successfully navigating this period.

CHILD-REARING PRACTICES: THE CENTRALITY OF THE MOTHER–DAUGHTER BOND

The family plays a pivotal role in fostering the girl's movement toward individuation. While all family members have the potential to influence development, the nature of parenting in our society establishes the mother–daughter bond as the crucial orbit out of which increased in-dividuation and a girl's fundamental sense of identity develop. Powerful at-tachments between mother and daughter provide the basis for empathy and establish a positive relational pathway of development (Surrey, 1984). These same powerful attachments can also serve as conduits of depression originating from personal or cultural forces. The primary psychosocial tasks of adolescence—separation-individuation and identity formation—must, for girls, be viewed within the larger framework of our culture's dictates for women and within the mother–daughter relationship.

Chodorow's (1978) writings on early child-rearing traditions and female development discuss how the nature of mothering in our society creates powerful attachments, which may impede normal strivings for autonomy and individuation. She argues that the likeness of sex and gender between mother and daughter and the differential treatment of boys and girls in child-rearing lead to a lack of separateness between mother and daughter. Developmentally, this close attachment and lesser degree of differentia-tion means that the girl "continues her preoedipal relationship with her mother for a long time and continues to experience herself as involved in issues of merging and separation, and in an attachment characterized by primary identification and the fusion of identification and object choice. By contrast, mothers experience their sons as a male opposite. Boys are more likely to have been pushed out of the preoedipal relationship, and to have had to curtail their primary love and sense of empathic ties with their mothers. A boy has engaged . . . [in] a more defensive firming of experi-enced ego boundaries. Issues of differentiation have become intertwined with sexual issues" (pp. 166–167). Thus, boys separate and differentiate themselves earlier and in a more delineated manner than girls; girls linger in the preoedipal period, gradually including father and siblings in their constellation of relationships, but never distinctly relinquishing their early connection with mother.

For Chodorow, the girl's prolonged preoedipal relationship with her mother provides the basis for empathy but also makes her quest for in-creased psychological separateness in childhood and in adolescence dif-ficult. For adolescent girls, the imperative to separate at this time creates great stress and seems to be even more difficult than for adolescent boys who had earlier practice with separation endeavors when changing primary identifications from mother to father during the first separation-individuation period and in subsequent childhood interactions encourag-ing separation and autonomy. For girls, a developmental constellation of growth within the context of relationships and a heightened attunement to the vicissitudes of relationships may lead to a more profound experience of loss associated with the separation aspects of increased individuation in adolescence.

The observation that girls may have greater difficulty than boys with separation has been offered by others (Greenhouse, 1977; Mahler, Pine, & Bergman, 1975; Taylor, Bogdanoff, Brown, Hillman, Kurash, Spain, Thacher, & Weinstein, 1978). An alternate interpretation of observed sex differences is that girls and boys have different "styles" of separation (Kurash, 1979), or, more generally, that girls and boys develop within different developmental constellations. A new framework from which to view female development has been offered by a group at The Stone Center, Wellesley College. They have proposed the construct of "self-in-relation" to describe the formation of a core sense of self organized and developed in the context of important relationships (Jordan, Surrey, & Kaplan, 1983; Kaplan, 1984; Kaplan & Klein, 1985; Miller, 1984; Surrey, 1984). "The notion of self-in-relation makes an important shift in emphasis from separation to relationship as the basis for self-experience and development. Further, relationship is seen as the basic goal of development: i.e., the deepening capacity for relationship and relational competence. The self-in-relation model assumes that other aspects of self (e.g., creativity, autonomy, assertion) develop within this primary context . . . and there is no inherent need to disconnect or to sacrifice relationship for self-development" (Surrey, 1984, p. 2). Surrey goes on to state that " . . . the adolescent does not necessarily want to 'separate' from her parents, but to change the form and content of the relationship in a way that affirms her own developmental changes and allows new relationships to develop and take priority. If this important need to continue the relationship but also to change the relationship is not honored, both daughters and mothers will feel shame and diminished self-worth" (p. 8). From this perspective, it is not through separation but rather through more highly articulated and expanded relational experiences that individual development takes place.

The self-in-relation framework, with its shift in emphasis from an autonomous, individual self to a more relational self, has implications regarding female adolescent development and depression. The girl's continuing attachments to her mother in adolescence are viewed, not as preoedipal remnants that indicate regression, but rather as the base of a positive relational pathway of development that has evolved and that will continue to evolve over time. Conflict between daughter and parent reflects a test of the fundamental integrity of the relationship, a fundamental aspect of engagement (Kaplan & Klein, 1985; Miller, 1976), and not a desire to disconnect and to separate. Against this backdrop, adolescent depression becomes pronounced under several conditions. Devaluation of relational aspects by the family and/or by society disconfirms the girl's core sense of self. At the same time, autonomy, self-assertion, and achievement, valued societal characteristics, are still viewed with mixed regard for adolescent girls. The dysjunction of developmental ideals for females (i.e., to become "independent," "sexual," and "autonomous" and also to remain "nurturant," "nonsexual," and "submissive") makes maturation difficult. Contradictory communications lead to confusion and inevitably impede individuation.

Thus, the nature of the mother–daughter bond impacts upon the separation-individuation process by virtue of its structure: in our culture, mothers are the primary caretakers; mothers and daughters, being of the same sex and gender, develop particularly close attachments that foster identification and projective identificatory processes (Kurash & Schaul, 1983; Podolnick, 1986). The mother–daughter bond will also impact upon the adolescent by virtue of its content: the kinds of communications imparted by mother to daughter will be of the utmost importance in facilitating either positive self-regard or in fostering depressive characteristics.

Several factors stemming from the mother's perceptions of herself and interactions with her daughter contribute toward increased depression in adolescent girls. These include ambivalence toward her womanliness and female sexuality, severe criticalness, her own depression with which the daughter will invariably identify, and vicarious ambitions for her daughter. A parent who is not affectively available or who responds to her teenager's impulses and attempts at contact with disdain, ridicule, or outright hostility will generate in the adolescent a hesitancy about herself as a potent and capable individual, shameful feelings about her sexuality, insecurity about how she will interact with the world outside of her family, and depression about herself as a young woman. As Menaker (1974) has described, an unfulfilled longing to be truly loved by a mother will leave a "melancholy imprint" on the daughter's character.

These mother–daughter interactions are not viewed as conscious communications that the mother willingly imparts. Rather, such communications are unconscious and subtle—communications that are imparted to women via cultural attitudes from generation to generation. The interplay of societal and personal factors makes the transmission of depression from mother to daughter a frequent occurrence. Societal values, as embedded in the construction of work and family roles, play a potent part in the internalization of personal values and the establishment of positive self-esteem. Menaker (1974) discusses the process by which society's underevaluation of women's role and position results in a denigrated self-image, which over centuries, has been, consciously and unconsciously, passed on from mother to daughter. The basis for female depression is rooted in the adolescent girl's dilemma: on the one hand, identification with the mother's negative attitude leads to feeling devalued and paves the way for depression, but keeps a close emotional connection; on the other hand, psychological separation from a mother whose unconscious attitudes include denigration of herself and her female child is a difficult struggle, involving significant loss. An oft-seen clinical phenomenon with the late adolescent girl is the desire for growth and change in tandem with her mother. Solitary change evokes feelings of abandonment and loneliness, whereas the hope of mutual growth enhances connectedness and self-esteem. Research supports clinical findings that close maternal relationships correspond to warm relationships with peers and to less depression (Gold & Yanof, 1985; Kandel & Davies, 1982). Thus, it is misleading to think in terms of a "hydraulic model" of interpersonal interaction (Kandel & Davies, 1982) where adolescent peer relations replace parental relationships. It appears that continuing warm relationships with mothers provide the foundation from which adolescent girls can successfully evolve other relationships. The extent to which the mother supports and encourages her daughter's autonomy, communicates positively about being female, both in biological and social spheres, and feels genuinely positive about herself as a woman will contribute to her daughter's ability to identify with and internalize positive attributes about herself and to develop positive relations with others.

The separation-individuation tasks involve a process of working through ambivalent feelings about parents so that selective identification with positive qualities can occur. Pathogenic family constellations characterized, for example, by rigid boundaries, hostility, psychopathology, and depreciation of feminine identity, often result in extreme ambivalence for the adolescent. The ability to remain affectively connected in a positive manner is made more difficult and the struggle for separation via rejection may present the sole hope for breaking the vicious intergenerational cycle of depression and establishing more healthful identificatory conditions for women. An extended network of other girls/women is important in providing the adolescent girl with a variety of positive role models and to assist her along the path of increased individuation through selective identification and internalization.

The importance of the availability of numerous role models is highlighted by the current cultural context. In the past, "most women's identities were achieved in the stereotypic ideals of their family roles" (Bardwick, 1979, p. 22). Girls would learn about becoming a woman directly from their mothers as traditions were passed on down through the generations. Today, early maternal identification may be incongruent with many of the choices to which adolescents will be exposed, and the components of a viable identity must be actively woven together, often independent of a prior or coincidental intimate attachment (Morgan & Farber, 1982). Thus, the present-day adolescent girl may have to make a greater separation from parents who are committed to adaptations to a different set of social conditions. Indeed, the rapidly changing context of our technological society has led to increased adolescent indifference to family values (not opposition, but indifference) (Bloom-Feshbach, 1981; Keniston, 1960; Lasch, 1979); and today's adolescents are often socialized more by peers than by parents (Bloom-Feshbach, 1981). These cultural conditions may set the stage for increased parent–adolescent alienation and increased adolescent depression.

ROLE OF THE FATHER

The father's perception of and relationship with his adolescent daughter is particularly important in facilitating the girl's sexual identity and in the formation of heterosexual relationships (Biller, 1981; Fisher, 1973; Lozoff, 1974). Paternal absence has shown to be associated with difficulties in interactions with boys (Hetherington, 1972), a major precipitant of female adolescent depression.

The management of interpersonal boundaries between father and daughter is a delicate balance in adolescence. Fathers must carefully nagivate between the Scylla of sexualized attention and the Charybdis of defensive remoteness. Adolescent girls are often acutely sensitive to their father's attentions, and fathers are often unaware of the impact of their criticism or disapproval at this time (Scarf, 1980). Not infrequently, fathers respond to the stirring of unacceptable feelings by withdrawal from the daughter, who, in turn, experiences him as suddenly rejecting and remote. The analytic literature is replete with references to pathological responses that are detrimental to the adolescent girl: insensitivity, rejection, overcriticalness, jealousy, overt interference in daughter's dating relationships (Machtlinger, 1981). The subtle and not so subtle devaluation of her femininity, sexuality, competence, and relational abilities communicate powerful messages, which become incorporated into her changing self-representation and affect her self-esteem.

PUBERTY

The impact of menarche and breast development, while biologically determined, is heavily colored by psychosocial influences. Maternal attitudes toward menstruation, which usually reflect her overall attitude toward sexuality (Berkovitz, 1979; Magrab, 1979), the father's acceptance of his daughter's burgeoning sexuality, and influences from the wider culture will all impact on the girl's experience of her bodily changes. Several authors and researchers report shifts in affect accompanying premenstrual hormonal changes including increased tension, decreased tolerance for frustration and a high degree of irritability (Feinstein, 1975; Ivey & Bardwick, 1968), and negative feelings about her body (Offer, Ostrov, & Howard,

1981; Whisnant & Zegans, 1981). Others report that the onset of menarche generates pride as well as anxiety and shame (Jacobson, 1964) and has a positive, organizing impact as a cornerstone of feminine identification (Kestenberg, 1961). Klerman and Weissman (1980) conclude, after a thorough exploration of the nature and causes of depression among women, that there is little to substantiate a relationship between mood change and altered endocrine balance, and that there is not sufficient evidence to conclusively link depression with the menstrual cycle.

SUMMARY AND CONCLUSION

Female adolescent depression is an interactive process that is invariably linked to the girl's relationships with her parents and to the culture in which she is maturing. Relational attunement, flexibility, and differentiation serve as a buffer against depression in adolescence. Relational indifference, rigidity, and narcissistic overinvestment provide conditions that lead to depression. As Stierlin (1977) has pointed out, the family's goal during the adolescent period is the continual movement toward mutual individuation and mature interdependence in which both the parent and child participate. The parents', and particularly the mother's, own degree of psychological individuation is a crucial variable in handling the daughter's adolescence. The extent to which the mother has come to terms with her own adolescence and (mid)adulthood, is capable of separating her needs from her daughter's, and can tolerate and respect differences affects her daughter's ability to formulate a mature, affirmative, and cohesive identity without undue depression. The twin dangers of narcissistic overinvestment and projective identification invariably contribute to depression. The ability to tolerate the adolescent's repudiation of unwanted parental projections and/or values and still remain affectively connected is a key dimension in allowing for successful individuation within the context of the parent–adolescent bond. Both partners benefit and both partners undergo a fundamental reorganization of self and object representations that correspond more accurately to the adolescent's new level of development, cognitive capacities, identity, and relational capabilities. This reorganization involves increased articulation, differentiation, and integration of previously organized representations for both mother and daughter.

A technological culture, as rapidly changing as ours, presents additional challenges to the adolescent who is already faced with the task of assimilating and synthesizing numerous personal changes. Increased internal stability is necessitated by everchanging demands that condense the "normative" adolescent tasks into a time-lapsed sequence. Numerous possibilities for identification and the necessity of making many selective decisions place extraordinary stress on the girl's synthetic function. Yet, at the same time, the number of options available and the multitude of possibilities that exist for developing different aspects of the self offer exciting opportunities for growth and change.

Mutual positive reinforcement between familial and societal values facilitate the adolescent girl's acculturation. Values that reflect positive, supportive, respectful attitudes ease the transition through the adolescent period, allowing the girl to assume a viable role as a young adult in our society. Values that reflect contradictory and conflictual positions create additional pressures and confusion, thwarting the development of a clear and positive sense of self and increasing the likelihood of depression.

REFERENCES

Bakwin, H. (1972). Depression—a mood disorder in children and adolescents. *Maryland State Medical Journal, 21,* 55–61.

Bardwick, J. (1971). *Psychology of women: A study of bio-cultural conflicts.* New York: Harper & Row.

Bardwick, J. (1979). *In transition.* New York: Holt, Rinehart & Winston.

Beck, A.T. (1972). *Depression: Causes and treatment.* Philadelphia: University of Pennsylvania Press.

Berkovitz, I.H. (1979). Effects of secondary school experiences on adolescent female development. In M. Sugar (Ed.), *Female adolescent depression* (pp. 173–200). New York: Brunner/Mazel.

Biller, H.B. (1981). The father and sex role development. In M.E. Lamb (Ed.), *The role of the father in child development.* New York: J. Wiley & Sons.

Blatt, S.J. (1974). Levels of object representation in anaclitic and introjective depression. *Psychoanalytic Study of the Child, 29,* 107–157.

Bloom, M. (1980). *Adolescent-parent separation.* New York: Gardner Press, Inc.

Bloom-Feshbach, J. (1981). Historical perspectives on the father's role. In M.E. Lamb (Ed.), *The role of the father in child development.* New York: J. Wiley & Sons.

Blos, P. (1962). *On adolescence.* New York: The Free Press.

Blos, P. (1967). The second individuation process of adolescence. *Psychoanalytic Study of the Child, 22,* 162–186.

Blos, P. (1979). *The adolescent passage: Developmental issues* (pp. 278–302). New York: International Universities Press, Inc.

Cantor, P.C. (1976). Personality characteristics among youthful female suicide attempters. *Journal of Abnormal Psychology, 85,* 324–329.

Chodorow, N. (1978). *The reproduction of mothering.* Berkeley: University of California Press.

Crook, T., & Raskin, A. (1975). Association of childhood parental loss with attempted suicide and depression. *Journal of Consulting and Clinical Psychology, 43,* 277.

Dorpat, T., Jackson, J., & Ripley, H. (1965). Broken homes and attempted and completed suicide. *Archives of General Psychiatry, 12,* 213–216.

Douvan, E., & Adelson, J. (1966). *The adolescent experience.* New York: J. Wiley & Sons, Inc.

Feinstein, S.C. (1975). Adolescent depression. In E.J. Anthony & T. Benedek (Eds.), *Depression and human existence* (pp. 317–336). Boston: Little, Brown.

Fibel, B. (1979). *Toward a developmental model of depression: Object representation and object loss in adolescent and adult psychiatric patients.* Unpublished doctoral dissertation, University of Massachusetts.

Fisher, S.F. (1973). *The female organs: Psychology, physiology, fantasy.* New York: Basic Books.

Freud, A. (1969). Adolescence as a developmental disturbance. In S. Lebovici & G. Caplan (Eds.), *Adolescence: Psychosocial perspectives.* New York: Basic Books.

Freud, S. (1917). Mourning and melancholia. *Standard Edition, 14.* London: Hogarth Press.

Glaser, K. (1967). Masked depression in children and adolescents. *American Journal of Psychotherapy, 21,* 565–574.

Gold, M., & Yanof, D. (1985). Mothers, daughters and girlfriends. *Journal of Personality and Social Psychology, 49*(3), 654–659.

Gove, W.R., & Herb, T.R. (1974). Stress and mental illness among the young: A comparison of the sexes. *Social Forces, 53,* 256–265.

Greenhouse, E. (1977). *Countertransference and transference issues of women in the supervisory relationship.* Unpublished paper.

Greenspan, S.I. (1979). Intelligence and adaptation: An integration of psychoanalytic and Piagetian developmental psychology. *Psychological Issues, XII* (3/4, Monograph 47/48).

Hetherington, E.M. (1972). Effects of father-absence on personality development in adolescent daughters. *Developmental Psychology, 7,* 313–326.

Holinger, P. (1977). Suicide in adolescence. *American Journal of Psychiatry, 134,* 1433–1434.

Inhelder, B., & Piaget, J. (1958). *The growth of logical thinking: From childhood to adolescence.* New York: Basic Books.

Ivey, M.E., & Bardwick, J.M. (1968). Patterns of affective fluctuation in the menstrual cycle. *Psychosomatic Medicine, 30,* 336–345.

Jacobson, E. (1964). *The self and the object world.* New York: International Universities Press.

Jacobson, E. (1966). Problems in the differentiation between schizophrenia and melancholic states of depression. In R.M. Loewenstein, L. Newman, L. Schur, & A.J. Solnit (Eds.), *Psychoanalysis: A general psychology.* New York: International Universities Press.

Jacobson, E. (1971). *Depression: Comparative studies of normal, neurotic and psychotic conditions.* New York: International Universities Press.

Jordan, J., Surrey, J., & Kaplan, A. (1983). Women and empathy. *Work in progress.* Wellesley, MA: Stone Center Working Paper Series.

Kandel, D.B., & Davies, M. (1982). Epidemiology of depressive mood in adolescents: An empirical study. *Archives of General Psychiatry, 39,* 1205–1212.

Kaplan, A. (1984). The "self-in-relation": Implications for depression in women. *Work in progress 84–03.* Wellesley, MA.: Stone Center Working Papers Series.

Kaplan, A., & Klein, R. (1985). Women's self development in late adolescence. *Work in progress.* Wellesley, MA.: Stone Center Working Papers Series.

Kaufman, B. (1979). Object removal and adolescent depression. In A.P. French & I.N. Berlin (Eds.), *Depression in children and adolescents.* New York: Human Sciences Press.

Keniston, K. (1960). *The uncommitted: Alienated youth in American society.* New York: Harcourt, Brace & World.

Kestenberg, J.S. (1961). Menarche. In S. Lorano & S. Schneer (Eds.), *Adolescents: Psychoanalytic approaches to problems and therapy.* New York: Hoeber.

Klerman, G.L., & Weissman, M.M. (1980). Depressions among women: Their natures and their causes. In M. Guttentag, S. Salasin, & D. Belle (Eds.), *The mental health of women* (pp. 57–89). New York: Academic Press.

Kurash, C.L. (1979). *The transition to college: A study of separation-individuation in late adolescence.* Unpublished doctoral dissertation, C.U.N.Y.

Kurash, C.L., & Schaul, J.F. (1983). The evolution of self-representations: Parent and adolescent. Paper presented at the Annual Meeting of the American Psychological Association, Anaheim, CA.

Lasch, C. (1979). *Haven in a heartless world: The family beseiged.* New York: Basic Books.

Lesse, S. (1974). Depressive equivalents and multivariant masks of depression. In S. Lesse (Ed.), *Masked depression.* New York: Aronson.

Litman, R., & Wold, C. (1974). Masked depression and suicide. In S. Lesse (Ed.), *Masked depression.* New York: Aronson.

Lozoff, M.M. (1974). Fathers and autonomy in women. In R.B. Kundsin (Ed.), *Women and success.* New York: Morrow.

Machtlinger, V.J. (1981). The father in psychoanalytic theory. In M.E. Lamb (Ed.), *The role of the father in child development* (pp. 113–153). New York: J. Wiley & Sons.

Magrab, P.R. (1979). Mothers and daughters. In C.B. Kopp & M. Kirkpatrick (Eds.), *Becoming female: Perspectives on development* (pp. 113 –132). New York: Plenum Press.

Mahler, M., Pine, F., & Bergman, A. (1975). *The psychological birth of the human infant.* New York: Basic Books, Inc.

Malmquist, C.P. (1972). Depressive phenomena in children. In B.B. Wolman (Ed.), *Manual of child psychopathology.* New York: McGraw-Hill.

McAnarney, E. (1979). Adolescent and young adult suicide in the United States—a reflection of societal unrest? *Adolescence, 14,* 765–774.

Menaker, E. (1974). The therapy of women in the light of psychoanalytic theory and the emergence of a new view. In V. Franks & V. Burtle (Eds.), *Women in therapy: New psychotherapies for a changing society* (pp. 230–246). New York: Brunner/Mazel.

Miller, J. (1975). Suicide and adolescence. *Adolescence, 10,* 11–23.

Miller, J.B. (1976). *Toward a new psychology of women.* Boston: Beacon Press.

Miller, J.B. (1984). The development of women's sense of self. *Work in progress 84:01.* Wellesley, MA.: Stone Center Working Papers Series.

Morgan, E., & Farber, B. (1982). Toward a reformulation of the Eriksonian model of female identity development. *Adolescence, XVII,* (65).

Neuringer, C. (1974). Problems of assessing suicidal risk. In C. Neuringer (Ed.), *Psychological assessment of suicidal risk.* Springfield, IL.: Charles Thomas.

Offer, D., Ostrov, E., & Howard, K.I. (1981). *The adolescent: A psychological self-portrait.* New York: Basic Books, Inc.

Peck, M. (1970). Research and training in prevention of suicide in adolescents and youths. *Bulletin of Suicidology, 6,* 35–40.

Petzel, S., & Riddle, M. (1981). Suicide's psychosocial and cognitive aspects. *Adolescent Psychiatry, IX,* 399–410.

Podolnick, E. (1986, April). *Parental narcissism in the etiology of eating disorders.* Paper presented at the Second International Conference on Eating Disorders, New York.

Radloff, L.S., & Rae, D.S. (1979). Susceptibility and precipitating factors in depression: Sex differences and similarities. *Journal of Abnormal Psychology, 88,* 174–181.

Root, N.N. (1957). A neurosis in adolescence. *Psychoanalytic Study of the Child, 12,* 320–334.

Sabbath, J.C. (1969). The suicidal adolescent—the expendable child. *Journal of the American Academy of Child Psychiatry, 8,* 272–289.

Sabbath, J.C. (1971). The role of the parents in adolescent suicidal behavior. *Acta Paedo-psychiatria, 38,* 211–220.

Scarf, M. (1980). *Unfinished business: Pressure points in the lives of women.* Garden City, NY: Doubleday.

Schaul, J. (1983). *Levels of object representation and cognitive structures in adolescent suicide.* Unpublished doctoral dissertation, C.U.N.Y.

Schrut, A. (1968). Some typical patterns in the behavior and background of adolescent girls who attempt suicide. *American Journal of Psychiatry, 125,* 107–112.

Seiden, R. (1969). Suicide among youth: A review of the literature 1900–1967. *Bulletin of Suicidology,* Supplement.

Seligman, M.E.P. (1975). *Helplessness.* San Francisco: W.H. Freeman.

Shapiro, R. (1963). Adolescence and the psychology of the ego. *Psychiatry, 26,* 77–87.

Sperling, M. (1959). Equivalents of depression in children. *Journal of Hillside Hospital, 8,* 138.

Spitzer, R. (1980). *Diagnostic and statistical manual of mental disorders* (3rd ed.). Washington DC: The American Psychiatric Association.

Stanley, E.J., & Barter, J.T. (1970). Adolescent suicidal behavior. *American Journal of Orthopsychiatry, 40*(1), 87–96.

Stierlin, H. (1977). *Psychoanalysis and family therapy.* New York: Aronson, Inc.

Sugarman, A., Bloom-Feshbach, J., & Bloom-Feshbach, S. (1980). The psychological dimensions of borderline adolescents. In J. Kwawer, H. Lerner, P. Lerner, &

A. Sugarman (Eds.), *Borderline phenomena and the Rorschach test.* New York: International Universities Press.

Surrey, J. (1984). The self-in-relation: A theory of women's development. *Work in progress 84:02.* Wellesley, MA: Stone Center Working Papers Series.

Taylor, S., Bogdanoff, M., Brown, D., Hillman, L., Kurash, C., Spain, J., Thacher, B., & Weinstein, L. (1978). By women, for women: A group relations conference. In G. Lawrence (Ed.), *Exploring individual and organizational boundaries.* New York: Wiley & Sons.

Teicher, J.D. (1970). Children and adolescents who attempt suicide. *Pediatric Clinics of North America, 17,* 687–696.

Teicher, J.D., & Jacobs, J. (1966). Adolescents who attempt suicide: Preliminary findings. *American Journal of Psychiatry, 122,* 1248–1257.

Teuting, P., Koslow, S.H., & Hirschfeld, R.M.A. (1981). *N.I.M.H. science reports: Special report on depression research.* Washington, DC: U.S. Department of Health and Human Services.

Toolan, J.M. (1962). Depression in children and adolescents. *American Journal of Orthopsychiatry, 32,* 404–414.

Toolan, J.M. (1971). Depression in adolescents. In J. Howells (Ed.), *Modern perspectives in adolescent psychiatry.* Edinburgh: Oliver & Boyd.

Weissman, M.M. (1980). Depression. In A. Brodsky & R. Hare-Mustin, (Eds.), *Women and psychotherapy: An assessment of research and practice.* New York: Guilford Press.

Weissman, M.M., & Klerman, G.L. (1981). Sex differences and the epidemiology of depression. In E. Howell & M. Bayes (Eds.), *Women and mental health.* New York: Basic Books.

Whisnant, L., & Zegans, L. (1981). A study of attitudes toward menarche in white middle class girls. In E. Howell & M. Bayes (Eds.), *Women and mental health.* New York: Basic Books.

■ 7
Eating Disorders: Why Women And Why Now?

SUZETTE FINKELSTEIN, Ph.D.

"You've come a long way, baby!" From hysteria in the late 19th century to eating disorders in the 20th. Hysterical paralyses have become psychiatric curiosities of the sort that anorexia nervosa was at the turn of the century. What has changed? What is there about life in the late 20th century that makes women in Western industrial societies reject hysteria in favor of eating disorders in their symptom choice? (No implication is intended that it is the same women who developed hysteria in the 19th century who would have developed eating disorders had they lived now.) This chapter will begin by summarizing some epidemiological and historical aspects of the disorder; it will go on to describe the principal clinical features of anorexia nervosa and bulimia, and then it will mention briefly some of the many theories called upon to explain it, including some that related it to depression. The chapter will conclude with some speculations as to what has changed so profoundly in women and in Western culture as to have altered the forms of our innermost human dilemmas, such as those involved in loving and eating.

There is no longer any doubt as to the increasing incidence and prevalence of eating disorders among women in Western industrialized societies (Casper, 1983; Halmi, Falk, & Schwartz, 1981; Garfinkel & Garner, 1982; Vandereycken & Meerman, 1984). The start of the current epidemic saw careful researchers (e.g., Theander, cited in Swartz et al., 1982) unwilling to conclude that the apparent increase in cases was not an artifact of increased public awareness and improved reporting, but subsequent work has left no doubt about the alarmingly increased prevalence of subclinical varieties of eating disorders in adolescent populations (Halmi et al., 1981; Hart & Ollendick, 1985; Katzman, Wolchik, & Brauer, 1984; Pope, Hudson, & Yurgelun-Todd, 1984) or about the vastly increased incidence and prevalence of full-blown eating disorders throughout the Western world (Bruch, 1973; Crisp, Palmer, & Kalucy, 1976; Garfinkel & Garner, 1982; Vandereycken & Meerman, 1984; Stangler & Printz, 1980; Swartz et al., 1983). Anorexia nervosa and bulimia or "bulimarexia" are typically afflictions of young people (preadolescent, adolescent, and young adult) (Bruch, 1973; Crisp, Hsu, Hording, Britta, & Hartshorn, 1980; Sours, 1974), typically from middle to upper class families (Crisp et al., 1976; Hart & Ollendick, 1985; Kalucy, Crisp, & Harding, 1977), and overwhelmingly female (10:1 to 20:1) (Bruch, 1973; Crisp et al., 1980). Only the incidence has changed; the sex-ratio and socioeconomic status of patients are fairly constant.

Anorexia nervosa was first described by Morton (1689), who called it "a nervous consumption" (cited in Sours, 1974). Leseque (1873) in France called it "hysterical anorexia," (cited in Sours, 1974), while Gull (1868) (cited in Sours, 1974) in England contributed the present name of the disorder. The clinical features described by these authors are similar to one another and to more contemporary observations. These early investigators were impressed by psychological difficulties and also by family conflict, especially between patients and their mothers, as well as by the intractability of the symptoms. These disorders have been so frustrating to clinicians and so puzzling to theorists that the appearance of a new etiological factor or a new theory or a new disease with similar symptoms has naturally lead to interest in its application to eating disorders. The history of attempts to understand these disorders is therefore a microcosmic history of psychiatry.

The initial phase saw some leaning toward a physical disease model, as in Morton's original name for the disorder, and as Bruch (1973) points out, this relationship to tuberculosis has cropped up again from time to time. A second biological theory was offered by Simonds in 1914 (Sours, 1974), which related the symptoms to panhypopituitarism on the basis of autopsy findings from one case. The initial enthusiasm for this explanation was soon found to be based on overgeneralization from very limited data.

Currently, we are experiencing another wave of enthusiasm for yet another biological model, this one relating eating disorders to affective disorders (Cantwell, Struzenberger, Burroughs, Salkin, & Green, 1977; Rivinus, Biederman, Herzog, Kemper, Harper, Harmaty, & Houseworth, 1984; Stern, Dixon, Nemzer, Lake, Sansone, Smeltzer, Lantz, & Schrier, 1984; Winokur, March, & Mendes, 1980). The evidence for this association comes from observations of depression in patients with eating disorders (Eckert, Goldberg, Halni, Casper, & Davis, 1982; Hatsukami, Eckert, Mitchell, & Pyle, 1984; Hendren, 1983; Hudson, Pope, Jonas, & Yurgelun-Todd, 1983; Rivinus et al., 1984; Stern et al., 1984), findings of depression on follow-up (Crisp et al, 1980; Hsu, 1980), neuroendocrine similarities of patients with eating disorders to patients with affective disorders (Biederman, Rivinus, Herzog, Harmatz, Shanley, & Yunis, 1984; Halmi, Dekirmenjian, Davis, Casper, & Goldberg, 1978; Vandereycken & Meermann, 1984; Winokur et al., 1980), unpredictable and unexplained positive response of some bulimic patients to antidepressants (Hudson, Pope, Jonas, & Yurgelun-Todd, 1983; Winokur, 1980), and overrepresentation of people with affective disorders in the families of patients with eating disorders, especially of bulimics (Cantwell et al., 1977; Crisp et al., 1980; Hudson et al., 1983; Rivinus et al., 1984; Stern et al., 1984; Strober, 1982). The biological findings are inconclusive, and there is no evidence for direct genetic transmission. The most cautious investigators (Hendren, 1983; Rivinus et al., 1984) propose a possible common genetic vulnerability of norepinephrine regulation between eating disorders and affective disorders; further study is clearly indicated before the role of these biological factors can be assessed.

Another, more psychological line of inquiry, has produced its own array of explanatory models. Questions of description, classification, and diagnosis, which dominated interest at the turn of the century (Sours, 1974), gave way to psychodynamic explanations. Waller, Kaufman, & Deutsch (1940), for example, explained anorexia nervosa as a defense against the forbidden wish for oral impregnation; other psychoanalytic writers, including some contemporary ones (Wilson, Hogan, & Mintz, 1983), have implicated various oral incorporative and oral sadistic wishes, as well as wishes from higher developmental levels, in the conflict underlying food refusal. Nemiah (1950) broadened the scope of observation and explanation by noting that these patients suffered not merely disorders of appetite, but of adaptation and of object relations, and like most other investigators, he noted their highly ambivalent and highly dependent orientation toward their mothers.

The psychoanalytic conflict model, in which symptoms are explained as compromises between expression and inhibition of forbidden wishes, was found an imperfect fit for clinical observations of eating disorders (Bruch, 1961, 1963; Nemiah, 1950; Galdston, 1974), and various object relations and ego deficit models have been proposed. Bruch's (1966) designation of anorexia nervosa as a primary diagnosis based on ego deficits related to processing of bodily sensations and emotions and consolidation of a sense of self was the first clearly articulated example. Other ego deficit and object relations etiologies have been proposed as these models have augmented and revised psychoanalytic theories of development. However, discussion of contemporary theories should await description of the typical clinical picture and family and developmental history associated with anorexia nervosa and bulimia.

Phenomenologically, anorexia nervosa is characterized by voluntary food restriction in the presence of normal and often gnawing appetite (Bruch, 1973; Crisp et al., 1980; Garfinkel & Garner, 1982). Some anorectics ("restricters") refuse food consistently, often especially carbohydrates but usually practically everything else as well. Others ("purgers and vomiters") also starve themselves, but have occasional or frequent bouts of bulimia, usually with purging and/or vomiting. Still others ("bulimics") gorge themselves on grotesquely large quantities of often high-calorie carbohydrates, but other foods as well, without restriction of intake; afterwards they induce vomiting and/or purge with laxatives. Mild cases have occasional eating binges; severe cases virtually devote their lives to continual eating and vomiting.

These bizarre eating behaviors reflect an obsessive preoccupation with weight, relentless pursuit of thinness, and morbid fear of being fat (Bruch, 1973; Crisp et al., 1980; Sours, 1974), which some writers characterize as a weight or fat phobia (Crisp, 1972; Wilson et al., 1983). Equally obsessive is their preoccupation with food and eating (Bruch, 1973; Crisp et al., 1980; Sours, 1974), exacerbated, but not wholly caused, by starvation. Anorectics often tyrannize their families by feeding them while they themselves abstain, or they occupy themselves with reading recipes and cooking food, which they do not eat (Galdston, 1974; Sours, 1974). They are often controlling and unreasonably demanding with respect to others' preparation of food for them and for other family members. Food must be prepared just so or served in a certain order, etc. (Wilson et al., 1983). They are also secretive and deceitful in maintaining their bizarre food behavior (Falstein, Feinstein, & Judas, 1956; Galdston, 1974; Bruch, 1973), the restricters hiding or vomiting food which they claim to have eaten and the bulimics often stealing money or food (Casper, Eckert, Holmi, Goldberg, & Davis, 1980) and almost always eating in secret.

Their characteristic concern with and relentless pursuit of thinness is given enormous urgency by distorted perception of their body size. Young women so emaciated that they look like concentration camp victims are distressed because they are sure they are fat (Bruch, 1973); the relentless hyperactivity of these skin-clad skeletons has astounded observers from the 17th century until now (Morton, 1689, cited in Bruch, 1973). Restricting anorectics and purgers and vomiters tend to have lower body weight than bulimics who often have normal body weight (Garfinkel, Moldofsky, & Garner, 1980; Pyle, Mitchell, & Eckert, 1981; Swift & Letven, 1984), but all three groups' estimates of their body size are unrelated to reality. They all feel fat, and they all see this as the most important issue in their lives (Bruch, 1973; Galdston, 1974; Garfinkel & Garner, 1982). The very emaciated restricters experience exalted self-esteem from control over their bodies (Sours, 1974), and the bingers seem to be tormented by shame and guilt (Casper et al., 1980).

The amenorrhea that accompanies anorexia nervosa is often attributed to loss of body fat, and its onset usually does follow severe weight loss and/or excessive exercise (Bruch, 1973). In the rare male case, a corresponding diminution of testosterone production following weight loss, and a resumption of normal levels upon refeeding has been noted (Crisp, Hsu, Chen, & Wheeler, 1982). However, in females, amenorrhea sometimes precedes any weight loss and continues after refeeding (Garfinkel & Garner, 1982). Hence, it cannot be attributed solely to excessive weight loss and exercise, but the physiological bases of these phenomena remain unclear.

These very severe and bizarre feeding abnormalities usually begin gradually and in benign-seeming ways. An adolescent girl, sometimes a bit plump, more rarely really obese, begins to diet, and perhaps to exercise as well (Bruch, 1973; Garfinkel & Garner, 1982; Sours, 1974). Or she begins by dieting, loses control and overeats, and reduces her subsequent panic about loss of control and fatness by inducing vomiting (Casper, 1983). The severe restricter gradually isolates herself from her friends and activities to a life of frantic exercise and calorie-counting, whereas the severe bulimic gradually reduces her life to bingeing and vomiting or purging (Pyle et al., 1981).

Just as the onset of the symptoms appears at first unremarkable, so do the precipitating events, insofar as they can be discerned (Galdston, 1974; Wilson et al., 1983). They appear to be of two sorts: losses of familiar situations or significant people whose presence turns out to have mattered more than could have been apparent, or blows to self-esteem such as those involved in moving from a small school where one is known and valued to a large school where one is unknown and less important. Such events do not appear on the face of it to involve major traumata; rather thay appear to be among the blows that inevitably accompany adolescence. But for those adolescents who develop eating disorders, such ordinary stresses are so apparently intolerable that they precipitate the narrowing of their lives to obsessive preoccupation with food, eating, and weight.

It is clearly personality differences that separate those young women who master adolescent stresses and who use diet and fitness to enhance the other pleasures of living from those who succumb to them and reduce their lives to bizarre exaggerations of weight control programs. Premorbidly, women with eating disorders tend to be rigid, perfectionistic, overachieving, compliant, "good" girls. They tend to have very harsh, punitive superegos, and to be preoccupied with dichotomous, "black and white" thinking about good and evil (and thin and fat) (Garfinkel & Garner, 1982). They also tend toward rigid, stereotyped views of other matters such as appropriate sex roles, familial obligations and the like (Striegel-Moore, Silberstein, & Rodin, 1986). They are usually very conforming and "good"; the onset of the eating disorder often brings seemingly unprecedented stubborn and oppositional attitudes and behavior and bizarre struggles about issues of autonomy and control, especially with respect to food (Bruch, 1973; Garner & Garfinkel, 1982). Under the mask of the perfect child and the achieving superstar, these young women hide (from themselves and others) feelings of inferiority, and in effectuality (Bruch, 1973), and powerless, helpless dependency on their intensely loved and hated mothers and/or fathers (Kalucy et al., 1977; Sours, 1974). Bulimic women tend to have the added problems of serious deficiencies of impulse control and tension regulation involving impulses at all developmental levels (Casper, 1983; Strober, Salkin, Burrough, & Morrell, 1982; Wilson et al., 1983) with no less harsh and primitive ways of judging themselves and their behavior.

The families that produce both types of young women are described in the literature as high-achieving, perfectionistic, invested in being the perfectly successful and perfectly harmonious family (Bruch, 1973; Garfinkel & Garner, 1982; Sours, 1974), intolerant of conflict and hence of autonomy in their children, and "enmeshed" (Minuchin, Rosman, & Baker, 1978), i.e., unable to respect or tolerate the separate self-hood of their members. In spite of their intrusive overconcern and frequent overprotectiveness (Bruch, 1973; Sours, 1974; Wilson et al., 1983), these families are often emotionally cold and unempathic (Sours, 1974), more invested in what one or both parents need their child to be for their own gratification or protection from discomfort than in the child as a growing person in need of support and validation or "mirroring" (Lerner, 1983; Swift & Letven, 1984). Alcoholism, depression, and marital conflict (often unacknowledged) (Garfinkel & Garner, 1982; Kalucy et al., 1977; Minuchin et al., 1978) are frequent, and intense overpreoccupation with food, eating, dieting, and weight are well nigh universal (Bruch, 1973; Sours, 1974; Wilson et al., 1983). A history of parental obesity and/or struggle against it are also very frequent (Bruch, 1973; Garfinkel et al., 1980; Kalucy et al., 1977), and even more so among families of bulimics where affective disorders, alcoholism, drug abuse, and other disorders of impulse control are characteristic (Casper, 1983; Strober et al., 1982). This ground is clearly very fertile for issues of autonomy to be bitter contests, and for control over eating to be an especially bitter autonomy issue between parents and children. Histories at intake tend not to reflect these premorbid early struggles (Bruch, 1973), but closer scrutiny during extended long-term treatment often brings them to light (Wilson et al., 1983).

Even descriptively, these phenomena provide highly complex and intriguing observations for the whole range of theorists and practitioners on the contemporary mental health scene. Biochemical models (Hudson et al., 1983), family dynamics (Minuchin et al., 1978; Palazzoli, 1974), psychodynamic developmental formulations of several varieties (Boris, 1984; Lerner, 1983; Rollins & Blackwell, 1968; Sours, 1974; Sugarman, Quinlan & Devenis, 1982; Swift & Letven, 1984; Wilson, Hogan & Mintz, 1983), and social psychological (Striegel-Moore et al., 1986) and sociocultural analyses (Schwartz, Thompson, & Johnson, 1982) have all found their way into the eating disorders literature, and each contributes something to our efforts to explain these phenomena and their current alarming increase. As interesting as these explanatory efforts are, it is not consistent with the purpose of this chapter to attempt exhaustive discussion of them. Rather, only those aspects of research and theorizing about eating disorders will be taken up which seem to shed light on why our current social climate encourages women to express their innermost adolescent dilemmas about loving and needing in the form of frantic efforts to be thin in the face of imperious urges to eat.

First, there are numerous references to a "cultural" explanation that notes the tremendous emphasis on thinness among contemporary women (Bruch, 1973; Garfinkel & Garner, 1982): fashion dictates thinness, social status requires it, and all women seem to value it. The oft-cited (e.g., Garfinkel & Garner, 1982; Striegel-Moore et al., 1986) *Playboy* centerfold's progress toward emaciation in the last 15 years is an example of this level of explanation. The recent *American Psychologist* paper by Striegel-Moore et al. (1986) is a vast compilation of descriptive statements about women with eating disorders, which portray them as subscribing more strongly and more rigidly than other women to traditional feminine role definitions and to attendant cultural pressures. These statements about the overvaluing of thinness, while they are descriptively very useful, are not explanations. On the contrary, they are part of what needs explaining. Why has thinness become so desirable? What has changed in our social institutions and in our culture to have produced so radically different an image of what is beautiful in women? We have rejected our formerly highly valued curves and softness in favor of a body reminiscent of a prepubescent boy's. How can we account for this change? Are the forces responsible for it the same forces (mediated through the family and the developmental process) that weigh more heavily on some women than on others, so that some are enriched by the fitness culture while others are enslaved by it? A true cultural explanation, which is beyond the scope of this chapter would involve answers to these questions. However, just posing them seems in itself a timely and worthwhile aim: timely because the increase in eating disorders is an important current concern, and worthwhile because the confounding of description with explanation hampers our efforts to understand why women are so especially prone to eating disorders and why so many more of them are succumbing now.

The more microcosmic theories, such as those related to family dynamics and to intrapsychic structural deficits arising from distortion of the normal developmental process, are potentially illuminating in this regard. Formulations of both family dynamics and of individual developmental deficits point to various ways in which women with eating disorders are incompletely developed with respect to one or more intrapsychic function necessary for stable, organized, autonomous adult functioning. Tension regulation (Swift & Letven, 1984), self-cohesion (Sours, 1974), self-esteem regulation (Lerner, 1983), affect modulation (Lerner, 1983; Swift & Letven, 1984), impulse control (Galdston, 1974; Swift & Letven, 1984), body image formation (Bruch, 1974), and self and object constancy (Rollins & Blackwell, 1968) are among the functions whose incomplete or distorted development have been implicated in the development of eating disorders. Family theories specify the transactions that make such achievements difficult, whereas psychoanalytic theories identify intrapsychic conflicts or developmental distortions with their resultant structural deficits, which promote symptom formation in lieu of mastery of developmental tasks.

It is particularly adolescent developmental tasks that women with eating disorders avoid (Crisp & Toms, 1972): independence from family and progress toward self-regulated functioning with respect to identity and sexuality. Developmental formulations tend to relate these individuals' inability to accomplish these tasks to an accumulation of deficits beginning in the earliest developmental phases and reaching an impasse at adolescence. Compliance and high-achieving "goodness" are revealed at adolescence as masks for multiple deficits in development of an independent and self-regulated self.

The process whereby independent self-regulation is achieved can be understood as one involving differentiation of self from other and of progressive reorganization and "decentering" of the units of self and nonself experience (Fast, 1984). The infant moves from an undifferentiated primary narcissistic state wherein the world of experience seems to be omnipotently created by her own action to one where she perceives the world and herself as an object in it as operating according to causal laws independent of her will or action. This shift from the narcissistic state in which the whole world of experience is construed as part of the self and subject to its omnipotence to a more mature and "decentered" state is a highly complex and difficult process even cognitively (Piaget, 1952); but even more so when cognition is about emotionally charged issues (Fast, 1974; Greenspan, 1979; Kohut, 1977; Mahler et al., 1975). Parental support and encouragement for the child's successful accomplishment of the numerous stages involved in this development make heavy demands on parents' maturity and level of self–other differentiation. If parents take their child's ambivalence or curiosity about the world or independent strivings as personal rejections, they will be unable to support their child's differentiation and integration of a separate self.

As we have seen, it is especially in these respects that parents of patients with eating disorders have particular difficulty: their narcissistic, intrusive, and unempathic overinvolvement with their children is an almost universal observation. Greenspan (1979), whose developmental theory attempts to integrate Piagetian and psychoanalytic developmental models, uses mothers of anorectics as a striking example of interference with self–other differentiation and self-structure formation by narcissistic projection of their own idiosyncratic constructions onto their daughters' experience in the earliest phases of the differentiation process where it has the most far-reaching consequences. Bruch's (1963) developmental formulation like-wise sees mothers as unable to tolerate or to validate child-initiated acts or affects. The daughter therefore never learns to process internal bodily sensations or affective cues well enough to use them to develop an effective sense of self capable of adaptive responsiveness to her own internal state. Clearly, parental failures of attunement cut short the child's developmentally necessary experience of omnipotence, leaving as a residue a pervasive sense of ineffectuality (Bruch, 1963) and vulnerability to humiliation (Kohut, 1977). Of particular relevance to the understanding of eating disorders are the observations of Perkins (1956) and Galdston (1974) that these earliest and most primitive and pathogenic mother–child transactions take place through the medium of food. Perkins hypothesizes that the more intense, exclusive, and food-dominated the exchange, the more likely it is to lead to an eating disorder rather than to some other distortion of object relations.

These failures of optimal parental functioning can have multiple effects on subsequent development, only three of which will concern us here because of their special relevance to the symptom picture in eating disorders. First, with respect to differentiation of self and nonself in the feeding situation, the discrimination of self, body-self, hunger sensations, affects such as longing, gratification, disappointment, humiliation, and the like are inadequately differentiated from one another and inaccurately located in various aspects of the feeding situation. For example, unappeased hunger and rage and helplessness may be a single experience perceived as located in the breast, which is construed to be part of the self. On this basis, it can make sense that appetitive strivings are disavowed, and fatness can be equated with helpless dependence and humiliation. Such failures of differentiation allow the body image to be responsive to subjective states rather than to actual body size, as when an anorexic patient reported feeling fat when she felt helpless and enraged at having been humiliated by a friend.

In addition to failure to differentiate self and nonself aspects of the feeding situation, the person with an eating disorder suffers from an inability to relinquish the omnipotent sense of self characteristic of primary narcissism (Fast, 1984). Only when in omnipotent control of the body and its appetites does she experience a sense of self; loss of control of the body, as in the bulimic episode, feels like loss of the self (Erard, 1985). The experience of neediness as in hunger and eating, or vulnerability as in object longing and loving, threaten the omnipotent self with intolerable feelings of powerlessness. Voluntary hunger and renunciation are defensively substituted for object longing because the breast must be repudiated unless it seems to be omnipotently controlled by the self (Boris, 1984). Omnipotent control of the body and repudiation of the object of longing obliterate feelings of vulnerability and powerlessness and imperfection. Omnipotent control of the body becomes a substitute for mastery of adolescent tasks, including acceptance of the limits on what one can be or aspires to be if one is to have a coherent identity.

Simultaneous longing and hatred for the object of longing, the ambivalence of the infant and toddler, is focal to Mahler et al.'s (1975) schema for the earliest developmental stages. Self and object constancy, the developmental achievement of the separation–individuation model, requires parental qualities which promote attunement in parent-infant transactions. Parents must be neither too narcissistic and intrusive nor too intolerant of the ambivalent toddler's alternating wishes to merge again with the symbiotic mother of infancy and to be free of her and leave her behind forever (as long as she stays nearby!). The pathogenic parenting we have already noted is a developmental impediment to the achievement of object constancy in that it heightens ambivalence to a problematical degree (Mahler, 1968; Bruch, 1973). Indeed, some writer (Rollins & Blackwell, 1968; Sugerman, Quinlan, & Devenis, 1982) see the symptom picture of anorexia nervosa primarily as a defense against anaclitic depression resulting from intrapsychic loss of the object whose loved and hated qualities are insufficiently integrated. The good object and the loving self are lost under the stress of adolescence; they are overwhelmed by hatred of the bad object and the bad self. Sours (1974) speaks of archaic states of dedifferentiation experienced by some anorectics who have never experienced the developmentally necessary separations. For these patients, the eating disorder represents a frantic effort to stave off fragmentation and loss of self because of inner emptiness (Lerner, 1983). Because they arise from similar developmental deficits that result in object loss, eating disorders and anaclitic depression can be thought of as two faces of the same intrapsychic adolescent dilemma, the one latent and the other manifest.

These failures of early differentiation processes, because of their relevance to female development as well as to the development of eating disorders, provide a possible clue to the special vulnerability of women to expressing their pathology through eating disorders. Numerous efforts at reformulation of the psychoanalytic developmental model as it relates to women (e.g., Chodorow, 1978; Fliegel, 1982; Notman, 1982) place special emphasis on the separation-individuation process and its particular "stickiness" for girls. Mothers are seen to have greater difficulty facilitating differentiation by daughters and differentiating themselves from daughters than from sons (Chodorow, 1978; Notman, 1982). They are more likely to engage in prolonged projective and identificatory processes with daughters than with sons (Chodorow, 1978; Torok, 1970), and the transactions these processes give rise to are of the sort that impede separation (Greenspan, 1979). In addition, Mahler et al. (1975) have observed that boys' greater reliance on gross motor activity during the rapprochement phase is an additional facilitator of separation that girls do not have. Another advantage of boys relative to girls in this regard is that boys leave their mothers to turn to their fathers as objects of identification (Fast, 1984). Girls remain identified with the mother, the object of primary identification, and thus they are in danger of not resolving completely enough this initial identification that precedes differentiation (Fast, 1984). They have a "softer" mother–daughter boundary (Fliegel, 1982), and an inherently more difficult time achieving the assurance that being like mother is not the same as being mother or being swallowed up by mother. The threat of swallowing and/or being swallowed up expresses the undercurrent pull to merge with the loved and feared and hated object. Girls who develop eating disorders presumably experience more of this pull to merge and more of its opposite than they can withstand without distortion of their development.

Changes in sex-role definitions of middle and upper class women exacerbate the conflict between the wish to merge with mother and the wish to be free and active, unfettered by constraining object ties. The expected social role of middle and upper class women is to be active, achieving, competitive, and sexual. These qualities are at odds with the merging, nurturing, affiliative qualities of the more traditional female role. The "stickiness" of the female separation-individuation process is necessary to create permeable ego boundaries for nurturing babies (Chodorow, 1978; Notman, 1982) and for women's special valuing of affiliative aims (Gilligan, 1982). Women aspire to build professional and business careers and relationship patterns like those of men on intrapsychic foundations culturally designed to make them mothers (Chodorow, 1978).

The dilemma of sexuality poses yet another conflict between the push of separation and the acquiescent, merging pull of mother. It is not only the competitive strivings of the Oedipal period that lead to conflict; it is also contemporary cultural pressure on, e.g., college students for free sexual expression without binding ties. Chassequet-Smirgel (1976) and Torok

(1970), in their efforts to contribute to a contemporary psychoanalytic formulation of female psychology, have interpreted penis envy as a way of contending with the power of the mother of early childhood. The young woman remains loyal and available to mother by substituting the wish for a penis for her wish to overthrow the power of the primitive mother image and to reject the primary tie to mother in favor of the sexual pleasure available from the man as primary object. Striving for achievement is less threatening to the primary tie to mother than is striving for sexual fulfillment, especially in a social and cultural context where sexuality has become more explicit and less binding. Penis envy can function to preserve the submissive bond with mother while disavowing both identification and sexual competition with her. It can effect a compromise in the conflict between independent, adult sexuality and the tie to the mother of childhood. While this conflict is not peculiar to women of the 20th century, contemporary pressures for both achievement and free sexuality in the context of the "sticky," "soft" mother–daughter bond, heighten it greatly. The ideal of the prepubescent male body, unencumbered by the softness in which she unconsciously wishes to lose herself, has great appeal for the woman who wants both her sexuality and to leave all that nurturant, affiliative nonsense behind.

The middle class culture of affluence and the frequent material overindulgence of middle class children by successful parents from deprived backgrounds is another contemporary phenomenon that may be seen as relevant for the development of eating disorders (Boris, 1984; Vandereycken & Meermann, 1984). Overindulgence can be a seductive, exploitive manipulation of the child's greed in order to gratify parental needs to overcome their own feeling of deprivation. The children rebel by renunciation, one variant of which is anorexia nervosa. Here again, as with the ideal body image, the eating disorder seems to represent an exaggerated version of a common social phenomenon, probably on the part of developmentally vulnerable women who experienced parental seduction not only with material things, but also with food.

Nineteenth-century women who developed neurasthenia or hysteria [Alice James (Strouse, 1980) is a vivid and highly articulate example] were biologically healthy women who "chose" to immobilize themselves with the burdens of illness. Their socially prescribed passivity was threatened from within by active, aggressive, achieving, and sexual aims; they disavowed these rebellious and instinctual strivings by becoming invalids. Twentieth-century women, having come a long way, find themselves disavowing their passive, affiliative nurturant strivings in favor of active, achieving, and sexual ones. This conflict is common to most contemporary middle and upper class women. It may be that the developmental deficits outlined above produce women in whom both sides of the conflict are particulary powerful, and that it is this increasingly larger group of women who develop not depression but eating disorders in lieu of mastering the conflicts inherent in coming into womanhood in this time and at this place.

REFERENCES

Biederman, J., Rivinus, T.M., Herzog, D.B., Harmatz, J.S., Shanley, K., & Yunis, E.J. (1984). High frequency of HLA-Bw16 in patients with anorexia nervosa. *American Journal of Psychiatry, 14*(9), 1109–1110.

Boris, H.N. (1984). The problem of anorexia nervosa. *International Journal of Psycho-Analysis, 65,* 315–322.

Bruch, H. (1961). Transformation of oral impulses in eating disorders: A conceptual approach. *Psychiatric Quarterly, 35,* 458–481.

Bruch, H. (1963). Disturbed communication in eating disorders. *American Journal of Orthopsychiatry, 33*(1), 99–104.

Bruch, H. (1966). Anorexia nervosa and its differential diagnosis. *Journal of Nervous and Mental Diseases, 141,* 555–564.

Bruch, H. (1973). *Eating disorders: Obesity, anorexia nervosa, and the person within.* New York: Basic Books.

Cantwell, D.P., Struzenberger, S., Burroughs, J., Salkin, B., & Green, J.K. (1977). Anorexia nervosa: An effective disorder? *Archives of General Psychiatry, 34,* 1087–1093.

Casper, R.C. (1983). On the emergence of bulimia nervosa as a syndrome. *International Journal of Eating Disorders, 2*(3), 3–15.

Casper, R.C., Eckert, E.D., Holmi, K.A., Goldberg, S.C., & Davis, J.M. (1980). Bulimia: Its incidence and clinical importance in patients with anorexia nervosa. *Archives of General Psychiatry, 37,* 1030–1035.

Chasseguet-Smirgel, J. (1976). Freud and female sexuality: The consideration of some blind spots in the exploration of the "Dark Continent." *International Journal of Psycho-Analysis, 57,* 275.

Chodorow, N. (1978). *The reproduction of mothering: Psychoanalysis and the sociology of gender.* Berkeley: University of California Press.

Crisp, A.H., Hsu, L.K.G., Chen, C.N., & Wheeler, M. (1982). Reproductive hormone profiles in male anorexia nervosa before, during and after restoration of body weight to normal: A study of 12 patients. *International Journal of Eating Disorders, 1*(3), 3–9.

Crisp, A.H., Hsu, L.K., Harding, B., & Hartshorn, J. (1980). Clinical features of anorexia nervosa: A study of a consecutive series of 102 female patients. *Journal of Psychosomatic Research, 24,* 179–191.

Crisp, A.H., Palmer, R.L., & Kalucy, R.S. (1976). How common is anorexia nervosa? A prevalence study. *British Journal of Psychiatry, 128,* 549–554.

Crisp, A.H., & Toms, D.A. (1972). Primary anorexia nervosa or weight phobia in the male: Report on 13 cases. *British Medical Journal, 1,* 334–338.

Eckert, E.D., Goldberg, S.C., Halni, K.A., Casper, R.C., & Davis, J.M. (1982). Depression in anorexia nervosa. *Psychological Medicine, 12,* 115–122.

Erard, R.E. (1985). *Body image and action maturity in eating disorders.* Unpublished manuscript, Orchard Hills Psychiatric Center, P.C., Farmington Hills, MI.

Falstein, E.I., Feinstein, S.C., & Judas, I. (1956). Anorexia nervosa in the male child. *American Journal of Orthopsychiatry, 26,* 751–772.

Fast, I. (1984). *Gender identity: A differentiation model. Advances in psychoanalysis: Theory, research & practice, Volume 2.* Hillsdale NJ: Analytic Press.

Fliegel, Z.O. (1982). Half a century later: Current Status of Freud's Controversial Views on Women. *The Psychoanalytic Review, 69* (Spring), 7–28.

Galdston, R. (1974). Mind over matter: Observations on 50 patients hospitalized with anorexia nervosa. *Journal of American Academy of Child Psychiatry, 13,* 246–263.

Garfinkel, P.E., & Garner, D.M. (1982). *Anorexia nervosa: A multidimensional perspective.* New York: Brunner/Mazel.

Garfinkel, P.E., Moldofsky, H., & Garner, D.M. (1980). The heterogeneity of anorexia nervosa. *Archives of General Psychiatry, 37,* 1036–1040.

Gilligan, C. (1982). *In a different voice: Psychological theory and women's development.* Cambridge, MA: Harvard University Press.

Greenspan, S.I. (1979). Intelligence and adaptation: An integration of psychoanalytic and Piagetian developmental psychology. *Psychological Issues, 12*(314), Monograph 47/48. New York: International Universities Press.

Halmi, K.A., Dekirmenjian, H., Davis, J.M., Casper, R., & Goldberg, S. (1978). Catecholamine metabolism in anorexia nervosa. *Archives General Psychiatry, 35,* 458–460.

Halmi, K.A., Falk, J.R., & Schwartz, E. (1981). Binge-eating and vomiting: A survey of a college population. *Psychological Medicine, 11,* 697–706.

Hart, K.J., & Ollendick, T. (1985). Prevalence of bulimia in working & university women. *American Journal of Psychiatry, 142*(7), 851–854.

Hatsukami, D., Eckert, E., Mitchell, J.E., & Pyle, R. (1984). Affective disorder and substance abuse in women with bulimia. *Psychological Medicine, 14,* 701–704.

Hendren, R.L. (1983). Depression in anorexia nervosa. *Journal of American Academy of Child Psychiatry, 22,* 59–62.

Hsu, L.K.G. (1980). Outcome of anorexia nervosa: A reveiw of the literature (1954 to 1978). *Archives of General Psychiatry, 37,* 1041–1046.

Hudson, J.I., Pope, H.G., Jonas, J.M., & Yurgelun-Todd, D. (1983). Family history study of anorexia nervosa and bulimia. *British Journal of Psychiatry, 142,* 133–138.

Kalucy, R.S., Crisp, A.H., & Harding, B. (1977). A study of 56 families with anorexia nervosa. *British Journal of Medical Psychology, 50,* 381–395.

Katzman, M.A., Wolchik, S.A., & Braver, S.L. (1984). The prevalence of frequent binge eating & bulimia in a nonclinical college sample. *International Journal of Eating Disorders, 3*(3), 53–62.

Kohut, H. (1977). *The restoration of the self.* New York: International Universities Press.

Lerner, H.D. (1983). Contemporary psychoanalytic perspectives on gorge-vomiting: A case illustration. *International Journal of Eating Disorders, 3*(1), 47–63.

Mahler, M.S. (1968). *On human symbiosis and the vicissitudes of individuation. Volume 1: Infantile psychosis.* New York: International Universities Press.

Mahler, M.S., Pine, F., & Bergman, A. (1975). *The psychological birth of the human infant: Symbiosis and individuation.* New York: Basic Books.

Minuchin, S., Rosman, B.L., & Baker, L. (1978). *Psychosomatic families: Anorexia nervosa in context.* Cambridge, MA: Harvard University Press.

Notman, M. (1982). Feminine development: Changes in Psychoanalytic theory. In M. Notman (Ed.), *The woman patient; Volume 2. Concepts of femininity in the life cycle* (pp. 3–29). New York: Plenum Press.

Nemiah, J.C. (1950). Anorexia nervosa: A clinical psychiatric study. *Medicine, 29,* 225–268.

Palazzoli, M.S. (1974). *Self-starvation: From individual to family therapy in the treatment of anorexia nervosa* (translated by A. Pomerans). New York: Jason Aronson.

Perkins, G.L. (1956). Discussion of Falstein et al., Anorexia nervosa in the male child. *American Journal of Orthopsychiatry, 26,* 770–772.

Piaget, J. (1952). *The origins of intelligence in children.* New York: International Universities Press.

Pope, H.G., Hudson, J.I., & Yurgelun-Todd, D. (1984). Anorexia nervosa and bulimia among 300 suburban women shoppers. *American Journal of Psychiatry, 141*(2), 292–294.

Pope, H.G., Hudson, J.I., Yurgelun-Todd, D., & Hudson, M.S. (1984). Prevalence of anorexia nervosa and bulimia in 3 student populations. *International Journal of Eating Disorders, 3*(3), 45–51.

Pyle, R.L., Mitchell, J.E., & Eckert, E.D. (1981). Bulimia: A report of 34 cases. *Journal of Clinical Psychiatry, 42*(2), 60–64.

Rivinus, T.M., Biederman, J., Herzog, D.B., Kemper, K., Harper, G.P., Harmaty, J.S., & Houseworth, S. (1984). Anorexia nervosa and affective disorders: A controlled family history study. *American Journal of Psychiatry, 141*(11), 1414–1418.

Rollins, N., & Blackwell, A. (1968). The treatment of anorexia nervosa in children and adolescents: Stage 1. *Journal of Child Psychology and Psychiatry and Allied Disciplines, 9,* 81–91.

Schwartz, D.M., Thompson, M.G., & Johnson, C.L. (1982). Anorexia nervosa & bulimia: The socio-cultural context. *International Journal of Eating Disorders, 1*(3), 20–36.

Sours, J.A. (1974). The anorexia nervosa syndrome. *International Journal of Psycho-Analysis, 55,* 567–576.

Stangler, R.S., & Printz, A.M. (1980). DSM-111: Psychiatric diagnosis in a university population. *American Journal of Psychiatry, 137*(8), 937–940.

Stern, S.L., Dixon, K.N., Nemzer, E., Lake, M.D., Sansone, R.A., Smelter, D.J., Lantz, S., & Schrier, S.S. (1984). Affective disorder in the families of women with normal weight bulimia. *American Journal of Psychiatry, 141*(10), 1224–1227.

Striegel-Moore, R.H., Silberstein, L.R., & Rodin, J. (1986). Toward an understanding of risk factors in bulimia. *American Psychologist, 41,* 246–264.

Strober, M. (1982). The significance of bulimia in juvenile anorexia nervosa: An exploration of possible etiologic factors. *International Journal of Eating Disorders, 1,* 28–43.

Strober, M., Salkin, B., Burrough, J., & Morrell, W. (1982). Validity of the bulimia-restricter distinction in anorexia nervosa: Parental personality characteristics & family psychiatry morbidity. *Journal of Nervous and Mental Disease, 170*(60), 345–351.

Strouse, J. (1980). *Alice James, A biography.* Boston: Houghton Mifflin.

Sugarman, A., Quinlan, D., & Devenis, L. (1982). Anorexia nervosa as a defense against anaclitic depression. *International Journal of Eating Disorders, 1*(1), 44–61.

Swartz, D.M., Thompson, M.G., & Johnson, C.L. (1982). Anorexia nervosa and bulimia: The socio-cultural context. *International Journal of Eating Disorders, 1*(3), 20–36.

Swift, W.J., & Letven, R. (1984). Bulimia and the basic fault: A psychoanalytic interpretation of the binge-vomiting syndrome. *Journal of the American Academy of Child Psychiatry, 23*(4), 489–497.

Torok, M. (1970). The significance of the penis envy in women. In J. Chassequet-Smirgel (Ed.), *Female sexuality* (pp. 135–170). Ann Arbor, MI: University Michigan Press.

Vandereycken, W., & Meermann, R. (1984). Anorexia nervosa: Is prevention possible? *International Journal of Psychiatry in Medicine, 14*(3), 191–205.

Van Thorre, M.D., & Vogel, F.X. (1985). The presence of bulimia in high school females. *Adolescence, 20*(77), 45–51.

Waller, J.V., Kaufman, M.R., & Deutsch, F. (1940). Anorexia nervosa: A psychosomatic entity. *Psychosomatic Medicine, 2,* 3–16.

Wilson, C.P., Hogan, C.C., & Mintz, I.L. (Eds.) (1983). *Fear of being fat: The treatment of anorexia nervosa & bulimia.* New York: Jason Aronson.

Winokur, A., March, V., & Mendels, J. (1980). Primary effective disorder in relatives of patients with anorexia nervosa. *American Journal of Psychiatry, 137*(6), 695–698.

■ Three
DEPRESSION IN ADULT WOMEN

■ 8
Episodic Mood Disorders In Women

RANDY S. MILDEN, Ph.D.

This chapter reflects on the coming of age of psychobiological perspectives on episodic affective disorders in women. Over the last 20 years, the contributions of biological psychiatric approaches to these disturbances have been impressive. Encouraged by the dramatic gains in understanding and treating endogenous depressions within this framework, researchers and clinicians have tried to extend this approach to depressions that fall short of the criteria for a major depressive disorder, but which have a similar, although attenuated shape and course (Spitzer, 1980; Spitzer & Robins, 1978). This latter category includes those disturbances of mood which, in the past, have been labeled characterological depressions and disorders, and in which a biological basis has been suspected. A prime example is premenstrual syndrome. We will discuss the application of contemporary biological psychiatric approaches to these two broadly defined categories of episodic mood disorders in women, that is, (1) endogenous depressions and (2) atypical depressions where descriptive definitions are more variable, pathophysiology less clearly known, and somatic treatment on the

The author wishes to acknowledge the contributions of Drs. Pamela Ludolph, Howard Lerner, Martin Mayman, Judith Ballou, Dennis Smith, and Miriam Rosenthal. This work was accomplished with the help of the Clinical Studies Unit, Department of Psychiatry, University of Michigan, and the Departments of Reproductive Biology and Psychiatry, Case Western Reserve University School of Medicine.

This chapter includes sections of a paper entitled, "Pseudoendogenous Depression in Patients with Borderline and Narcissistic Character Disorders," presented as part of a symposium on "Some Character Types Met with in Psychoanalytic Work: An Update," at the annual meeting of the American Psychological Association in Toronto, Canada, on August 26, 1984.

whole less effective. Our observations will focus on (1) the state of scientific progress and (2) the effect of changes in our approaches on the patient's subjective experience of her illness and her sense of self.

This chapter concentrates on episodic affective illness in women for a number of reasons. It has been well established that the incidence of these illnesses is significantly greater in women than in men (Weissman & Klerman, 1977; Radloff & Rae, 1979). Breaking down the incidence of depression by diagnostic category, women have a higher rate of major depressive illness than men, with a slightly greater incidence of bipolar disease (1.2:1) and substantially greater incidence of unipolar depression (2:1) (Hirshfeld & Cross, 1982). When one examines less severe but persistent depressions, a preponderance of women is also found.

By virtue of their numbers, women are a natural focus in any discussion of the impact of new approaches to depression. As we consider how psychobiological perspectives on depressive illness shape a patient's sense of herself, the rationale for such a focus becomes more compelling. We will suggest that, in some of these patients, the meaning of the biologically defined disease becomes interwoven with the meaning of being female. Thus, although the way in which an illness is defined certainly affects patients of both sexes, women may experience such definitions in a unique way.

We will first consider the impact of the burgeoning development of biological psychiatry in the arena of endogenous depressive illness. In 1980, one of the pioneers in the field of biological psychiatry, Snyder, reflecting on the advances of neurobiological work in this area, concluded as follows:

> The mental health professions can be proud that mechanisms of action of psychotropic drugs are probably at least as well worked out as the mechanisms for many of the principal drugs in medicine. Identifying specific sites of actions of drugs at molecularly defined receptors permitted the tailoring of drugs with greater therapeutic potency and fewer side effects. Classification of neurotransmitter synthesis, release, and inactivation has considerably enhanced our understanding of how the brain processes emotional behavior. Genetic studies have increased our appreciation of what determines vulnerability to various forms of major mental illness. In a word, the biological and psychological aspects of mental disorders have been drawn closer. (Snyder, 1980, p. viii)

It is not our intention to present an exhaustive summary of these clinical and investigative efforts. That has been done and done well (Baldessarini, 1983; Cooper, Bloom, & Roth, 1982; Davis & Maas, 1983; Paykel, 1982; Snyder, 1980). It is sufficient for our purposes to acknowledge that, based on these advances, there has been a growing reliance in most academic psychiatric domains on neurobiological explanations for cyclic affective disease. Much of the funding for psychiatric research that remains in the wake of extensive cutbacks supports biological psychiatric explorations. A majority of the articles published in the most highly regarded psychiatric professional journals address psychobiological questions.

This shift in orientation has carried over to clinical settings involved in the evaluation and treatment of major depressive illness. Psychiatric assessments in these institutions are characteristically based less on depth-psychological studies and more on descriptive symptom tallies and laboratory (sleep EEGs, dexamethazone suppression tests). Somatic treatments (antidepressant medication, ECT) may be used exclusively or in combination with psychotherapy. Snyder's celebration of the scientific gains in this area is echoed by clinicians who are treating endogenous unipolar and bipolar affective patients with the benefit of psychobiological advances. Somatic therapies do not cure the disease—they effect a remission of an episode of symptoms—and rates of effectiveness in symptom remission vary (Baldessarini, 1983; Davis & Maas, 1983; Paykel, 1982). Nevertheless, these approaches can successfully alleviate cycles of mood disturbance in patients who, in the past, received limited help from psychotherapy. Bipolar patients who endured years of mood swings can now be stabilized on lithium and lead fulfilling, balanced lives. Unipolar depressives who at one time might have remained depressed and virtually nonfunctional for months are now back to work in three weeks, the time it takes for a depressive episode to respond to a course of tricyclic antidepressants.

The scientific and clinical benefits of these treatments of endogenous depression are well documented. What does the literature say about the impact of a biological psychiatric approach on a patient's experience of herself? Little has been written directly on that topic. In the earlier days of psychopharmacological management of depressed patients, many concerns were raised about the dangers of reliance on drugs for treatment. Those writing from a political perspective decried somatic therapies as potentially coercive—agents not of healing but of social control (Meerloo, 1955; Szasz, 1957). Some psychoanalytic observers, skeptical of non-psychoanalytic approaches, argued that medications would interfere with the gains from psychoanalysis or psychoanalytic psychotherapy (Ostow, 1975). Klerman (1976) and Klerman and Schechter (1982) catalogued these concerns, listing the following objections analysts have raised regarding psychobiological treatment. Specifically, some analysts have been concerned about a negative placebo effect with pharmacotherapy, which could mobilize countertherapeutic, regressive transferences. Some fear that symptoms, in particular anxiety, will be allayed by medication, with the patient no longer motivated to continue therapy. Moreover, defenses might be undercut by drug treatment; the rapid eliminations of symptoms could disrupt the patient's psychic equilibrium and lead to decompensation. Patients might negatively evaluate the recommendation for medication, considering themselves of lesser value than others for whom insight-oriented treatment is prescribed.

Most writers today agree that the negative effects of drug treatment have been overstated and have little basis in fact. Some writers have called for an integration of drug treatment with psychotherapy (Cooper, 1985; Ostow, 1975; Pfefferbaum, 1977). Others have addressed the issue empirically, examining the effects of drugs and psychotherapy, alone and in combination, with patients with depressive disorders (Covi, Lipman, Derogatis, Smith, & Pattison, 1974; DiMascio, Weissman, Prusoff, Neuzwillig, & Klerman, 1979; Elkin, Parloff, Hadley, & Autry, 1985; Friedman, 1975; Klerman, DiMascio, Weissman, Prusoff, & Paykel, 1974; Luborsky & Singer, 1975; Murphy, Simons, Wetzel, & Lystman, 1984; Prusoff, Weissman, Klerman, & Rounsaville, 1980; Rounsaville, Klerman, & Weissman, 1981; Shakir, Volkmar, Bacon, Pfefferbaum, 1979; Weissman, 1978, 1979, 1983; Weissman, Prusoff, DiMascio, Neu, Gorklaney, & Klerman, 1979). Although the final research results are not in, the consensus is that medications and psychotherapy work well in combination. Some studies postulate an additive effect, in which each mode of intervention targets a different constellation of symptoms. Klerman and Schechter (1982) state categorically that, despite the concerns that have been raised, "there was no evidence in any of the studies for a negative interaction between drugs and psychotherapy" (p. 335).

Much of the work that these authors summarize is sensitive and sophisticated. The mobilization of solid research to answer difficult theoretical and clinical questions is certainly welcome. There is always a danger, however, that data-based conclusions, even when drawn from well-designed studies may miss subtle and elusive clinical phenomena. There are aspects of psychological experience that are difficult to tap in a questionnaire or to tease out in a statistical analysis. Drug therapies may have an impact—on how patients think and feel about their problems and themselves, which is not easily measurable and, in fact, often unknown to investigators and even to the patients themselves. These less obvious effects may have particular relevance to the treatment of depressed women.

We will consider these more subtle psychological "side effects" at the same time as we appreciate the main effects of biological interventions. It is clear that women with endogenous affective illness need somatic therapies. Drug treatment is useful in caring for these patients and can be integrated with psychotherapeutic modalities. Based on the clinical assessment and treatment of depressed patients and the preliminary analysis of data from a Rorschach study, it has also been my observation that biological therapies affect the way in which these patients think about themselves

(Milden, 1984; Milden, Ludolph, & Lerner, in press). Some patients can directly report about these effects, others report them projectively on a test like the Rorschach. A number of characteristics emerge: many patients undergoing somatic treatment for episodic endogenous depressions describe difficulty feeling complete and in control of themselves. They have been told that they are ruled, during an episode, by their neurotransmitters, and that they are rescued by medication. They understand that they are neurobiologically incomplete, and they need external materials to complement what they perceive as their deficient selves. When the medicine is continued prophylactically between episodes, patients are constantly reminded of their need for exogenous substances to feel whole. Patients who, prior to the onset of illness, were relatively self-sufficient in terms of mood-state regulation now are forced to rely on medication and on a physician to administer and supervise it. This new reliance may be experienced by such patients as a prescription for regression.

This sense of narcissistic vulnerability may be a direct result of experiencing mood swings, regardless of how they are understood or treated. This aspect of postepisode symptoms has been noted by Akiskal (1983) and others. In some patients, such feelings are also undoubtedly related to a premorbid difficulty with self-integrity and self-sufficiency, a problem which, one might speculate, has contributed to a vulnerability to depression. In addition, for most patients, such feelings are also a result of the biological approach to depression.

Such subjective reactions no doubt exist in men as well as in women. Yet it is the women who talk about it more easily and directly, and who relate these feelings about self-integrity to their sense of themselves as women. Many of these women are characterologically passive and far from self-reliant before they are ever depressed. Flooded with affect in an episode, affective inhibition characterizes their state not only after an episode but also before. There is a continuity between their premorbid lack of self-definition and the messages they hear about the causes and treatments of their psychiatric disorder. As we explore, in psychotherapy, women's feelings about their biologically defined disease, they begin to talk about some of their more basic difficulties with self-control and self-integrity. What they have been told is missing neurobiologically becomes a metaphor for a sense of a core deficiency or inferiority. The diagnosis of a biological defect may give rise, in some women, to a sense of overall incompleteness or inadequacy. As women confront the effects of a biologically defined affective illness on their sense of self, many of these women are able for the first time in their lives to begin to change their more primary sense of being deficient and passive.

It is of general importance to underscore that, in the absence of psychodynamic approaches, drug treatment alone may relieve symptoms, but may also affect sense of self, lower self-esteem, and lead to a depression with a psychological foundation. Thus, pharmacotherapy that can allow depressed women to lead more productive lives may unwittingly encourage personality features that may interfere with a remission of the depressive episode and make a recurrence more likely.

Let us now look at those patients we have identified as not meeting criteria for a major depression, who find themselves in the purview of biological psychiatry. As noted earlier, with these patients whose depressions are less severe or prolonged, definitions are less clear and reliable, their etiology is speculated upon but not well understood, and somatic treatments are less certain to be beneficial.

A biological approach has been applied to depressions that have been labeled characterological, neurotic, endogenomorphic, and cyclothymic (Akiskal, 1983; Akiskal, Djenderedjian, & Rosenthal, 1977; Akiskal, Rosenthal, Haykal, Lemmir, & Rosenthal, 1980; Klein, 1974; Klerman, Endicott, Spitzer, Hirshfeld, 1974). These writers raise the interesting theoretical and clinical possibility that some depressive illnesses thought to be psychologically based may, in fact, bear a resemblance to full-blown endogenous depression, sharing a common pathophysiology, which is also responsive to drug treatment. Although this view has its proponents, more work is required before we can understand these conditions more fully. It is presently not clear what substantive contributions biological psychiatry can make to this cluster of atypical affective disorders. Drug treatment is used with benefit by some patients but does not help others, and biological forays in this area remain exploratory.

Similar conclusions may be drawn in the other type of mood disorder we have included in this nonendogenous group of depressions—premenstrual syndrome. Unlike the more broadly framed nonendogenous depressions, which have only recently received attention from those working from a biological perspective, premenstrual syndrome has for decades been thought to have a neuroendocrine basis (Frank, 1931; Reid & Yen, 1981). Despite hundreds of papers over the last 50 years that have explored biological aspects of premenstrual syndrome, little is definitively known. Although the scientific quality of these studies has improved, serious methodological problems exist in many such investigations (Rubinow & Roy-Byrne, 1984). It is hardly surprising that, in an area in which we have difficulty defining what it is we are studying, we are far from knowledgeable about etiology or treatment, biological and nonbiological. Although many complex etiologies have been proposed, including the linking of the underpinnings of premenstrual syndrome with endogenous depression, none have been supported by data. And while many drug treatments, including tricyclic antidepressants and lithium, have been tried with patients suffering from premenstrual syndrome, none have been shown to be effective in a double-blind, placebo-controlled, cross-over research design.

Despite this discouraging lack of clarity, and continuing methodological difficulties, we shall briefly review the work that does link premenstrual syndrome with affective disorders. Halbreich and Endicott, perhaps the most prolific proponents of a relationship between premenstrual syndrome and affective disorders, highlight methodological concerns in their efforts to tease out this link (Endicott, Halbreich, Schacht, Nee, 1985, 1981; Halbreich & Endicott, 1985, 1982; Halbreich, Endicott, & Nee, 1983). These authors subtype premenstrual syndrome (as well as other affective illness): "almost no women have a premenstrual endogenous depressive syndrome. However, women have premenstrual dysphoric changes that resemble other subtypes of depressive disease" (Halbreich & Endicott, 1985, p. 332). Researchers have tried to explore the link suggested by this resemblance in a number of ways. As noted above, they have attempted unsuccessfully to demonstrate a common pathophysiology or treatment response in the two groups. Although some researchers have found that depressed patients seek acute psychiatric care in the premenstrual phase of their cycle, others have found that this pattern occurs across diagnostic groups or at different cycle phases (Abramowitz, Baker, & Fleischer, 1982; Glass, Heninger, Lansky, & Talan, 1971; Jacobs & Charles, 1970; Janowsky, Gorney, Castelnuovo-Tedesco, & Stone, 1969; Zola, Meyerson, Reznikoff, Thornton, & Concool, 1979). There has also been a lack of consensus among studies that have looked at the frequency of premenstrual syndrome in depressed patients and controls. Some researchers have found that patients with affective disorder have a higher incidence of premenstrual difficulties. Others have concluded that the incidence is the same as in normals, and less than in other clinical populations, notably among neurotic patients (Coppen, 1965; Diamond, Rubenstein, & Dunner, 1976; Gregory, 1957; Price & DiMarcio, 1986). Finally, there does seem to be a link (ranging from a trend to a significant result) between a diagnosis of premenstrual syndrome and a past or future episode of affective illness (Endicott et al., 1981; Halbreich & Endicott, 1985, 1982; Halbreich, Endicott, & Nee, 1983; Kashiwagi, McClure, & Wetzel, 1976; Logue & Moos, 1986; McClure, Reich, & Wetzel, 1971; Schuckit, Daly, Herrman, Hineman, 1975; Wetzel, Reich, McClure & Wald, 1975).

What is the experience of patients without a clear-cut endogenous depression treated in a psychobiological framework? Again, it is striking that there is little information on this topic. In discussing the absence of a clear neurobiological formulation of premenstrual syndrome, some writers emphasize the need to focus on psychological aspects, i.e., aspects determined by a woman's expectations and attitudes about her problems (Parlee, 1973,

1982). For the most part, however, this approach to the woman's response to these problems has been descriptive or psychosocial rather than psychodynamic. In addition, there has been a tendency to focus either on biological or psychological explanations, rather than on an integration of approaches. Little has been written on the psychological effects of biological approaches. Although many researchers have tried to establish a link between hypothesized neurobiological causes and the cures for nonendogenous depression, no one has tried to understand the patient's experience of premenstrual syndrome or characterologic depression and its pharmacologic remedies with an eye to the experience of patients with more classical biologically defined mood disorders.

Although their responses overlap with those of endogenous patients, the reactions of patients with nonendogenous depression are also different in fundamental ways. In contrast to its confidence in treating endogenous depression, biological psychiatry explains and treats nonendogenous, characterological depressions or premenstrual symptoms with less certainty. Whatever promise these new approaches might hold for the endogenous patient, they cannot, at least at this point, provide similar help for the nonendogenous patient. Patients' response to this difference are in part influenced by such reality factors as treatment effectiveness. We no longer make the arbitrary distinction that endogenous patients are, by definition, free of personality problems and life stress, while only the nonendogenous patients are reactive to psychological stress and environmental factors. We assume that, whether or not there is a biological component to their disorders, both groups of patients may have intrapsychic and interpersonal difficulties. As we have suggested, the psychological issues that endogenous patients bring to the experience of a biological treatment are shaped by what the treatment can and typically does provide. The patient with a characterological depression or premenstrual syndrome who comes to a clinic for a biological assessment and somatic therapy must deal with both the wish that her "chemical imbalance" can be righted, as well as the high probability that she will not get a simple biological fix.

There are many patients with premenstrual complaints or characterological depressions who seek no treatment, coping more or less well on their own. Those patients, however, who do select a biological approach and formulation are affected by its important personal meaning. When one interviews an endogenously depressed patient in an episode of depression, there is often a sense that a psychodynamic assessment would be futile. Meaning and thematic depth are frequently buried beneath a pressing litany of descriptive concerns and recovered gradually as the episode remits. With the patient who presents in a biological psychiatric setting with a nonendogenous depression, on the other hand, meanings seem closer to the surface at the time. It is important to understand patients' symbolic and transferential communications. In proclaiming, "I am biologically ill," many of these patients are announcing, "I am empty and incomplete. I am helpless, out of control." Their fantasy is to be filled up and contained, allied with what they imagine is the providence and power of psychobiological intervention. Popular descriptive methods are more compelling than psychodynamic, in part because a focus on surface rather than underlying meaning corresponds to the patients' own sense of themselves as lacking depth and coherence. They are telling the therapist that there is something wrong with their bodies. They have decided they have a hormonal problem, one related to their biological femaleness.

As we have noted earlier, some of these issues arise with endogenously depressed patients. With those patients who appeal to biological psychiatry for help with premenstrual syndrome and characterological depression, however, there is another chapter to the story, often a disheartening denouement. These are patients who are presenting to professionals who will, in many cases, not be able to help them. They have chosen a mode that offers a quick, passive infusion of a relieving substance. It contains possibilities, if not promises, that arouse in many women longings for nurturance and vicarious power. And it is a mode that is, for many of these women, disappointing in the end. When the lithium or progesterone does not make patients with cyclothymic disorder or premenstrual syndrome well, or results in a temporary respite from symptoms which then return, patients may feel betrayed. The transference skid from idealization to devaluation is one that is especially painful, and there can be considerable anger at the physicians who, no matter how carefully they cautioned against unduly high expectation, may be accused of creating a wish that they could then not gratify. Our attempts to relieve nonendogenous depressions may also reinforce those aspects of personality that created some of the psychological (i.e., narcissistic) underpinnings of a depression in the first place. Biological approaches stir up a nonendogenous patient's sense of being needy and, in many cases, let down, and these are themes to which psychotherapists must be sensitive.

Although psychobiology has much to offer women who are trying to overcome endogenous and nonendogenous depressions to lead productive and fulfilling lives, there is always the danger that we may unwittingly engender in these women a new kind of biological determinism. Biology is a woman's destiny only if its meaning to her is not understood. It is important, in working with these women, that we appreciate the symbolic power of our approaches, even and especially when the care provided has a descriptive rather than depth-psychological foundation.

REFERENCES

Abramowitz, E.S., Baker, A.H., & Fleischer, S.F. (1982). Onset of depressive psychiatric crises and the menstrual cycle. *American Journal of Psychiatry, 139,* 475–478.

Akiskal, H.S. (1983). Dysthymic disorder: Psychopathology of proposed chronic depressive subtypes. *American Journal of Psychiatry, 140,* 11–20.

Akiskal, H.S., Djenderedjian, A.H., & Rosenthal, R.H. (1977). Cyclothymic disorder: Validating criteria for inclusion in the bipolar affective group. *American Journal of Psychiatry, 134,* 1227–1233.

Akiskal, H.S., Rosenthal, T.L., Haykal, R.F., Lemmi, H., & Rosenthal, R.H. (1980). Characterological depressions. *Archives of General Psychiatry, 37,* 777–783.

American Psychiatric Association (1980). Diagnostic and statistical manual of mental disorders (3rd ed.), Washington, D.C.

Baldessarini, R.J. (1983). *Biomedical aspects of depression and its treatment.* Washington, DC: American Psychiatric Press.

Cooper, A.M. (1985). Will neurobiology influence psychoanalysis? *American Journal of Psychiatry, 142,* 1395–1402.

Cooper, J.R., Bloom, F.E., & Roth, R.H. (1982). *The biochemical basis of neuropharmacology,* New York: Oxford University Press.

Coppen, A. (1965). The prevalence of menstrual disorders in psychiatric patients. *British Journal of Psychiatry, 111,* 155–167.

Covi, L., Lipman, R.S., Derogatis, L.R., Smith, J.E., & Pattison, J.H. (1974). Drugs and group psychotherapy in neurotic depression. *American Journal of Psychiatry, 132,* 191–198.

Davis, J.M., & Maas, J.W. (Eds.). (1983). *The affective disorders,* Washington. DC: American Psychiatric Press.

Diamond, J.B., Rubenstein, A.A., & Dunner, D.L. (1976). Menstrual problems in women with primary affective illness. *Comprehensive Psychiatry, 17,* 541–548.

DiMascio, A., Weissman, M.M., Prusoff, B.A., Neu, C., Zwillig, M., Klerman, G.L. (1979). Differential symptom reduction by drugs and psychotherapy in acute depression. *Archives of General Psychiatry, 36,* 1450–1456.

Elkin, I., Parloff, M.B., Hadley, S.W., & Autry, J.H. (1985). NIMH treatment of depression collaborative research program. *Archives of General Psychiatry, 42,* 305–316.

Endicott, J., Halbreich, U., Schacht, S., & Nee, J. (1985). Affective disorder and premenstrual depression. In H.J. Osofsky, & S. J. Blumenthal (Eds.), *Premenstrual syndrome: Current findings and future directions.* (pp. 3–11). Washington, DC: APA Press.

Endicott, J., Halbreich, U. Schacht, S., & Nee, J. (1981). Premenstrual changes and affective disorders. *Psychosomatic Medicine, 43,* 519–529.

Frank, R.J. (1931). The hormonal causes of premenstrual tension. *Archives of Neurology and Psychiatry, 26,* 1053–1057.

Glass, G.G., Heninger, G.R., Lansky, M., & Talan, K. (1971). Psychiatric emergency related to the menstrual cycle. *American Journal of Psychiatry, 128,* 705-711.

Gregory, B.A. (1957). The menstrual cycle and its disorders in psychiatric patients—II. *Journal of Psychosomatic Research, 2,* 199-224.

Halbreich, U., & Endicott, J. (1982). Classification of premenstrual syndromes. In R. Friedman (Ed.), *Behavior and the menstrual cycle* (pp. 243-265). New York: Marcel Dekker.

Halbreich, U., Endicott, J., & Nee, J. (1983). Premenstrual depressive changes. *Archives of General Psychiatry, 40,* 535-542.

Halbreich, U., & Endicott, J. (1985). Methodological issues in studies of premenstrual syndrome. *Psychoneuroendocrinology, 10,* 15-32.

Halbreich, U., & Endicott, J. (1985). The relationship of dysphoric premenstrual changes to depressive disorders. *Acta Psychiatrica Scandinavica, 71,* 331-338.

Hirschfeld, R.M., & Cross, C.K. (1982). Epidemiology of affective disorders. *Archives of General Psychiatry, 39,* 35-46.

Jacobs, T.J., & Charles, E. (1970). Correlation of psychiatric symptomatology and the menstrual cycle in an outpatient population. *American Journal of Psychiatry, 126,* 1504-1508.

Janowsky, D.C., Gorney, R., Castelnuovo-Tedesco, P., & Stone, C.P. (1969). Premenstrual–menstrual increases in psychiatric hospital admission rates. *American Journal of Obstetrics and Gynecology, 103,* 189-191.

Kashiwagi, T., McClure, J.N., & Wetzel, R.D. (1976). Premenstrual affective syndrome and psychiatric diseases. *Diseases of the Nervous System, 37,* 116-119.

Klein, D.F. (1974). Endogenomorphic depression: A conceptual and terminological revision. *Archives of General Psychiatry, 31,* 447-454.

Klerman, G.L. (1976). Psychoneurosis: Integrating pharmacotherapy and psychotherapy. In J.L. Claghorn (Ed.), *Successful psychotherapy.* (pp. 69-91). New York: Brunner/Mazel.

Klerman, G.L., DiMascio, A., Weissman, M., Prusoff, B.P., & Paykel, E.S. (1974). Treatment of depression by drugs and psychotherapy. *American Journal of Psychiatry, 131,* 181-186.

Klerman, G.L., Endicott, J., Spitzer, R., & Hirshfeld, R.M.A. (1979). Neurotic depressions: A systematic analysis of multiple criteria and meanings. *American Journal of Psychiatry, 136,* 57-61.

Klerman, G.L., & Schechter, G. (1982). Drugs and psychotherapy. In E.S. Paykel (Ed.), *The handbook of affective disorders* (pp. 329-337). New York: The Guilford Press.

Logue, C., & Moos, R.H. (1986). Perimenstrual symptoms: Prevalence and risk factors. *Psychosomatic Medicine, 48,* 388-414.

Luborsky, L., & Singer, B. (1975). Comparative studies of psychotherapies. *Archives of General Psychiatry, 32,* 995-1008.

McClure, J.N., Reich, T., & Wetzel, R.N. (1971). Premenstrual symptoms as an indicator of bipolar affective disorder. *British Journal of Psychiatry, 119,* 527-528.

Meerloo, J. (1955). Medication into submission: The danger of therapeutic coercion. *Journal of Nervous and Mental Disease, 122,* 353–360.

Milden, R.S. (1984). Affective disorders and narcissistic vulnerability. *American Journal of Psychoanalysis, 44,* 345–353.

Milden, R.S., Ludolph, P.S., & Lerner, H.D. (in press). The role of projective testing in a descriptive psychiatric model. In H.D. Lerner & P.M. Lerner (Eds.), *Primitive mental states and the Rorschach.* New York: International Universities Press.

Murphy, G.E., Simons, A.D., Wetzel, R.D., & Lustman, P.J. (1984). Cognitive therapy and pharmacotherapy: Singly and together in the treatment of depression. *Archives of General Psychiatry, 41,* 33–41.

Ostow, M. (1975). Psychological considerations in the chemotherapy of depression. In E.J. Anthony & J. Benedeck (Ed.), *Depression and human existence* (pp. 461–481). Boston: Little, Brown.

Parlee, M.B. (1973). The premenstrual syndrome. *Psychological Bulletin, 80,* 454–465.

Parlee, M.B. (1982). The psychology of the menstrual cycle: Biological and physiological perspectives. In R. Friedman (Ed.), *Behavior and the menstrual cycle* (pp. 77–99). New York: Marcel Dekker.

Paykel, E.S. (Ed.). (1982). *The handbook of affective disorders.* New York: The Guilford Press.

Pfefferbaum, A. (1977). Psychotherapy and psychopharmacology. In J.D. Barchas, P.A. Berger, R.D. Ciaranello, et al. (Eds.), *Psychopharmacology: From theory to practice* (pp. 481–492). New York: Oxford University Press.

Price, W.A., & DiMarcio, L. (1986). Premenstrual tension in rapidly cycling bipolar affective disorder. *Journal of Clinical Psychiatry, 47,* 415–417.

Prusoff, B.A., Weissman, M.M., Klerman, G.L., & Rounsaville, B. (1980). Subtypes of depression. *Archives of General Psychiatry, 37,* 796–801.

Radloff, L.S., & Rae, D.S. (1979). Susceptibility and precipitating factors in depression: Sex differences and similarities. *Journal of Abnormal Psychology, 8,* 174–181.

Reid, R.L., & Yen, S.S.C. (1981). Premenstrual syndrome. *American Journal of Obstetrics and Gynecology, 139,* 85–104.

Rounsaville, B.J., Klerman, G.L., & Weissman, M.M. (1891). Do psychotherapy and pharmacotherapy for depression conflict? *Archives of General Psychiatry, 38,* 24–29.

Rubinow, D.R., & Roy-Byrne, P. (1984). Premenstrual syndromes: Overview from a methodologic perspective. *American Journal of Psychiatry, 141,* 163–171.

Schuckit, M.A., Daly, V., Herrman, G., & Hineman, S. (1975). Premenstrual symptoms and depression in a university population. *Disease of the Nervous System, 36,* 516–517.

Shakir, S.A., Volkmar, F.R., Bacon, S., & Pfefferbaum, A. (1979). Group psychotherapy as an adjunct to lithium maintenance. *American Journal of Psychiatry, 136,* 455–456.

Snyder, S.H. (1980). *Biological aspects of mental disorders.* New York: Oxford University Press.

Spitzer, R.L., & Robins, E. (1978). *Research diagnostic criteria*. New York: Biometrics Research Evaluation Section, New York State Psychiatric Institute.

Szasz, T.S. (1957). Some observations on the use of tranquilizing drugs. *Archives of Neurology and Psychiatry, 77*, 86–92.

Weissman, M.M. (1978). Psychotherapy and its relevance to the pharmacotherapy of affective disorders: From ideology to evidence. In M.A. Lipton, A. DiMascio, & K.F. Killam (Eds.), *Psychopharmacology: A generation of progress* (pp. 1313–1321). New York: Raven Press.

Weissman, M.M. (1979). The psychological treatment of depression. *Archives of General Psychiatry, 36*, 1261–1269.

Weissman, M.M. (1983). Psychotherapy in comparison and in combination with pharmacotherapy for the depressed outpatient. In J.M. Davis (Ed.), *The affective disorders* (pp. 409–418). Washington, DC: American Psychiatric Press.

Weissman, M.M., & Klerman, G.L. (1977). Sex differences and the epidemiology of depression. *Archives of General Psychiatry, 34*, 98–111.

Weissman, M.M., Prusoff, B.A., DiMascio, A., Neu, C. Goklaney, M., & Klerman, G.L. (1979). The efficacy of drugs and psychotherapy in the treatment of acute depressive episodes. *American Journal of Psychiatry, 126*, 555–558.

Wetzel, R.D., Reich, T., McClure, J.N., & Wald, J. (1975). Premenstrual affective syndrome and affective disorder. *British Journal of Psychiatry, 127*, 219–221.

Zola, P., Myerson, A.T., Reznikoff, M., Thornton, J.C. & Concool, B.M. (1979). Menstrual symptomatology and psychiatric admission. *Journal of Psychosomatic Research, 23*, 241–245.

■ 9
Childbirth: Happiness, Blues, or Depression?

RUTH NEMTZOW, C.S.W.

The first part of this chapter discusses current research on postpartum depression and highlights psychosocial stressors that significantly impinge on the experiences of new mothers. The second part of the chapter presents material from New Mothers groups (organized by the author) and examines the ways in which the groups served as social support networks.

The birth of a child, the beginning of a new life, generally regarded as a joyous event, paradoxically brings with it increased risks of emotional illness to the mother. The transition to motherhood—pregnancy, delivery, and the postpartum period—constitutes a series of stressful events in the life cycle of a woman. Postpartum depression is viewed as the most common of the serious psychiatric syndromes of women. During the first month postpartum, women are at the highest risk in their entire lives for psychiatric hospitalization, although few have had a prior psychiatric history (Inwood, 1985).

The high incidence of postpartum depression raises concern regarding the emotional health and well-being of the new infant as well as of the new mother and the family (Hopkins, Marcus, & Campbell, 1984). The importance of early mother–child attachment has been well documented (Robson & Kumar, 1980). The infant's early experiences in relationship to the mother form a prototype for subsequent social relationships. Since the infant's earliest attempts to manipulate the environment and to develop competence are directed toward the mother, her reactions are a major influence on the infant's development. The depressed mother's feelings of helplessness and inadequacy may lead her to view herself as an unsatisfactory mother and cause her to emotionally withdraw from her infant.

Since postpartum depression often occurs unexpectedly and a woman's functioning may become impaired precisely when her responsibilities are greatest, prediction as to which pregnant women are at risk is obviously critical.

HISTORY

The link between emotional disturbance and childbirth has been recognized for thousands of years. The first description of postpartum illness is found in Hippocrates' (4th century B.C.) speculations that suppressed lochial discharge (blood flow) following delivery could be carried to the head and result in agitation, delirium and attacks of manias (Hamilton, 1962).

With the exception of sporadic references in the medical literature, an abiding interest in postpartum illness did not emerge until the 19th century. In 1838, Esquirol, a French psychiatrist, described postpartum mental disorders he observed among his patients. He attributed the cause to hereditary predisposition, traumatic life events, and previous postpartum illness, a view not markedly different from contemporary thinking. In 1858, Esquirol's student Marcé identified symptoms still considered to be accurate descriptions of postpartum psychosis: mood lability, confusion, delirium, and hallucinations.

Early investigators associated the physiology of reproduction with psychiatric symptoms. Marcé described instances in which the progression of psychiatric symptoms paralleled physical changes in childbirth: the onset of lactation and prolonged amenorrhea coincided with emotional disturbance. Marcé, whose work may be considered an antecedent of endocrinology, concluded that there was "something" connecting childbirth to abnormal behavior; he labeled it *"sympathie morbide."*

Research in postpartum depression was virtually dormant between the mid-1800s and 1962 when Hamilton (1962) first published *Postpartum Psychiatric Problems*, maintaining that the field of medicine had seriously neglected this women's ailment. Hamilton also supported the concept prevalent in the late 19th and the early 20th century that postpartum disorders were unique syndromes with specific organic etiologies. However, that concept was replaced with the view of postpartum disorders as identical to standard psychiatric illnesses (Brown & Shereshefsky, 1972).

In the 1970s, the National Health Systems of England and other European countries brought together data revealing the high incidence of emotional problems relating to childbearing, once again drawing medical attention to this phenomenon. Concurrently, the emergence of the Women's

Movement directed attention to the medical, psychological, and social problems of women and identified societal biases affecting women's problems.

This feminist view emphasized the experience of childbirth in a male-dominated medical setting in which childbirth was manipulated to suit institutional requirements, and, accordingly, the woman was pressured to accept a passive dependent role. The "medicalization of birth" and the technology of medicine removed control from the mother to the "medical expert," thereby detaching the mother from the experience of childbirth and rendering her vulnerable to helplessness and depression (Oakley, 1980).

Postpartum illness has been conceptualized within the framework of various psychological theories. According to some psychoanalytical formulations, depression is related to unresolved conflicts regarding feminine identification, nurturance and dependency, and the woman's relationship to her own mother (see J. Charone-Sossin & K.M. Sossin, *this volume*). Behavioral theorists relate postpartum depression to a woman's lack of social skill in eliciting positive reinforcement from others, i.e., support. Cognitive theorists hypothesize that it is related to a depressive cognitive and attributional style, such as the belief that one's own efforts are useless in effecting positive changes in one's life.

CLASSIFICATION

The research on postpartum depression varies in definitions and methodology and includes contradictory findings (Cutrona, 1982). However, most writers agree with a delineation of three different levels of postpartum depression (Brown, 1979; Paykel, Emms, Fletcher, & Rassaby, 1980).

A. Fifty to 70% of postpartum women experience a brief transitory depression known as "maternity blues." The onset occurs within the first 10 days postpartum, usually the third or fourth day, coinciding with the onset of lactation. The dysphoric symptoms may lift within a week, and the condition is usually self-limiting. A wide spectrum of symptoms has been identified: crying spells, often unpredictable and for seemingly trivial reasons, anxiety, depressed mood, fatigue, headaches, hypochondriasis, restlessness, irritability, feelings of unreality and confusion, and, less frequently, feelings of depersonalization, guilt, self-dislike, and negative feelings toward the husband and infant. Feelings toward the infant show considerable variation, with some women expressing distress about their lack of maternal feelings in the first few postpartum days (Robson & Kumar, 1980).

Weeping in the postpartum period has been explored cross-culturally (United States, Europe, West Indies, Tanzania), with the same reported incidence of 50 to 70% (Stein, 1982). Still unresolved is the question of whether the "blues" are environmentally determined or due to endocrine or metabolic changes, or both. The "blues" are more common in primiparous women (Gelder, 1978; Nott, Franklin, Armitage, & Gelder, 1976; Yalem, Lunde, Moos, & Hamburg, 1968) and may therefore be associated with the adjustment to parenthood.

For a small subgroup the "blues" may signal the onset of a clinical depression. Paykel et al., (1980) found that 85% of postpartum women who developed a clinical depression had suffered earlier from the "blues," while only 35% of nondepressed women had experienced "blues."

B. A sizable minority of postpartum women, 10 to 20%, experience a moderate to moderately severe depression, lasting from six weeks to a year or longer. Symptoms, similar to other depressive states, include feelings of inadequacy and inability to cope, tearfulness, lability, despondency, listlessness, apathy, self-derogatory feelings, indecisiveness, inability to concentrate, and multiple somatic complaints. However, it is the specific ideas accompanying these symptoms that distinguish the postpartum depression from other depressions—anxiety concerning the infant's well-being and self-doubts about the capacity for "normal" maternal feelings.

Symptoms may not be severe enough to interfere with functioning, and many women in this category do not come to professional attention, and thus do not receive help at this crucial time in their lives.

C. A small number of postpartum women, 0.01 to 0.02%, experience a debilitating psychotic illness, which renders the new mother nonfunctional and often requires hospitalization. This occurs within 6 weeks of delivery, but most frequently between the third and 14th day postpartum. The two groups of women at highest risk are (1) women who have had a previous postpartum psychotic episode, and (2) women who have a history of manic-depressive illness (Brockington & Kumar, 1982; Paffenbarger, 1982; Paykel et al., 1980; Reich & Winokur, 1970). Despite the severity of symptoms, prognosis for recovery is considered to be very good (Brockington & Kumar, 1982; Hamilton, 1985).

The characteristic symptoms of a nonpsychotic postpartum depression may very quickly intensify into a qualitatively different phenomenon. Symptoms of insomnia, exhaustion, agitation, restlessness and irritability, and rapidly alternating states of elation and depression may progress to states of confusion, irrationality, incoherence, delirium, and hallucinations. Thus, suspiciousness and undefinable feelings of apprehension may develop into refusal to eat, a distrust of others, and panic regarding the infant and herself. Sudden aversions, confusion between nightmares and reality, and obsessional concerns over minor matters occur. Delusional material may involve the idea that the baby is dead; suicidal and infanticidal ideation may occur.

Whether postpartum psychosis constitutes a specific entity separate from other forms of psychosis remains controversial. A five-year study in the psychiatric Mother and Baby Unit in Sheffield, England (Sneddon & Kerry, 1982) supports the position that postpartum psychosis differs from other psychoses in that symptoms become acute and develop more rapidly than in other psychiatric illnesses, in most instances with no forewarning and no prior history. Sneddon and Kerry believe that the attendant symptom of confusion may be organically based. Symptoms appear with the onset of lactation, with virtually no cases in which symptoms appear in the first two postpartum days.

CURRENT RESEARCH ISSUES

The degree to which biological factors impinge on the psychological aspects of childbirth remains a primary concern of investigators. Dramatic changes in hormone levels occur soon after conception when estrogen and progesterone increase; when women go into labor, the levels are 50% higher than before pregnancy. The delivery of the placenta results in a sharp decline in plasma estrogen and progesterone. These changes also affect thyroid, pituitary, and adrenal functions, as well as the function of the hypothalamus neurotransmitters, which result in mood alterations (Treadway, Kane, Jarrahi-Zadeh, & Lipton, 1969). There have been findings associating changes in tryptophan metabolism with postpartum "blues," although the results are not generalizable to other types of postpartum depression (Handley, Dunn, Waldisu, & Baker, 1980; Stein, Milton, Bebbington, Wood, & Coppen 1976).

While many researchers agree that it is likely that postpartum depression is related to rapid hormonal changes, direct evidence is lacking (Brockington & Kumar, 1982; Nott et al., 1976). No consistent differences have been found with respect to the hormone level rate of change which distinguish those who suffer from postpartum depression from those who do not.

The assumptions of this chapter are that biological and psychosocial stressors converge, overloading the circuits as it were. Some women's constitutional and/or personal/familial history render them susceptible to the stress of childbirth and to the postpartum period.

SOCIAL FACTORS

The perception that the adjustment to motherhood belongs solely in the medical and psychiatric realm has been disputed by feminist writers. According to their view, the role of women in reproduction is as much an issue for the social sciences as it is for the biological sciences. Women's subordinate societal status is a major factor leading to the fragility of their self-esteem and renders them vulnerable to stress at each turn of life events, particularly childbirth. Oakley (1980) expresses this position as follows:

> Because women's biological reproductivity has a social function—the reproduction of a society—difficulties women have with motherhood constitute a "social problem." Science, responding to the agenda of social concerns, has provided the label "postnatal depression" as a pseudo-scientific tag for the description . . . of maternal discontent. Thus labeled, maternal difficulties remain impervious to male scientific understanding. Only if childbirth is placed in its larger context—human reactions to life events—will it be understood and dealt with.

In addition to Oakley (1980), Dix (1985), Kitzinger (1978, 1982), and Scarf (1980) have made significant contributions in removing the stigma of pathology from the experience of childbirth.

Although no studies have shown a relationship between postpartum depression and socioeconomic status (Brown & Harris, 1978; Paykel, 1979), statistics on nonpostpartum depression show it to be more prevalent among lower socioeconomic groups. Despite the absence of a correlation between the two, one suspects its existence. For example, Blumberg (1980) found a strong correlation between postpartum depression and the delivery of infants at high risk for medical and developmental disorders. A disproportionately large number of these vulnerable infants come from minority and low-income families.

Vulnerability to postpartum depression, in the three degrees of severity, is related to a number of factors: constitutional predisposition, personal and family history, the abrupt biochemical changes following childbirth, psychosocial events, as well as intrapsychic meanings of pregnancy and childbirth. The actual and perceived losses associated with childbirth are considerable. Personal freedom is a primary loss. Additionally, losses may be felt in career curtailment, the exclusivity of the marital relationship, and in social contacts. The gaining of a child and the rewards of motherhood may not be immediately felt as compensating for these losses.

The correlation between specific psychosocial stressors and postpartum depression is well established. Four major stressors have been identified (Paykel et al., 1980; Scott & Steiner, 1986): (1) early life events, (2) the new mother's state, (3) recent life events, and (4) the presence and degree of support systems.

Early Life Events

Early Life Events. Events relevant to subsequent postpartum depression include (1) childhood bereavement—loss of a parent or separation from a parent in childhood or adolescence; (2) history of turbulent relation to either parent resulting in an impaired identification with the mother; (3) history of deprivation, particularly the lack of nurturing and stability in childhood; (4) negative attitudes to child-rearing in family of origin; (5) early history of violence or neglect; and (6) sexual abuse as a child.

Psychological State of the New Mother. Psycological attitudes of the new mother that were found to correlate with postpartum depression are (1) unwanted pregnancy; negative attitudes toward pregnancy and childbirth; (2) unrealistic expectations of motherhood; anxiety about motherhood and inadequate psychological preparation; (3) conflict with other role interests; (4) depressive feelings, self-reproach, inappropriate guilt, and self-worthlessness; (5) lack of satisfaction in educational or marital status; (6) intolerance of infant's needs because of mother's own unmet dependency needs; and (7) feeling unloved by spouse.

Recent Life Events. The actual experiences of pregnancy and childbirth frequently produce elevated stress: fears concerning the physical rigors of delivery, possible complications for the mother, and delivery of an infant with defects. Concerns about body changes are common in pregnancy, emphasized also by a culture that overvalues thinness. Some women suffer marked narcissistic injury due to body changes, whereas others are able to derive gratification as their changing shape reflects their growing infant.

Research on the effects of stressful deliveries and other obstetric risks is as yet equivocal. However, these factors, when added to preexisting stresses, may exceed the new mother's threshold.

The integration of an infant into a previously dyadic family system may provoke crisis as life routines are disrupted and freedom is decreased. Marital conflict, especially the lack of physical and emotional support, is significantly associated with postpartum depression. Studies have found a correlation between postpartum depression and divorced status (O'Hara, Rehms, & Campbell, 1983), single status (Blake, 1982), and delivery of an infant with medical or developmental problems (see J. Charone-Sossin & K.M. Sossin, *this volume*). Recent undesirable events such as bereavement, onset of illness, or financial problems obviously interfere with postpartum adjustment.

Social support. Supportive interpersonal relationships prevent or reduce depressive reactions even when circumstances are adverse (O'Hara, Rehm, & Campbell, 1983). Weiss (cited in Mueller, 1980) identifies six characteristics of social support: (1) attachment—provided by an intimate relationship in which the individual receives a sense of security and safety; (2) social integration—a network of relationships in which individuals share interests and concerns; (3) the opportunity for nurturance—each feels responsible for the well-being of the others; (4) reassurance of worth—relationships in which a person's skill and abilities are acknowledged; (5) reliable alliance—individuals can count on others for assistance, and (6) guidance.

To address the need for social support networking, New Mother–New Baby groups were organized by several of the YM-YWHA Community Centers on Long Island, New York, and were led by the author, a social worker from Jewish Community Services of Long Island. These groups fulfilled, to varying degrees, the functions outlined by Weiss for social support.

These groups consisted of six to 12 members and met weekly over a period of 12 weeks. The members were suburban working class and middle class women, without psychiatric history, their ages varied from mid 20s to early 40s, with the majority in their early to middle 30s, who were from two weeks to five months postpartum. All had been employed prior to motherhood, many as professionals. Many had recently moved to the suburban communities from New York City; some had families nearby. With few exceptions, all were mothers for the first time. Almost all had taken childbirth preparation classes and had had high expectations of the childbirth process and of motherhood. Many had joined the groups because they were experiencing difficulties in adjusting to their babies and to their new roles as mothers and felt isolated and overwhelmed. It soon emerged that a significant number reported anxiety states, role conflict, and mild to moderate depressed mood, suggestive of postpartum depression. Thus, these women had symptoms described in classifications A and B above.

The case of Peggy points up the psychodynamic, familial, and social contributions to postpartum depression.

> Peggy is a 36 year-old former speech therapist, the wife of a systems analyst, and mother of a 3½-year-old daughter. She experienced a postpartum depression lasting six months after the birth of her second child, a boy. Peggy, the oldest of three daughters, had a turbulent relationship with her mother, and perceived her as demanding and punitive. She internalized her mother's critical attitudes towards her. Peggy married a man who was intensely preoccupied with his career, and, therefore, household management and the

parenting of their children were mainly Peggy's responsibility. Although Peggy resented her husband's lack of involvement in the household, her own overinvolvement with her daughter in effect excluded her husband.

The birth of the first child had been a difficult one with life-threatening complications for Peggy, including toxemia, high fever, and convulsions. She was hospitalized for three weeks, and the infant was kept in the hospital nursery. Despite these difficulties, her postpartum mood was euphoric rather than depressed. She derived gratification from her daughter, whom she perceived as filling her own needs for nurturance, and she became intensely involved with her child.

Peggy's second pregnancy was planned but discussed in terms of her "daughter's need" for a sibling, societal expectations, and the pressure of her "biological clock." Changes were particularly difficult for Peggy, and her established routines were disrupted by the course of her second pregnancy. In her fifth month, contractions started, leading to medical recommendations for complete bed rest for the duration of the pregnancy. Labor was induced and was extremely painful.

Peggy was disappointed that the baby was a boy, and, in her words, "very ugly." From the outset she was aware of her detached feelings toward the infant. The baby was colicky, allergic to milk, and had episodes of intense screaming, a temperament that evoked no immediate affectionate response. Peggy experienced little support from her husband, who continued to work long hours, and her mother absented herself. Intensely self-critical about her feelings of detachment, Peggy felt guilty and inadequate as a mother. Her depressed mood, irritability, withdrawal from husband and friends, sense of depersonalization, and somatic complaints persisted for six months. To outward appearances, Peggy went through the motions of caring—bathing and dressing the baby—and never permitted anyone else to feed him. She was aware of her detachment and felt that her oversolicitous care of her infant's physical needs was an effort to allay her guilt.

Within the group, Peggy came to understand that her reactions were not unique and that her experience with her own mother affected her differential reactions to her daughter and son. The group helped her to realize her capacity to establish herself as a mother in a style different from that of her own mother. She formed close personal relationships with several group members who provided her with warmth, support, and acceptance. After several weeks, she was able to allow a homemaker to help with the baby's care and with the establishment of routines. Although the depressive symptoms accompanying the birth of the second child lifted, the more complex issues of her relationship to her mother and her husband were not addressed by the group.

The group acknowledged the stress inherent in new motherhood: the high incidence of depressed feelings, anxiety about the infants, physical fatigue, and feelings of being overwhelmed. This acknowledgement in and of itself was an important factor in mitigating feelings of personal deficiency.

Some individual group members had difficult labor and delivery: fetal distress, acute toxemia, prolonged labor, cesarian sections, postnatal infections, and premature deliveries. Several had infants with significant medical problems. These women came to the group with strong unresolved feelings of anger, disappointment and guilt concerning their experiences. Additionally, many had to reconcile disappointment in that their childbirth experiences did not measure up to the high expectations raised by their childbirth preparation classes.

> Marge, a university librarian prior to motherhood, had always been very achievement oriented. "I took Lamaze the way I always do everything: thoroughly. I read all the books, I practiced the exercises diligently, I watched my diet. I worked hard at being pregnant the right way. Then when the labor started, I freaked out. After four hours of labor, instead of breathing I was screaming. I wanted drugs, anything so that it would be over. When they gave me Leslie to hold, all I could think of was that I flunked Labor and Delivery: I'm joking about it now but I still feel like my best wasn't good enough. I carry around a feeling that I'm not strong the way everyone I admire seems to be."

Many women experienced complex and ambivalent feelings toward motherhood and the group provided a nonjudgmental and supportive atmosphere for such expression. Some women were shocked and frightened that they did not experience a simple outpouring of positive maternal feelings.

> Phyllis: I looked at this stranger with his squashed nose and pointy head and felt, I'm ashamed to admit, revulsion. Then when Matt and his parents came to the hospital beaming and gleaming, I felt like some kind of a monster. I couldn't tell anyone and when they left I really panicked about whether I could be a mother.

The group's laughter and subsequent recital of similar reactions did much to diffuse Phyllis' discomfort. Accepting the complexity of their feelings may have helped the mothers ward off potentially more serious depression.

Mothers were encouraged to examine their past histories in reference to current feelings about themselves as women and mothers. Many connected their histories as daughters with their new role as mothers, examining how they themselves had been nurtured.

> Linda expressed a common fear: Am I going to be just like my mother? "My mother worried about everything. Nothing was lighthearted or fun. She always imagined disasters. I couldn't go swimming, I couldn't roller skate, I couldn't even go on a class trip in a school bus. In all my memories of childhood, I feel my mother hovering. I promised myself I'd be different.

Now I'm scared that I'm the same. I worry for an hour whether the baby needs a sweater. I don't want to be like this. All this worrying exhausts me."

The group helped Linda see herself as distinct from her mother and capable of setting a different course for herself in motherhood.

The spousal relationship was a major factor in determining which women were at greater risk for depression. Some women had strong relationships, others troubled ones. Whether women received emotional and physical support from their mates was critical to their emotional states. The group members helped each other in formulating strategies to elicit help in infant care from the fathers or other close persons.

Closely related was the issue of father–baby bonding. Some fathers couldn't wait to be with their newborn and were responsive to their baby's needs, others were minimally involved and contributed little to infant care.

Many mothers experienced difficulty in finding the time or energy to devote to their relationship, and resumption of sexual relations was often problematic. Fatigue and physical discomfort were exacerbated by mothers' anger toward their partners for not sharing infant care.

Another issue was fathers' jealousy of mothers' deep involvement with the baby. Mothers struggled to find a balance between the demands of parenthood and the couple's relationship.

Tensions were often relieved when couples were able to spend time together away from the baby. Group members encouraged and assisted each other in making childcare arrangements toward this end. The practical difficulties in finding childcare often masked strong separation anxiety, which the group could then address.

Martha's marriage was one of the more troubled ones. At six months postpartum, she became seriously discouraged about the future of her marriage. "Jeff complains to me that the baby wakes him up. I'm the one who gets up to feed her. I feed the baby twice during the night, and I try not to wake him. But he never worries about my getting any sleep. He shows no concern about what's happening to me. I feel like I have two babies, only one isn't little and cute. Before the baby was born, I knew he could be selfish, but we also had a lot of good times together. I thought being parents was something we'd do together but I wonder if it would be that much worse to take care of the baby without him."

Although the group was empathic, they urged Martha to allow herself more time to evaluate her marriage. Over several weeks, as various marital issues were discussed, Martha continued to address the weaknesses and strengths of her marriage. The group members also helped her to look at the financial and practical problems of single parenthood. Having a forum helped Martha to feel less desperate for an immediate resolution.

Social isolation was a strong factor for many women. For some, the isolation inherent in infant care was exacerbated by loneliness due to relocation. Being home with an infant all day without adult company was a new experience. Their loneliness contributed to depressed mood, and joining the group in itself served to mitigate their isolation.

Group members faced the task of integrating the parental role into their own identities. For some, motherhood quickly became the center of their identity and was emotionally satisfying to them. For others, the process was more complex and problematic, particularly for those who experienced feelings of loss of status due to leaving work.

> Lucy: When I was a city planner, I had important responsibilities, and when I finished a project I felt great and got recognition for it. Now, understanding a baby who can't express what's wrong except by crying is harder than my job was. Even when I can solve a problem, another appears, and I can never say, "That's finished. Well done."

The group encouraged these mothers to maintain former interests and contacts, both professional and nonprofessional. A recurrent theme was allocating time for those interests that best helped the mother to retain her sense of self.

Conflict about returning to work was frequently expressed. Many women had moved from two incomes to one at a time when their financial responsibilities increased. For some, the option to stay home with their child, though desired, was impossible. Others missed the professional stimulation and chose to work. For the latter group, there was more guilt since their decision was made to meet personal needs.

> Meryl was 38 when her infant was born. She and her husband built up and ran an employment agency for 12 years. Although she was ambivalent about having a child she went ahead feeling it was "now or never." She had planned to take a year's leave to devote her full energies to motherhood. To her distress, after six weeks, she felt she was "losing it." "I awake each day with dread. I can't face another day of feedings and diapers and small excursions to the neighborhood park. The best I could look forward to was getting the baby dressed to go to the supermarket. I feel myself getting unhinged. Each day is endless and like the day before. This is not for me. I feel I made a terrible mistake."

In the groups, returning to a career or staying at home were seen as valid alternatives. Although many mothers did not share Meryl's feelings, they expressed awareness of individual needs.

Many women needed support to reduce the demands they made on themselves for housekeeping tasks. They all acknowledged their own reduced physical and emotional stamina. Approval and support were given for easing up on housekeeping standards, a factor that was pivotal in helping new mothers to take care of themselves. The group members' priorities became taking care of their infants and themselves, with other chores relegated to a lower priority.

Concrete aid and advice were immensely helpful, particularly for the relocated women. The women exchanged information about pediatricians, baby sitters, and other specific resources. They passed along experiences with formulas, pacifiers, and infant toys, and often felt greatly relieved to leave the group meeting with the solution to a concrete problem.

Significantly, each of the groups continued to meet regularly on an informal basis after the formal sessions ended, reflecting the mothers' need for ongoing social support. Short-term New Mothers Groups may well be an excellent model for primary prevention of mild-to-moderate postpartum depression, and may also be effective in the prevention of more serious pathology.

REFERENCES

Blake, J. (1982). Demographic revolution and family evolution: Some implications for American women. In P.W. Berman & E.R. Ramsey (Eds.), *Women: A developmental perspective* (pp. 299–311). Washington DC: U.S. Dept. of Health & Human Services.

Blumberg, N.L. (1980). Effects of neonatal risk, maternal attitude, and cognitive style on early postpartum adjustment. *Journal of Abnormal Psychology, 2,* 139–150.

Brockington, I.F., & Kumar, R. (Eds.). (1982). *Motherhood and mental illness.* New York and San Francisco: Grune & Stratton.

Brown, G.W. (1979). A three-factor causal model of depression. In J.E. Barrett (Ed.), *Stress and mental disorder* (pp. 111–120). New York: Raven Press.

Brown, G.W., & Harris, T. (1978). *Social origins of depression: A study of psychiatric disorder in women.* New York: Free Press.

Brown, W.A., & Shereskefsky, P. (1972). Seven women: A prospective study of postpartum psychiatric disorders. *Psychiatry, 35,* 139–158.

Cutrona, C.E. (1982). Nonpsychiatric postpartum depression: A review of recent research. *Clinical Psychology Review, 2,* 487–503.

Dix, C. (1985). *The new mother syndrome coping with postpartum stress and depression.* Garden City, New York: Doubleday.

Gelder, M. (1978). Hormones & postpartum depression. In M. Sandler (Ed.), *Mental illness in pregnancy and the puerperium* (pp. 80–90). Oxford: Oxford Medical Publications.

Hamilton, J.A. (1962). *Postpartum psychiatric problems.* St. Louis: C.V. Mosby Co.

Hamilton, J.A. (1985). In D.G. Inwood (Ed.), *Recent advances in postpartum psychiatric disorders.* Washington, DC: American Psychiatric Press.

Handley, S.L., Dunn, T.L., Waldisu, G., & Baker, J.M. (1980). Tryptophan, cortisol, and puerperal mood. *British Journal of Psychiatry, 136,* 498–508.

Hopkins, J., Marcus, M., & Campbell, S.B. (1984). Postpartum depression: A critical review. *Psychological Bulletin, 95*(3), 498–515.

Inwood, D.G. (Ed.). (1985). *Recent advances in postpartum psychiatric disorders.* Washington, DC: American Psychiatric Press.

Kitzinger, S. (1978). *Women as mothers.* New York: Random House.

Kitzinger, S. (1982). *Birth over thirty.* New York: Penguin Books.

Mueller, D.P. (1980). Social networks: A promising direction for research on the relationship of the social environment to psychiatric disorder. *Social Science Medicine, 14a,* 147–161.

Nott, P.N., Franklin, M., Armitage, C., & Gelder, M.G. (1976). Hormonal change and mood in the puerperium. *British Journal of Psychiatry, 128,* 279–283.

Oakley, A. (1980). *Women confined.* New York: Schocken Books.

O'Hara, M.W., Neunaber, D.J., & Zekowski, E.M. (1984). Prospective study of postpartum depression: Prevalence, course, and predictive factors. *Journal of Abnormal Psychology, 93*(2), 158–171.

O'Hara, M.W., Rehm, L.P., & Campbell, S.B. (1983). Postpartum depression: A role for social network and life stress variables. *The Journal of Nervous and Mental Disease, 171*(4), 336–341.

Paffenbarger, R.S., Jr. (1982). Epidemiological aspects of mental illness associated with childbearing. In I.F. Brockington & R. Kumar (Eds.), *Motherhood and mental illness.* New York and San Francisco: Grune & Stratton.

Paykel, E.S. (1979). Contribution of life events to causation of psychiatric illness. *Psychological Medicine, 8,* 245–253.

Paykel, E.S., Emms, E.M., Fletcher, J., & Rassaby, E.S. (1980). Life events and social support in puerperal depression. *British Journal of Psychiatry, 136,* 339–346.

Reich, T., & Winokur, G. (1970). Postpartum psychoses in patients with manic depressive disease. *Journal of Nervous & Mental Disease, 151,* 60–68.

Robson, K.M., & Kumar, R. (1980). Delayed onset of maternal affection after childbirth. *British Journal of Psychiatry, 136,* 347–353.

Scarf, M. (1980). *Unfinished business: Pressure points in the lives of women.* Garden City, New York: Doubleday.

Scott, M., & Steiner, S.C. (1986). Social support and psychopathology: Interrelations with preexisting disorder, stress of personality. *Journal of Abnormal Psychology, 95*(1), 29–39.

Sneddon, J., & Kerry, R.J. (1982). The psychiatric mother and baby unit: A five-year study. In D.G. Inwood (Ed.), *Recent advances in postpartum psychiatric disorders.* Washington, DC: American Psychiatric Press.

Stein, G. (1982). The maternity blues, in motherhood and mental illness. In I.F. Brockington (Ed.), *Motherhood and mental illness*. New York: Grune & Stratton.

Stein, G., Milton, F., Bebbington, P., Wood, K., & Coppen, A. (1976). Relationship between mood and disturbances and free and total plasma tryptophan in postpartum women. *British Medical Journal, 2,* 457.

Treadway, C.R., Kane, F.J., Jarrahi-Zadeh, A., & Lipton, M.A. (1969). A psycho-endocrine study of pregnancy and puerperium. *American Journal of Psychiatry, 125,* 1380–1386.

Yalem, I.D., Lunde, D.T., Moos, R.H., & Hamburg, D.A. (1968). "Postpartum blues" syndrome: A description and related variables. *Archives of General Psychiatry, 18,* 16–27.

■ 10
Depressive Reactions to the Birth of A Handicapped Child

**JAN CHARONE-SOSSIN, Ph.D. and
K. MARK SOSSIN, Ph.D.**

The psychological process involved in the earliest relationship between mother and infant—that between a mother-to-be and her growing fetus—needs to be better understood, particularly in light of how this process is torn asunder following the birth of an impaired child. We shall not draw a profile of mothers of handicapped infants, as Lyon and Preis have done (1983); nor do we suggest a universal response to the birth of a damaged child, as maternal attitudes vary widely. Our goal is to explore the dynamics of depressive reactions following the birth of a less-than-perfect baby.

We have drawn on our clinical experience as psychologists in the Infant/Toddler Development Program of the Division of Child Development at Schneider Children's Hospital, Long Island Jewish Medical Center, where we observed various psychological reactions of parents to the assessment of their baby (regarding approximately 150 infants) as in some way disabled. We closely followed 35 parents who had particular difficulty in their adaptation to this devastating reality.

In this chapter, we shall address the distinction between depressive symptoms that are reactive, similar to those following any loss, from those that are pathological. The complexity of constitutional, interpersonal and environmental influences on the stress experienced by family members of a handicapped child is well documented (Beckman, 1984).

Parents of an impaired child mourn the loss of the wished-for child while simultaneously adapting to a love relationship with a child who brings fear and disappointment (Solnit & Stark, 1961). Some parents do not merely mourn; they will experience depression, since the self itself is entwined with the ideal object representation of the child who is experienced as lost.

We propose that, among maternal reactions, there are indeed types of "adaptive depression," which can be crucial to the success of the evolving relationship between the mother and her handicapped infant. Our observations of these "adaptive depressions" point to the necessity of their outbreak and resolution during the first few months of the infant's life, or in the case of later determinations, in the first few months after a child is diagnosed as handicapped. When the adaptive depression cannot be resolved, pathological functioning begins to dominate and a clinical depression may unfold. In examining these nonpathological and pathological depressions, we shall focus on predisposing traits and experiences, defensive maneuvers, consequences for mother–child relationships, and implications for early intervention.

PREGNANCY AS A STAGE OF EMOTIONAL VULNERABILITY FOR THE MOTHER-TO-BE

The state of being pregnant has been compared to adolescence as a developmental stage that triggers a major upheaval and reorganization in a woman's psyche (Bibring, 1959). The 40 weeks after conception serve a function beyond the development of the fetus: they permit the woman time to prepare her new identity as a mother. Some aspects of pregnancy that contribute to the emotional vulnerability of the mother-to-be include the revival of receptive-dependent needs, an inner-directedness, a regressive pull, together with mood swings from the narcissistically elated to the anxiously depressive, intensification of receptive and retentive tendencies, as well as a specific regression to the oral phase (Benedek, 1970). Bibring (1959; Bibring, Dwyer, Huntington, & Valenstein, 1961) stressed the need for the pregnant woman to reorganize her psychic equilibrium by the time the child is born to facilitate desirable attunement between mother and infant. Mothers who fail to achieve this reorganization by birth are at risk in their interactions with their young infants.

Bibring et al. (1961) suggest that there are two psychological stages that a mother-to-be must successfully resolve. The first stage is marked by the need to accept the intrusion represented by the impregnation and to successfully incorporate a "foreign object" as her own. After the mother experiences the baby's first discernible movements, a second stage ensues, in which the mother perceives of the baby as another object, readying her for separation and the development of her relationship to the offspring. It is the actual birth of a healthy newborn that cements the success of this second stage, demonstrating that the mother has adequately differentiated her baby from herself.

Kestenberg (1976, 1980) has posited that pregnancy, as an adult developmental stage (see also Bibring, 1959), normally involves regression to earlier phases of development. Through the course of a successful pregnancy there are various regressions, progressions, and reintegrations. To some extent these developments are foiled with the birth of an impaired child. Pregnancy normally offers the prospective mother a chance to resolve old conflicts with her own mother—especially as the woman's pregnancy usually gratifies two childhood wishes: her wish to have a baby, and her wish that her mother *not* have a baby. The pregnant woman often develops an identification with the unborn fetus (Lax, 1972). There is a looking inward toward the uterus, some withdrawal from external objects, and a transfer of narcissistic libido to a new internal object. In the last trimester, there is often "a new wave of identification with the mother" (Kestenberg, 1976, p. 244), serving to counteract or deny fears of death, prematurity, injury to the child, etc.

Certain normal regressions prior to actual delivery underscore the marked vulnerability of the mother who finds her newborn child disabled. According to Kestenberg (1976, 1980), some mothers fear separation from the fetus or its loss; some fear being injured by the baby, or losing their genitals with the baby's birth. Under normal circumstances, these regressions lead to a creative and adaptive resolution with birth, from which the mother is able to attune to the needs of her infant. Such a mother may be better able to imagine what her baby is feeling as a consequence of the regression she herself experienced. With the birth of an impaired baby, however, some of the regressive fears are often felt to be substantiated. The new mother's readiness to identify and even merge with her new baby is interrupted when an impaired baby bears little resemblance to the mother's dreams and fantasies.

The physical changes created by the pregnancy demand that the woman come to accept herself in a new way. By bypassing one mode of narcissistic[1] gratification acquired from the successful presentation of one's sexual self to the outside world, the woman must reinvest her body cathexis, focusing less on her own physical attractiveness and more on how her new shape both allows her to carry her child and prepares her for taking adequate care of her newborn. This transition in cathexis is attended by the woman's growing identification with her unborn baby (Lax, 1972); she takes pride in what her body is producing to the extent that she begins to care for the

---

1. The term narcissism is used in accord with the definition of Stolorow and Lachmann (1980): "mental activity is narcissistic to the degree that its function is to maintain the cohesion, stability, and positive affective coloring of the self representation" (p. 26).

fetus as a new love object.

By the end of pregnancy, the woman has ideally accepted the limitations and discomforts of her now swollen shape for the sake of the baby she expects to love and cherish. The success of this narcissistic shift is dependent on the birth of a normal baby, who will fulfill the mother's wishes for a perfect child, who will somehow compensate for her own lack of perfection endured in her life, and especially during pregnancy. There is a particular psychic vulnerability at birth in that a healthy baby can offer narcissistic gratification as well as promoting resolution of the conflicts intrinsic to pregnancy. Conversely, a less than perfect baby can bring narcissistic injury by deflating the mother's sense of self, thus exacerbating those conflicts.

IDENTIFICATION WITH THE IMPAIRED BABY

Identification with the healthy baby as a means toward restoration of narcissistic balance (Reich, 1953) may not be available when the baby's deficits are significant. A mother may devalue herself and her infant, and experience intense ambivalence in her attachment. A woman is particularly vulnerable when the anticipated baby represents a narcissistic ideal. Instead, the impaired baby brings narcissistic injury to the mother by stirring her feelings of being given less than she is entitled to, of powerlessness and helplessness and failure. Parents of handicapped infants may see disavowed aspects of themselves in the baby, which are reinforced by the reality of the infant's deficits.

As described by Lax (1972), who considered this type of narcissistic trauma for the mother of an impaired child: "the mother feels as if she created what she always, unconsciously, felt she is rather than what she hoped for." The severity of the depressive reaction is a function of the degree to which "the mother unconsciously perceives the child as an externalization of her defective self and the extent to which the mother is simultaneously symbiotically linked to her child" (p. 340).

Although parents' reactions differ, a primary one is mourning the loss of the anticipated healthy child (Solnit and Stark, 1961). This experience is accompanied by guilt, anger, shame, and fear, and as with other personal catastrophes, may lead to reactive depression. Moreover, given the vulnerable psychic structure that accompanies entrance or re-entrance into the phase of motherhood, identity disturbances may ensue.

Part of a woman's developing pride in herself as a mother-to-be involves her growing identification with her own mother. The woman either feels closer to her mother, sharing with her a positive excitement in her new role as a mother, or she retreats from her mother, choosing instead to be everything that her mother was not (of course, these are polarities on a continuum). Thus, her maternal identity may evolve from a positive or negative identification. Either way, the mother's success with these identifications and the subsequent emergence of her new role as a mother is dependent on a healthy baby who will respond to her newly developed mothering skills. When the baby is damaged, the mother's new and fragile concept of herself as a mother is threatened. She may lose her faith in her ability to mother, and begin to feel hopeless, desperate, and depressed.

When the baby is impaired, the mother's perception of the baby may regress to an earlier stage, when the baby was a part of herself, thus intensifying her feeling that she herself is damaged. Or, the mother may return to her initial perception of the fetus as a foreign "other-than-me" phenomenon from which she can retreat in anger and dismay, disclaiming her initial tie.

Mrs. K.

Mrs. K. found out immediately after birth that her son had Down's syndrome. Her first reaction was to deny and disclaim any tie that she might have to her son. Mrs. K. felt an overwhelming anger at what had happened; she made plans to rid herself of the baby, disposing of it as an other-than-me phenomenon, whose disappearance would allow her to resume her life. She defensively sought to rid herself of what she would otherwise perceive as her own disability. In the next few days, she discovered that the impaired baby was, in fact, lovable. Mrs. K. then reestablished a connection to her son as a part of herself, opening herself up to narcissistic injury for having given birth to a less-than-perfect child. By reowning the baby, Mrs. K. could no longer give him up; rather, she took the baby home and began to mother him, working through a process of mourning and depression for the loss of the perfect baby she had awaited.

Mrs. S.

Mrs. S.'s baby was also born with a genetic disorder, although in her case the diagnosis was not made until a few weeks following delivery. An intelligent, devout woman who had successfully raised other children, Mrs. S. had sought to have another child over her husband's objection because raising children was for her most gratifying and enhancing of self-esteem. She did not know what to do without another child, and her investment in her capacity to have a well baby, as well as her bond to this baby, were shattered upon diagnosis. In her anguish, she wished the baby as well as herself dead. She blamed herself for the impairment, but found justification in her religious convictions. Her depression was manifested in all areas of her functioning. Her anger, although failing to diminish her self-hatred, came to be externalized and displaced onto her husband, toward other parents whom she perceived as passive and uninvolved with their children's welfare, toward therapists working with her son because they did not show enough care or expertise, and against the system that would penalize her son unless she could prevent it. In fact, as she mobilized herself, she became expert on her son's condition and on interventions to aid his development. She became active in advocacy and educational groups as she moved out of depression and away from self-blame.

Both mothers experienced profound feelings of rejection toward their impaired children, which gave way to more adaptive modes of caring and interacting. Turning passive to active, channeling aggression in a defined and self-chosen external direction, and becoming acquainted with the more intact aspects of the child are prerequisites for this transition. The capacity for such transition underscores the fact that parental actions toward a child at any one time do not necessarily reflect or predict the parent's adaptive potential (Anthony & Benedek, 1970).

MOURNING THE LOSS

According to Solnit and Stark (1961), psychological preparation for a new child during pregnancy involves both the wish for a perfect child and the fear of a damaged child. If the mother gives birth to a defective child, she mourns the loss of the anticipated healthy child. Following initial numbness and disbelief, she becomes aware of disappointment and a feeling of loss, often accompanied by affective and physical symptoms. The mother reacts with grief, reexperiencing her memories and expectations until her wish for an ideal child gradually fades away. Solnit and Stark outline two patterns that could interfere with the mother coming to terms with her grief. In one pattern, the mother is overwhelmed by guilt feelings. She consequently dedicates herself unremittingly and exclusively to the welfare of the impaired child. In the other pattern, she becomes intolerant of the child and wants to deny her relation to the child.

According to Bibring et al. (1961), the guilt reaction stems from identifying the fetus as one's own and thus as one's own responsibility if something goes wrong with the child. The second reaction of intolerance and denial may stem from the mother's initial perception of the impregnation as an intrusion. Both patterns may serve to ward off depression.

IMPACT OF MATERNAL DEPRESSION ON MOTHER–CHILD INTERACTIONS

In a study comparing the interactions of mothers with infants having "short" illnesses versus those having "long" illnesses, Minde, Trehub, Corter, Boukydis, Celhoffer, & Marton (1978) and Minde (1982) report that mothers of infants with short illnesses increased their interactions, but the mothers of infants with long illnesses did not change their behavior over time. Minde suggests that mothers of seriously ill infants withdraw emotionally and fail to perceive changes in their babies.

The development of empathy and trust between infant and primary caregiver and the fine tuning that occurs in the normal dyadic relationship has been highlighted by numerous writers (Beebe & Gerstman, 1980; Kestenberg, 1975; Kestenberg & Beulte, 1977a, b, 1983; Stern, 1971). Serious handicaps on the part of the infant lead to an interference in this interaction, and trust is not elicited. In view of the fact that the regulation of excitation, arousal, activation, stimulation, and tension are atypical amongst handicapped babies, there is a high risk for disturbance in what Stern (1985) calls "core-relatedness" between parent and infant. The infant's unresponsiveness, disengagement, and frequent distress may take their toll on the mother, exacerbating her depression and leading to her disengagement from the infant.

ISSUES PERTAINING TO SELF-ESTEEM REGULATION

Mintzer, Als, Tronick, and Brazelton (1984) examined the effects on parents of the birth of a defective infant. In particular, they observed the manner in which parents experienced a series of assaults to their sense of self that affected self-esteem and interfered with the parenting process. They identified 3 stages regarding the family's reactions: (1) an initial sense of shock, (2) a period of intrapsychic disequilibrium, and (3) if all goes well, restoration of the intrapsychic equilibrium.

Other authors have similarly suggested a predictable order in reaction and adaptation to a handicapped child. For example, Rosen (1955) suggests that parents show awareness and then recognition of the problem, followed by a search for a cause, search for a cure, and then acceptance. Many factors, both internal and external, create obstacles to such acceptance. Although a medical cause is sometimes immediately established (e.g., chromosomal abnormalities), parents continue to search for causes ("why me?"). When no cause is found, and only a functional diagnosis can be offered, denial often follows. Some parents have expressed relief at hearing a serious diagnosis, because only then did they feel they could start dealing with what happened.

Parents generally experience an enormous let down—a severe injury to their sense of self-worth. Roos (1963), with the insight of a parent of a handicapped child, describes parental emotional traumata such as loss of self-esteem, shame, ambivalence, depression, a need for self-sacrifice, and defensiveness. Some parents already have deficits in their sense of self-worth prior to the birth of a disabled baby. One mother's reaction to her child's serious metabolic disorder renewed her feeling of "being the baby my parents never wanted." Another mother, whose child had a genetic disorder, brought childhood feelings of "not being intelligent enough" to the fore, and became unable to make any decisions without being frozen with self-doubt.

PARENTS' COPING STYLES

The particular parental reaction shown depends on many factors, including personality makeup and identifications that have already taken shape prior to the infant's birth. Mintzer et al. (1984), like Lax (1972), observed that the parents' capacity to parent is partly a function of the extent to which parents view the infant as a negative part of themselves, i.e., as an embodiment of their own inadequacies. These investigators view the adaptive task for parents (1) to identify positive aspects of the infant, (2) to view the infant as a separate person, and (3) to grieve the loss of the wished-for relationship. Factors bearing on intrapsychic organization, the quality of object relations, the degree of narcissism, and the nature of limited or distorted parent–child interactive patterns determine the eventual adaptation.

Parents expect personal gratifications with the birth of their baby, linked closely to the newborn's well-being. Losing the source of this gratification with the birth of a handicapped child may lead to a parent's self-perceptions of weakness and helplessness. This process is similar to the reaction of the bereaved to the loss of persons who were the suppliers of gratification (Horowitz, Wilner, Marmar, & Krupnick, 1980; Osterweis, Solomon, & Green, 1984). Horowitz et al. (1980), who investigated grief reactions, suggested that those particularly vulnerable to difficulties viewed themselves as incompetent, bad, or hurtful. Bereavement pertaining to a child gives rise to self-blame, guilt, and lost hope reactions, which also appear when the child is alive but disabled.

Pathological deviations that result from a mother's less successful efforts to cope with the birth of her impaired or premature baby are addressed by Caplan, Mason, and Kaplan (1965) and Kaplan and Mason (1960). They describe four psychological tasks essential to the mother's attainment of mastery of the crisis of the premature birth and in the establishment of a healthy mother–child relationship: (1) at the time of delivery, preparation for the possible loss of the child (including the anticipation of grief); (2) facing and acknowledging her failure to deliver a normal, full-term baby, usually followed by grief and depression; (3) while the baby is in the hospital, a resumption of the relationship to the baby; and (4) coming to understand how a premature baby differs from a normal baby in terms of its special needs and growth patterns.

Two pathological deviations that can arise from the mother's failure to cope with the crisis evoked by the birth of the impaired child include (1) denial of the real threat to the baby, or (2) failing to respond with hope to indications of survival and to the actual developmental gains of the infant. Such parents are often too depressed to respond positively, and use denial to ward off the conflictual feelings pertaining to the baby's survival. Although Kaplan and Mason refer specifically to the reactions of mothers to their premature infants, the four psychological tasks and the two pathological outcomes they outline can readily be adapted to the birth of an impaired child.

Four areas of assessment pertain to the mother's success or failure in coping with the birth trauma: (1) her cognitive grasp of the crisis situation (Caplan, Mason, & Kaplan, 1977), (2) the extent of her activity in searching for information about her baby, (3) the degree to which she is aware of, or denies, her negative feelings, and (4) her ability to obtain help—for the infant and for herself.

ROLE OF DENIAL

The psychological state of the mother depends on the severity of her depression and degree of denial used. Denial may be viewed on a continuum, i.e., some denial may be essential to surviving the crisis and thus may represent healthy psychological functioning. At the other end of the continuum, massive denial may interfere with everyday functioning. One typical form of denial is the mother's resistance to any information that might show the baby to be damaged. Lax (1972) described how "denial of the reality of the child's condition occurs in cases where the acceptance of reality might lead to a possible psychic breakdown of the mother" (p. 341).

Mrs. C.

Mrs. C. failed to see anything really wrong with her baby daughter, who showed little evidence of vision or hearing or independent movement (e.g., she did not pull up, sit, crawl, or stand) at the age of 15 months. Mrs. C. stated that her daughter could simply grow out of any of her present problems, insisting she knew of a baby similar to her own who was now a physician. This denial of the reality of her baby's condition interfered with her intellectual processing; she seemed flat and affectless, remaining detached from both her daughter and other mothers in the parent group she attended. She wandered around in a fog, appearing almost oblivious to others. Mrs. C.'s depression did not lift until she was able to acknowledge the reality of her daughter's condition—when she became able to externalize the blame for her daughter's condition onto her obstetrician, thus giving a direction to her anger. Only then could Mrs. C. begin to interact with her daughter and with other parents in her group.

Mrs. C.'s denial did not ward off her depression. Rather it was the gradual giving up of her denial of her daughter's condition that allowed her to be less depressed. Our observations suggest that the use of denial may not be as successful in warding off depression as Solnit and Stark (1961) suggest. On the other hand, we shall describe a case in which denial was more specific and less massive, involving only resistance to the child's ultimate prognosis.

Mrs. L.

Mrs. L. was initially quite depressed with the birth of a severely impaired baby with a host of cardiac, neurological, and gastrointestinal problems. The infant was not expected to live. Mrs. L. showed many signs of a clinical depression, including poor appetite, disturbed sleep/wake patterns, and negligence in self-care. During this stage of "anticipatory grief reaction" (Rose, 1961), Mrs. L. felt helpless and ineffective in coping with her baby's profound disability and anticipated early death. Gradually, her sadness changed to anger; she began to take a critical view of the medical staff, to whom she had previously turned for direction—they were not taking good enough care of her baby. When it was discovered that a mistake had actually been made by one of the baby's surgeons, Mrs. L. became mobilized to fight. She actively pursued all information regarding her baby's condition, becoming an expert in the infant's daily medical condition and nursing care. In her anger, she only used denial specifically to block out the baby's poor prognosis. With regard to all other medical facts, Mrs. L. became determined and even ruthless in her pursuit of the truth. Her anger fueled her hope that the doctors were wrong and that her baby would live, and would gain some sense of self through cognitive, motor, and social attainments.

As her determination grew, Mrs. L.'s depression lifted and she began to interact more successfully with her baby and the outside world.

Mrs. Z.

When V. was 8 months old, she was still on the neonatal unit demonstrating few organized responses. She was gavage fed (through a tube directly passing into her stomach) and showed hyperextensive arching. Her mother stood by for seemingly endless periods, frequently suctioning the baby's heavy mucus accumulations. Neurological involvement included brain-stem dysfunction, quadraparesis, and ocular motor apraxia. Pediatric therapy was begun on the neonatal unit and then carried on in the out-patient Infant Program. Mrs. Z. participated in therapy sessions and learned how to assist in normalizing V.'s muscle tone and increasing her postural control. Originally V. was hyporesponsive to handling; Mrs. Z. experienced pleasure when V. began to complain. Facial paralysis greatly limited V.'s expression of clear affect. Mrs. Z.'s depressed feelings pertained not only to V.'s deficits, but to her feelings of abandonment resulting from the withdrawal of friends and family who shielded themselves from the tensions surrounding V.'s handicaps. Mrs. Z. felt that family and friends were fearful of V. especially of the tube feedings. For more than two years she maintained the belief, contradicted by the evidence, that eventually V. would develop normally. Her trust in a benevolent world was perhaps founded on early good experiences with her own caretakers. She secretly believed that, if only V. would eat by mouth, all other deficits would disappear.

Mrs. Z.'s denial, though strong, did not diminish a realistic appraisal of V.'s day-to-day functioning, nor of V.'s needs. Her hope was also sustained by the realistic recognition that she could positively influence V.'s development.

Denial that sustains hope (Solnit and Stark, 1961) may successfully ward off depression. This kind of denial is quite distinct from another type not sustaining hope, sometimes observed in parents who feel incapable of influencing the course of their child's development. Such parents' denial may lead to distortions of reality as all their energies are spent on reparative fantasies.

CONCLUSION

We have reviewed the role of depression and denial, in both their pathological and nonpathological forms, in a mother's adjustment and reaction to the birth of an impaired child. While fathers undergo many of the same developmental crises and resolutions (cf. Herzog, 1982), that topic would be beyond the scope of the present chapter. It is important to keep in mind that depression implies a certain degree of ego strength. Winnicott (1954–55, 1965) reminds us that in reaction to an experienced loss, "depression is a healing mechanism; it covers the battleground as with a mist, allowing for a sorting out at a reduced rate, giving time for all possible defenses to be brought into play, and for a working through, so that eventually there can be a spontaneous recovery" (1954–55, p. 275). A mother can tolerate depression without being paralyzed by it only if she retains a solid sense of self, and if she regains a sense of control over the environment, especially a sense of competence in the care of her child.

We have highlighted cases in which depression and denial served a critical role in eventually facilitating the mother's attunement to her child. A protracted stage of adaptive depression, in the face of the grim reality of an impaired baby, may be a necessity. This type of depression may be viewed as a period of accommodation to the child as he/she is.

Certain implications follow for the treatment and/or facilitation of the depessed mother of an impaired baby. Mintzer et al. (1984) indicate that, for grief work to occur, parents need to view their infant as separate and not as a negative extension of the self. We have found that a focus on the infant's specific abilities and patterns of individuality and cueing help to foster this recognition of the infant as separate. We wish to emphasize the importance of the adaptive and beneficial aspects of denial and depression, and the need to differentiate these from more pathological states. For the purpose of early intervention, this differentiation is a crucial one.

REFERENCES

Anthony, E.J., & Benedek, T. (1970). Maternal rejection, overprotection and perplexity. In E.J. Anthony & T. Benedek (Eds.), *Parenthood: Its psychology and psychopathology* (pp. 373–375). Boston: Little, Brown.

Beckman, P.J. (1984). A transactional view of stress in families of handicapped children. In M. Lewis (Ed.), *Beyond the dyad* (pp. 281–298). New York: Plenum.

Beebe, B., & Gerstman, L.J. (1980). The "packaging" of maternal stimulation in relation to infant facial-visual engagement: A case study at four months. *Merrill-Palmer Quarterly, 26,* 321–339.

Benedek, T. (1970). The psychobiology of pregnancy. In E.J. Anthony & T. Benedek (Eds.), *Parenthood: Its psychology and psychopathology* (pp. 137–152). Boston: Little, Brown.

Bibring, G.L. (1959). Some considerations of the psychological processes in pregnancy. *Psychoanalytic Study of the Child, 14,* 113–121.

Bibring, G.L., Dwyer, T.F., Huntington, D.S., & Valenstein, A.F. (1961). A study of psychological processes in pregnancy and of the earliest mother-child relationship. *Psychoanalytic Study of the Child, 16,* 9–27.

Caplan, G., Mason, E.A., & Kaplan, D.M. (1977). Four studies of crises in parents of prematures. In J.L. Schwartz & L. Schwartz (Eds.), *Vulnerable infants: A psychosocial dilemma.* New York: McGraw-Hill.

Herzog, J. M. (1982). Patterns of expectant fatherhood: A study of the fathers of a group of premature infants. In S. H. Cath, A. R. Gurwitt, & J. N. Ross (Eds.), *Father and child: Developmental and clinical perspectives* (pp. 301–314). Boston: Little, Brown.

Horowitz, M., Wilner, N., Marmar, C., & Krupnick, J. (1980). Pathological grief and the activation of latent self-images. *American Journal of Psychiatry, 137,* 1157–1162.

Kaplan, D.M., & Mason, E.A. (1977). Maternal reactions to premature birth viewed as an acute emotional disorder. In J.L. Schwartz & L.H. Schwartz (Eds.), *Vulnerable infants: A psychosocial dilemma.* New York: McGraw-Hill.

Kestenberger, J.S. (1975). *Children and parents.* New York: Aronson.

Kestenberg, J.S. (1976). Regression and reintegration in pregnancy. *Journal of the American Psychoanalytic Association, 24,* 213–250.

Kestenberg, J.S. (1980). Maternity and paternity in the developmental context. *Psychiatric Clinics of North America, 3,* 61–79.

Kestenberg, J.S., & Buelte, A. (1977a). Prevention, infant therapy and the treatment of adults. 1: Toward understanding mutuality. *International Journal of Psychoanalytic Psychotherapy, 6,* 339–366.

Kestenberg, J.S., & Buelte, A. (1977b). Prevention, infant therapy and the treatment of adults. 2: Mutual holding and holding-oneself-up. *International Journal of Psychoanalytic Psychotherapy, 6,* 367–396.

Kestenberg, J.S., & Buelte, A. (1983). Prevention, infant therapy and the treatment of adults. 3: Periods of vulnerability in transition from stability to mobility and vice versa. In J.D. Call, E. Galenson & R.L. Tyson (Eds.), *Frontiers of infant psychiatry* (pp. 200–216). New York: Basic Books.

Lax, R. (1972). Some aspects of the interaction between mother and impaired child: Mother's narcissistic trauma. *International Journal of Psycho-Analysis, 53,* 339–344.

Lyon, S., & Preis, A. (1983). Working with families of severely handicapped persons. In M. Seligman (Eds.), *The family with a handicapped child: Understanding and treatment* (pp. 203–232). New York: Grune & Stratton.

Minde, K. (1982). The impact of medical complications on parental behavior in the premature nursery. In M. Klaus & M. Oschrin Robertson (Eds.), *Birth, interaction and attachment* (pp. 98–104). Skillman, NJ: Johnson & Johnson.

Minde, K., Trehub, S., Corter, C., Boukydis, C., Celhoffer, L., & Marton, P. (1978). Mother-child relationships in the premature nursery: An observational study. *Pediatrics, 61,* 3733–3739.

Mintzer, D., Als, H., Tronick, E., & Brazelton, T.B. (1984). Parenting an infant with a birth defect: The regulation of self-esteem. *Psychoanalytic Study of the Child, 39,* 561–589.

Osterweis, M., Solomon, F., & Green, M. (1984). *Bereavement: Reactions, consequences and care.* Washington, DC: National Academy Press.

Reich, A. (1953). Narcissistic object choice in women. In *Psychoanalytic contributions* (pp. 179–208). New York: International Universities Press, 1973.

Roos, P. (1963). Psychological counseling with parents of retarded children. *Mental Retardation, 1,* 345–350.

Rose, J.A. (1961). The prevention of mothering breakdown associated with physical abnormalities of the infant. In G. Caplan (Ed.), *Prevention of mental disorders in children.* New York: Basic Books.

Rosen, L. (1955). Selected aspects in the development of the mother's understanding of her mentally retarded child. *American Journal of Mental Deficiency, 59,* 522–528.

Solnit, A.J., & Stark, M.H. (1961). Mourning and the birth of a defective child. *Psychoanalytic Study of the Child, 16,* 523–537.

Stern, D.N. (1971). A micro-analysis of mother-infant interaction: Behaviors regulating social contact between a mother and her three-and-a-half-month-old twins. *Journal of the American Academy of Child Psychiatry, 10,* 501–517.

Stern, D.N. (1985). *The interpersonal world of the infant.* New York: Basic Books.

Stolorow, R.D., & Lachmann, F.M. (1980). *Psychoanalysis of developmental arrests.* New York: International Universities Press.

Winnicott, D.W. (1950–55/1975). Aggression in relation to emotional development. In *Through pediatrics to psychoanalysis* (pp. 204–218). New York: Basic Books.

Winnicott, D.W. (1954–55/1975). The depressive position in normal emotional development. In *Through paediatrics to psychoanalysis* (pp. 262–277). New York: Basic Books.

Winnicott, D.W. (1965). Psychiatric disorder in terms of infantile maturational processes. In *The maturational processes and the facilitating environment* (pp. 230–241). New York: International Universities Press.

■ 11
Silencing the Self: The Power of Social Imperatives in Female Depression

DANA JACK, M.S.W., Ed.D.

For women, entry into the adult years carries a significant risk of becoming depressed. Research suggests that the risk is associated with a woman's socioeconomic status, and varies with the roles she occupies. Poverty, the presence of three or more children under 14, the lack of a supportive, confiding relationship with a partner, the death of a mother before 11, and/or the lack of a job increase the likelihood of becoming depressed (Brown & Harris, 1978). Entry into marriage appears to increase the possibility of depression, leading researchers to observe that "elements of the traditional female role" may contribute to depression (Klerman & Weissman, 1980).

Though certain niches in society are particularly hazardous to women's mental health, depression crosses socioeconomic lines to affect a broad spectrum of women in differing contexts—from rich to poor. Its incidence among women peaks during the ages 25 to 44 (Weissman, Myers, & Thompson, 1981). These are the years of full engagement in whatever roles a woman chooses (still most often those of wife and mother), and are critical for her adult development. Because women in all contexts are more vulnerable to depression than men, it appears that certain cultural imperatives attached to being female are interacting with the developmental demands of adulthood to create symptoms of helplessness, low self-esteem, and hopelessness.

This chapter is based on the author's doctoral dissertation at Harvard University. Helpful comments from Carol Gilligan and Deborah Belle on an earlier draft of this paper are gratefully acknowledged.

This chapter explores how cultural forces interact with women's adult development and their normal experience of self to create a vulnerability to depression. Findings from a longitudinal study of clinically depressed women (Jack, 1984) provide the basis for my observations. The theoretical framework for understanding normal female development and a woman's sense of self comes from recent research by the self-in-relation theorists (Chodorow, 1978; Gilligan, 1982; Miller, 1976, 1984; see also D. Jack, Chapter 3, *this volume*). This new model of women's psychology, in conjunction with the examination of depressed women's self-evalaution, affords a different way of understanding women's vulnerability to depression.

FEMALE PERSONALITY IN SOCIAL CONTEXT: AN EXPLORATORY STUDY

Critical to an understanding of depression is how women's orientation to relationships and their moral emphasis on care interact with cultural values, social contexts, and the roles they occupy. To observe these issues, I explored 12 women's experiences of depression in a longitudinal, exploratory study. Prior to referral to the study all 12 subjects had been diagnosed as depressed by physicians and clinicians according to DSM III (1980) for depression. The women were interviewed when actively depressed, and then reinterviewed approximately two years later in order to observe changes in their depression and accompanying social, cognitive, and emotional changes. All subjects were Caucasian, ranging in age from 19 to 55, with socioeconomic status spanning poverty (on welfare) to upper class. Nine of the women had children, and only one woman was not partnered or married when first interviewed.

Intensive, semistructured interviews were used to gather data for the study. Questions did not supply categories to frame responses. Allowing women to speak in their own terms, I listened to their conflicts and concerns, and derived concepts from their descriptions. In the spirit of an anthropologist seeking knowledge of other cultures, I viewed these women as "informants" from women's sphere (Bernard, 1981), trusting they would locate and describe the stresses that rendered them vulnerable to depression. The observations from the study are not generalizable to all depressed women. Rather, they supply conceptualizations that clarify the phenomenology of female depression, particularly the interactions of role, morality, and culture with women's relational sense of self.

SELF-EVALUATION AND DEPRESSION

Self-evaluation provides a window through which to observe both the dynamics of depression and the interaction of culture and personality. As this study confirms, self-evaluation holds the key to understanding gender differences in the prevalence and dynamics of depression.

In depression, self-evaluation is invariably negative. This negative self-assessment is central to depressive symptoms and dynamics. It affects self-perception, self-esteem, anger directed toward the self, and feelings of worthlessness, hopelessness, and paralysis. Among the diagnostic symptoms of major depression, DSM III (1980) lists the effects of negative self-evaluation as follows: "self-reproach, inappropriate guilt, feelings of worthlessness" (p. 214). Clinicians describe the phenomenology of depression as characterized by a fall in self-esteem, and a self-deprecating sense of worthlessness and hopelessness (Klerman, Weissman, Rounsaville, & Chevron, 1984). In 1917, Freud (1961) wrote that the "most outstanding feature" of the clinical picture was the patient's "dissatisfaction with the ego on moral grounds" (pp. 247–248). Freud also asserted a difference in moral development and superego activity between men and women. Yet the illness in which the superego is most active—depression—has not been explored in terms of gender difference, nor with regard to gender-specific standards women may use to evaluate themselves.

Other theorists point to the importance of self-evaluation for understanding the dynamics of depression. From an ego-psychological perspective (Bibring, 1953), the low self-esteem and feelings of worthlessness characteristic of depression stem from an impossible gap between the self one would like to be (the ego ideal) and the self one perceives one is. The greater the discrepancy between the self one aspires to be and the self one perceives one is, the lower the self-esteem. Despite important differences, Kohut (1980; Kohut & Wolf, 1978; Alice Miller, 1981), and Winnicott (1965) agree that depression results from an early environment where the child learned that his/her actual self was unacceptable, and developed a false self to present to the world, becoming self-alienated and cut off from emotions in the process.

Conflict between actual and ideal ego states provides a model to observe how social role and social context interact with the developing personality to create depression. The interaction appears in the person's self-reproach, where standards for the ideal self are used to judge the actual self. These standards come form two major sources: the individual's family and the wider culture. Accordingly, the standards include both personal constructs that incorporate the moral "shoulds" and idiosyncratic values of the family, and social constructs acquired from the culture. The two sets of standards constantly interact to confirm, disconfirm, or distort each other (S. Miller, 1985). Thus, self-evaluation provides a two-way mirror reflecting, on the one hand, outer social norms and cultural tradition regarding feminine goodness and correct behavior; and, on the other, the woman's inner imperatives that direct her understanding of how she "should" be in relation to others. If the family standards and the cultural norms reflect and magnify each other, the woman may find it difficult to challenge these standards on the basis of her personal experience.

My work reveals that when women try to fit their relational capacities and needs into the roles of "wife" and "good woman," defined by society as self-sacrificing and oriented to the needs of others, they run the risk of self-alienation and inauthenticity. Evaluating themselves by such societal standards, they feel "worthless," and express a sense of "failure as a wife, as a mother, as a woman, I guess." Valuing relationships, these women adapted to the needs of those around them so that they experienced a loss of self within their roles of wife and mother.

When the relationship is troubled by lack of intimacy, by disruption and separation, the woman may feel her basic sense of self to be threatened. At the same time, observing herself from the perspective of the culture, the woman may judge herself to be a failure according to the social standards of adult independence and achievement. In the case of such women, depression appeared overdetermined when, in addition, their mothers modeled selflessness as an ideal in the role of wife, a standard that is unattainable and self-defeating in heterosexual relationships. And when being "selfless" in relationship is linked in the woman's mind with "goodness" (morality), with femininity (out of identification with a mother who was "selfless" in relationship), and with intimacy (providng safety from abandonment), she must deny whole parts of herself, including negative feelings and direct self-assertion.

From the outside, the woman's behavior may look "passive," "dependent," and "helpless." But on the inside, the selfless role requires tremendous cognitive and emotional activity to curb the self in order to live out its vision of goodness. The woman must actively silence her negative feelings, which she (and society) considers unacceptable, and begins to experience self-condemnation, inner division, and depression.

RELATIONSHIPS AND DEPRESSION

Eleven of the 12 women described their depression as arising out of problems in unsatisfactory relationships. In agreement with findings from other studies (Belle, 1982a; Brown & Harris, 1978; Van Fossen, 1981; Weissman & Paykel, 1974), they describe relationships characterized by financial dependence (10/12), emotional coldness (11/12), physical brutality (3 of 12), and inhibited communication (12/12). The women described an inability to say what they were thinking and feeling to their husbands or partners, an inability to "be themselves" in marriage, a constant necessity to monitor the expression of their feelings. Described by the clinical literature as enmeshed in relationships where they are overdependent and overdemanding, these women portray themselves as isolated and lonely within relationships of inequality and emotional distance.

Other studies confirm that when a woman is married or partnered, the quality of her relationship with her partner is the critical variable that appears either to precipitate or protect against depression. Brown and Harris (1978) describe issues of loss and disruption of relationship as the central features of most events bringing about clinical depression in a sample of low income women in London. But they found that a confiding, intimate relationship with the partner, even in the face of stressful conditions such as poverty, inadequate housing, young children, illness, or other vulnerability factors, protected against depression. This critical variable, *the quality of the woman's relationship with her partner,* appeared most strongly to mediate her experience of painful events and/or chronic conditions. Similarly, in Belle's (1982) study of 40 low income families, the factor that appeared to protect against depression was intimate, supportive relationships with others. Pearlin (1980) found that perceived failure of a spouse to fulfill role expectations, to exercise reciprocity in the relationship, and to recognize and accept their partner as their "'real,' quintessential self" (p. 177) were more strongly related to stress leading to depression than divorce, separation, or widowhood. These studies confirm Bowlby's (1980) observation that "In most forms of depressive disorder . . . the principal issue about which a person feels helpless is his ability to make and to maintain affectional relationships" (p. 40).

In addition, 10 of the 12 women I interviewed were not working, so they were financially dependent on unsatisfactory relationships. Being financially dependent affected these women's perceptions of their prerogatives within marriage, as well as their ability to leave unsatisfactory relationships. Brown and Harris (1978) found that employment halved the woman's risk of depression by providing her with an additional role identity and more social contacts.

MODEL OF GOODNESS

Each of the interviews were filled with moral language—words such as "should," "ought," "good," "bad," "selfish"—centering on how to resolve conflicts in heterosexual relationships, and how to evaluate the self. Specifically, such self-evaluative statements as "I feel like I'm a failure," "I don't measure up," "I'm a liar, a cheat, and I'm no good" point to the importance of uncovering the beliefs that guide such harsh self-judgment.

Searching for the standards depressed women use to judge themselves negatively, I repeatedly found the norms of the "good wife" and "good woman." The women expressed similar beliefs about self, care, relation-ships, and role—a network of ideas which interlock to compose their model of goodness. It is this model of goodness, in conjunction with limit-ing social conditions, that restrains and confines depressed women's per-ceptions of their alternatives.

Most broadly stated, the model of goodness is composed of the woman's beliefs about how one "should" care for others and be cared for in return, and is particularly focused on her roles of wife and mother. These beliefs form part of her ego ideal, the self she would like to be. The beliefs are in-formed by cultural norms, and by her mother's actions in relationship with her father, internalized as part of her feminine gender identification with the mother's role and affective behaviors.

As I talked with these depressed women over time, I was impressed with the tenacity and power of their "model of goodness." Its stability appears to stem from several factors. First, the interlocking nature of the ideas—care, role, marriage, self—implies that changing one idea challenges the whole model. Part of the difficulty lies in the culture's reflection of these ideas and behaviors as normal for women: something is "wrong" with her if she does not like them. Although women have other cultural images available from which to choose, the traditional model, learned from the family and reinforced by the culture, is so strong that they do not embrace other op-tions. Nor do they give credence to their own personal experiences that challenge the model of goodness by demonstrating that it leads to hurt to the self. In addition, the depressed women describe being unable to challenge the traditional role out of fear of negative consequences, such as an increase in conflict with the spouse, or a withdrawal of affection and financial support.

The moral themes throughout these interviews point to the second reason for the model's power and stability: it is part of the self, part of the ego ideal, formed out of early learnings of how to be a good female. The close tie between the developing female superego and a context of ongo-ing attachment with the preoedipal mother leads to a mingling of relational issues with moral issues. It can also result in role imperatives such as "put the man first," "go along with his wishes and interests," becoming moral-ized so that the imperatives are indistinguishable from moral standards. Women have appeared to lack their own standards and to take on the values of their spouses precisely because of the content of their own moral beliefs, which direct them to do so. Thus, part of the difficulty in challeng-ing the model of goodness comes from the mental pain of feeling low self-esteem, guilt, and self-doubt created if one behaves in ways the ego ideal judges as immoral.

SCHEMAS OF CARE AND INTIMACY

As noted above, the women interviewed had a distinct view of themselves as morally lacking, as not living up to the standards of their model of goodness. Central to the model of goodness was the women's ideal of care. Eleven of the 12 women I interviewed understood care to mean being "unselfish," "giving," and "self-sacrificing." These same 11 women spontaneously tied their behavior in their marriages to the model of goodness and the image of the relationship they observed their mother living out in her unequal marriage with the father. For example, talking about their marriages, the women said.:

> In terms of my priorities, I would have to say first comes my husband, well, my home and my husband and then me. I've thought a lot about—you asked me last time what's good for me and maybe I don't consider that enough. Because, you know, I apply the word selfish to that. (Laura, age 32, pregnant with second child).

> I just put everybody else first. . . . You know I was just busy with raising a family and looking after my husband and I guess I just put me back. (Anna, age 55, married 36 years, with two children.)

These women try to accomplish their goals—to establish intimacy and keep the husband happy—through fulfilling the role of the traditional "good wife." Their beliefs about feminine behavior are reinforced by a social context that has equated traditional feminine goodness with the injunction to care for others before the self. Traditional feminine virtues are stated in a language of constraint, which implies an eclipse of the woman's self by merits that overshadow initiative: self-restraint, self-denial, self-sacrifice, self-effacement. Depression similarly connotes a diminution in the experience of an active self and its possibilities. Because these women measure their effectiveness from the perspective of others (being there for others, nurturing others, pleasing others), they begin to listen to others' demands and requirements more than to their own feelings and needs. When this occurs without mutuality or reciprocity, they experience a loss of self—they feel disconnected, unsupported, and self-alienated.

Yet the willingness to give to others does not necessarily lead to self-alienation and depression. Critical is the context within which the giving occurs, and the giver's ability to *choose* when, how, and in what form to care. If the imperative to care is experienced as an obligation, which has the character of a moral absolute, then the woman becomes subservient to others' needs, and becomes increasingly angry, resentful, and confused. In addition, these women's ego ideal contains the image of self as one who is loving and loved, who is competent in relationships. Faced with unsatisfactory relationships, these women held themselves responsible for the difficulties, reflecting the cultural norm that women are more responsible for the affective side of relationships.

Intimacy, the goal of these women's "selfless," caring behavior, is an ongoing task that organizes their adult development. In Western society, marriage is the social arrangement within which most adults expect to fulfill their needs for intimacy. The "good wife" role, a historical legacy from the 19th century, still carries certain moral values attached to its behaviors. Ideals of submissiveness, selflessness, and responsiveness to the needs of others inform its actions. Indicators of being a successful wife lie outside the self—in a "happy," loving husband, well-adjusted children, a clean house—so that a woman accordingly looks outside to measure her achievement in the role. Belle (1982) reviews literature which confirms that women most often provide emotional and physical support to other family members without receiving it in return. High levels of stress, with resulting mental and physical health costs, stem from women's social role as the primary provider of support to others.

Intimacy is only one organizing aim of adult life. The other lifelong task is to develop and express one's unique capacities and interests: to be authentic, to be a self. The adult years bring the full development and integration of intellectual and physical capacities that enable people to express their abilities through purposeful, organized activity. Yet again, gender, the immediate family context, and the larger social environment all affect the individual's possibilities.

The tasks of intimacy and identity merge when one is able to be a growing, changing self within an ongoing relationship, when intimacy facilitates the developing authentic self, and the developing self deepens the possibilities of intimacy. In our culture, women often experience these necessities for healthy adult development—intimacy and authenticity—as in conflict. In their interviews, the depressed women feared that if they tried to be themselves, they would lose their marriages; yet they described having lost themselves in an attempt to achieve an intimacy that was never attained. They portray how striving toward intimacy through the traditional role constrains and compromises their own continually developing sense of self. Conversely, their capacity for intimacy is diminished by their compromised self-development. Part of the sense of hopelessness and helplessness in their depression stems from the sense that moving toward one major life goal forecloses the other. Thus, the cultural imperatives attached to the roles adult women occupy interact with their personal values and their developmental tasks to create a vulnerability to depression.

MORALITY AND ROLE

Observing women's orientation to relationships as normal, yet considering the problematic nature of these women's marriages, the interesting question becomes: Why do women stay in defeating relationships? Beyond the important economic issues, the answer requries a further look at how role becomes associated with morality and intimacy in women's thought.

Through her developmental history, a girl learns to value care as the means by which relatedness to others occurs. She learns how to care, the gender-specific caring behaviors acceptable in our culture, through observing her parents' relationship and through the media, religion, school, etc. In adulthood, the marital role offers to women a socially patterned, acceptable way to express their value on care and relationships. The women I studied believed that following the traditional role behaviors would lead to intimacy, and that failure to achieve intimacy stemmed from their inability to care enough, or in the "right" ways. They had changed and adapted themselves to fulfill the imperatives of the wife *role*, rather than changing and adapting the wife role to suit themselves and their relationships.

Developmentally, a woman is particularly vulnerable to depression when she equates goodness with self-sacrifice, which Gilligan (1977, 1982) describes as the conventional construction of care. From the conventional perspective, goodness is understood as conformity to social norms and values, as fulfilling the obligations and functions of the roles one occupies: wife/mother/daughter/woman. At this point in development, the imperatives attached to the traditional female role converge with the woman's internal standards for caring and responsibility. Goodness, defined as selfless giving in relationships, joins with the stereotypic role prescriptions for women's behavior to create a powerful bind for self-expression and recognition of anger. In tandem with social conditions that limit their self-concept and expression, this ideal of goodness renders women particularly vulnerable to loss of self, to depression.

Further, within the personality, moral values and ideals perform an integrative and a defensive function. Morality integrates outer demands for conformity to social roles with the individual's personal valuing of those roles. By seeing self-sacrifice as what the "good woman" does, a woman accepts it as a legitimate, positive way of being in a relationship with a man. In its defensive function, the "good woman" morality operates to ward off feelings of anxiety: it provides a cognitive schema of specific behaviors and responses in heterosexual relationships that guide the woman's actions to keep her "safe" from anxiety about abandonment. Selflessness operates defensively against her fear of loss of love, and against the fear that others will judge her negatively. The women believe that if they love "well enough," that is, selflessly enough, they will be loved in return. Thus, deviation from the ideal of selflessness in relationship feels so frightening to the women because external and internal imperatives recite in unison the consequences—loss of relationship—that may result.

Since no one can be selfless all the time, the ideal of selflessness contributes to a woman's negative self-evaluation. The women in this study describe a growing resentment from continually setting their own needs and wishes aside and from the lack of empathy or mutuality in the relationship. In an effort to conform to the cultural prohibition on female anger, they deflect their anger from their spouses toward themselves. Blaming the self rather than the other for problems reinforces inequality, and, perceiving herself as "inferior" to her husband, the woman tries even harder to please in order to avoid conflict and to prevent separation.

The resentment finally erupts in angry outbursts, followed by periods of self-blame and guilt. The outbursts "prove" to the woman her selfishness and inability to love and care, so she redoubles her efforts to give, to please, and the cycle begins again. Clarice, 38, described her interactions with her husband:

> I know that part of the problem was the lack of communication where I did not express my real feelings. I was just wanting to do certain things and not wanting to do what he wanted me to do, but not telling him why I did not want to. . . . I think I was generally pretty submissive but then I would feel resentments inside and leave them inside until all of a sudden it got to me and I would be very aggressive.

Other women described holding in their anger in accord with their idea of the woman's role as "submissive." The idea of selflessness was reinforced by their fear of physical abuse, or being emotionally and/or financially abandoned. Maya, age 33, described her view of woman's role as

> being submissive. I thought all women were like that. I never thought couples ever fought with each other or disagreed. That was my view of marriage and then when I got married I found that in order to maintain that, I had to be quiet and not say anything to avoid arguments. And that's when I started stepping back into that real submissive role and losing, and not being able to speak out.

About her anger and its inhibition, she said:

> I just kept it inside. I didn't let my anger out. And just holding these feelings in just made me sick, made me want to die.

One of the inherent problems with the ideal of selflessness is that it is believed to enhance the possibility of closeness in a relationship where, in fact, it threatens intimacy. The threat to intimacy lies in the woman's belief that she should silence herself when she differs from the spouse in order to maintain harmony. The silencing is reinforced by the belief that it is selfish (immoral) to consider and act on her own needs. This silencing precludes engagement by which two individuals continually become known to each other, and by which two realities are accommodated in the relationship.

FAMILY HISTORY

Eleven of the 12 women I interviewed described their mother as the submissive one in a clearly dominant/submissive relationship with the husband. This pattern of personal history of depressives was also found by Slipp (1976) and Arieti and Bemporad (1978) who reported that "for most but not all mild depressives the father rather than the mother was the dominant parent." The mother is described as "loving though weak and submissive" (Arieti & Bemporad, 1978, pp. 183–184).

Children whose parents have a dominant/submissive relationship will observe the mother's powerlessness in relation to the father. When the girl identifies with the mother, she also has either to identify with or to reject the mother's position and role. These women incorporated the awareness of their mother's hierarchical position and role along with their mother's values, choices, and behavior in relationship. Thus, they learned to value the role and the morality enacted within the role. As girls, they learned to associate giving to others with *subservience* to others, and giving and caring for others carried the implicit arrangement of putting others first and discounting the needs of the self. If the girl learns that others' needs come first, then the unspoken (and perhaps unconscious) corollary is: "my needs are less important than those of others and they will never be met; or will be met reciprocally only as I care for others." This childhood learning, passed on through mother–daughter identification, and in tandem with a social structure that reflects women's lesser position, lays the basis for an unspecified but pervasive low self-esteem. These women described a sense of self-diminution that occurs from continually seeing themselves reflected as less important in their relationships. Investing a large amount of self into their marriages, they felt a gradual "loss of self" through continually compromising the expression of their feelings and needs, and through evaluating themselves as incompetent in their marriages.

These same 11 women reported homes where parental conflict was not overt, where the mother appeared compliant to what the father wanted. Observing the mother's outer compliance, not knowing her inner frustration, these daughters mistakenly learned it was good for relationships to silence themselves when they disagreed with their husband/partners.

The depressed women also described that, as girls, they did not have a warm affectionate relationship with their fathers. In such family situations, the father is not "real" to the girl through her experience. Instead, she can easily idealize and fear him as she identifies with her mother's position and sees her father through her mother's eyes. In this idealization, however, there is the implicit recognition that the father is vulnerable in certain ways, and the woman is to protect him from his vulnerability by "letting" him feel strong, in control, powerful, and that she has her role to play in order to keep him "strong." But the girl/woman comes to believe in the male's magical strength herself and loses sight of the fact that she, by her actions, is helping him play the role and occupy the position.

Susan's themes illustrate the interaction of family history, the "model of goodness," and social norms. At age 32, married seven years and the mother of two daughters, Susan reflects on her own mother:

> My mother was always a giver, giver-type person. She was always a helper of people, and I learned early that you get happiness from giving happiness. I never learned to be a taker, and my mother would often say, "you know, you have to give and sacrifice," and these kinds of concepts were ones I grew up with.

Susan describes her father as a man who "emotionally abused" her and her mother. Her mother did not leave him, so Susan saw the abuse throughout childhood and adolescence. Witnessing the situation of her mother's giving within such a context affected Susan's understanding of strength and weakness:

> And so, at the same time I was mad at her for her subservience in her relationship with my father, I also emulated and respected the fact that she was such a loving, giving person. She was a person who had, in a way, great strength inside, a peace inside herself; and yet, now that I look back on it, she may have been very weak too, in some areas. And that's why she did just—I think she has a lot of fears, maybe of loneliness and being without my dad— she would never consider separating or leaving him.

Susan was left with a basic confusion about whether her mother was strong or weak in her capacity to give so much. She learned that to be safe in relationship—to avoid the possibility of separation—that one should not speak one's opinion or confront the partner. Also, Susan saw both sides of her mother's caring: its strength—active love and care for others—and its weakness—the incapacity to care for herself, coinciding with the fear of loss.

As an adult, Susan is "mixed up" about what goodness is because the model she was taught by her mother allows no way to include her needs and wants within a relationship. Instead she must "be for the other guy."

She (mother) never, never dared rock the boat or express needs or say, "I want this." You never say, "I want," you always find out what the other person wants and . . . You don't desert somebody just because they have a weakness or a sickness. There again, you be the servant or the keeper or the brother or we must be serving of one another. That was the constant thought that came through everything she taught. *Always serve and be for the other guy. Never, ever dare think about yourself.*

Being taught to respond to external expectations and to ignore the self's needs and feelings emerges as a crucial issue in each of these depressed women's psychological development. For each woman it leads to loss of awareness of their own needs and feelings. Susan learned that pleasing others, giving to others was more important, more *good*, than listening to herself. She learned that thinking about herself, or asking for her needs to be met, was "selfish" and by implication, bad. If the girl has learned that her needs are less important than those of her mate, that she has no "right" to her needs, then she has learned the basis of low self-esteem.

For Susan, the morality of goodness as self-sacrifice her mother taught led directly to emotional and physical hurt. In addition to the "battered woman syndrome" (Walker, 1979), a general pattern of reaction to physical and psychological abuse inflicted on a woman by her spouse, these childhood learnings about goodness—that "you don't desert somebody just because they have a weakness or a sickness"—bind the woman to a hurtful spouse with the wish to "help" him. In addition to this teaching, Susan had a model whom she admired and loved who "stuck it out in a bad marriage." Explaining why she did not call the police when her husband became physically violent, Susan says:

I'm sure a lot of it is that same old thing I was brought up with. . . . it was what I saw, my model at home for 18 years was a woman who was getting walked on. A doormat, living with a man who was constantly putting her down, belittling her, making fun of her, hurting her in front of other people, and she took it and took it and took it, and she was the "good" person—and so there I go.

Susan saw her mother not voicing her feelings in order to stay in relationship with her father. The equation became: silence yourself and stay in relationship, or speak your feelings and lose the relationship. The identification with a submissive, loving mother, the wish to be good, the uncertainty of her "right" to her own needs and integrity, financial dependence, and fear are some of the factors that led Susan to remain in an unsatisfactory marriage and to become clinically depressed.

Susan feels betrayed by her mother's teachings since what she believed to be her mother's strength she now considers a weakness, and she becomes confused about what constitutes strength and weakness within herself.

> My father would get very belligerent. Never physically, but he would get extremely belligerent and extremely insulting and whatever to my mother. Her friends, everything about her, and she would just sit there and take it. That's what I was brought up to see as being good, and being good is what we all want to be, right? Well, I don't believe in that anymore. Just like I don't believe in fairy tales. I don't believe that being good means you allow yourself to be walked on and manipulated, put down, victimized, that is not being good. I feel it's being weak, and I see that I am weak in some areas like that.

In this passage, Susan equates goodness with "taking it" and "taking it" with weakness. She is attempting to separate her own definition of goodness from that of her mother, but has not yet found a replacement. To act in her own self-interest is to be like her father and her husband, both of whom hurt people with their "selfish" actions. Yet she observes that being good leads to hurt to the self.

If women cannot exercise power without (in their minds) causing hurt, they may choose to remain powerless for what feel like moral reasons, rooted in social inequality. Susan is confused about how she can be good without becoming a victim, and how she can act in her own best interests without being "bad," that is, causing hurt to others. These childhood learnings lead to women's common difficulty in separating an understanding of healthy self-assertion from aggression, which hurts others. These childhood learnings also contribute, in a direct way, to answering the question of why women stay in nonintimate, self-defeating relationships and do not perceive other choices that may be open to them.

EITHER/OR OF NO CHOICE

The women's feelings of being hopeless and helpless, their inability to perceive choice, also derives from their absolutist, either/or thinking. The understanding of goodness as selflessness, which characterizes these women's thinking, creates a paralyzing either/or that yields loss on either side of the contradiction:[1]

---

[1]Beck (1979) and Kris (1977) have described the absolutist, either/or thinking of depressed people, but do not specify a gender-specific content of their thought. In the depressed women's narratives, the either/or thinking was characterized specifically by their understanding of care.

Either care for the other/or care for the self

which has as its corollary that one:

Either excludes the self from one's care/or excludes the other from one's care

From the perspective of the traditional "good woman," these positions are construed as:

Selfless (and good)/or selfish (and bad)

These women describe seeing no way to care for themselves—to attend to their needs and feelings without severing connection; and no way to care for another person without losing themselves. They perceive two visions of relationship: either isolation or subordination. These ideas are structured in the women's thought as follows:

Either	*Or*
Stay in relationship	Act on my own needs, speak my own feelings
means	*means*
Be responsive to his needs in his terms	Be responsible to myself
and	*and*
He is in control of me	I am in control of myself
and	
Sacrifice my own needs and feelings, and silence my voice	
leads to	*leads to*
Loss of self and subordination	Loss of other and isolation

This structure of thought about the self-in-relation does not allow the person to integrate self and other—to hold the self's and the other's needs in view at the same time. When a woman is living out the "selfless" side of the equation, her depression appears to be the "overdependent" type: she focuses on the important other, fears the loss of the relationship but experiences a loss of self. When she has decided to care for herself first, her depression often looks hostile, angry, and defiant: she fears the loss of self if she cares for another, yet she feels isolated.

This split in thought is overdetermined by a social context that presents women with competing alternatives for adulthood which seem to cancel each other out: either achievement *or* relationships; either superwoman *or* traditional homemaker; either authenticity *or* submissiveness. Anna provides an example of the "selfless" depression and its either/or thought construction, framed in the language of inequality:

> I was telling my daughter-in-law, "I guess I was just born to serve others."
> Bless her heart, she said, "Well I wasn't." I said that to Ann and she said,
> "Good for her!" Because we shouldn't be born to serve other people, we
> should look after ourselves.

The double bind in Anna's thought is that if she "serves other people," she
excludes her self, but if she "looks after herself," she excludes other people.
Each alternative is insufficient as a guide for how to deal with competing
needs in relationships, and each side of the dichotomy holds loss: the
choice is either loss of self or loss of other.

The rigid, exclusionary construction of either/or is insufficient to ap-
prehend a reality of paradox, contradiction, and change that challenges it.
The woman experiences the either/or as a double bind, as requiring a
choice between two alternatives which are equally valued yet so equally
lacking that a self-perpetuating vacillation is begun by any act of choice between them. The fact that she must choose between incompatible alternatives causes despair and confusion. Both sides of the either/or are
valued: care for the other (goodness, responsiveness), and care for the self
(survival, authenticity), but each alone is insufficient because both are required for health. The fact that she cannot communicate within her
relationship about the double bind she experiences perpetuates the either/
or and the continual vacillation between its alternatives. It is this either/or
thought construction—where either choice results in loss—which allows
the woman to feel like a victim.

Within marriage, the woman's choices about how to respond when the
husband's wishes and needs conflict with her own are guided by this
either/or schema of care. In putting the husband first these women are not
passively subordinating their wishes to others. Rather, they describe a
moral conviction that caring for others first is a vital, positive expression of
self that furthers intimacy. While initially putting the husband first is
valued, the women describe the dawning realization that it does not lead to
reciprocity or mutuality, that their actions seem devalued. They describe
feeling betrayed, and resentful over the sacrifice of their own growth and
development, while a part of the self still values the caring activity of putting others first. The social support for this action derives from the
stereotype of the good woman and the inequality between the sexes, which
reinforces the view that the male's needs, wishes, and opinions are somehow more important or worthwhile.

ACTIVITY REQUIRED TO BE PASSIVE: SILENCING THE SELF

Repeatedly the women describe how they silence their voices in relationship, discounting and monitoring their feelings, ignoring and critiqu-

ing them according to their ideas of "goodness." In this process, we can see the cognitive activity required to inhibit both outer actions and inner feelings. Statements such as "I have to walk on eggshells in dealing with my husband" and "I have learned 'don't rock the boat'" shows their awareness of their actions and their intended effect: not to cause difference or disharmony.

These efforts to keep harmony make the women look outwardly conforming and compliant; yet inwardly, a different dynamic appears. The inner dynamic is apparent in sections of the interviews where the women try to change their thoughts, where they tell themselves how they "ought" to feel, and where they take their husbands' perspective or the culture's perspective on their feelings and condemn them. Here one can observe the tremendous activity it requires to be submissive. All the cognitive activity results in what appears to be "passivity," whereas, in reality, what occurs is continual thought-monitoring and assertion by the ideal (conventional) self against the actual (authentic) self. For example, Clarice voices some forbidden feelings in the interview and then reveals how she controls her thinking:

> Like for a while, I was just down on all men, they're all no good. And sometimes I still catch myself thinking that, you know, generalizing and saying to myself that, well, you know a wife gives herself a lot more than a man. And that's probably not true, but I catch myself reliving old hurts. And the more you think about them, the worse they get. *So I just force myself to quit thinking about them.* Because I know it's not going to do me any good. Let alone anybody else.

Forcing themselves to stop thinking and judging their own thoughts are methods by which the women inhibit their anger and resentment in order to live out their view of traditional marriage. The conventional self, with prohibitions about how one "should" think and feel, throws a wet blanket over the inner world of feeling and dampens its vitality (Winnicott, 1965).

The active silencing of the self leads to the inner split of the depressive, the condition of self-alienation. Living out the model of goodness, the woman begins to experience two opposing selves: an outwardly conforming, compliant self, and an inner, secret self who is angry and resentful. This inner division was evident as each woman described her life and her conflicts. The outwardly conforming self accepts the social norms for female goodness and tries to comply with them in order to achieve intimacy; the actual, authentic self observes the problems in relationship, and how her own needs remain unmet. The conventional self silences the authentic self with shoulds about how to think and feel:

> And so, when he speaks to me in a harsh tone, or scolds me for something that I have done wrong or haven't done or whatever, I've tended to think to myself, "now you're supposed to be submissive, so just ignore him." Just, you know, don't confront the issue sort of a thing.

In this process, the woman becomes separated from her own feelings and may experience a sense of guilt for not being true to herself.

The inner split affords two different perspectives from which the woman evaluates herself and her experience. The actual self's perspective is based on personal experience, feelings, and observations. It is at odds with the "ideal" or conventional, role-determined way to think about how relationships "should" be and what is a "good" woman. These two perspectives result in a disparity between what the woman sees and knows from her own experience and what she thinks she *should* think and feel. The handling of this disparity regarding how to evaluate her self and her experience is central to the course of the woman's depression in terms of whose reality she acts on—her own or others'. Evaluating her self in her husband's terms or the culture's terms, the woman can come to judge her healthy wish for intimacy as weakness, as signifying immaturity. Using the standards of the model of goodness, the woman can judge her own needs and the anger resulting from their frustration as selfish and bad.

Given the disconfirmation of the authentic self in her relationships, from her childhood learnings, and from the stereotype of the "good woman," the authentic self becomes silent to protect the integrity of its own vision from judgment. What is paralyzing and leads to the sense of hopelessness in depression is the sense of not being heard, not being recognized or loved for the self one "really" is, and the belief that if one were heard, one would not be understood but rather be called immoral, selfish, and be abandoned. Thus, the authentic self goes into hiding and feels angry, resentful, hopeless. The conventional self takes this authentic self as its object and evaluates it as morally lacking. I suggest it is at this point of inner division created by the silencing of the self in relationship, influenced by moral understanding and social role imperatives, that women are most vulnerable to depression.

CONCLUSION

In order to understand women's vulnerability to depression during their adult years, we must look through the window of morality—specifically through the woman's self-evaluation—to observe the interaction of the relational sense of self with social norms for feminine behavior. In the present study, the women's accounts of their depression concur with certain aspects of the clinical literature, and do not concur with others. According to the clinical literature, depressed women have a problem with separation and self-esteem because of excessive dependence on their relationships; these women describe their problem as one of establishing and maintaining connection. The women in this study depict their depression as precipitated not by the loss of affiliation, but by the recognition that they have lost themselves in the process of trying to establish an intimacy they never attained. For these depressed women, the sense of hopelessness and helplessness stems from despair about the possibility of being an authentic, developing self within an intimate marriage, and from their equation of failure in relationship with moral failure.

The woman's normal, relational sense of self with its wish for closeness and intimacy joins with a culturally defined way to care that shapes the form of the woman's thoughts and behaviors in relationship. And this role-defined way to care—in tandem with social conditions which limit women's freedom and self-concept—generates self-defeating behaviors and paralyzing conflicts that lead to depression. These women reveal depression as a frustration of healthy attachment needs, as an absence of intimacy and dialogue with others, and an absence of creative dialogue with the self who knows itself through others. Since these women consider intimacy to be achieved and maintained by dialogue, the silencing of the self in relationship not only renders the self powerless in the relationship but eliminates the very possibility of intimacy the woman is trying to achieve.

The anger turned against the self, described by many theorists, stems from the following factors: (1) The women's anger is, in part, an anger that their needs for relationship have not been met. Their unacceptable anger at the partner's limitations is turned into an anger at the self's "weak" or "selfish" needs for closeness, needs that are labelled dependent by the culture and their male partners. They begin to feel the self that is silent, if revealed, would be condemned as selfish, aggressive, and bad. (2) The woman is angry at herself for having abandoned her own feelings, thoughts, and goals she may have had for herself, but not expressed in her relationship. She feels a sense of not developing, not growing, and a loss of self from continually having put others first. (3) She is angry at others (her husband, her parents, religion, society) who prescribe what she should be like, who condone selfless, self-sacrificing behavior as morally good and condemn active self-assertion, including setting one's own goals, as selfish. She is trying to defend herself against a morality and social norms that support the very destruction of her authenticity through rendering her self-less, labelled "good" and "normal" for women. And the act of self-sacrifice—of literally putting herself aside to try to live up to these standards of goodness—is the act that leads to anger at those (including herself) who prescribe that act and label it morally good. But at the same time she adheres to these standards and judges herself as bad and wrong for her anger. These women are trying to defend themselves against a morality of goodness that condones the destruction of their authenticity, and this is the source of their confusion. Thus, the women both silence themselves and are silenced by the social context within which they live.

Depressed women reveal how a network of interlocking ideas—femininity, goodness, wife, intimacy—tightly binds them, restricting the options they see and restraining their inner and outer vitality. Like the historical practice of footbinding in China, the culture of inequality prevents women from taking steps in their own behalf—toward authenticity, toward relationships of mutuality and equality. Despite the women's movement, the model of goodness is overdetermined for women in our society because of the convergence of historical, religious, social, and familial norms for feminine behavior. In conjunction with relationships of inequality and affectional deprivation, conditions of social and economic discrimination, and cultural mandates to achieve in male terms but with feminine values, these ideas lead women to a vulnerability to paralysis and depression.

REFERENCES

Arieti, S., & Bemporad, J. (1978). *Severe and mild depression: The psychotherapeutic approach.* New York: Basic Books.

Beck, A.T., Rush, A.J., Shaw, B.F., & Emery, G. (1979). *Cognitive therapy of depression.* New York: The Guilford Press.

Bernard, J. (1981). *The female world.* New York: The Free Press.

Belle, D. (Ed.). (1982a). *Lives in stress: Women and depression.* Beverly Hills, CA: Sage Publications.

Belle, D. (1982b). The stress of caring: Women as providers of social support. In L. Goldberger & S. Breznitz (Eds.), *Handbook of stress: Theoretical and clinical aspects* (pp. 496–505). New York: The Free Press.

Bibring, E. (1953). Mechanisms of depression. In P. Greenacre (Ed.), *Affective Disorders* (pp. 13–48). New York: International Universities Press.

Bowlby, J. (1980). *Loss (Vol. 3).* New York: Basic Books.

Brown, G.W., & Harris, T. (1978). *The social origins of depression: A study of psychiatric disorder in women.* London: Tavistock Publications.

Chodorow, N. (1978). *The reproduction of mothering: Psychoanalysis and the sociology of gender.* Berkeley, CA: University of California Press.

Diagnostic and statistical manual of mental disorders. (1980). (With annotations by R.L. Spitzer & H.B. Williams). Washington, DC: American Psychiatric Assoc.

Freud, S. (1961). Mourning and melancholia. In J. Strachey (Ed. and Trans.), *The standard edition of the complete psychological works of Sigmund Freud, (Vol. 14)* (pp. 237-258). London: Hogarth Press. (Original work published in 1917.)

Gilligan, C. (1977). In a different voice: Women's conception of the self and of morality. *Harvard Educational Review, 47,* 481-517.

Gilligan, C. (1982). *In a different voice: Psychological theory and women's development.* Cambridge, MA: Harvard University Press.

Jack, D. (1984). *Clinical depression in women: Cognitive schemas of self, care, and relationships in a longitudinal study.* Unpublished doctoral dissertation, Harvard University, Cambridge MA.

Klerman, G., & Weissman, M.M. (1980). Depressions among women: Their nature and causes. In M. Guttentag, S. Salasin, & D. Belle (Eds.), *The mental health of women* (pp. 57-92). New York: Academic Press.

Klerman, G., Weissman, M.M., Rounsaville, B.J., & Chevron, E.S. (1984). *Interpersonal psychotherapy of depression.* New York: Basic Books.

Kohut, H. (1980). Reflections on advances in self-psychology. In A. Goldberg (Ed.), *Advances in self-psychology* (pp. 473-554). New York: International Universities Press.

Kohut, H., & Wolf, E. (1978). The disorders of the self and their treatment: An outline. *International Journal of Psychoanalysis, 59,* 413-424.

Kris, A.O. (1977). Either/or dilemmas. *The Psychoanalytic Study of the Child: Vol. 32* (pp. 91-117). New Haven: Yale University Press.

Mendelson, M. (1974). *Psychoanalytic concepts of depression* (2nd ed.). Flushing, New York: Spectrum Publications.

Miller, A. (1981). *The drama of the gifted child* (R. Ward, Trans.). New York: Basic Books. (Original work published in 1979.)

Miller, J.B. (1976). *Toward a new psychology of women.* Boston: Beacon Press.

Miller, J.B. (1984). *The development of the feminine sense of self.* Work in Progress, Paper #12; available from The Stone Center for Developmental Services and Studies, Wellesley College, Wellesley, MA.

Miller, S. (1985). *The shame experience.* Hillsdale, NJ: The Analytic Press.

Pearlin, L. (1980). Life strains and psychological distress among adults. In N. Smelser & E. Erikson (Eds.), *Themes of work and love in adulthood* (pp. 174-192). Cambridge, MA: Harvard University Press.

Slipp, S. (1976). An intrapsychic–interpersonal theory of depression. *Journal of the American Academy of Psychoanalysis, 4,* 398-410.

Van Fossen, B.E. (1981). Sex differences in the mental health effects of spouse support and equity. *Journal of Health and Social Behavior, 22,* 130-143.

Walker, L. (1979). *The battered woman.* New York: Harper and Row.

Weissman, M.M., Myers, J.K., & Thompson, W.D. (1981). Depression and its treatment in a U.S. urban community, 1975-1976. *Archives of General Psychiatry, 38,* 417-421.

Weissman, M.M., & Paykel, E.S. (1974). *The depressed woman.* Chicago: University of Chicago Press.

Winnicott, D.W. (1965). *The maturational process and the facilitating environment.* New York: International Universities Press.

■ 12
The Role of Shame in Depression in Women

HELEN BLOCK LEWIS, Ph.D.

In this chapter, I shall develop the thesis that attention to the phenomena and dynamics of shame helps us to understand the dynamics of depression. In particular, attention to shame, beginning with childhood, helps us to understand why adult women are more prone to depression than adult men. Although it has been common observation, beginning with Darwin (1872), that women are more prone to shame than men, the psychology of shame has not been much studied. Perhaps, as a consequence, women's greater susceptibility to depression (Cytryn, McKnew, Zahn-Waxler, & Gershon, 1986; Lewis, 1976) has not been well understood.

I have suggested that women's greater sociability and lesser aggression, together with their second-class citizenship in the world of power, increases their tendency to experience shame. Men, in contrast, on the basis of their lesser sociability and greater aggression, together with their unjust position of superiority in the world of power, are more susceptible to guilt. The indirect evidence that adult women are more prone to shame than men is very compelling (Lewis, 1971, 1976) and, despite little direct evidence, the few empirical studies that do exist yield results in the expected direction (Binder, 1970; Gottschalk & Gleser, 1969; Lewis, 1986).

Until recently, there has been both a neglect and a misunderstanding of shame in both psychoanalytic and behavioral theory. Understanding shame has been made more difficult by the adherence of both psychoanalytic and behavioral theory to a view of human nature as essentially individualistic or "narcissistic" (Lewis, 1984). Shame, although it catches the self "at the quick," to use Lynd's (1958) accurate term, is also quintessentially other-connected. Although shame is about the self, shame is not just a "narcissistic" reaction. With information about the life-long importance of the attachment emotions (Bowlby, 1969, 1973, 1980) as our species' basic human endowment, there has also come the realization that threats to these life-long ties evoke shame. Shame is one of our species' inevitable responses to loss of love, whether in early childhood or in old age. This view differs from that of shame as a defense against the childish "partial instinct" of exhibitionism (Freud, 1905a).

This chapter is divided into five parts. The first part discusses the neglect and misunderstanding of shame in psychoanalytic theory. It suggests that sexism has been one factor influencing the neglect of shame. The second part discusses the connection between shame and the attachment emotions. In a new theoretical framework offered by the concept of life-long affectional ties, shame is understood to be one means by which we seek to maintain attachment bonds. The third part briefly reviews the important distinctions between guilt and shame in depression. The fourth part shows how attention to the role of shame in depression is helpful in understanding problems that arise in both psychoanalytic and behavioral theories of depression. Finally, in the fifth part, some clinical examples show how the neglect of shame hinders therapeutic progress. Freud's (1905c) case of Dora is cited as one example. Excerpts from a woman's dynamic psychotherapy sessions conducted by an experienced (male) therapist will also show how the failure to recognize the concomitants of shame can lead to a renewal of symptoms.

NEGLECT AND MISUNDERSTANDING OF SHAME IN PSYCHOANALYTIC THEORY

When I first published *Shame and Guilt in Neurosis* (Lewis, 1971), I found only eight references to shame as compared to 64 references to guilt. Although Miller (1985) reports that attention to shame has increased in recent years (Broucek, 1983; A. Morrison, 1983; N. Morrison, 1985; Würmser, 1981), it is worth considering some of the reasons for the continuing neglect of shame.

Shame is an acutely painful experience that we wish to end quickly. Shame, moreover, tends to be contagious. The witness to it tends to look away, and psychoanalysts are no exception to this tendency. Although analysts expect to find guilt in their patients' communications and help their patients understand the unconscious hostility that is the source of guilt, they rarely look for shame, partly because shame has been ignored in psychoanalytic theory.

A second set of reasons for both the neglect and misunderstanding of shame may be found in the way that Freud and his followers incorporated evolutionary theory into psychoanalytic theory. Freud (1914) evolved a theory of "primary narcissism" as fundamental to human nature, based on the notion that the "ego-instincts" are as necessary for individual survival as the "sexual instincts" are for species survival. What this theory of primary narcissism ignored, however, was the role of the nurturant female in survival of the individual and the species.

Mahl (1985) has documented the relative infrequency with which Freud refers to mothers. Even more important, Freud's (1900) view of the mother–infant relationship was that it starts with deprivation (see Lewis, 1983). He postulated that infants learn to love their mothers because their mothers feed them. This is the "cupboard love" theory, and it reflects the marketplace values of *quid pro quo*. In this view, "orality" and "dependency" are "primitive" states and their occurrence in adulthood signifies "regression." Implied in this view is a pejorative attitude toward human attachment as well as denigration of (women's) nurturance. It is an instance of the androcentric bias in science, which has resulted, also, in a pejorative attitude toward shame.

By the time Freud had come to write on the origin of guilt in *Totem and Taboo* (1913), he had adopted a male model of human development in which guilt arises out of the resolution of the oedipus complex, with its implied castration threat. In the absence of the castration threat, he thought, women's "superego is never so inexorable, so impersonal, so independent of its emotional origins as we require it to be in men" (Freud, 1925, p. 257). In fact, Freud's (1923) description of the psychology of women insists that women are shame-prone. "Shame, which is considered to be a feminine characteristic par excellence ... has as its purpose, we believe, concealment of genital deficiency" (p. 132).

What was harmful to women was the place assigned to shame, with the implication that women are inherently more "narcissistic" (Freud, 1914), more prone to neurotic symptoms (Freud, 1905a), and more difficult to treat (Freud, 1933).

That these views are still held by respected classical analysts is a measure of the tenacity with which Freudian theory resists change. For example, Anthony (1981) still believes that "the course of analysis is likely to be more difficult and more complicated" in women. "Because of the prolonged preoedipal attachment to the mother ... and because of the woman's preference for passive behavior and passive aims, the treatment may appeal profoundly to her passive, dependent and submissive needs, and make her disinclined to give it up.... The powerful masochistic impulses ... make women more prone to interminable analyses.... The cycle of masculinity and femininity during the analysis ... and the cycles of drive, fantasy and dream that alternate during the course of the month in every woman . . . may loosen them up, leaving the analyst bewildered by the facile regressions to the preoedipal phase . . . the sudden abject moments of surrender, and most puzzling of all, . . . episodes of shamelessness during which habitual modesties are overwhelmed and vulgarizations, disturbing for the male analyst, may display themselves. Shame follows rapidly in the wake of such exhibitions" (p. 195).

The essential misunderstanding of shame that is apparent in this description of women's behavior is the implied hierarchy, in which shame is "preoedipal" while guilt is "oedipal." This hierarchy is based on the assumption that shame is more "primitive"—an assumption that is easy to make since shame feels "childish" and "irrational." But there is no evidence that shame precedes guilt in development. On the contrary, it seems likely that both shame and guilt "messages" are exchanged, beginning with the mother's response to her infant's crying, during the infant's earliest days. A theoretical system that is based on the primacy of the attachment emotions will include shame as an inevitable and appropriate response to threatened attachment.

SHAME AND THE ATTACHMENT EMOTIONS

The concept of an attachment system (Bowlby, 1969; Harlow & Mears, 1979) that is biologically grounded and necessary for species survival is based on new information. In this new framework, shame and guilt can be understood to function as the means by which we maintain our fundamental affectional ties.

Why, then, should shame be the response to loss of love? And what role does humiliated fury play? Somehow, in a way that has puzzled psychoanalysts beginning with Freud, losing an attachment figure evokes humiliated fury because it feels like a loss of self-esteem. Shame is the empathic experience of the other's rejection of the self. Vicarious emotional experience is the foundation of attachment (on both sides), and it is the price we pay for it. Shame is the state in which one "accepts" the loss of the other as if it were a loss in the self. Humiliated fury, which is the inevitable accompaniment of shame, angrily protests the loss at the same time that it demands restitution of the other's positive feeling. But being angry at and wanting the love of the same person is inherently disorganizing; it is a useful reaction only if the other person is actually stably affectionate. In that case, the guilt that comes with humiliated fury is a useful reminder of affectional ties. When the other person is always rejecting, or unable to be stably affectionate, humiliated fury is useless and will not effect the required change in feeling. Fury only leads back into shame, more humiliated fury, and chronic "irrational" guilt.

DIFFERENCES BETWEEN SHAME AND GUILT

My attention to the differences between shame and guilt developed out of a confluence of influences from my clinical practice as a psychoanalyst and my research into the cognitive style called "field dependence" (Witkin, Lewis, Hertzman, Machover, Meissner, & Wapner, 1954). In my clinical work, my attention was drawn to the few but disturbing cases for whom analysis at first seemed successful but then turned out to have failed. In each of these "returned" patients, the superego was even more vicious than it had been before analysis began. Analysis had only increased the patient's vocabulary of self-derogation. It gradually became apparent to me that these patients were suffering from unanalyzed shame in the transference, or more accurately, in the patient–therapist relationship. In some instances, the unanalyzed shame was concealed by intractable guilt.

In clinical accounts of psychoanalytic work with neurotic patients (Lewis, 1958, 1959), I used field dependence as a "tracer element" for following characteristic behavior and transference phenomena during the treatment. In particular, the patients' cognitive styles focused attention on the manner and extent of the relationship between the self and significant others. A field-dependent patient was described as readily merging herself with the surround. She was self-effacing; when she was self-conscious it was in an awkward and shy way. A field-independent patient, also a woman, was described as having an organized self which took the initiative in vigilantly defending her place in the field. Differences between field-dependent and field-independent patients were also traced in the organization of the self in their dreams.

From observations of an embarrassed four-year-old girl, a patient, who watched me vigilantly and continuously, I suggested (Lewis, 1963) that shame functions particularly as a protection against the loss of self boundaries that is implicit in absorbed sexual fantasy, that is, in states of longing for attachment figures. Shame brings into focal awareness both the self and the other, with the imagery that the other rejects the self. It thus helps to maintain the sense of separate identity. This notion about shame is similar to Lynd's (1958) description of how shame can spur the sense of identity. It also parallels Erikson's (1956) observation that shame is the opposite of autonomy, but with the emendation that it is the autonomy of the self that is at issue, not the autonomy of the ego.

Making a link between characteristics of the self and characteristic functioning of the superego was one step in a line of reasoning which supposed that the superego functioned differently in field-dependent and field-independent patients. A field-dependent mode would be shame; a field-independent mode, guilt. Both modes of functioning represent an equally developed superego. Both modes could be associated with an equally severe or malfunctioning superego. An empirical study was undertaken to test these hypotheses, and they were confirmed (Witkin, Lewis, & Weil, 1968). The 180 transcripts obtained in this study formed the source material for my description of the differences between shame and guilt.

Shame involves more self-consciousness and more self-imaging than guilt. The experience of shame is directly about the *self,* which is the focus of a negative evaluation. In guilt, the self is not the *direct* object of negative evaluation, but, rather, the *thing* done (or not done) is the focus of experience.

Shame is the self's vicarious experience of the other's negative evaluation. In order for shame to occur, there must be a relationship between the self and the other in which the self *cares* about the other's evaluation.

Shame has a special affinity for stirring autonomic reactions, including blushing, sweating, and increased heart rate. Shame usually involves greater body awareness than guilt, as well as visual and verbal imagining of the "me" from the "other's" point of view. The self is the focus of a variety of noxious stimuli that catch the self "at the quick" and can be experienced as paralyzing the self. This special position of the self as the target of attack makes shame a more acutely painful experience than guilt.

Shame and guilt are often fused and therefore confused. This is a result of their common origin as modes of repairing lost affectional bonds. The clearest example of their fusion occurs when both states are evoked by a moral transgression. The two states then tend to be perceived as fused under the heading of guilt.

Shame is about the self; it is therefore global. Guilt is more specific, being about events or things. Adults regard shame as an "irrational" reaction that is more appropriate to childhood, especially if it occurs outside the context of moral transgression.

The self-reproaches likely to be formed as guilty ideation develops might run as follows: How could I have *done that*? What an injurious *thing* to have done. How could I *hurt so-and-so*? What a moral lapse that *act* was. What will become of *that* or of *him/her* now that I have neglected *to do it,* or injured *him/her*? How should I be *punished* or *make amends*? Simultaneously, ashamed ideation says: How could *I* have done that? What an *idiot I am*—how humiliating. What a *fool,* what an *uncontrolled person*—how mortifying, how unlike so-and-so, who does not do such things. *How awful and worthless I am.* A current of aggression has been activated against the whole self, in both one's own and the "other's" eyes. This current of shame can keep both guilty ideation and shame affect active even after appropriate amends have been made.

The stimulus to shame is two-fold: moral and nonmoral shame. Shame may be evoked in connection with guilt, or it may be evoked by competitive defeat, sexual rebuff, social snub, invasion of personal privacy, or being ridiculed. Shame thus has a potential for a wide range of connections between transgressions and failures of the self. Shame for defeat or snub generalizes and also evokes guilt for transgression. Shame and guilt states are thus easily confused with one another by the experiencing person, although an observer may have a clearer view.

A wide variety of painful superego states exists, in which shame is merged with guilt in varying degrees. Feeling ridiculous, embarrassment, chagrin, mortification, humiliation, and dishonor are all variants of shame states, each with its own admixture of guilt and hostility. Embarrassment or chagrin, evoked without too much underlying guilt, can yield to good-humored laughter. When one has trouble righting oneself after feeling ridiculous or embarrassed, there is usually underlying guilt. Dishonor is the most serious shame state, since it carries the clear implication of personal guilt, signifying both a serious crime and a personal failure.

Adults regard shame as a primitive reaction, in which body functions have gone out of control. It is regarded as an irrational reaction for this reason as well. Except for ideation that is often identical with that of guilt, shame is a relatively wordless state. The experience of shame often occurs in the form of imagery, of looking or being looked at. Shame may also be played out in imagery of an internal colloquy, in which the whole self is condemned by the "other." There is, however, a relatively limited vocabulary of scorn. The wordlessness of shame, its imagery of looking, together with the concreteness of autonomic activity make shame a primitive, "irrational" reaction, for which a rational solution is found only with difficulty.

Shame-rage, which originates about the self, is discharged upon the self. Whether it is evoked in the context of moral transgression or outside it, shame involves a failure of the central attachment bond. This failure evokes rage, as does the painful experience of lost attachment because one is unable to live up to the standards of an admired image. It is the feeling state to which one is more susceptible when one has fallen in love. The "other" is a prominent and powerful force in the experience of shame.

In shame, hostility against the self is experienced in the passive mode. The self feels not in control but overwhelmed and paralyzed by the hostility directed against it, or wants to "sink through the floor," or "die" with shame. The self feels small, helpless, and childish. In cases of unrequited love, the self feels crushed by the rejection.

Thus, for shame to occur there must be an emotional relationship between the person and the "other" such that the person cares about a negative evaluation by the "other." In this affective tie, the self does not feel autonomous but dependent and vulnerable to rejection. A "righting" tendency is often evoked by shame in the form of "turning of the tables." Evoked hostility presses toward triumph over, or humiliation of the "other," i.e., to the vicarious experience of the other's shame. But the "other" is simultaneously beloved or admired, so that guilt is evoked for aggressive wishes.

A prediction that results from this phenomenological analysis is that there should be a particularly strong association between shame and self-directed hostility. This prediction was confirmed in our therapy study (Witkin et al., 1968), and in subsequent studies by Smith (1972) and Safer (1975).

Table 12.1 summarizes the distinctions between shame and guilt.

THE ROLE OF SHAME IN DEPRESSION

Empirical evidence for the importance of shame in depression has been building steadily in the last two decades. Izard's (1972; Izard & Schwartz, 1986) carefully developed instruments for studying the affective phenomenology of depression have continued to show that shame/shyness is an important component of the "emotion-profiles" of depressive experience. Other direct evidence for the role of shame in depression comes from a study by Smith (1972). Forty men and 30 women, all patients at a pastoral counseling center, were assessed for shame or guilt proneness by several reliable methods. As predicted, persons adjudged relatively shame-prone were more likely to be suffering from depression. This result held more strongly for women. In addition, as predicted, shame-prone patients showed more self-directed hostility. Hoblitzelle (1982) is in the process of evolving a self report measure for shame and guilt proneness. She has obtained results that show a significant correlation between her shame measures and depression.

Excellent indirect evidence for the role of shame in depression comes from studies using the reformulated "learned helplessness" theory (Abramson, Seligman, & Teasdale, 1978). Strong evidence has accumulated for a connection between depression and a tendency to attribute negative events to one's own failings. This tendency for the person to make *internal, stable, global* attributions for failure (ISG attributions) shows good connections to depression. A paradox has been shown, however, in the evidence for a connection between ISG attributions and depression: if depressed people are as helpless as they appear, logic dictates that they should not feel self reproaches for what they are unable to control (Abramson & Sackeim, 1977; Peterson, 1979; Rizley, 1978). This paradox vanishes if we assume that what depressed people are helpless to do is change the vicarious experience of the other's negative evaluation— in short, to get out of a state of shame.

There is other, indirect evidence for a connection between shame and

TABLE 12.1 Summary of the phenomenology of shame and guilt

	Shame	Guilt
Stimulus	Disappointment, defeat or moral transgression	Moral transgression
	Deficiency of *self*	*Event* or *thing* for which the self is responsible
	Involuntary: self *unable*, as in unrequited love	Voluntary: self *able*
	Encounter with the other *or* within the self	Within the self
Conscious content	Painful emotion	Affect may or may not be present
	Autonomic responses: rage, blushing, tears	Autonomic responses absent
	Global characteristics of *self*	Specific *activities* of self
	Identity thoughts	No identity thoughts
Position of self in the field	Self passive	Self active
	Self focal in awareness	Self absorbed in action or thought
	Self-imaging and consciousness; multiple functions of self	Self intact, functioning silently
	Vicarious experience of other's negative view of self	Pity, concern for injury to other
Nature and discharge of hostility	Humiliated fury	Righteous indignation
	Discharge blocked by guilt and/or love of other; self-directed	Discharge on self *and* other
	Discharge in good-humored and/or shared laughter	Discharge in *acts* of reparation
Characteristic symptoms	Depression; hysteria; "affect disorder"	Obsessional; paranoia, "thought disorder"
Variants:	Humiliation, mortification, embarrassment, chagrin, shyness	Responsibility, obligation, fault, blame

depression. Beck's (1967) study of depressed patients' dreams portrayed them as "recipients of rejection, disappointment and humiliation" (p. 217). Blatt (1974) distinguishes between anaclitic and introjective depression, a distinction that has some parallels to the distinction between shame and guilt (see B. Fibel Marcus, *this volume*).

An empirical study of guilt and conscience in the major depressive disorders suggests that negative self-esteem rather than guilt is basic to depressed patients of all types (Prosen, Clark, Harrow, & Fawcett, 1983). Shame is the affective-cognitive state of low self-esteem.

Finally, there is the fascinating indirect evidence on the role of shame in depression that comes from the pioneering studies of Brown (Brown, Harris, & Bifulco, 1986). Brown and associates have been studying the long-term effects of early loss of parent (before age 11) on the development of depression in women. They have also been studying the "vulnerability factors," such as lack of an intimate tie with husband, having three children below the age of 14, as well as the "provoking agents" that precipitate depression. "Provoking agents" are such events in life as severe loss or disappointment, encompassing not only personal loss but the loss of a role or even an idea.

SOME CLINICAL EXAMPLES OF THE NEGLECT OF SHAME

The Case of Dora

Perhaps the clearest way to illustrate the clinical implications of recognizing the role of shame in depression, especially in women, is to review a much studied case, the case of Dora (Freud, 1905c). The difficulty Freud experienced in treating his young depressed-hysterical woman patient, Dora, is a classic example of the neglect of shame, and a classic example, as well, of sexism in psychotherapy, which is still apparent today.

Even though Dora had experienced personal betrayal at the hands of the three people she loved most dearly—her father, Herr K., and Frau K.— both Freud and Dora missed her most powerful feeling: the shame of personal betrayal, that is, of lost trust or broken attachment. Even when they explicitly named her feeling "mortification" (a shame variant), neither Freud nor Dora permitted themselves to take it "seriously." Because they were both unable to deal with Dora's shame, except to deprecate the rage it evoked as "exaggerated," Dora unexpectedly left treatment in what Freud felt, quite accurately, was a burst of revenge. But Freud had no idea of what he had done to deserve it. And Dora must have come away from the experience with the feeling that she could not find vindication anywhere, while still being ashamed of wanting it. Twenty-five years later, when Deutsch (1957) was called into psychiatric consultation for her, Dora was still struggling with feelings of mortification.

Dora's actual situation at the time of her suicide note was this: her father was having an affair with Frau K. Because of this affair with his friend's wife, it was convenient for Dora's father to ignore Herr K.'s sexual advances toward his adolescent daughter. When Dora told her father about being molested by Herr K., her father said he did not believe her, although she knew quite well that he actually *did* believe her. His disbelief was dishonest, and thus represented a double personal betrayal. Frau K., whom Dora loved and for whose children she had often been a devoted "sitter," also disbelieved her. And Herr K., in whose affection for her she had once trusted, had become a sexual molester, not an indulgent father-figure. It is fascinating to realize the profound influence of the patriarchal system in which these events took place. Freud himself believed that the normal "female" response to Herr K.'s advances should have been pleasure, and that Dora's disgust was a measure of her unconscious guilt arising from her oedipal fantasies. That her inevitable response to personal betrayal would be shame-rage was simply not recognized by either Freud or Dora, although Dora was clearly in the grip of humiliated fury. Freud puts it this way: "When she was feeling embittered, she used to be overcome by the idea that she had been handed over to Herr K. as the price of his tolerating the relations between her father and his wife; and the rage at her father for making such use of her was visible behind her affection for him. At other times she was quite well aware that she had been guilty of exaggerating in talk like this. The two men had, of course, *never made a formal agreement in which she was the object of barter*; her father in particular would have been horrified at any suggestion" (p. 83, italics added). There was clearly no place in Freud's cognitive system for the shame-rage that broken attachment evokes. Dora was also all too ready to repair her attachment bond with her father by exculpating him and blaming herself, a state that generated her depression as well as her hysterical symptoms. Although Freud intuitively connected her symptoms to the molestation she had suffered, it was his neglect of shame in both the sexual abuse and the personal betrayal that made the analysis a failure.

A Young Woman Depressive

Some excerpts from the transcripts of dynamic psychotherapy sessions with a 21-year-old woman, a college senior, illustrate with great clarity the neglect of shame. The excerpts also illustrate that pejorative attitudes toward attachment and shame are still current in psychoanalytic psychotherapy nearly 100 years after Freud treated Dora.

The patient had applied to an urban outpatient clinic for treatment of her depression and for the alleviation of the facial tics she had been afflicted with since childhood. She is in treatment with an older man, a psychoanalyst by training. The first excerpt illustrates how acutely painful a shame reaction can be. Although the patient is describing acute shame in a metaphor of death, the therapist's response is not an empathic one; he counters by questioning her metaphor. The patient dutifully retreats to a literal meaning, but continues to express her shame in another metaphor ("crawl through a hole"). She also indicates quite clearly that her tics are increased when she is in a shame state, but the therapist does not pursue the connection. Throughout the lengthy transcript from which this excerpt is derived neither the patient (P) nor the therapist (T) actually labeled her state as shame.

> P. When I find somebody looking at me (at her tics) I could die.
> T. Could die?
> P. Well, not literally (slight laugh) that's when I sort of have the feeling that I could crawl through a hole. That's when I do these habits the most.

The second excerpt illustrates the way in which laughter tends to relieve shame. Once again, however, the therapist takes a questioning rather than an empathic stance toward the patient's laughter. Once again, the patient dutifully agrees that "it's not funny," but continues to describe how laughter relieves shame. The patient makes very clear as well how shame dissipates when she is reassured that an important affectional tie—to her boyfriend—is no longer in jeopardy. The therapist, however, interprets her shame about her tics as if it were irrational, "a way of keeping other people from knowing about it," rather than as a natural means to an end—the concealment of defects to maintain affectional bonds. The patient had been describing how her mother used to shame her about the tics. "I was told that I was very stupid, and, if I only knew how I looked, I wouldn't do it, you know (slight laugh). So I mean if my own mother told me that it looks horrible, I believed her (laugh). . . . "

> P: I was always very self-conscious with people around, and always imagining that I looked horrible. And as I said, I don't really know how I look. It's just, well you know—and it disturbs me a lot. And as I said I feel very—like when people kept looking at me (slight laugh).
> T: Feel like everybody's looking at you?
> P: Yeah. I feel like, you know, I'm such an oddity that everybody's looking. "What is that girl doing?—(laugh) you know."
> T: But you sort of smile and laugh as you say that—
> P: Well . . . (slight laugh) not that I think it's funny, but it's a curious, you

know, feeling that I have, I, I perhaps can laugh. I can laugh about it now, more than I could even last year. I mean up until last year I couldn't even talk about it, much less laugh about it. You know it was a very, very sensitive sore spot, and uh, the reason I can more or less laugh at it—if you want to call it that—it's not really funny, but I started talking about it with my boy-friend. . . . He was the first one I ever discussed it with; and it was so hard for me I couldn't even look him straight in the face. It was just really a horrible experience, but after I spoke about it, I felt much better and uh . . .

T: Do you think it made any difference to the twitches?

P: No, it didn't (slight laugh). It didn't disappear. It didn't subside or anything. The only difference it made was in how I felt about having them myself, and the fact that I didn't have to worry about my boyfriend. He knew about it and he didn't care.

T: It sounds as if you're not talking about it, it's just some kind of way of keep-ing other people from knowing about it.

The next excerpt illustrates the way in which the patient's depression is evoked in direct response to her mother's shaming of her boyfriend. She is describing her mother's disapproving reaction to the patient's engagement to be married. The sequence from humiliated fury into depression is discernible.

P: As a child . . . I—we—were very affectionate, we were very close. We were just about inseparable. But as I got older and I started dating . . . well, sud-denly so much dissension and disagreement and not getting along . . . She doesn't let me feel optimistic in any way . . . .She has no faith in me, and she has no faith in my boyfriend. And she doesn't know how I feel . . . about con-stantly ridiculing and criticizing him. Even if she feels that it's true and that she's justified, I don't feel she should do it. Because if I love him, I feel she should take it into consideration and try to give me more confidence in myself and him. She doesn't. No confidence. Constantly criticizing and doom doom doom . . . and I start to believe it because I hear it all the time. And then, if my boyfriend happens to go down in the dumps—oh boy, I go right with him. I mean I need him; he's my morale . . . he's gotta be there to tell me that things will be allright and that we will have money and that we will be happy. Because when I'm with my family—I might just lay down and die.

T: You take on your mother's opinion?

P: Yeah, I can't help it. I try to fight against—when I'm with them I'll fight down to the end, and yet when I leave I get so depressed, I'm so down in the dumps. . . . And I feel inside of me, a kind of sickness comes over me, and they always do this to me.

The next excerpt illustrates clearly the sequence from shame into humiliated fury and thence into guilt for unjust rage. The patient is describing her reaction to the therapist's failure to keep an appointment without notifying her.

> P: But just waiting for the bus—oh (laugh). You know I was really uh . . . upset (slight laugh) because I, I was very, I was upset at the time; I was on the verge of tears I was so upset because I had this test. I hate just wasting time. I generally am a great time-waster anyway, but, oh, I can blame no one but myself. But here I have no control over the situation. You know, I hate that feeling. I hate the feeling of being helpless, and not being able to do anything about. I guess everyone hates that feeling. But, uh . . . it just wore off you know—given a few days it generally wears off. . . . But the point is, . . . I knew that you couldn't be here, you know? I was just, just angry at the situation in general, that you weren't here and I had wasted the day. And things like this often happen and I, I just hate, I just hate the feeling of not being able to do anything. I, I don't know, it's a sort of like the whole world's against me (slight laugh), you know that feeling?
> T: The whole world instead of me?
> P: Yeah, you know, just things in general—just things like that, and there's no one really you can blame . . . rationally, you know and really feel right about blaming the person. . . . In fact, if I had blamed you, I would have felt downright guilty, because I feel I had no grounds. I would have no grounds to be angry at you because you couldn't help it. . . . But it still doesn't take away the feeling of the anger, or of, or of, I guess, the frustration.

The final excerpt illustrates the patient's natural tendency to "turn the tables" on the therapist and his neglect of this aspect of the shame-rage sequence. As we shall see, the consequence is an increase in the patient's symptoms. In this instance, shame in the patient–therapist relationship is probably compounded of the (mutual) assumption of the therapist's "superior wisdom" and the fact that he is an older man.

The patient has told the therapist about how easily her mother makes her feel guilty and how "silly" she knows it is for her to feel this way, but she can't help it. As an example, the patient had offered the therapist the prediction that her mother would make her feel guilty about having Thanksgiving dinner with her boyfriend, away from home. The therapist, responding in the spirit of minimizing the mother's power, had suggested that the patient was "worrying too much in advance." The patient's opening comments in the next session, although phrased as a trivial point, were to the effect that the therapist was "wrong." The patient was "right"; her mother did make her feel guilty. The therapist caught on that he was being disputed. The patient was signalling to him by her embarrassed laughter that she was making a trivial point—one that he would "hardly later remember." She was already ashamed (guilty) of her need to put him down, but this aspect of the shame-rage sequence went by him. He interpreted her need to show him wrong as a neurotic defense (of which he obviously disapproved). In the next moment, the patient was apparently having some tics. And she was terribly disconcerted by the therapist's calling them to her attention. She actually thought that he might be out to trick her, but for benign therapeutic reasons! She then lost her train of thought, and within moments was off on a depressed train of thought about her many failings: lapses of memory, inability to keep things organized, and excessive anxiety. These failings even include her inability to keep her appointments straight—the very lapse the therapist had made when he had failed to keep their appointment without notifying her. In other words, under the press of unanalyzed shame vis-à-vis the trusted male therapist, the patient experienced a temporary increase in her neurotic symptoms.

Later in the session we find the patient talking about her many failings.

> P: Another thing that you know I find—like when I happen to have a lot of things to do, not even in school, but just in general—well, I should say, not tests, but, you know, but making appointments to see people, and um, but to see more than one person, and doing little things that—unless I make a long list of things that I have to do, I'm constantly rehashing it in my mind. And I go crazy, I just—I get so nervous, and I do it over and over and over again, and I leave one out and then I have to go back and do it all over again. And I say there is supposed to be 10 and I can only count nine. You know, I really can't take it. I really get, uh, very upset when I have a lot of things to think about. I just can't handle it (pause). And that's what I have now. I'm very—that's what happens to me, all sorts of things pile up. And papers to do and tests and all sorts of things that I've stuck—and I'm always afraid that I'm gonna forget to do them. Even *forget to go to an appointment* (italics added).

The sequence from shame in the patient–therapist relationship, into humiliated fury, with its natural impulse to "turn the tables," thence into guilt for "unjustified anger" is thus apparent. The patient is now back down into her familiar state of low self-esteem. And neither the therapist nor the patient is aware that in what is a rational-sounding "primary process transformation," the *patient* is failing in the ability to keep appointments, not the therapist.

And so we are reminded of Freud's (1917) original, brilliant clinical observation that, in depression, the self-reproaches are unconsciously meant for "someone whom the patient loves or has loved or should love. Everytime one examines the facts this conjecture is confirmed" (p. 248).

REFERENCES

Abramson, L., & Sackeim, H. (1977). A paradox in depression: Uncontrollability and self blame. *Psychological Bulletin, 84,* 838–857.

Abramson, L., Seligman, M., & Teasdale, J. (1978). Learned helplessness in humans: Critique and reformulation. *Journal of Abnormal Psychology, 87,* 49–74.

Anthony, E. (1981). Shame, guilt and the feminine self in psychoanalysis. In S. Tuttman, C. Kay, & M. Zimmerman (Eds.), *Object and self: A developmental approach.* New York: International Universities Press.

Beck, A. (1967). *Depression: Clinical, experimental and theoretical aspects.* New York: Harper and Row.

Binder, J. (1970). *The relative proneness to shame of guilt as a dimension of character style.* Dissertation Abstracts International.

Blatt, S. (1974). Levels of object representation in anaclitic and introjective depression. *Psychoanalytic Study of the Child, 29,* 107–157.

Bowlby, J. (1969, 1973, 1980). *Attachment and loss, Vols. 1, 2, and 3.* New York: Basic Books.

Broucek, J. (1983). Shame and its relationship to early narcissistic development. *International Journal of Psychoanalysis, 65,* 369–378.

Brown, G., Harris, T., & Bifulco, A. (1986). Long-term effects of early loss of parent. In M., Rutter, C., Izard, & P., Read (Eds.), *Depression in young people.* New York: Guilford.

Cytryn, L., McKnew, D., Zahn-Waxler, C., & Gershon, E. (1986). Developmental issues in risk research: The offspring of affectively ill parents. In M. Rutter, C. Izard, & P. Read (Eds.), *Depression in young people.* New York: Guilford.

Darwin, C. (1872). *The expression of the emotions in man and animals.* London: Murray.

Deutsch, F. (1957). A footnote to Freud's "Fragment of an analysis of a case of hysteria." *Psychoanalytic Quarterly, 26,* 159–167.

Erikson, E. (1956). Identity and the life-cycle. *Journal of the American Psychoanalytic Association, 4,* 56–121.

Freud, S. (1900). The interpretation of dreams. *Standard Edition, Vol. 4.* London: Hogarth Press.

Freud, S. (1905a). Three essays on the theory of sexuality. *Standard Edition, Vol. 7.* London: Hogarth Press.

Freud, S. (1905c, 1953). Fragment of an analysis of a case of hysteria. *Standard Edition, Vol. 7.* London: Hogarth Press.

Freud, S. (1913). Totem and taboo. *Standard Edition, Vol. 13.* London: Hogarth Press.

Freud, S. (1914). On narcissism. An introduction. *Standard Edition, Vol. 14.* London: Hogarth Press.

Freud, S. (1923). The ego and the id. *Standard Edition, Vol. 19.* London: Hogarth Press.

Freud, S. (1925). Some psychological consequences of the anatomical distinction between the sexes. *Standard Edition, Vol. 19.* London: Hogarth Press.

Freud, S. (1933). New introductory lectures on psychoanalysis. *Standard Edition,* *Vol. 22.* London: Hogarth Press.

Gottschalk, L., & Gleser, G. (1969). *The measurement of psychological states through the content analysis of verbal behavior.* Berkeley, CA: University of California Press.

Harlow, H., & Mears, C. (1979). *The human model: Primate perspectives.* New York: Wiley.

Hoblitzelle, W. (1982). *Developing a measure of shame and guilt.* Unpublished predissertation, Yale University.

Izard, C. (1972). *Patterns of emotions: A new analysis of anxiety and depression.* New York: Academic Press.

Izard, C., & Schwartz, G. (1986). Patterns of emotion in depression. In M. Rutter, C. Izard, & P. Read, (Eds.), *Depression in young people.* New York: Guilford.

Lamont, J. (1973). Depressed mood and power over other people's feelings. *Journal of Clinical Psychology, 29,* 319–321.

Lewis, H. (1958). Overdifferentiation and underindividuation of the self. *Psychoanalysis and the Psychoanalytic Review, 45,* 3–24.

Lewis, H. (1959). Organization of the self as reflected in manifest dreams. *Psychoanalysis and the Psychoanalytic Review, 46,* 21–35.

Lewis, H. (1963). A case of watching as a defense against an oral incorporation fantasy. *Psychoanalytic Review, 50,* 68–80.

Lewis, H. (1971). *Shame and guilt in neurosis.* New York: International University Press.

Lewis, H. (1976). *Psychic war in men and women.* New York: New York University Press.

Lewis, H. (1983). *Freud and modern psychology, Vol. 2. The emotional basis of human behavior.* New York: Plenum.

Lewis, H. (1984). Freud and modern psychology: The social basis of humanity. *Psychoanalytic Review, 71,* 7–26.

Lewis, H. (1986). The role of shame in depression. In M. Rutter, C. Izard, & P. Read (Eds.), *Depression in young people.* New York: Guilford Press.

Lewis H., & Franklin, M. (1944). An experimental study of the role of the ego in work: II. The significance of task orientation in work. *Journal of Experimental Psychology, 34,* 195–215.

Lynd, H. (1958). *On shame and the search for identity.* New York: Harcourt Brace.

Mahl, G. (1985). Freud, father and mother: Quantitative aspects. *Psychoanalytic Psychology, 2,* 99–115.

Miller, S. (1985). *The shame experience.* Hillsdale, NJ: Analytic Press.

Morrison, A. (1983). Shame, the ideal self and narcissism. *Contemporary Psychoanalysis, 19,* 295–318.

Morrison, N. (1985). Shame in the treatment of schizophrenia. The reheal considerations with clinical illustrations. *Yale Journal of Biology and Medicine, 58,* 289–297.

Peterson, C. (1979). Uncontrollability and self blame in depression: Investigations of the paradox in a college population. *Journal of Abnormal Psychology, 88,* 620–624.

Prosen, M., Clark, D., Harrow, M., & Fawcett, J. (1983). Guilt and conscience in major depressive disorders. *American Journal of Psychiatry, 140,* 839–844.

Rizley, R. (1978). Depression and distortion in the attribution of causality. *Journal of Abnormal Psychology, 87,* 32–48.

Safer, J. (1975). *The effects of sex and psychological differentiation response to a stressful group situation.* Unpublished doctoral dissertation, The New School for Social Research.

Smith, R. (1972). *The relative proneness to shame and guilt as an indicator of defensive style.* Unpublished dissertation, Northwestern University.

Witkin, H., Lewis, H., Hertzman, M., Machover, K., Meissner, P., & Wapner, S. (1954). *Personality through perception.* New York: Harper.

Witkin, H., Lewis, H., & Weil, E. (1968). Affective reactions and patient-therapist interactions among more or less differentiated patients early in therapy. *Journal of Nervous and Mental Disease, 146,* 193–208.

Würmser, L. (1981). *The mask of shame.* Baltimore: Johns Hopkins University Press.

■ 13
Female Depression: Self-Sacrifice and Self-Betrayal in Relationships

HARRIET GOLDHOR LERNER, Ph.D.

Depression is one form of emotional reactivity associated with loss. In this chapter, I shall address female depression as it relates to a particular aspect of loss that occurs as women betray or sacrifice the self in order to preserve relationship harmony. In attempting to navigate the delicate balance between the "I" and the "we," women frequently sacrifice the "I" in the service of "togetherness," thus assuming a de-selfed position in relationships. Depression may result from the sacrifice of self and the concomitant loss of self-esteem, which accompanies the unconscious awareness of self-betrayal.

Excessive self-sacrifice or de-selfing occurs when too much of the self (one's beliefs, convictions, wants, priorities, ambitions) becomes negotiable under relationship pressures. The de-selfing process begins in the first family and is continued most conspicuously in women's relationships with men. In previous work, I have illustrated the complex pressures on women to assume such a position in adult heterosexual relationships and the powerful intrapsychic, familial, and cultural forces that mitigate against change (Lerner, 1983, 1985).

The following case fragment depicts how female depression is inextricably interwoven with the sacrifice of self that occurs in key relationships and the related fear of object loss. The conceptual links among depression, anger, and women's "relationship-orientation" will also be clarified.

CASE EXAMPLE

Ms. R., a 35-year-old homemaker with ten-year-old twin girls and a four-year-old son, sought psychotherapy for depression and marital unhappiness. She had deliberately selected a therapist with a feminist orientation, and she arrived at her first session complaining of her husband's chauvinist attitudes and outrageous deeds. Her own part in the marital drama was a common one for women; she complained about her husband and blamed him for her unhappiness, but nonetheless accommodated to his demands and remained profoundly resistant to examining and modifying her own position in the relationship.

Ms. R.'s symptomatic depression was associated with her experience of being caught in a very narrow space in which she could not move. The circumstances of her marriage were so intolerable to her that she could no longer continue in the old ways; yet, she would not even consider the possibility that she wanted out. She was not ready to face the risk of putting her husband and herself to the test of whether change was possible and she had already convinced herself that the relationship could not tolerate much change. She was unable to say to herself "I am choosing to stay in this unhappy marriage," nor could she clarify her bottom line and say, "If these things do not change, I will leave."

Ms. R.'s depression placed her in the role of the "sick one" and obscured marital issues, yet it also served as an indictment of the system in which she was operating, drawing attention to its unworkable nature. Paradoxically, her depression served both to protect and protest the status quo, forcing change while holding the clock still. For example, the severity of her symptom undermined her competence to manage her home and children, and thus allowed her to go on strike against her "sacred calling," which she was unable to protest more directly. Her husband, who had formerly avoided all family responsibility, now put the children to bed at night and occasionally made their breakfast in the morning because otherwise these tasks would not get done. He did so, however, to fill in for his dysfunctional wife, and not because Ms. R. had openly challenged the old rules of the relationship by clarifying her own needs and redefining what she would and would not do.

For many women, depression serves to bind anger and obscure its sources so that they may deny marital difficulties entirely and maintain a singleminded focus on the question, "What's wrong with me?" In Ms. R.'s case, however, her depression did not block her from experiencing and expressing rage at her spouse. Yet, she protected both of them from the threat of serious dialogue by venting her anger in a manner that would invite him to ignore her or write her off as "irrational," "hysterical," or "sick."

For example, Ms. R. was furious with her husband for his condescending and patronizing treatment of her. When she finally addressed this issue with him, she "lost control" of herself and began yelling hysterically, thus confirming that she was, indeed, the weak and irrational child he needed her to be. Her husband listened coolly to her outburst and then sympathetically asked her whether she had taken her medication that day. Therapeutic exploration revealed that Ms. R. was afraid to state her position in a way that would ensure that she could not so easily be written off. She preferred to be in the one-down position, rather than to put her husband on the spot by identifying her dissatisfaction in a firm, calm, and articulate manner and insisting on real dialogue. She was unconsciously convinced that her husband could tolerate only an accommodating child-wife, and she was correct. When, later in treatment, Ms. R. began to function at a higher level of self-assertion and maturity, her husband distanced, had an affair, and threatened to dissolve the marriage.

For Ms. R., as for many women, remaining "the sick one" or "the depressed one" was easier than clarifying the sources of her dissatisfaction and moving out of a de-selfed position. This is not because she gained masochistic gratification from being in a victimized or abused position, but because she was unconsciously convinced her most important relationship could only survive if she continued to maintain the status quo. To become clearer, to act stronger, to be more separate, assertive, and self-directed were all equated with a castrating, destructive act that would diminish and threaten her partner who might then retaliate or leave. This unconscious belief is common, if not universal, for women (Lerner, 1980, 1983, 1985).

Although she had not consciously articulated her dilemma for herself, Ms. R. was convinced that she had to choose between having a marriage and having a self. Rather than encourage her in a particular direction, therapeutic work on the marital relationship involved systemic questioning, which helped Ms. R. to identify the systems maintaining function of her depressed stance and the positive, protective function that it served for both herself and her husband. The actual and fantasized risks of moving out of a de-selfed position were explored as carefully as the costs of maintaining sameness.

During the early phase of therapeutic work it was crucial that I appreciated the fact that making waves in her marriage was not an option for Ms. R. as she equated aloneness with psychological and even physical death. This high level of anxiety had its roots in her difficulty in achieving separateness and autonomy from her first family, as well as in problems evoked and maintained by the institution of marriage. Ms. R. had spent years cloistered in the home and had no marketable skills, few support systems, and little confidence that she could provide for herself and her children in the case of divorce. The loss of her husband threatened her not only with a loss of identity but also with the actual loss of economic security and social status. Although she possessed considerable internal strengths and resources, they were obscured from her experience, in part, by entrenched dysfunctional marital patterns in which she occupied an underfunctioning position. Only after Ms. R. was confident that she could survive without her marriage was she able to move differently within it.

SELF-SACRIFICE IN THE FAMILY OF ORIGIN

To help Ms. R. more clearly define herself in her marriage and give voice to previously denied aspects of self, considerable therapeutic time was spent exploring her depression and patterns of self-sacrifice within the context of her first family. In previous work (Lerner, 1979, 1980), I have suggested that a woman's de-selfed position in adult relationships is associated with an earlier de-selfing with mother; that is, daughters frequently thwart their own autonomy and growth, and sacrifice valued aspects of the self (e.g., ambition, sexuality, creativity, and zest) in order to protect a special bond with mother who is unconsciously perceived as unable to tolerate the daughter's moves toward separateness and success. I have also stressed that such difficulties (which leave the woman vulnerable not only to depression but also to other symptoms and dysfunctional behaviors) are not an inherent or "natural" aspect of the mother–daughter relationship, but, rather, reflect larger systems issues including the structuring of gender roles over many generations and women's subordinate status (Lerner, 1978, in press).

From my current perspective, however, this narrow theoretical and clinical focus on mothers (even when the role of culture is acknowledged) is problematic. On the one hand, the mother–daughter dyad is often the most intense and conflictual in the family. At the same time, this relationship cannot be isolated or understood apart from other family relationships or from multigenerational patterns that give shape and form to the family. While many psychotherapists appreciate this systemic view in theory, they are often at a loss to put it into practice, especially when the client's own focus on her mother is intense and other family members are presented as shadowy or unimportant. In my clinical experience, the use of the genogram and a multigenerational perspective helps clinicians put mothers and daughters back in context and mitigates against the tendency to overfocus on this dyad at the expense of exploring other interlocking family relationships. It is from this perspective that I shall discuss historical facts and family patterns that were linked to Ms. R.'s self-sacrificing behaviors in her own family and ultimately to her de-selfed and depressed position in her marriage.

MS. R.'S FAMILY OF ORIGIN

Below is a partial genogram of Ms. R's family of origin that I collected during our initial meetings (Figure 13.1). The limited amount of family information included here highlights key relationships, dates, and patterns associated with Ms. R.'s depression. Readers unfamiliar with the construction of a genogram see McGoldrick (McGoldrick & Gerson, 1985).[1]

As the family diagram illustrates, Ms. R.'s entrance into the family system was colored by loss. At the time of her birth, her mother (Mary) was still under the emotional sway of a second-trimester miscarriage that occurred 15 months earlier. Father's mother (Katherine) died from a protracted illness only weeks before Ms. R. was born, and mother's father (Andrew) was killed in a car accident shortly after her first birthday. These three significant losses—a miscarriage and the deaths of two grandparents occurring around the time of Ms. R.'s birth and first year of life—influenced family relationships and intensified key family triangles linked to Ms. R.'s vulnerability to depression.

Ms. R.'s father, John, managed the powerful affects generated by his mother's death, coinciding in time with the arrival of his firstborn child, by distancing from both his wife and new daughter. In addition to intensifying work-related pursuits, he became increasingly preoccupied with the well-being of his widowed father, Joe, and his relationship with his oldest sister, Lois, became increasingly conflictual as they argued about issues surrounding their mother's death and their father's financial situation. The growing marital distance compounded mother's sense of loss, and she became increasingly focused on, and protective of, her new daughter. As the family diagram illustrates, the firstborn daughter in mother's own sibling group (Rosemary) had died an untimely death, which undoubtedly further increased Mary's anxious preoccupation with her firstborn child.

Evidence of mother's intense focus on Ms. R. was more than apparent. For example, until the birth of her brother Alan, she was frequently brought to sleep in her parents' bed when she fussed during the night. Mary's explanation for this practice was that Ms. R. was a fearful baby and

---

[1]Squares stand for males and circles for females. The horizontal line connecting a square and circle indicate a marriage. Children are drawn on vertical lines coming down from the marriage line, in chronological order, beginning with the oldest on the left. An X inside a circle or square indicates the person has died.

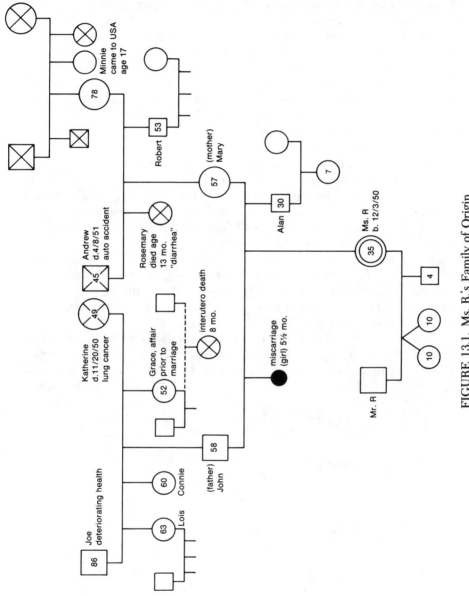

FIGURE 13.1. Ms. R's Family of Origin

child who "refused" to sleep alone when she was upset. John also participated in this arrangement perhaps because the intensity in the mother–daughter dyad helped him maintain emotional distance from both females. John's withdrawal and Mary's intense focus on Ms. R. did not lessen over time. Once Ms. R. asked her mother if she had ever considered working or having a career when she was younger. Mary replied, "I would first be dead before I would leave my children with some stranger. Also your father could never deal with you and Alan, so I had to be two parents in one."

This key triangle, consisting of distant father, a distant marital relationship, and overintensity between mother and daughter (Figure 13.2), became increasingly entrenched over time.

The arrows in Figure 13.2 illustrate the circularity of family relationships, i.e., it is no more correct to suggest that mother "caused" Ms. R.'s difficulties or father's outside position in the family, than it is to say that father "caused" mother's overinvolvement with Ms. R. by creating an emotional vacuum in his relationships with both daughter and wife. Each side of the triangle is both the cause and the effect of the other two sides, and no family member, mother included, has unidirectional power over the whole. The ability to fully appreciate the circular connectedness of family relationships helps the therapist avoid questions and interpretations that hold one family member implicitly responsible for another's symptoms and behaviors (Lerner & Lerner, 1983).

After her marriage, Ms. R. participated in a similar triangle with her husband in the outside position. She frequently complained to her mother about her husband's domineering and unfair behavior in a manner that in-

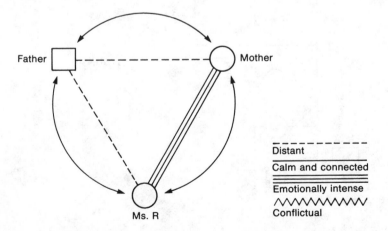

FIGURE 13.2. Circularity of Family Relationships.

vited mother to be her ally at the expense of both her marriage and mother's relationship to her son-in-law. When marital tensions mounted between Ms. R. and her husband, she sometimes "disappeared" with her children to her parents' home. Mother went along with these disappearing acts (although there was no threat of violence), blaming Mr. R. for her daughter's difficulties and feigning ignorance when he telephoned looking for his wife and children. At these times, father managed his own anxiety through extreme emotional distancing. He did not ask his daughter why she and her children were temporarily camping out in their home, nor did he clarify with either his wife or daughter his position regarding Ms. R.'s behavior and whether he was comfortable keeping such a big secret from his son-in-law. During these times, Ms. R. and mother would have intense conversations about Ms. R.'s unhappy marriage; father would read in the next room acting as if nothing was happening, solidifying his odd-man-out position in the family.

While Ms. R. was not consciously sacrificing her own self to protect relationship ties in her family of origin, she nonetheless participated in patterns and triangles that thwarted her own growth and left her depressed. Her position in her family, as in her marriage, was an accommodating one in which she unconsciously went along with family roles and rules at the expense of differentiating a self. Much emotional energy went into "being for" mother and protecting father from dealing with emotional issues in his relationships with wife and daughter. Like many daughters, Ms. R. had a radarlike sensitivity to underground issues in the family and unconsciously felt that significant changes on her part would threaten family stability and shatter the security of predictable family ties, including her parents' marriage and her fused relationship with mother. She was also unconsciously aware both of her parents' vulnerability to depression and of the important losses they each had suffered around the time of her entrance into the family.

In my clinical experience, therapeutic work derived form Bowen Family Systems Theory (Bowen, 1978) is especially useful in helping women to identify and move out of dysfunctional family patterns that contribute to de-selfing and depression in adulthood. One aspect of this work is gathering family facts, which allows the woman to put her current struggles and relationship patterns into a broader multigenerational perspective.[2] What follows is a brief picture of patterns in the previous generations that bear on the key triangle diagrammed in Figure 13.2, and on Ms. R.'s related dif-

---

[2]For those unfamiliar with the systemic theory that underlies the clinical use of the genogram, see Kerr (1981) and McGoldrick and Gerson (1985).

ficulty in assuming a more separate and differentiated position in both her first and second families (Figure 13.3).

Ms. R.'s mother, Mary, had an overly intense and enmeshed relationship with her own mother, Minnie. Mary criticized Minnie constantly to other family members, yet accommodated to her demands and behaved as if she was single-handedly responsible for her mother's well-being. Mary's long-standing sense of responsibility for her mother was intensified following her father Andrew's death, at which point mother alternated between distancing from her mother on the one hand, and trying to "fix" her loneliness and depression on the other. When Ms. R. was born, Minnie had just become a widow and mother hoped her new daughter, the first grandchild, would cheer Minnie up and give her a purpose for living, which contributed further to Ms. R's role as an overfocused-upon child.

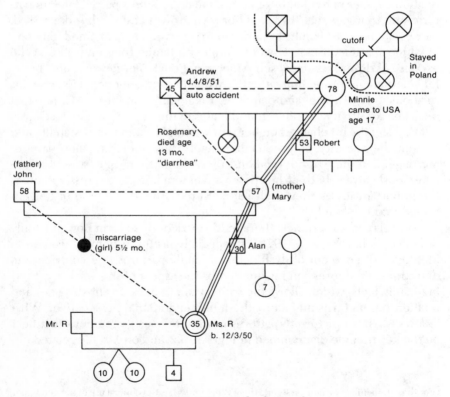

FIGURE 13.3. Mother's Family.

Grandmother Minnie had experienced a traumatic migration from Poland at age 17. After being sent to America with her older brother, her parents and two younger siblings were unable to leave the country as had been planned. Minnie had been in love with a Polish farmer whom her parents had forbidden her to see and who died in a motorcycle accident the day following Minnie's one-year anniversary in America. Minnie told her children that she married Andrew "for convenience, not love," and she confided in Mary that she had never gotten over the Polish farmer whom she had known for all of a month. Undoubtedly, Minnie's inability to emotionally let go of this young Polish man was connected to the devastating loss of her parents, two siblings, and her homeland. At the time of Minnie's marriage to Andrew, she burned a box containing all of her family photographs from Poland, stating that they were too painful to look at and "there was no point in dwelling on the past." At the same time she kept in her possession a gift from the Polish farmer. Not surprisingly, Minnie's marriage to Andrew was both distant and mutually dissatisfying.

The severe geographical and emotional cutoff that Minnie experienced from important members of her family of origin emotionally overloaded her relationships with her children. The fact that Minnie had lost her firstborn daughter at 13 months further heightened both the anxiety and the fusion in Minnie's relationship with Mary. Minnie overprotected Mary as if she might disappear at any moment; Mary had slept with Minnie for much of her young life, each worrying about the well-being of the other. As an adult woman, Mary still remained her mother's child, maintaining the fusion between them by failing to openly define differences or address significant relationship issues. For example, Mary did not attend church regularly but lied to her mother about this and other facts, claiming that Minnie would be "too upset" by the truth.

Over time, Ms. R. explored the ways in which her relationship with her mother was similar to her mother's relationship to Minnie, and she obtained a clearer, more factual picture of the broader context that shaped family relationships over several generations. In so doing, she became increasingly observant of her own part in repeating a multigenerational triangle in which mothers and daughters were especially intense and mutually protective at the expense of father–daughter relatedness, marital satisfaction, the pursuit of personal goals, and the clarification of self.

Ms. R.'s father, John, was the third child and only boy in a sibling group of four. He was mother's "special son" whom she both overprotected and turned to as her "best friend" in the family. Father's pattern was also one of overintensity with mother and a complementary distance from father (Figure 13.4).

John's special position with his mother, Katherine, emotionally charged

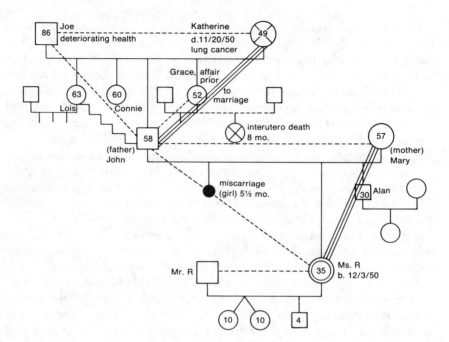

FIGURE 13.4. Father's Family.

his relationships with his three sisters. Lois, the firstborn, was particularly vocal about John being "spoiled" and privileged, while she had excessive family and domestic responsibilities. Because John was also looked to by mother as her "advisor," Lois received the burdens but not the benefits of her firstborn status. When Ms. R. began therapy, her father and Lois were involved in a heated struggle about managing their aging father's care. In the children's growing up years, Lois was the closest to father and often assumed the role of justifying or trying to explain his behavior to other family members.

Father's parents, Katherine and Joe, managed intensity in their relationship through marital distancing and child-focused triangles in which John played a key role. Katherine's role in her marriage was an accommodating one; she failed to voice her own needs or complaints, and she did not articulate her own life goals or plans. Marital dissatisfaction and anger was bound by her intensifying her relationship with her son John and turning to him as a special ally and confidante.

This pattern, beginning early in John's life, continued into his adulthood. For example, Grace, John's youngest sister, became pregnant out of wedlock the first year she moved from the family home to a distant city. She made plans to give the child up for adoption, but aborted a month short of full term. Mother warned Grace against sharing this information with other family members including father, who did not even know of the pregnancy. Mother then confided the whole story to John but forbade him to talk about it. John, on his part, failed to take a stand with his mother that he would not be able to keep such a big secret, and more than three decades later he had never discussed it. This example was one of many illustrating the entrenched and toxic triangle in which John had an overly intense tie with one family member (in this case, mother) at the expense of other crucial family relationships. Now in his second family, married to Mary, he had flipped positions from "insider" to "outsider," replicating the position of his own father; the basic triangle, however, remained intact.

FAMILY OF ORIGIN WORK

Over the course of therapy, Ms. R. began to view her unsatisfactory marriage in the context of the broader family picture. The legacy of the previous generations included unsatisfying marriages managed by fathers/husbands through distancing and by mothers/wives through child-focus. Ms. R. entered the family at a time of loss for both her parents, which further intensified this triangle; when Ms. R. entered therapy she was solidly entrenched in the role of mother's emotional ally while collaborating with father's distant odd-man-out position; the triangle stabilized her parents' marriage but thwarted the growth of all involved.

Rather than working to challenge the status quo in her own marriage, Ms. R. complained to her mother and therapist in a manner that replicated the old triangle and only served to hold the clock still. The invisible threads that bound mother and daughter together were tightened as the two women consolidated their closeness around their disappointment in men and their exclusion of them. The men in turn participated actively in creating and maintaining their part in this drama, which had deep roots in their own family of origin as well as the prescriptions of culture. Ms. R.'s symptomatic depression similarly kept her bound to mother, who focused her "worry energy" more on her daughter's depression than on her own problems. Because Ms. R.'s depression kept her stuck in all arenas, it also served as an oath of fidelity to her mother that Ms. R. would never really grow up and leave home.

Ms. R. was able to think clearly about her own situation and perceive new options for her own behavior after she obtained a picture of the multigenerational system and understood the current interactional context in which her symptomatic depression occured. At the same time, the seemingly simple task of obtaining family facts inevitably forced a shift in entrenched patterns. For example, Ms. R. learned about her Aunt Grace's pregnancy and loss as well as other family "secrets" by questioning her father and his siblings about their family history. In so doing, she herself moved against the long legacy of father–daughter distance and began, for the first time, to address emotionally important issues with John. This experience allowed her to observe firsthand the extremely high level of anxiety and resistance that was evoked in all family members, herself included, by this change; it also challenged her fused position to mother since the overintensity in this relationship was inextricably interwoven with a complementary disengagement from her father.

Over the course of therapy, Ms. R. slowly continued to change her own part in the entrenched family triangle; for example, she stopped engaging her mother in intense marathons about her depression and miserable marriage in which both women implicitly or explicitly agreed that Ms. R.'s husband was to blame and that Ms. R.'s father should not be told. Instead, Ms. R. connected with each of her parents separately, and, in a calm factual way, shared something of her perspective on her marital difficulties and her own contribution to them. She stopped telling her mother "secrets" that were not for father's ears, and she slowly challenged the legacy of secret-keeping in the extended family. When her marriage heated up, she still sought temporary distance from her husband, but she no longer took her three children to her parents' home or otherwise invited them to join with her in an alliance against their father.

As Ms. R. made these and other changes, previous unconscious material emerged full force. As she worked toward establishing more of an emotional connection with both father and husband, a profound sense of guilt and disloyalty towards mother emerged. Ms. R.'s fears that her moves toward greater separateness and differentiation would injure her mother were reinforced by strong "Change back!" reactions from both parents as well as by Ms. R.'s own separation anxiety and resistance to change that she projected onto mother, which further increased Mary's fragility in Ms. R.'s eyes. In addition, Ms. R.'s changed behavior destabilized the family and predictably had profound reverberations throughout the system. First, marital issues between her parents surfaced full force as Ms. R. moved out of the old triangle. Ms. R.'s father confessed to his wife that he had been having a homosexual affair for several years, and the couple began a marital therapy process that continued on after Ms. R.'s psychotherapy terminated. Mother was confronted with emotional issues in the relationship with her own mother, Minnie, as Ms. R. began to interact with both mother and grandmother in a more differentiated fashion. Father had a similar challenge of renegotiating relationships with members on his family tree as his daughter began to challenge a long legacy of cut-offs and secret-keeping. For example, shifts in father's hostile, blaming relationship with Lois and in his distant relationship with his younger sister Grace (with whom he had never discussed her traumatic pregnancy and loss) occurred over time as Ms. R. worked to establish a person-to-person relationship with each of her aunts that was relatively free from the intense emotional field of father's reactivity to both. Certainly, Ms. R. could not have successfully initiated or sustained the significant changes she made in her family of origin until after she had spent considerable time in therapy gathering family facts, understanding multigenerational patterns and triangles, and gaining a calm and more objective perspective on the part she played in them.

As a result of the work Ms. R. did in her own family of origin, she was able to consolidate a clearer, more separate sense of self, and her depression lifted. She adopted a more thoughtful, responsible, and less reactive stance to her marital problems, and she was able to better observe marital interactions free from the screen of old family scripts (e.g., her need to be "for mother" at the expense of other relationships). Yet, as Ms. R.'s clarity and objectivity about marital issues sharpened, her resistance to moving out of the role of the accommodating and de-selfed spouse also mounted. I wish to briefly focus on one underpinning of resistance that is frequently overlooked or minimized in therapeutic work derived from a psychodynamic or family systems model. I refer here to the far-reaching implications of women's economic dependence on men.

IMPACT OF ECONOMIC DEPENDENCE

Ms. R.'s lack of economic independence was a crucial factor underlying her unconscious dread of clarifying a bottom line position with her husband. ("These are the things that must change in order for me to continue in this relationship." "These are the things that I will no longer do.") As noted earlier, Ms. R. dared not make waves in her marriage until she was confident that she could survive without it, if need be. Even after she had worked through internal barriers to change, a factor in Ms. R.'s stuck position in her marriage was the devasting statistics on the poverty and plight of divorced women with dependent children. I believe this factor is universally so for unemployed homemakers or those locked into low-paying jobs. While women tend not to articulate this dilemma to themselves or others ("Doing what I need to do for myself may eventually lead to the dissolution of my marriage, which will plunge me into a condition of poverty and insurmountable stress"), they may be blocked from moving forward until it is identified and addressed in the therapeutic process.

In Ms. R.'s case, I kept the issue out on the table by continually questioning the implications of either changing or maintaining her current economic situation. These questions were raised in the context of Ms. R.'s own complaints that she seeemed unable to do the very things in her marriage that she eventually recognized as necessary for her to move beyond her depression and accompanying feelings of anger and bitterness. For example, one obvious source of Ms. R.'s depression stemmed from her overfunctioning and overresponsible position on the domestic scene. Over the course of therapy she became aware that this situation would change not from her symptomatic position and tearful arguments with her husband, but rather from her own resolve to stop overfunctioning in this arena. However, when she planned even a small specific change in this direction (e.g., telling her husband that she would no longer make his lunches or do his laundry because she was tired and needed to take better care of herself), she would not stay on course. In response to Mr. R.'s predictable anxiety and countermoves, Ms. R. would reinstate the status quo and lapse back into depression and bitterness. At such times I would engage in careful systemic questioning designed to clarify exactly how Ms. R. saw the consequences of such changes on this relationship system. Through such questioning, Ms. R. came to recognize that her worst fear was that continued changes on her part might cost her her marriage.

I did not shy away from asking specific questions about how Ms. R. would take care of herself if she ended up without a husband and exactly what short- and long-term plans she would make for herself. I was clear that I was not predicting divorce but rather taking her own anxieties seriously, particularly in light of current divorce statistics and the facts available about the poverty conditions of divorced mothers with dependent children. The more I specifically questioned her in this area, the more clearly it emerged that Ms. R. simply did not think in terms of planning personal life and career goals for herself. The product of generations of sex-role socialization, Ms. R. had been raised to believe that she would marry and be taken care of, and that all her needs would be met through her husband and children. Instead, she found that she was taking care of everybody else and no one was taking care of her—except for the minimal secondary gains that her symptomatic depression evoked. Yet she could not begin to take care of herself when she feared that changes on her part might destabilize a marital arrangement that was for her not only a crucial emotional relationship but a matter of survival.

I believe that a woman cannot save an unhappy marriage until she can save her own self. I also believe that nothing is more important for women than having a life plan that neither requires nor excludes marriage or life-long partnership. This statement reflects more than my conviction that both men and women without long-term personal and work goals are especially vulnerable to depression and other symptoms and dysfunctional behaviors. More to the point, the issue is that of economic survival. Statistics suggest that, if current trends continue, single women with dependent children as well as older women will constitute almost all of our nation's poor by the turn of the century. While it is not a psychotherapist's job to encourage women to seek employment, in my experience careful and systematic questioning (which includes questioning about the legacy of work and career in the previous generations of women) will lead patients to eventually think through their own position on this issue, based neither on a need to conform to or to rebel from cultural pressures and the wishes and expectations of others (Lerner, in press).

In Ms. R.'s case, she chose not to formulate career plans during the course of her work with me. She did, however, more clearly articulate her fear that she was one husband away from a welfare check, and she explored the impact on her marriage of her economic dependence and her choice of having all her eggs in the basket of one role. As her self-esteem and belief in her own resources mounted, she became more confident that she could find a way to survive on her own if need be, and she no longer needed to maintain her marriage at whatever cost to herself. Thus, she was able to relinquish her role of blaming her husband while accommodating to him, and to assert herself on a number of "hot issues" in their relationship, including her overresponsible position on the domestic scene. While her changed behaviors did precipitate a marital crisis, which included the threat of divorce from her husband who started a brief affair, their marriage eventually weathered the high stress of change and was ultimately strengthened. A year following Ms. R.'s termination from treatment, she wrote me that her family had relocated because of her husband's job promotion. She was entering a master's program in counseling psychology, and, although she was struggling, she was far from clinically depressed.

DEPRESSION AND ANGER

In both the popular (Rubin, 1970) and classical psychoanalytic literature (Abraham, 1927; Freud, 1956), depression has been linked to the avoidance of the awareness and expression of anger. Depression has been conceptualized as "anger turned inward" or "anger turned against the self," as if repressed aggression is the actual source of depression and depression, in turn, can be lifted by the mere venting of one's anger or rage at the appropriate object. More recently the old anger-in/anger-out theory, which states that "letting it all hang out" offers protection for the psychological hazards of keeping it all pent-up, has been challenged by both empirical data and clinical experience (Lerner, 1985; Tavris, 1982; Weissman & Klerman, 1984).

Obviously, the ability to voice anger and protest on one's own behalf is essential for maintaining one's dignity and self-regard and is a crucial vehicle for both personal and social change. Before the second wave of feminism, depressed women like Ms. R. felt personally to blame for their own unhappiness and presented in our consulting rooms with a single-minded focus on their personal neurosis or, alternately, they blamed their mothers. In contrast, contemporary women recognize that "the personal is political," and they have begun to challenge and change the roles and rules that have falsely defined, constricted, and misnamed women's lives. Short of this process of consciousness-raising and social/political change (in which the awareness of anger plays a crucial role), depression is nothing less than a universal aspect of the female condition. Bernardez (1978) was the first to explore the powerful internal and cultural prohibitions against female anger and the psychological consequences of such injunctions, of which depression is one.

While depression may serve as an indirect form of protest, it may also bind anger and obscure its sources. In Ms. R.'s case, her symptomatic depression forced change in the marital relationship (e.g., Mr. R. began to do housework and childcare to fill in for his underfunctioning wife), but it also protected Ms. R. from clearly articulating her grievances and openly challenging the status quo. Ms. R.'s position as the "sick one" or the "depressed patient" in the family further lowered her self-esteem and sense of competence, making it even less likely that she would have a sense of legitimacy about voicing her complaints and taking a new and different action on her own behalf.

At the same time, venting anger does not offer women protection against depression. Ms. R., for example, was not helped by the fact that she blamed her husband for her unhappiness and solidified her bond with her mother by complaining about him. Depressed women frequently participate in endless cycles of fighting, complaining, and blaming that go nowhere and only reinforce the woman's feelings of helplessness, powerlessness, and low self-regard.

Feelings of depression, low self-esteem, self-betrayal, and even self-hatred are inevitable when women fight but continue to submit to unfair circumstances, when they complain but participate in relationships that betray their own beliefs, values, and personal goals, or when they find themselves fulfilling society's stereotype of the bitchy, nagging, bitter, or destructive woman.

In Ms. R.'s case, as in most, her depression was not mitigated by voicing her anger at significant others, e.g., her husband, for his sense of entitlement and patronizing attitudes, her mother for her possessiveness and overinvolvement, her father for his distance and emotional nonavailability. Rather, her anger was a piece of a larger process in which Ms. R. became a better observer of larger relationship patterns and became more aware of the necessity for her to change her part in them. For example, Ms. R.'s repetitive angry complaints in therapy regarding her father's emotional absence did little to help her depression. What was significant was her ultimate ability to slowly connect with him over time despite the high level of resistance evoked from within and without. Such a change on Ms. R.'s part was possible only after she had spent considerable time in psychotherapy, gathering information about family facts, patterns, and triangles, which allowed her to put father's distancing in a broader systemic framework in which no one individual was viewed as the cause of family problems.

In sum, depression is not "anger turned inwards," although the denial of anger and lack of awareness of its sources can reinforce depression and mitigate against effective action. Clinical depression and chronic anger and bitterness occur together, signaling (among other things) the necessity for change in a relationship system that is unconsciously viewed as lacking the flexibility to tolerate that change. While anger is other-directed ("If it weren't for him . . . ") and depression is self-directed ("What's wrong with me . . . "), both forms of emotional reactivity become less intense when the woman is able to identify and change her part in the relationship patterns and triangles that keep her stuck and when she is able to become more expert on the needs, wants, and priorities of the self.

If feelings of depression or anger ultimately move the woman in the direction of positive change, they have served a crucial purpose. Repetitive expressions of emotional intensity, however, have little inherent therapeutic value and often block the patient's ability to think about her dilemma rather than simply react to it. Therapists who work to uncover angry feelings in depressed patients (as a therapeutic end in itself) or operate primarily as sympathetic listeners to their patient's grievances about other family members may replicate a dysfunctional triangle in which therapist–patient closeness operates at the expense of the patient's relationship with that other family member who is viewed as bad, sick, or the one to blame (Lerner & Lerner, 1983).

DEPRESSION AND WOMEN'S RELATIONSHIP ORIENTATION

Feminist writers suggest that women differ from men in their stronger need to affiliate with and care for others (Gilligan, 1983; Miller, 1976). The notion that emotional ties are more central to a woman's sense of self than they are to her male counterpart has been evoked to explain research findings indicating women's greater vulnerability to depression—a vulnerability that cuts through both economic class and all phases of the life cycle (Scarf, 1980). Although feminist theorists view women's affiliative stance as a strength rather than a weakness, their work has nonetheless been interpreted to suggest that a primary commitment to relationships is an emotional health hazard and a key factor in female depression. Some experts (Scarf, 1980) suggest that women have a biologically based "people-orientation" that predispose them to depression when relationships fail, whereas other authors have invoked nurture rather than nature in concluding the same (Braverman, 1986).

While there is clearly a link between female depression and women's position in relationships, such a generalization is imprecise and misleading. The valuing of marriage, family, intimacy, and attachment is a mental health asset, not a liability; a strong relationship orientation will hardly predispose an individual to depression even when that relationship ends. In fact, research unequivocally demonstrates that women do far better without men than men do without women, despite women's financial disadvantages (Bernard, 1973). As every insurance company knows, men without wives are the single most vulnerable group to an alarming range of emotional and physical disorders. Men need women as much or more as women need men, although male dependence needs are more likely to be hidden (Lerner, 1983). Contrary to popular mythology, the male sex is far more vulnerable to dysfunction when alone.

In sum, it is not women's "affiliative needs" or "relationship-orientation" that predisposes females to depression, for emotional connectedness is a basic human need as well as a strength. Rather, it is what *happens* to women in relationships that deserves our attention. Here the structuring of gender roles and the profound impact of women's subordinate and devalued status have far-reaching implications for a woman's vulnerable position in her family of origin and in marriage (Carmen, Russo, Miller, 1981; Lerner, 1985). In countless ways, women learn that their own ambition, achievement, and self-enhancement will hurt and threaten others rather than strengthen and consolidate their most important ties. Self-sacrifice and self-betrayal are culturally prescribed for women, and have strong roots in previous generations. The ways in which women have suffered from the traditional structure of marriage and motherhood have been well documented by scholars from numerous disciplines (Bernard, 1973; Carmen, Russo, Miller, 1981; Rich 1976) and need not be elaborated here. While women's higher incidence of depression has many sources, the primary valuing of relationships (when relatedness does not occur at the expense of the self) is part of the solution, not the problem.

POSTSCRIPT: "THE PERSONAL IS POLITICAL"

As a psychologist and psychotherapist, my primary focus in working with depressed women is on intrapsychic factors that are inextricably interwoven with dysfunctional family patterns. It is important to recognize, however, that individual and family dysfunction are inseparable from the dysfunction of patriarchal culture (Carmen, Russo, Miller, 1981; Lerner, 1978). Ms. R.'s position in her family of origin is a case in point. The all-too-familiar dance—repetitively reenacted by the distant husband/father, the child-focused wife/mother, and the symptomatic daughter who is too loyal to grow up herself—is prescribed and perpetuated by the patriarchal societal system just as this particular type of family organization reinforces and perpetuates that same societal dysfunction. As long as men are the makers and shapers of culture in the world outside the home, as long as women are not free to define the terms of their own lives, as long as society continues to convey the message that mother *is* the child's environment, then the basic dysfunctional triad of distant father, emotionally intense, overinvolved mother with a child with little room to grow up, is a natural outgrowth and microcosm of the culture (Lerner, in press).

Family structure and societal structure form a circular, self-perpetuating, downward spiraling cycle (Lerner, 1978). The more women are blocked from proceeding with their own growth and excluded from positions of power and authority outside the home, the more they become excessively child-focused and the more likely they are to thwart the differentiation of their children. As emotional intensity and intimacy increasingly reside within the mother–child dyad, the distance and emotional isolation of the husband/father becomes more entrenched. In turn, children growing up within this context develop a dread of the "destructive" powers of women and, in a defensive attempt to further confine and constrict women's spheres of activity and control in their own adult lives, move toward patriarchal solutions of their own. For men, these solutions include participating in cultural adaptations that restrict women's avenues of growth and opportunity as well as devaluing and disowning "feminine" aspects of self. For women they include tacitly supporting restrictive and oppressive cultural arrangements and their "willingness" to de-self themselves by avoiding and suppressing areas of activity and competence that threaten men. The "solution," of course, only perpetuates the problem and contributes, among other things, to the high incidence of female depression.

How does one disrupt such cycles and where does one intervene to effect change? With Ms. R. much of my work was focused on the rigid patterns and structures that inhibited her growth in her family of origin and her marriage. In my clinical experience, individual work derived from a family systems model is particularly effective in fostering the differentiation of self and altering psychic structures and distorted internalized object representations that have origins in early family experience. Yet individual and family dysfunction cannot be understood without thoroughly examining the meanings and implications of patriarchal systems that give shape and form to the family and to the very process of differentiation of self. While therapists need not be social activists to effect change, the failure to attend to the consequences of patriarchal structure on individual and family functioning can only result in partial and inaccurate theories of female depression.

REFERENCES

Abraham, K. (1927). *Notes on the psychoanalytic investigation and treatment of manic-depressive insanity and allied conditions. Selected papers.* London: Hogarth Press.

Bernard, J. (1973) *The future of marriage.* New York: Bantam Books.

Bernardez, T. (1978). Women and anger: Conflicts with aggression in contemporary women. *Journal of the American Medical Women's Association 33,* 215–219.

Bowen, M. (1978). *Family therapy in clinical practice.* New York: Jason Aronson.

Braverman, L. (1986). The depressed woman in context: A feminist family therapist's analysis. In M. Ault-Riche (Ed.), *Women and Family Therapy* (pp. 90–99). Rockville, MD: Aspen Publications.

Carmen, E., Russo, N.F., Miller, J.B. (1981). Inequality and women's mental health. *American Journal of Psychiatry, 138*(10), 1319–1330. Also in P.P. Rieker & E. Carmen (Eds.), *The gender gap in psychotherapy: Social realities and psychological processes* (pp. 125–138). New York: Plenum.

Freud, S. (1956). Mourning and melancholia. In E. Jones (Ed.), *Collected papers (Vol. 4).* London: Hogarth Press.

Gilligan, C. (1983). *In a different voice.* Boston: Harvard University Press.

Kerr, M. (1981). Family systems theory and therapy. In A. Gurman and D. Knistern (Eds.), *Handbook of Family Therapy* (pp. 226–364). New York: Brunner/Mazel.

Lerner, H.G. (1978). On the comfort of patriarchal solutions: Some reflections on Brown's paper. *Journal of Personality and Social Systems, 1*(3), 47–50.

Lerner, H.G. (1979). Effects of the nursing mother–infant dyad on the family. *American Journal of Orthopsychiatry, 49*(2), 339–348.

Lerner, H.G. (1980). Internal prohibitions against female anger. *The American Journal of Psychoanalysis, 40*(2), 137–148.

Lerner, H.G. (1983). Female dependency in context: Some theoretical and technical considerations. *American Journal of Orthopsychiatry, 53*(4), 697–705. Also in P.P. Rieker & E. Carmen (Eds.), (1984). *The gender gap in psychotherapy: Social realities and psychological processes* (pp. 125–138). New York: Plenum.

Lerner, H.G. (1985). *The dance of anger: A woman's guide to changing the patterns of intimate relationships.* New York: Harper & Row.

Lerner, H.G. (in press). Work and success inhibitions in women. *Bulletin of the Menninger Clinic.*

Lerner, S., & Lerner, H.G. (1983). A systemic approach to resistance: Theoretical and technical considerations. *American Journal of Psychotherapy, XXXVII*(3), 387–399.

McGoldrick, M., & Gerson, R. (1985). *Genograms in family assessment.* New York: Norton & Company.

Miller, J.B. (1976). *Toward a new psychology of women.* Boston: Beacon Press.

Rich, A. (1976). *Of woman born.* New York: Norton & Company.

Rubin, T. (1970). *The angry book.* New York: Collier.

Scarf, M. (1980). *Unfinished business.* New York: Doubleday.

Tavris, C. (1982). *Anger: The misunderstood emotion.* New York: Simon & Schuster.

Weissman, M., & Klerman, G. (1984). Sex differences and the epidemiology of depression. In P.P. Rieker & E. Carmen (Eds.), *The gender gap in psychotherapy: Social realities and psychological processes* (pp. 160–195). New York: Plenum.

■ 14
Socialization of Women: A View From Literature

MARILYN MAXWELL, M.A.

Recent empirical research correlating depression with socialization factors associated with the feminine stereotype (dependency, passivity, submissiveness) suggest that depression may, in fact, be a political malady (Levitt, Lubin, & Brooks, 1983; Wetzel, 1984). The hypothesis that depression may be a symptomatic response to an unequal distribution of power that affects those who are most vulnerable—the oppressed members of society—provides the literary critic with a new interpretive lens through which to "re-view" most, but not all, fictional women. While there are a variety of possible critical approaches to any one work of fiction, the following discussion employs a realistic approach and uses psychological concepts to illuminate the description of depressed women in literature.

By viewing three works of fiction as metaphoric case studies, I have focused upon the degree to which a female character's oppression within various social institutions contributes to her depression. For, as Showalter (1981) has pointed out, since both mental illness and femininity are culturally defined, their relationship must be analyzed within the social framework. Two 19th century novels—Jane Austen's *Mansfield Park* and Charlotte Bronte's *Villette*—and one modern play—Eugene O'Neill's *Long Day's Journey Into Night*—each portray a woman who manifests, in varying degrees, the symptoms of depression: fear, crying, anxiety, pessimism, anger, guilt, withdrawal, impoverished speech, negativity, fragmented self-image, recurrent thoughts of death and suicide, and fatigue (Wetzel, 1984; DSM III, 1980). The analyses of these three protagonists reveal that despite their different historical contexts, socioeonomic levels, and ages, these women face the same fundamental conflict inherent in being female in a patriarchal environment. For each woman lives in a society that marshals institutions which strive to socialize women into conforming to the feminine stereotype of dependency, submissiveness, passivity, and silence.

It is within such oppressive institutional contexts as government, education, religion, finance, and the family that the fictional women portrayed derive their sense of subordinate self and lack of significant place in the power structure. While all of the women discussed in this chapter share the same affliction—depression—they display different strategies to cope with their oppressors. Mary Tyrone's depressive anger and her awareness of her subjugation (*Long Day's Journey into Night*) lead to her self-destructive drug addiction as an act of covert rebellion against her subordinate role in the Irish Catholic family. Unlike Mary Tyrone, Fanny Price (*Mansfield Park*) and Lucy Snowe (*Villette*) seek to assimilate themselves into the existing power structure in exchange for economic survival and financial security. Through an unconscious identification with the aggressor, both women conform to the feminine stereotype of dependency upon a male for self-definition, a strategy which, by requiring one to repress the human desire for self-autonomy, proves inimical to psychological well-being.

"CREEPMOUSE": FANNY PRICE

Jane Austen's *Mansfield Park* provides the opportunity to view a depressed woman as she unfolds within the confines of a 19th century upper middle class family. "Orphaned" by her own family and sent to live with more affluent relatives so as to improve her social status, nine-year-old Fanny Price arrives at the Bertram home feeling very much alone and uncertain. While living with Sir Bertram, his wife, their four children, and their Aunt Norris, Fanny, for much of the novel, receives the "kindness" accorded to an outsider who straddles the line between a step-child and a servant. Her gradual assimilation into the Bertram family (and English society) culminates in her marriage to Edmund, the oldest son.

As a Cinderella figure hovering on the periphery of the Bertram family circle, Fanny, not surprisingly, exhibits many symptoms of depression. Much of her behavior throughout the novel is punctuated by episodes of unhappiness, fear, shame, despondency, self-abnegation, tears, and self-blame:

> afraid of everybody, ashamed of herself . . . she could scarcely speak . . . without crying. (p. 50)

Fanny was . . . forlorn, finding something to fear in every person and place. (p. 51)

What right had she to be of importance to her family? . . . She only was to blame. (pp. 375–376)

The depth of her psychological impoverishment is best summarized in her image of herself as "foolish and awkward," an image which leads her to state, "I can never be important to anyone" (p. 61).

It is very tempting to attribute Fanny's depression solely to her child-hood experience of dislocation and her perceived "abandonment" by her family. Yet, a closer look at the Bertram family as it embodies the sexist attitudes of Victorian society will reveal that much of Fanny's depression results from her being (1) reduced to a commodity in the marriage market (as one critic notes, "men and not women in Victorian society had the right of choice of a mate," Tanner, in Austen, 1966, p. 45), (2) required to relinquish any bid for psychological independence in exchange for financial security as an emotionally dependent spouse, and (3) socialized into conforming to male-imposed roles of inferiority in the family and social hierarchy.

The very first page of *Mansfield Park* introduces the theme of women's enforced dependency upon men to obtain, through marriage, an economically secure place in society. For, of the Ward sisters, Maria had the good fortune to marry well by "captivating" Sir Thomas Bertram, thereby being raised to a Baronet's Lady (p. 41). Fanny's mother, however, married a Marine "without connections" (p. 41), a fact that accounts for Fanny's being wrenched away from her family and sent to the more prestigious Bertram home. That is to say, Fanny must suffer her psychologically traumatic separation from her own family because she, as the female off-spring of a relatively "poor" marriage, will herself someday be dependent upon a husband to raise her social status. The Bertram social environment will improve her chances of meeting wealthy suitors.

The dehumanizing reduction of women to pieces of male-owned property contributes to the low self-image and self-alienation underlying female depression. In *Mansfield Park*, the capitalist view of marriage as an economic alliance in which women are reduced to marketable commodities is endorsed by Sir Bertram when he "advises" Fanny to accept the marriage proposal of the affluent Sir Henry Crawford. Such advice, we are told, is the "advice of absolute power" (p. 285), for it is spoken by the unquestioning "master of Mansfield Park" (p. 365). Already committed in her heart to Edmund and distrustful of Crawford, Fanny disobeys Sir Bertram, but pays a heavy emotional price: "Her heart was almost broke by [the] picture of what she appeared to him" (p. 319). For Sir Bertram accuses Fanny of failing to consider the financial advantages of such a marriage *for her family,* of putting her own feelings ahead of her family's economic well-being, of being "willful, perverse and too independent," "disgusting," and "offensive" (p. 318). Fanny's depression and its accompanying shame and guilt result from her having internalized the negative image of herself as presented by the patriarchal other, of seeing herself as deceptive, and as failing to conform to what he feels she should be: submissive and *self*-less. Dependent upon Sir Bertram's acceptance of her and devoid of an autonomous, independent sense of self, Fanny fears for her future: "she had lost his good opinion. What was to become of her?" (p. 319).

Because she is a woman, Fanny, like Mary Tyrone in *Long Day's Journey Into Night,* has been socialized to sacrifice her "self" for the benefit of others. The depression that results when Fanny fails to live up to the "feminine ideal" is the price of disobedience. Her defiance of Sir Bertram, however, should not be interpreted as a bid for psychological autonomy, for in her heart she has already abdicated her "self" to Edmund, and is only too anxious to subjugate herself to his will, desires, and needs.

Though perhaps more subtle than his father in the wielding of power, Edmund Bertram, nonetheless, embodies the same sexist assumptions of Victorian society. Like his father, he will be the voice of authority not only from his future position as titular head of the family but also from the Anglican pulpit once he is ordained. As a representative of a patriarchial religion that "entombs women in sepulchers of silence" (Daly, 1973, p. 151), Edmund, like Paul Emmanuel in *Villette,* believes that "girls" should not be too talkative, never loud, sharp, or coarse.

Edmund perpetuates his father's double standard that encourages boys to act, recite, and speak well, but frowns upon girls doing the same (p. 152). It is Fanny who, throughout the novel, strives to conform to this stereotype by silencing her own voice and reducing herself to an echo and mirror image of Edmund. By the end of the novel, Fanny has succumbed to a "dependence upon (Edmund's) words" (p. 445). Having internalized the sexist assumptions of her society and repressed her own individuality, Fanny is only too willing to allow Edmund to "form her mind" (p. 95) so that she can think like him:

> [Fanny's] heart beat for [Edmund] . . . and felt what his sensations must be. (p. 163)
> [Fanny's] glad to like whatever was liked by [Edmund]. (p. 221)

Such self-*effacing* behavior leads to a dissolution of Fanny's individuality as she even begins to take on Edmund's *facial* expressions. Willing to negate her own identity in order to become a Bertram, Fanny conforms to the feminine ideal by sacrificing her *self* for Edmund.

Fanny's acceptance into the patriarchal family is achieved, therefore, through her gradual abdication to male power, to Edmund's will, that is, through denying her own autonomy and psychological integrity. Such denial, however, exacts a heavy psychological price, and it is not surprising to find Fanny "feeling herself becoming too nearly nothing" (p. 189) and feeling "sad and insignificant" (p. 180). Fanny is plagued by a pervasive sense of her own nothingness and insignificance—clear symptoms of depression. In an episode of the novel that is perhaps emblematic of her present status as well as her future role as Mrs. Edmund Bertram, Fanny is asked to play the part of the Cottager's wife in a theatrical performance arranged by the Bertram children and the Crawfords:

> "It is nothing of a part, a mere nothing, not above a half-dozen speeches altogether, and it will not much signify if nobody hears a word you say, so you may be as creepmouse as you like, but we must have you to look at." (p. 168)

As Edmund's future wife, Fanny will undoubtedly be content to remain silent, ornamental, and self-effacing; she will continue to "creepmouse" around in the shadow of his existence and to negate her human desire to be a psychologically independent, substantial self. In exchange for the economic security that such a marriage will afford her, Fanny will continue to be haunted by that pervasive sense of nothingness, by the depression that accompanies dependency and the annihilation of *self*.

THE SELF-SWINDLER: LUCY SNOWE

If Fanny Price's all too eager acceptance of her subordinate place in the Bertram hierarchy arouses in the modern reader feelings of impatience or disappointment, Lucy Snowe's "solution" to her precarious position as a female living on the periphery of the male-defined institutions of religion and education leaves us with a sense of terror and pity. Like *Mansfield Park*, Charlotte Bronte's *Villette* depicts the plight of a young Victorian woman who, deprived of her own family, exists, throughout much of the novel, as the "outsider," as one defined in terms of who she is *not* and what she does *not* possess. Lucy's struggle to survive within the misogynistic setting of a Catholic girl's school in Brussels not only leads to her severe depression, but also to her apparent subsequent affirmation of the very forces that oppress her.

Prior to her arrival at Madam Beck's school in Brussels, Lucy undergoes two significant experiences that lay the foundation for her negative self-image and her feelings of inadequacy and alienation. During her brief stay with her godmother, Mrs. Bretton, and her godmother's son, Graham, Lucy retreats into passivity, solitude, and relative silence, a demeanor that, indicative of depression, contrasts with the behavior of the young girl Polly, who is also living with the Brettons. For amidst Polly's activity and passionate attachment to Graham, Lucy remains "calm," unobtrusive, and awkwardly unsure of herself, that is, outside the center of emotional activity. Furthermore, it is during her stay at the Brettons that Lucy begins to experience herself as a "lack" by internalizing the negative perceptions of the male power figure. Overhearing Graham tell his mother that "Polly amuses [me] a great deal more than Lucy Snowe" (p. 85), Lucy comes to view herself as deficient, as devoid of the male-prescribed attributes necessary to win approval. As a *non*-Bretton and a relatively *un*amusing female, Lucy begins to construct her negative self-image out of negative cognitions, reinforcing her own susceptibility to depression.

Lucy's next role as caretaker for the invalid Mrs. Marchmont solidifies her negative self-image, for she is encouraged to identify with her female patient's passivity, weakness, frailty, and withdrawal, characteristics that are not only symptoms of depression but also components of the female stereotype. Lucy, like Fanny, is indeed being socialized into depression. Furthermore, with no independent sense of selfhood to fall back upon, Lucy eagerly redefines herself according to Mrs. Marchmont's perceptions, viewing herself as Mrs. Marchmont does—as a "worn-out creature, faded and hollow-eyed" (p. 96). Content to derive her sense of self from a restrictive environment fraught with disease and decay— a "crippled old woman" living in "two rooms" (p. 97), Lucy, like Fanny, shrinks to an almost parasitic dependence upon an oppressive figure:

> Her service was my duty—her pain, my suffering . . . her anger my punishment. I forgot that there were fields, woods, rivers, seas . . . outside this sick chamber. All within me became narrowed to my lot. (p. 97)

Willing to "narrow" and stifle herself in exchange for financial security and emotional connection, Lucy begins to exhibit a propensity typical of women who have been socialized into a dependence upon others for their definition of self—namely, a tendency to resign and assimilate themselves to their oppressive surroundings. "I would have crawled on with her for twenty years," Lucy horrifyingly admits (p. 97). This strategy of identifying with the oppressive Other and of internalizing the Other's negative perceptions triggers Lucy's severe depressive episodes in her next "home" at Madame Beck's school.

Hired by Madam Beck first as a lady's maid and then as a teacher, Lucy again must confront the loneliness and alienation of the "outsider," of one who is defined in terms of what she is not. As a *non*-Catholic who does *not* speak French, Lucy immediately experiences herself as not belonging, of being out of place in a French, Catholic school. During her stay at the school, Lucy continues to exhibit her propensity to internalize others' negative reflections. Ginerva, a young student, cruelly describes Lucy in terms of what she lacks:

> I suppose you are nobody's daughter . . . you have no attractive accomplishments. As to admirers, you hardly know what they are . . . you sit dumb when other teachers quote their conquests. I believe you were never in love and never will be. (p. 215)

Lucy's rather pathetic but predictable response, "A good deal of what you say is true" (p. 216), reveals the depth of her psychological impoverishment and lends credibility to one critic's assessment of *Villette* as providing the "most moving and terrifying account of female deprivation ever written" (Gilbert & Gubar, 1979, pp. 399–400).

It is within the confines of Madam Beck's school, a sociopolitical microcosm of Victorian society, that Lucy's depressive symptoms manifest themselves most clearly. She falls prey to feelings of negativity, pessimism, withdrawal, insignificance (p. 208), and a profound sense of despair:

> The negation of pure suffering was the nearest approach to happiness I expected to know. (p. 140)
> A sorrowful indifference to existence often pressed on me—a despairing resignation to reach betimes the end of all things earthly. (p. 228)

Unquestionably the profile of a depressed personality, these symptoms reflect Lucy's childhood experiences of alienation and deprivation. As seen in *Mansfield Park*, to be a female alone in the world, "abandoned" by family and friends, is to be susceptible to dependency and to depression. However, just as Fanny Price's oppression within the patriarchal family significantly contributes to her depression, so similarly is Lucy Snowe's exploited status in the educational hierarchy the catalyst for her overt, depressive episodes.

Madam Beck's school reflects the patriarchal assumptions of Christian society and perpetuates the female stereotype of dependency, passivity, withdrawal, fearful submission, and resignation, thereby contributing to the process of socializing women into depression. Required to live in confining, "oppressive" nuns' cells (p. 130), Lucy and the female students are constantly being reminded of the penalty awaiting women who break the rules imposed upon them by male power-holders. For haunting the atmosphere of the school is the legend of the nun who, failing to abide by her sacred vows, was buried alive (p. 172). Furthermore, despite the fact that the school is run by a woman, Madam Beck proves to be a "man in woman's clothing," whose violation and exploitation of Lucy contribute to the latter's low self-esteem and depression. Perceived by Lucy as displaying a masculine demeanor (p. 141), Madam Beck not only violates Lucy's privacy by eavesdropping, spying, and rummaging through her personal belongings, but also exploits Lucy by forcing her to become a teacher and paying her *half* the salary of her *male* predecessor (p. 144)!

The violation and exploitation of Lucy by masculine power-holders leave her frighteningly aware of her own vulnerability in a patriarchal environment. For Lucy, however, the consciousness of her own vulnerability and the anxiety and depression it triggers are apprehended and reflectively expressed in a thinly disguised, sexually violent image: "like a tiger crouched in a jungle, [t]he breathing beast of prey was in my ears always . . . I knew he waited for sundown to bound ravenous from his ambush" (p. 122).

As a metaphor for the ubiquitous male predator stalking his female prey, the "ravenous tiger" thematically anticipates the character of Paul Emmanuel, the "tiger-Jesuit" (p. 574), who sadistically exploits Lucy to further his own egotistic ends. Paul, the "tyrannical" teacher and "lay Jesuit" (p. 457), accosts Lucy and forces her, at the last minute, to assume a role in his play, substituting for a student who has become ill. "Play you must" he orders Lucy and then proceeds to lock her in the attic, among the cockroaches and mice, and "forgets to feed her," so she will learn her lines. Like the tiger ready to "bound ravenous from his ambush," Paul is seen by Lucy as the "violent and implacable" force of the oppressor whose "irritable nature glowed in his cheeks" (p. 202).

In *Villette*, Paul Emmanuel wields his power to thwart Lucy's intellectual development, that is, to silence her. Consistent with his misogynistic view, Paul tells Lucy that a "woman of intellect is a sort of *lusus naturae*," that is, a "luckless accident" who does not "fit in creation, wanted neither as wife, nor worker" (p. 443). In other words, Lucy's demonstrated success in the classroom and her very human desire to learn render her a superfluous and aberrant creature in the eyes of a patriarchal religion. In order to bar her from the exclusively male domain of intellectual achievement and to keep her in her subordinate place, Paul, as Lucy's tutor, displays paternal compassion when she fails and patriarchal wrath when she succeeds academically (pp. 439–440). Aware that he wants her to fail (p. 446), Lucy alludes again to an intuitive apprehension of imminent violence: "I was vaguely threatened with, I know not what doom, if I ever trespassed the limits proper to my sex" or "conceived an appetite for unfeminine knowledge" (p. 440).

The "doom" awaiting intelligent women who struggle to realize their intellectual potential is often ridicule, ostracism, frustration, and, of course, depression. Judged as being unfeminine by the male power structure, the intellectual woman, according to the 19th century male medical establishment, risked "atrophying the uterus through too much mental exercise" (Ehrenreich & English, 1973). It is not surprising, then, that Lucy's combative, tutorial encounters with Paul leave her feeling unfulfilled, inadequate, depressed, and convinced that "learning is not happiness" (p. 440). Yet it is to Paul Emmanuel that Lucy eventually commits herself in what appears to be an overt act of abdication to emotional tyranny and an endorsement of the very forces that oppress her.

When viewed in terms of the construct of depression, Lucy's choice of Paul Emmanuel reflects her previously established pattern/strategy of succumbing to an oppressive power-figure in order to construct a sense of self. She began her psychological journey as an *un*amusing, *non*Bretton and moved on to become a reflection of the *un*healthy Mrs. Marchmont. Initially perceiving herself as Ginerva defined her—the creation of lack— Lucy does seem to emerge at the end of the novel with a glimmer of a positive self-image in her role as a teacher. Placed by Paul at the head of her own school, Lucy manages to disinter herself from the "sepulchre of silence" of the nuns' cell and to experience professional success. That her first taste of happiness as something more than the "negation of suffering" should occur during Paul's three-year absence from Brussels is significant. For, in effect, his absence reflects the removal of the emblem of oppression in Lucy's struggle to construct a positive sense of self. With the oppressive "Other" gone, her depression abates: "few things had importance to vex, intimidate, or depress me: most things pleased—mere trifles had a charm" (p. 594).

"Mere trifles had a charm"—indeed a symptom of happiness! Yet, for Lucy, such happiness may be short-lived, for she seems to adopt the all-too-common, self-effacing female stance, indicative of low self-esteem and depression, that attributes success and happiness to external factors rather than internal strengths and resources. "The secret of my success did not lie so much in myself" but in Paul, who, if we are to believe Lucy, seems to have been suddenly and miraculously transformed into a loving, sensitive, tolerant human being (p. 504).

However, can we believe Lucy, or is she, in fact, unconsciously resorting to a defense that is often strategically employed by depressed, intelligent women when attempting to render their situations more tolerable? If Paul has tempered his despotic wielding of power, perhaps it is due not to a radical change in *his* personality but rather to Lucy's identification with him as the aggressor, and to her abdicating to his will by subjugating herself: "He was my king; royal for me had been that hand's bounty; to offer homage was both a joy and a duty" (p. 587).

One shudders to hear Lucy proffer a desire to submit joyfully to the "Tiger-Jesuit." Such a strategy of assimilation, of course, will guarantee her, as it did Fanny, a place in the patriarchal system; it will enable Lucy to teach, for Paul has rewarded her obeisance by giving her her own school. However, to deceive herself into thinking that such dependency on the sexist Jesuit will flood her life with joy is a ruse that threatens to exact a heavy psychological price in the form of depression. In what appears, in retrospect, to be a poignantly prophetic insight, Lucy, herself, reflects earlier in the novel upon the dangers of self-deception:

> And he is a poor self-swindler who lies to himself and . . . sets down under the head happiness that which is misery . . . Falsify, insert "privilege" where you should have written "pain" and see if your mighty creditor will allow the fraud to pass. (p. 451)

Fanny Price paid for her abdication to Edmund Bertram through an increasing sense of her own nothingness; one can only conjecture that if Paul does return to Lucy (and the author seems ambivalent about her protagonist's situation, leaving Paul's fate on the stormy sea-voyage open to question), her "joyful" submission to the patriarchal other will eventually be exposed as psychologically fraudulent behavior that will leave her financially secure but fundamentally depressed.

"YOU'VE LOST YOUR TRUE SELF FOREVER": MARY TYRONE

Neither Fanny Price nor Lucy Snowe rebel against their subordination by the male power structure. Rather, by conforming to their expected sex-role stereotypes, both women exhibit a learned dependency upon the patriarchal society that guarantees them economic security but which leaves them highly vulnerable to depression.

In contrast, Mary Tyrone in O'Neill's *Long Day's Journey Into Night* struggles against her oppressive situations. Mary's covert rebellion through drug addiction can be viewed as an act of protest.

against oppressive institutions that foster dependency and depression in women.

Psychologists or literary critics interested in studying female depression will find no better case study than *Long Day's Journey Into Night*. As the archetypal female who is surrounded by males, Mary Tyrone emerges as the victim of a sexist ideology which, through the institutions of family and religion, socializes women into positions of dependency and depression.

Mary Tyrone displays four stereotypically female traits that have been correlated with depression in women. First, like Fanny she is very *dependent* (Wetzel, 1984) upon male approval for her sense of self and self-worth, much of which results from her internalizing the male's perceptions of her physical appearance. Second, Mary suffers the pain of *alienation* (Wetzel, 1984) when she is rejected by her family for failing to conform to the male-prescribed image of her as wife/mother. Like Fanny Price, and Lucy Snowe, Mary is plagued by an oppressive loneliness, an almost claustrophobic sense of isolation that leaves her feeling "cut off" from her real self and from others. Having always been excluded from the male domain of business/money of the "outside world" by virtue of her gender, and having fallen from grace in the eyes of a patriarchal religion because of an addiction to morphine, Mary Tyrone, once she internalizes the rejection by her family, is left completely bereft of any positive, sustaining sense of self. Third, by subordinating her own dreams and desires to those of her family's, Mary conformed for many years to the societally imposed female role that demanded the *delayed gratification* (Wetzel, 1984) of a woman's needs in order to satisfy the needs of others. Not only has Mary sacrificed her *self* for the males in her family, she has also been sacrificed by them for their own selfish purposes. It is this ongoing process of female sacrifice and self-sacrifice that has been found to lead to depression in women and that accounts for the fourth correlate of female depression, namely, Mary's *inability to feel "at home"* in a male-dominated environment. For her failure to perceive the external surroundings as stable and *"home-like"* stems, in part, from an unconscious projection of her own lack of internal stability; that is to say, it reflects the *absence of an abiding sense of self* (Miller, 1976). An examination of these four correlates of human depression strongly suggests that Mary's psychological distress results, to a great extent, from her being female and that her drug addiction reflects, in part, the deleterious effects of her subordinate position in the male power structure.

That Mary is dependent upon the Tyrone men for her feelings of self-worth is apparent throughout the play in the numerous references both to her physical appearance and to her self-conscious demeanor when in their presence. The very first two lines of the play draw attention to Mary's figure and capture the sense of her dependence upon her husband's approval:

> Tyrone: You're a fine armful now, Mary, with those twenty pounds you've gained.
> Mary: I've gotten too fat, you mean, dear. I really ought to reduce.

Although this reflects a light, affectionate exchange between husband and wife, it does establish and foreshadow the thematic importance of Mary's physical appearance in the play. As one critic has noted, Mary's appearance will deteriorate as her drug intake grows more acute (Tornqvist, 1969). An equally important consideration, and one overlooked by critics, is that this opening dialogue also reveals the stereotypically female dependence upon the approval of the male for her own self-esteem, a dependence that is inimical to psychological well-being and conducive to depression. Not only does Mary suffer the withdrawal of male approval during the course of the play, but she also dangerously constructs her sense of self upon her family's perceptions of her most ephemeral attributes—her physical features.

While it is obviously true that the Tyrone men condemn Mary because of her drug addiction and not because of her aging, the fact remains that the attention accorded to her changing physical characteristics— her failing eyesight, her greying hair, and her rheumatoid hands—serves the dual thematic purpose of symbolizing her unhealthy dependency not only upon an external substance (morphine), but also upon an external figure of approval (Tyrone). Her initial need for morphine to assuage physical pain has developed into a dependency upon the drug to maintain a superficial semblance of psychophysical composure; similarly, her dependence upon male acceptance to construct a sense of self has developed in a reliance upon a self-identity tenuously built upon transient, superficial, physical attributes. Withdrawal from morphine initially leads to pain and depression; as we shall see, withdrawal of male approval leaves Mary feeling psychologically impoverished in her present, male-dominated existence.

For many women whose identities rest solely upon their conforming to the role of wife-mother, withdrawal of family approval proves to be a psychologically devastating occurrence, leading to alienation, loneliness, and depression. Like many women living in the early part of the 20th century, Mary Tyrone, for the most part, was socialized to direct her energies inward to the home and discouraged any development of a sense of independent self. Mary has been psychologically suffocated by the men in her life, a fact that is reflected in the play's references to various claustrophobic settings, each of which symbolizes Mary's loneliness, dependency, and bondage.

The very setting of *Long Day's Journey Into Night*—the summer home—manifests an oppressive, claustrophobic atmosphere, more so for Mary than for the others. For as one critic points out, the fact that we see all men leave the house at some point during the play but never see Mary leave conveys the impression that for her the house is inescapable (Tiusanen, 1976): the summer house for Mary is a psychological prison, where she is often abandoned by the men, who, because they are men, seek activity outside the home, whether it is gardening, transacting business or drinking with "the boys." Mary complains about this societal double standard to Edmund: "Your father goes out. He meets his friends in barrooms or at the Club. You and James have the boys you know. You go out. I am alone. I've always been alone" (p. 46). Mary's sense of confinement to the summer house leaves her with an increasing awareness of her own loneliness and alienation, thus exacerbating her depression and fostering her drug dependency. "I feel so lonely," she tells Edmund (p. 45); as the men leave her alone in the house at the end of Act II, she mutters to herself, "It is so lonely here . . . Why do I feel so lonely?" (p. 95). None of the Tyrone men actively seek to alleviate her loneliness but rather try to escape from her drug addiction by leaving the house or by turning to their own drug—liquor.

Mary's abandonment by Tyrone to a claustrophobic space is a theme that carries retrospective import in *Long Day's Journey Into Night*, for as the play progresses, we discover that Tyrone often left Mary alone in cheap hotel rooms when she accompanied him on his acting tours in the early days of their marriage. Feeling alienated from the rough, hard-drinking male world of Tyrone's theatre group, Mary frequently suffered the humiliation of being abandoned by her husband while he sought the cameraderie of his barroom friends: "I remember the first night your barroom friends had to help you up to the door of our hotel room . . . We were still on our honeymoon" (p. 113). Mary's painful memory takes on an added poignancy when she then reveals that the honeymoon incident was merely the first in a series of abandonments: "I didn't know how often that was to happen in the years to come, how many times I was to wait in ugly hotel rooms" (p. 113). It is Mary Tyrone, of course, who was also "abandoned" by her family to the stifling enclosure of the sanitarium, a place where she was made to feel like a criminal (p. 74).

Whether it is the summer house, the hotel room or the sanitarium, Mary Tyrone is the character most closely associated with oppressive, claustrophobic settings. As a female "imprisoned" by males, Mary Tyrone, when failing to conform to societal expectations, has been "locked away" in confined spaces. Her drug addiction is obviously incompatible with the traditional female role of wife/mother and accounts, to a great extent, for her suffering the punishment of isolation that has been imposed upon her by her family.

By sacrificing her *self* for her husband and later for her sons, Mary Tyrone, prior to her drug addiction, fulfilled the traditional Madonna-like female role of being defined solely in relation to the men in her life (Daly, 1973), that is, in her self-sacrificing role of the wife/mother. While some critics have noted the importance of the religious dimension of *Long Day's Journey*, none, to my knowledge, has viewed Mary's psychological plight and drug addiction as possibly being symptomatic of her alienation within the oppressive confines of patriarchal, Irish Catholicism. The sexist ideology perpetuated by traditional Catholic doctrine limits the possible female modes of existence to that of either the Madonna or the whore. This simplistic dichotomy is symbolically represented in the play by the Virgin Mary and Fat Violet, respectively, both of whom, although physically absent from the stage, function, nevertheless, as ubiquitous reminders of the limited options available to women in traditional Christian culture.

In the eyes of Catholicism, Mary's addiction to morphine precipitates her "sinful fall" from the sanctified roles of wife/mother to the whorish existence of the drug addict and moral reprobate. Mary is perceived by the men not as a victimized, complex human being in distress, but as a shattered ideal or a fallen Madonna who, in Jamie's mind, becomes explicitly linked with his whore, Fat Violet: "I thought only whores were drug addicts," utters Jamie (p. 163). By associating drug addiction with prostitution and moral decadence, the Tyrone men can perceive Mary not as a victim but as a sinner. Tyrone, Jamie, and Edmund constitute a harshly critical, judgmental trinity, for each of them, despite his feeble protests to the contrary, holds Mary morally culpable for her addiction. Tyrone maintains that if Mary had only *prayed* and not forgotten her *faith*, she could have conquered the addiction (p. 78). Edmund, like Dr. Hardy at the sanitarium, *preaches sermons* on will power (pp. 74, 92). That she has internalized their moral condemnation is revealed in her expression of regret at having given birth to Edmund: "I should never have borne him. . . . He wouldn't have had to know his mother was a dope fiend—and hate her" (p. 122).

If Mary, in effect, has been sacrificed by a religious ideology that denies women power over their own lives and that fails to recognize women as complex human beings who overflow simplistic, female stereotypes, then her use of morphine could be interpreted as an unconscious act of rebellion against the oppressive, secular trinity of her family. That is to say, Mary's drug use, during the course of the play, could represent her grabbing for control or her attempting to usurp the power held by the men.

Mary's angry rebellion against her family and her unconsciously manipulative use of morphine to gain control over the men are reflected in her cutting revengeful remarks. For example, in response to their suspicions about her drug relapse, Mary states, "It would serve all of you right if it was true" (p. 47). Such hostility is an understandable reaction from someone who has been victimized by others. For not only was Mary betrayed in the past by her husband's penuriousness, but she is also suffering in the present from the men's overt use of alcohol in the house. Both situations are inextricably linked to her drug addiction. For it was Tyrone's notorious "niggardliness" that resulted in her being introduced to morphine in the first place, when he allowed a cheap, unscrupulous hotel doctor to give Mary the drug to alleviate her pain following the birth of Edmund. In addition, the Tyrone men, in a perverse sense, encourage Mary's relapse through their own explicit dependence upon alcohol. The Tyrone home environment is characterized by a dependency upon alcohol, which, as a critic notes, only reinforces her inclination to resume morphine (Bloom, 1984). The fact that the Tyrone men do not stop drinking at home reveals the subordinate, powerless position of Mary in the family. As the depressed victim of an oppressive, male household, Mary has been selfishly sacrificed by others.

Like many women of her era, Mary sacrificed any possibility for an independent, autonomous sense of self by conforming, for the most part, to her subordinate role of wife/mother in the early years of her marriage. The depression that attends such a sacrifice of one's needs and dreams is exacerbated, in Mary's case, by the present withdrawal of male approval of her in the role of wife/mother. The irony, of course, lies in their condemning and isolating her because of her drug addiction, a situation for which they bear a great deal of responsibility.

In addition to signifying an act of covert rebellion, Mary's morphine addiction represents her attempt to escape not only from the unpleasant reality of Edmund's tuberculosis but also from her own inner vacuity. Just as the morphine assuages the pain of her rheumatoid hands, so too does it dull the aching awareness of loss of *self*, that abiding sense of an internal permanence or psychological "home" that sustains one when the external support systems of "props" are wrenched away. Mourning her loss of self, Mary poignantly observes that: "None of us can help the things that life has done to us. They're done before you know it . . . until at last . . . you've lost your true self forever" (p. 61).

It is this loss of self that undoubtedly underlies Mary's profound depression, symptomatically manifested by her pessimism, despair, and drug addiction, and by her inability to feel "at home" in the summer house. The fact that the summer house is, by definition, a transient setting, does not fully account for her failure to perceive it as a home. Neither the summer house nor any house would ever come to connote or represent a home for Mary, because any external environment would be perceptually imbued with the stark, cold hollowness of her emotional state. If a "house" suggests transience and a "home" permanence for Mary, then the depressive awareness of her own lack of an inner core of identity will leave her feeling fundamentally "not at home" in the world and, like Willy Loman, in *Death of a Salesman,* "kind of temporary about herself" (p. 24).

CONCLUSION

The preceding discussion of three fictional women illustrates the connection between female depression and the culturally-determined feminine stereotype during the 19th and 20th centuries. When illuminated against the backdrop of the novel or play's misogynistic institutions, these women emerge as victims—whether they conform to the externally imposed feminine stereotype by repressing the desire for autonomy and environmental mastery, or whether they struggle to become part of the sociopolitical framework and forge an independent, integrated sense of self in a society that systematically strives to render women dependent, submissive, and manageable. Whatever strategy is described—whether it be Fanny Price's rather passive assimilation, Lucy Snowe's identification with the aggressor, or Mary Tyrone's escape through drug addiction, each woman, through her depression, pays the price of having been socialized as a female.

REFERENCES

American Psychiatric Association (1980). Diagnostic and statistical manual of mental disorders (3rd ed.). Washington, DC.

Austen, J. (1966). *Mansfield park,* edited with an introduction by Tony Tanner. New York: Penguin Books.

Bloom, S.F. (1984). Empty bottle, empty dreams: O'Neill's use of drinking and alcoholism in *Long day's journey into night.* In J. Maritine (Ed.), *Critical essays on Eugene O'Neill* (pp. 159–177). Boston: G.K. Hall & Co.

Brontë, C. (1979). *Villette,* edited by Mark Lilly with an introduction by Tony Tanner. New York: Penguin Books.

Daly, M. (1973). *Beyond God the father: Toward a philosophy of women's liberation.* Boston: Beacon Press.

Ehrenreich, B., & English, D. (1973). *Complaints & disorders: The sexual politics of sickness.* Old Westbury, NY: The Feminist Press.

Gilbert, S., & Gubar, S. (1979). *The madwoman in the attic: The woman writer and* the 19th century literary imagination. New Haven, CT: Yale University Press.

Levitt, E.E., Lubin, B., & Brooks, J.M. (1983). *Depression: Concepts, controversies and some new facts.* Hillsdale, NJ: Laurence Erlbaum Associates.

Miller, A. (1976). *Death of a salesman.* New York: Penguin Books.

Miller, J.B. (1976). *Toward a new psychology of women.* Boston: Beacon Press.

O'Neill, E. (1955). *Long day's journey into night.* New Haven, CT: Yale University Press.

Showalter, E. (1981). Victorian women and insanity. In Andrew Scull (Ed.), *Madness, mad-doctors and madmen: The social history of psychiatry in the Victorian era* (pp. 313–331). Philadelphia: University of Pennsylvania Press.

Tiusanen, T. (1976). Through the fog into the monologue: *Long day's journey into night.* In Ernest G. Griffin (Ed.), *Eugene O'Neill: A collection of criticism* (pp. 114–129). New York: McGraw Hill Book Company.

Tornqvist, E. (1969). *A drama of souls: Studies of O'Neill's supernaturalistic technique.* New Haven, CT: Yale University Press.

Wetzel, J.W. (1984). *Clinical handbook of depression.* New York: Gardner Press, Inc.

■ 15
Suicidal Self-Destruction In Women

CHARLES NEURINGER, Ph.D.

Interest in the demographics, psychodynamics, and prevention of female suicide has lagged behind that directed towards males. There are several reasons for this disparity. The rate of suicidal deaths in men far outstrips that of women, rendering male self-destructive behavior more visible than that of females. Because of our current male-dominated cultural orientations, male deaths usually have a greater impact on the family, the economy, and society than do the suicides of women.[1]

Research in female suicide has also lagged behind that of men for the same reason. Suicide research in males is more easily accomplished than in females because of the availability of a large centralized deposit of data on suicidal males. Due to recent wars, many male suicidal patients reside in Veterans Administration Hospitals. Many other veterans who are (or have been) suicidal maintain a connection to the Veterans Administration through its many outpatient and posthospitalization care programs. The Veterans Administration Hospital system's patient load and records are available for retrospective and prospective research. Meaningful suicide research is methodologically difficult (Neuringer, 1962) and becomes even more difficult when the number of subjects is low as is the case with women who commit suicide.

Suicide prevention agencies have rapidly increased in number since the

[1]It may also be true that these same social attitudes lead physicians, coroners, and medical examiners to discount or ignore suicidal behavior in women. These authorities may, because of their attitudes, assign the death to other modalities (natural, accident, homicide, etc.). As will be demonstrated later, there is evidence of the existence of a social orientation about female passivity which leads to a conclusion that women are physically and psychologically incapable of active suicidal behavior.

early 1960s. It was only after their establishment that the enormity of non-fatal suicidal behavior in women came to light. Even though fewer women successfully commit suicide, the incidence of their other self-destructive behavior is disturbingly high. Accurate information about the number of women making suicidal threats, gestures, and attempts is hard to come by. However, unofficial estimates of such activities range upwards to ten times as many as the "known" rates to be described below.

The specific gathering of data about female suicide is a relatively new activity as compared to that for males. Demographic data on self-destructive women was previously gathered only as an adjunct for male comparison purposes. But some studies of the relationship between women's physiology and their suicidal behavior had been conducted prior to the current upsurge in interest in female suicide.

We still have little idea of the variables that give rise to suicidal decisions in women and those that differentiate suicidal males from females.[2] We therefore have very little information about socioeconomic status and its variations among suicidal women. What does seem to have captured the interest of many investigators is the low suicidal death rate in women. This interest is probably spurred by a desire to find a set of variables, suspected to exist in women, that offers "protection" against killing themselves. These researchers are, in one sense, chasing after the "secret" that protects women from suicidal death.

There is a growing urgency compelling those interested in saving lives to make rapid progress. The absolute number of female suicidal deaths is rising, especially among adolescent girls and women in the work force. The number of female threats and attempts is also rising in all age groups, with a particularly large upsurge among adolescents.

DEMOGRAPHICS OF FEMALE SUICIDE

When Durkheim (1951) published his pioneer study of suicide in 1897, he declared that femininity was a protection against suicide. His declaration was based on the then available demographic data. Subsequent demographers have continued to report lower suicide rates in women than in men.[3]

Male predominance in suicidal statistics is of very long standing, and ex-

[2]There is some evidence that the paucity of findings of differential suicidal psychodynamic patterns between men and women may be due more to the non-existence of such differentiators rather than to sparseness of research efforts (Neuringer & Lettieri, 1982).
[3]However, the reader should keep in mind that there is evidence of this sex differential's gradual disappearance.

ists regardless of race or marital status. However, the male/female suicide death rate differential increases with age: 21-year-old men kill themselves about twice as often as 21-year old women, but ten times as many 60-year-old males kill themselves as 60-year-old women (Johnson, 1979). Men who commit suicide tend to use highly lethal methods (firearms, jumping, and hanging), whereas women tend to use less lethal, but equally effective methods, such as the ingestion of barbiturates and toxic substances (Davis, 1967; Dublin, 1963; Lester, 1972; Maris, 1969; Marks & Abernathy, 1974; Marks & Stokes, 1976). Davis (1983), on the other hand, recently reported a dramatic rise in the use of the more lethal self-destructive methods by adolescent suicidal females.

The sex-differential is reversed for suicide attempts. In general, about three times as many women attempt suicide as do men (Dorpat & Boswell, 1963; Hendin, 1950; Lendrum, 1933; Maris, 1969; Phillips & Muzaffer, 1961). Adolescent women make ten times as many attempts as comparably aged males (Balser & Masterson, 1959; Davis 1983). Although older women make fewer suicide attempts and threats than younger ones, their self-destructive maneuvers are more serious than those of younger women (Neuringer, 1982b).

The predominance of male suicidal deaths seems to be slowly eroding. In 1950, there was a 12.5 per 100,000 population predominance of male over female suicidal deaths. By 1969, this difference had shrunk to 9.2 per 100,000 population (Department of Commerce, 1975). Neuringer (1968b) compared Los Angeles suicidal death rates for the years 1959 and 1966. During this period female suicide in general rose 39%, with an 83% rise among young females. Smaller increases were found for males. Similar findings have been reported elsewhere (Davis, 1983; Hendin, 1985). While total population male/female percentage ratio differences are slowly closing, the absolute number of female suicide deaths has rapidly increased. Frederick (1985) reported a 200% increase in the number of female adolescent suicide deaths since 1968. Cantor (1972) reported that adolescent females comprise 90% of the client population of suicide prevention centers. Davis (1981) found a dramatic rise in suicides of women in the labor force between the years 1950 to 1969 while also reporting a slight diminution of suicidal deaths in men during that period.

There seems to be growing evidence that female suicidal deaths are increasing at a faster rate than male suicidal deaths.

CHARACTERISTICS OF SUICIDAL WOMEN

The results of various studies that have attempted to distinguish the characteristics of female suicide attempters and committers from nonsuicidal women reveal little that is surprising. The most commonly reported variables of both attempters and committers include social isolation, interpersonal difficulties, loss of one or more parents before age twenty, previous suicide attempts, psychiatric disturbance, alcoholism, marital, physical, and health problems (Adam, Bouckoms, & Streiner, 1982; Bassuk, Schoonover, & Gill, 1982; Berglund, 1984; Borg & Stahl, 1982; Braucht, Loya, & Jamieson, 1980; Choron, 1972; Crook & Raskin, 1975; Farber, 1968; Goldeny, 1981; Goldeny, Adam, O'Brien, & Termansen, 1981; Hawton, 1982; Hendin, 1982; Johnson, 1979; Lester, 1979; McCulloch & Philip, 1972; Trout, 1980; Worden, 1976). After comparing these and other possible warning signs of female suicide to those found for males, Neuringer and Lettieri (1982) found no profound suicidogenic differences between males and females: women die by their own hands for the same reason as men do (i.e., despair, hopelessness, guilt, self-loathing, pain, remorse, fear, rage, etc.).

In order to develop a set of characteristics to reliably identify suicidal individuals, it is necessary to find some psychological functions that seem to appear exclusively (or almost exclusively) in self-destructive people and exist rarely (or not at all) in nonsuicidal persons. The characteristics discussed above have only limited utility because of their frequent occurrence in nonsuicidal individuals. However, two variables seem, at this time, to meet the criteria of independent occurrence between suicidal and nonsuicidal men and women. One is "dichotomous thinking," a particular cognitive style of organization of meaning. The second variable is a special affect configuration that, as far as is now known, seems to exist exclusively in suicidal women.

DICHOTOMOUS THINKING

In 1957, Shneidman suggested that a study of how suicidal people think might prove to be more productive in terms of understanding (and thus preventing) self-destructive behavior than investigations of personality variables.

Shneidman's notion was expanded upon and investigated by Neuringer (1961, 1964b, 1967, 1968a, 1979). From these studies Neuringer concluded that suicidal individuals have a predilection towards organizing their value systems in extreme bipolar opposites. Suicidal individuals tend to see people, activities, ideas, or goals as either "very good" or "very bad" with little moderation between these bipolar opposites. Nonsuicidal, or "normal," individuals have the capacity to moderate this self-destructive cognitive style. Even nonsuicidal at-risk populations seem to resist the encroachments of bipolar value organization to a greater degree than self-destructive people. Neuringer adopted a term coined by Shneidman (1957) to describe this particular cognitive style: "dichotomous thinking." Neuringer found this variable to be present in seriously suicidal males to a greater extent than in less seriously suicidal, nonsuicidal but psychiatrically ill, and normal males. He also reported that this style of organizing the world was a personality trait and resistant to change.

The above cited conclusions were based on studies of male suicidal individuals. Neuringer and Lettieri (1971, 1982) turned their attention to suicidal women in order to ascertain whether this cognitive orientation also existed and played a suicidogenic role in females. Their findings for women were identical with those found for suicidal males. As was true for the men, severely suicidal women think more dichotomously than low- or no-risk women. They tend to view everything in terms of bipolar opposites. If objects, thoughts, ideas, things, etc., are not completely good, beautiful, and ecstatic, they can only become extremely ugly or disgusting. Therefore, the *only* alternative to expectations of complete success in love, career, marriage, social aspiration, etc., are feelings of complete failure. There is no room in their value systems for moderate or mild success. It is a case of needing to be "first," and being "second" is the equivalent of being "last." Since the world cannot ever gratify such grandiose expectations, most people have consciously or unconsciously learned how to adjust their expectations. Suicidal men and women do not seem to have learned this primary lesson of life and expect and demand perfection from themselves and others. Their levels of aspiration are inordinately high. And when they are disappointed (as surely they must be), they respond as if they had failed completely or had been utterly rejected. For them everything is spoiled because nothing turns out to be perfect. They become depressed and unhappy as an inevitable consequence of their dichotomous thinking. Extreme dichotomous thinking is dangerous because it jeopardizes one's capacity to live in the real world (i.e., to make compromises, change viewpoints, or accept new alternatives). Neuringer (1964a, b) found these same individuals to be very rigid in both their dealings with other people and in their use of problem-solving strategies. High-risk suicidal men and women show more dichotomous thinking than other populations ever evaluated in suicide research. There is no significant diminution of dichotomous thinking over time in any of the high-risk women. This cognitive organization may be so ingrained that it leads these women into impossible emotional *cul-de-sacs* from which the only escape is death. The effects of dichotomous thinking are seen more clearly when one examines the findings for the affect configuration in suicidal women.

A SUICIDAL AFFECT CONFIGURATION IN WOMEN

A unique affect configuration exists in seriously suicidal women, which is not found in normal, nonsuicidal but psychiatrically disturbed women, or even in mildly suicidal "gesture"-making women (Neuringer, 1982b; Neuringer &Lettieri, 1982). Suicidal women were found to have a set of intense negative emotions and orientations not matched by other women. Compared to other women, (1) they feel that life is duller, emptier, and more boring; (2) they are less interested and responsive to people and to events; (3) they feel angrier, they have less interest in and are more dissatisfied with their work; (4) they report that thinking is a great effort; their thought processes are slow and sluggish; (5) they feel their ideas lack value, and they lack intellectual self-confidence; (6) they feel more guilt-ridden and are less self-approving; (7) they feel inadequate and helpless; and (8) they feel more depressed and weary.

Nonserious suicidal women experience some of these affects but not all, and not as intensely as seriously suicidal women. Nonsuicidal women report feelings of internal and external constraint, which are absent in the seriously suicidal women. These high levels of constraint may dampen action potentials, thus mitigating against acting-out behavior or actual self-destructive behaviors in the nonsuicidal but psychiatrically disturbed women. The absence of such constraints coupled with lack of interest and responsiveness to the environment, as well as the intense emotions experienced by the seriously suicidal women make it possible for suicidal acting-out behaviors to occur. What emerges is a configuration that has interrelated components of intense withdrawal (loss of interest), extreme depression (emptiness, mental sluggishness, guilt, self-loathing, undischarged anger), alienation (little or no allegiance to, or interest in particular people or ideas), and diminished acting-out inhibition (little or no sense of being constrained to take into regard the wishes and feelings of friends and family). Once this "I-don't-care" or "nothing-matters-to-me" attitude develops, nothing appears to stop the suicidal women from escaping from the misery engendered by the configuration. It appears that the suicidal women are not concerned with others' feelings nor with how their own behavior will affect others.

One other disturbing finding has been reported. The continued intensity of the affects in the configuration over time augurs poorly for the future of highly suicidal women as it suggests to them that relief from their intensely negative feelings is slow in coming. This may be the result of the cognitive style discussed earlier. Dichotomous thinking, the inflexible and polarized thinking of suicidal individuals, is impervious to change (Neuringer, 1979). It may well be that the inflexible and polarized thinking perpetuates and maintains for long periods of time the high levels of crisis (i.e., the high level of negative affect) experienced by seriously suicidal women.

Thus, suicidal women are caught in a negative affect web that appears to be unending. That is, their pain never really diminishes long enough for relief to be felt. If the cognitive style does indeed sustain negative affect, it may explain why suicidal individuals feel so hopeless and why they have such difficulties envisioning a future in which they could feel better (Neuringer & Levenson, 1972). It may also explain why seriously suicidal threateners and attempters go on to commit overt suicidal acts. No comparable evaluation of the emotional organization of suicidal men has, as yet, been done. However, based on previous male–female suicidal comparison studies of personality organization, it is highly probably that such a configuration also exists in self-destructive men.

SUICIDAL BEHAVIOR ACROSS THE LIFESPAN

Suicidal activity across the lifespan follows different curves for men and women. For men, the number of suicidal deaths is low during adolescence and continues to rise, reaching a peak around age sixty. Fatal suicidal activity in women also is low in adolescence, then slowly rises, reaching a peak around age 20 and from then on becomes fairly stable. As mentioned above, twice as many 20-year-old men kill themselves as do women. By age 60, this gap has widened to ten to one in favor of men.

Middle age seems to be a most dangerous time for men in regard to suicide. Surprisingly, this is not true for middle-aged women. It is surprising since age-related physical ills and stresses seem to occur in both groups (physical illness and deterioration, mental slowing down, loss of family and friends, widowhood, etc.). What causes this differential response to aging? Women may be better prepared to handle the crises associated with the aging process than are men, or perhaps their view of the aging process is not as devastating as is that of men. Males in our society are expected to have achieved certain material and social goals by retirement time. Their sense of self-worth is often dependent upon those socially mandated goals. If these goals are not achieved by age sixty or so, then feelings of frustration, failure, and decline shake men's sense of self-worth. Older women may be protected from this situation because society does not urge them to be as success oriented as men.

Another factor to be considered is that women develop more friendships than men. These friendships also seem to be more intimate and supportive than those found between men (Brehm, 1985). Women, therefore, have greater opportunity to share experiences, feelings, seek support, and be dependent upon others than do men. For most men, their friends are acquaintances formed in the work place. With retirement, concomitant diminution of contact with others occurs. For women, the loss of a spouse can be partially compensated for by friendships. For men, the loss of a spouse often means social isolation and loneliness. In addition, the expression of emotion is socially sanctioned for women, but discouraged for men.

Most overt, but nonlethal, suicidal risks occur in adolescent girls. Their emotional expressiveness, more than a desire to die, may account for their high rate of suicide attempts. However, the suicidal death rate in young girls and older women is rising. As current female adolescent suicide attempters get older, their self-destructive behaviors may continue to be expressed as suicide attempts or take on more lethal forms.

WOMEN AND SUICIDAL BEHAVIOR

Researchers are trying to fathom the "secret" of what protects women from choosing to end their existence. Two questions are frequently asked: "Why has the occurrence of suicide in women been traditionally lower than that of males?" and "Why do so many more women than men threaten and attempt suicide?" Various answers to these questions have been offered by a variety of theorists and, the explanations can be roughly divided into physiological and psychosocial explications.

Physiological hypotheses argue that the lower suicide rate in women is intimately related to the differences in biological structures and physiological activities of men and women. Some argue that the fatal suicide rate in women is low because of their muscular weakness (Lester, 1972). This hypothesis holds that women are not physically strong enough to utilize the fatality-producing self-destructive methods. When they do attempt to use these methods, they usually fail to kill themselves. These failures would also explain the high attempt rate in women as being due to lack of success rather than "cries-for-help" or "manipulation-of-others" strategies. However, skepticism about this hypothesis is called for since it takes very little physical strength to pull the trigger of a gun or step off the ledge of a high building.

Pregnancy has been mentioned as a protection against suicide (Barno, 1967). Surveys have reported that suicidal deaths are rare in pregnant women (Resnik, 1971; Rosenberg & Silver, 1965; Sim, 1963; Whitlock & Edwards, 1968). Approximately 2% of all women who kill themselves are pregnant, far below the general suicide rate in women. Several explanatory hypotheses have been offered. It may be that pregnancy abates the action of hormonal menstrual irritants (Smith, 1975). It may also be that many psychologically disturbed women feel that the forthcoming child may strengthen a failing relationship. It is also possible that pregnant women may have scruples about destroying the burgeoning life within them. One must also consider the possibility that the low rate of self-destruction in pregnant women is due to a disinclination on the part of unhappy women to become pregnant and take on the responsibility for rearing children. These speculations about the low rate of suicidal activity in pregnant women are psychologically oriented. At this time, there is no evidence that hormonal changes associated with pregnancy cause any chemically induced diminution of grief or anxiety.

However, some pregnant women do kill themselves. The death usually occurs during the last two trimesters (Goodwin & Harris, 1979). About half of the pregnant suicidal women were unmarried (Rosenberg & Silver, 1965; Whitlock & Edwards, 1968), suggesting that feelings of guilt, shame, and entrapment were the prime motivations for their deaths. Stern (1968) used psychoanalytic theory to explain self-destructive behavior in pregnant women as a displacement of hostility, originally connected with the husband or lover, onto the fetus. He stated that the pregnant woman's death was a symbolically displaced murder and that her death was an unfortunate but incidental outcome.

Various hypotheses relating to "feminine psychological traits" and to their social role behavior have been put forth to account for the low suicidal death incidence in women. Durkheim (1951) argued that women were less intellectually adventurous than men and therefore more accepting of fate. He suggested that women were more passively accepting of the blows of life than men. This, coupled with their alleged intellectual passivity, makes it difficult for them to contemplate suicide. Davis (1904) suggested that women had a naturally stronger religious faith than men, which served as an inhibitor of self-destructive behavior. Schneider (1954) argued that women were more distractable than men, and therefore not able to intellectually plan a successful suicide. Diggory and Rothman (1961) felt that women are more vain than men and therefore reject any behavior that would mar their bodies or bring their name into ill-repute. Stengel (1954) hypothesized that women were more manipulative than men and therefore would not use direct methods to deal with their self-loathing. Berkowitz (1962) ascribes the lower suicide rate in women to their being naturally less aggressive than men.

Social role explications of the lower suicide rate in women seek to explain this phenomenon in terms of the social expectancies imposed on women. Henry and Short (1965) pointed out that women have traditionally had little to do with the operations of the business cycle, and that there is an intimate relationship between suicide and the business cycle. Since women are peripheral to the cycle, they do not get caught in its maws. This is no longer true today. More and more women are entering the work force, and more of these working women are killing themselves (Davis, 1981).

Lester (1972), Maris (1969), Marks and Abernathy (1974), and Marks and Stokes (1976) argued that in our society women are not as well acquainted with guns and other deadly paraphenalia as are men. Because of this ignorance, they will not choose such self-destructive methods if they are contemplating suicide. Rather, they will prefer to use the less dangerous techniques in their self-destructive adventures, thus incidentally inflating the suicide attempt rate because of the inefficiency of these methods.[4] Hamblin and Jacobson (1972) offer an interesting speculation concerning the low suicide rate in women: our society disapproves less of drug habituation in women than in men. They imply that there exists tacit approval (and even encouragement) of pill taking in women while at the same time such behavior in males is prohibited. Sims (1974) reported that there is a much higher rate of legal drug prescriptions for women than for men. Both Sims and Hamblin and Johnson feel that the higher rate of drug habituation in women, as compared to men, offers women a protective alternative to suicide. Men, in our society, are not allowed this protective substitute.

MENSTRUATION

While researchers have found women to be predisposed to suicidal attempts during menstruation, MacKinnon and MacKinnon (1965), on the basis of evidence from autopsies, document that most of the suicidal women in their survey were in the ovulation phase. The bulk of the research with female suicide attempters indicates that suicidal activity occurs during the flowing stage (Dalton, 1959; Mandell & Mandell, 1967; Tonks, Rack, & Rose, 1968; Trautman, 1961; Wetzel & McClure, 1973).

Menstrual pain may act as a physiological stressor, especially on an already disintegrating personality structure. Smith (1975) reported that approximately one-third of all women feel somewhat depressed and irritable during the flowing stage. If the current reports about the deleterious effects of the premenstrual syndrome are reliable, then the physical and .

---

[4]Again one has to be dubious about the validity of this hypothesis because of the wide availability of firearms and the ease of using them.

psychological stressors associated with menstruation may be greater than previously suspected.

The above comments (except those on menstruation) have focused on the hypothesized reasons for the traditionally low rate of suicidal fatality and high suicide attempt levels in women as compared to men. However, evidence, cited earlier, indicates that this traditional suicidal disparity between men and women is beginning to disappear.

CONCLUSIONS

Our society values material possessions, intellectual accomplishments, job success, and sexual and athletic prowess—all traditionally the province of men. Contemporary women aspire to assume more and more prerogatives from which they have historically been excluded. However, women who aspire to the same goals as men may also become vulnerable to the pressures and demands that have plagued the lives of men. In addition, the current ideal of the new woman demands that she have two occupations, one being her career and the other as a homemaker, retaining her traditional role. Women have been more effective in their efforts to attain equal opportunity in the marketplace than in having society accept sex-equality in the domestic sphere. Society, by means of the media, and in particular television programs and commercials, has portrayed the new role model of a "Superwoman" who can do everything—manage a company, be a gourmet cook, a competent and loving mother, an immaculate housekeeper, and still be an ever-ready and enthusiastic sex partner.

Women are asked to fulfill the demands of the traditional female role without much emotional support. But an easing of the demands of these roles is necessary for woman's psychological as well as literal survival. Without help in the domestic sphere, equality will not exist, especially as concomitant changes in male roles have not occurred. Today's women are being asked to be *more* able than men—a new and subtle form of discrimination. Women's failure to live up to the new ideal can engender feelings of guilt, inadequacy, and low self-esteem, and may contribute to the current and dramatic rise in the suicide rate.

REFERENCES

Adam, K.S., Bouckoms, A., & Streiner, D. (1982). Parental loss and family stability in attempted suicide. *Archives of General Psychiatry, 39,* 1081–1085.

Balser, B.H., & Masterson, J.F. (1959). Suicide in adolescents. *American Journal of Psychiatry, 116,* 400–404.

Barno, A. (1967). Criminal abortion deaths, illegitimate pregnancy deaths and suicide in pregnancy. *American Journal of Obstetrics and Gynecology, 98,* 356–357.

Bassuk, E.L., Schoonover, S.C., & Gill, A.D. (1982). *Lifelines: Clinical perspectives on suicide.* New York: Plenum.

Berglund, M. (1984). Suicide in alcoholism: A prospective study of 88 suicides. *Archives of General Psychiatry, 41,* 888–891.

Berkowitz, L. (1962). *Aggression.* New York: McGraw-Hill.

Borg, S.E., & Stahl, M. (1982). Prediction of suicide: A prospective study of suicides and controls among psychiatric patients. *Acta Psychiatrica Scandinavica, 65,* 221–232.

Braucht, G.N., Loya, F., & Jamieson, K.J. (1980). Victims of violent death: A critical review. *Psychological Bulletin, 87,* 309–333.

Brehm, S.S. (1985). *Intimate relationships.* New York: Random House.

Cantor, P. (1972). The adolescent attempter: Sex, sibling position and family constitution. *Life Threatening Behavior, 2,* 252–261.

Choron, J. (1972). *Suicide.* New York: Scribners.

Crook, T., & Raskin, A. (1975). Association of childhood parental loss with attempted suicide and depression. *Journal of Consulting and Clinical Psychology, 43,* 277–287.

Dalton, K. (1959). Menstruation and acute psychiatric illness. *British Medical Journal, 1,* 148–149.

Davis, E. (1967). The relationship between suicide and attempted suicide. *Psychiatric Quarterly, 41,* 752–765.

Davis, P.A. (1983). *Suicidal adolescents.* Springfield, IL: C.C. Thomas.

Davis, R.A. (1981). Female labor force participation, status intergration and suicide, 1950–1969. *Suicide and Life-Threatening Behavior, 11,* 111–113.

Department of Commerce (1975). *Historical statistics of the United States: Colonial times to 1970.* Washington, DC: U.S. Printing Office.

Diggory, J.C., & Rothman, D.Z. (1961). Values destroyed by death. *Journal of Abnormal and Social Psychology, 63,* 205–210.

Dorpat, T.L., & Boswell, J.W. (1963). An evaluation of suicidal intent in suicide attempts. *Comprehensive Psychiatry, 4,* 117–125.

Dublin, L.I. (1963). *Suicide: A sociological and statistical study.* New York: Ronald Press.

Durkheim, E. (1951). *Suicide.* New York: Free Press.

Farber, M.L. (1968). *Theory of suicide.* New York: Funk and Wagnalls.

Frederick, C.J. (1985). An introduction and overview of youth suicide. In M.L. Peck, N.L. Farberow, & R.E. Litman. (Eds.), *Youth suicide* (pp. 1–16). New York: Springer.

Goldney, R.D. (1981). Attempted suicide in young women: Correlates of lethality. *British Journal of Psychiatry, 139,* 382–390.

Goldney, R.D., Adam, K.S., O'Brien, J.C., & Termansen, P. (1981). Depression in young women who have attempted suicide: An international replication study. *Journal of Affective Disorders, 3,* 327–337.

Goodwin, J., & Harris, D. (1979). Suicide in pregnancy: The Hedda Gabler syndrome. *Suicide and Life Threatening Behavior, 9,* 105–115.

Hamblin, R.L., & Jacobson, R.B. (1972). Suicide and pseudocide: A reanalysis of Maris's data. *Comprehensive Psychiatry, 13,* 99–104.

Hawton, K. (1982). Annotation: Attempted suicide in children and adolescents. *Journal of Child Psychology and Psychiatry, 23,* 497–503.

Hendin, H. (1950). Attempted suicide. *Psychiatric Quarterly, 24,* 39–46.

Hendin, H. (1982). *Suicide in America.* New York: Norton.

Hendin, H. (1985). Suicide among the young: Psychodynamics and demography. In M.L. Peck, N.L. Farberow, & R.E. Litman (Eds.), *Youth suicide* (pp. 19–38). New York: Springer.

Henry, A.F., & Short, J.F. (1965). *Suicide and homicide.* New York: Free Press.

Johnson, K.K. (1979). Durkheim revisited. Why do women kill themselves? *Suicide and Life Threatening Behavior, 9,* 145–153.

Lendrum, F.C. (1933). 1000 cases of attempted suicide. *American Journal of Psychiatry, 13,* 479–500.

Lester, D. (1972). *Why people kill themselves.* Springfield, IL: C.C. Thomas.

Lester, D. (1979). Sex differences in suicidal behavior. In E.S. Gomberg & V. Franks. (Eds.), *Gender and disordered behavior: Sex differences in psychopathology* (pp. 86–92). New York: Brunner/Mazel.

MacKinnon, P.C.B., & MacKinnon, I.L. (1956). Hazards of the menstrual cycle. *British Medical Journal, 1,* 555.

Mandell, A.J., & Mandell, M.P. (1967). Suicide and the menstrual cycle. *Journal of the American Medical Association, 200,* 792-795.

Maris, R. (1969). *Social forces in urban suicide.* Homewood IL: Dorsey Press.

Marks, A., & Abernathy, T. (1974). Towards a sociocultural perspective on means of self-destruction. *Life Threatening Behavior, 4,* 3–17.

Marks, A., & Stokes, C.S. (1976). Socialization, firearms and suicide. *Social Problems, 5,* 622–639.

McCulloch, J.W., & Philip, A.E. (1972). *Suicidal behavior.* Oxford: Pergamon Press.

Neuringer, C. (1961). Dichotomous evaluations in suicidal individuals. *Journal of Consulting Psychology, 25,* 445–449.

Neuringer, C. (1962). Methodological problems in suicide research. *Journal of Consulting Psychology, 26,* 318–326.

Neuringer, C. (1964a). Reactions to interpersonal crisis in suicidal individuals. *Journal of General Psychology, 71,* 45–55.

Neuringer, C. (1964b). Rigid thinking in suicidal individuals. *Journal of Consulting Psychology, 28,* 54–58.

Neuringer, C. (1967). The cognitive organization of meaning in suicidal individuals. *Journal of General Psychology, 76,* 91–100.

Neuringer, C. (1968a). Divergencies between attitudes towards life and death among suicidal, psychosomatic and normal hospitalized patients. *Journal of Consulting and Clinical Psychology, 32,* 59–63.

Neuringer, C. (1968b). Suicide certification as a diagnostic method. In N.L.

Farberow (Ed.), *Proceedings of the fourth international conference for suicide prevention* (pp. 34–35). Los Angeles: Delmar Publishing Company.

Neuringer, C. (1979). Relationships between life and death among individuals of varying levels of suicidality. *Journal of Consulting and Clinical Psychology, 47*, 407–408.

Neuringer, C. (1982a). Suicidal behavior in women. *Crisis, 3,* 41–49.

Neuringer, C. (1982b). Affect configurations and changes in women who threaten suicide following a crisis. *Journal of Consulting and Clinical Psychology, 50,* 182–186.

Neuringer, C., & Levenson, M. (1972). Time perception in suicidal individuals. *Omega, 3,* 181–186.

Neuringer, C., & Lettieri, D.J. (1971). Cognition, attitude and affect in suicidal individuals. *Life Threatening Behavior, 1,* 106–123.

Neuringer, C., & Lettieri, D.J. (1982). *Suicidal women: Their thinking and feeling patterns.* New York: Gardner Press.

Phillips, R.H., & Muzaffer, A. (1961). Some aspects of self-mutilation in the general population of a large psychiatric hospital. *Psychiatric Quarterly, 35,* 421–423.

Resnik, H.L. (1971). Abortion and suicidal behaviors. *Mental Hygiene, 55,* 10–20.

Rosenberg, A., & Silver, E. (1965). Suicide, psychiatrists and therapeutic abortion. *California Medicine, 102,* 407–411.

Schneider, P.B. (1954). *La tentative de suicide.* Paris: Delachaux et Niestle.

Shneidman, E.S. (1957). The logic of suicide. In E.S. Shneidman & N.L. Farberow (Eds.), *Clues to suicide* (pp. 31–40). New York: McGraw-Hill.

Sim, M. (1963). Abortion and the psychiatrist. *British Medical Journal, 2,* 145–148.

Sims, M.A. (1974). Sex and age differences in suicidal rates in a Canadian province. *Life Threatening Behavior, 4,* 139–159.

Smith, S.L. (1975). Mood and the menstrual cycle. In E.J. Sachor (Ed.), *Topics in Psychoendocrinology* (pp. 208–228). New York: Grune and Stratton.

Stengel, E. (1964). *Suicide and attempted suicide.* Baltimore, MD: Penguin Press.

Stern, E.S. (1968). The Medea complex: Mother's homocidal wishes towards her children. *Journal of Mental Science, 94,* 321–331.

Tonks, C.M., Rack, P.H., & Rose, M.L. (1961). Attempted suicide and the menstrual cycle. *Journal of Psychosomatic Research, 11,* 319–323.

Trautman, E.C. (1961). The suicidal fit. *Archives of General Psychiatry, 5,* 76–83.

Trout, D.L. (1980). The role of social isolation in suicide. *Suicide and Life-Threatening Behavior, 10,* 10–23.

Wetzel, R.D., & McClure, J.N. (1973). Suicide and the menstrual cycle. *Comprehensive Psychiatry, 13,* 369–374.

Whitlock, F.A., & Edwards, J.E. (1968). Pregnancy and attempted suicide. *Comprehensive Psychiatry, 9,* 1–12.

Worden, W. (1976). Lethality factors and the suicide attempt. In E.S. Shneidman (Ed.), *Suicidology: Contemporary developments* (pp. 131–138). New York: Grune and Stratton.

■ Four
DEPRESSION AND THE AGING WOMAN

■ 16
Depression and Menopause: A Socially Constructed Link

RUTH FORMANEK, Ph.D.

This chapter will examine the historical development of the connection between menopause and depression which begins with ancient fears of menstruation and its cessation. Societal views of women and their functioning, medical and psychoanalytic approaches to menopause will be summarized and compared to empirical findings. No empirical support has been found for the connection between menopause and depression.

DEFINITIONS

The word "menopause" derives from *meno,* monthly, and from *pausis,* referring to cessation. A recently invented term, it was preceded by a number of metaphors including the term "change of life." The word "climacteric" derives from the Latin *klimakter,* rung of the ladder, presumably the top rung.

The present definitions of the climacteric and menopause derive from the First International Congress on the Menopause (Utian & Serr, 1976): 1. The climacteric is that phase in the aging process of women marking the transition from the reproductive stage of life to the nonreproductive stage. 2. The menopause refers to the final menstrual period and occurs during the climacteric. 3. The climacteric is sometimes, but not necessarily always,

Miriam Formanek-Brunell's assistance is gratefully acknowledged.

associated with symptomatology. When this does occur it may be termed the "climacteric syndrome."

Climacteric symptoms and complaints are regarded as being derived from three main sources:

1. Decreased ovarian activity with subsequent hormonal deficiency, resulting in early symptoms (hot flushes, perspiration, and atrophic vaginitis), and late symptoms related to metabolic changes.
2. Sociocultural factors determined by the woman's environment.
3. Psychological factors, dependent on the woman's character.
4. Combinations of the above.

An understanding of attitudes toward the menopause and the development of a link between menopause and depression requires an excursion into history. It is the contention of this chapter that the link between menopause and depression was invented, that it served a number of social purposes, that it expresses still-prevailing notions about women. In other words, to understand particular views of the menopause one must consider views of women of the same historical time period.

HISTORICAL ACCOUNTS

Before 1800

Freind's book on menstruation was the first on this topic published in English (1729). He cites the Greek physician Galen (between 130 and 200 A.D.), who had a theory about the menopause that became most influential: "The Menses are given to Women, that they may be evacuated for their Healths sake; and yield Nourishment to the Embryo, when suppressed by Conception." Galen believed that a plethora existed, an accumulation of blood which was periodically discharged until at a certain age "the Fibres of the Vessels grow more rigid and hard; so that a Plethora can neither be accumulated at that Age, nor if it be, can it be discharged, because of the tenacity of the Vessels . . . elderly Women are more dry and abound less with Blood" (p. 59). No connection between menopause and emotional disturbance, however, is found in Freind's book except that "many Women, as soon as they are destitute of their Menses, contract a fuller habit, and grow fat" (p. 62).

This somewhat mechanical view of women's functioning was accepted with minor modifications until the discovery of hormones was able to explain the phenomena of menstruation and menopause. Although little was known about the menopause, its negative effects were widely speculated on and accepted as fact. Beginning in the late 18th century, menopause was viewed as a catastrophe for women.

The exact origin of the alleged association between menopause and symptoms of emotional disturbance is unclear. It is first found in the years following publication of Freind's book. John Leake (1777) believed that "At this *critical time of life* (his italics) the female sex are often visited with various diseases of the *chronic* kind. . . . Some are subject to pain and giddiness of the head, hysteric disorders, colic pains, and a female weakness . . . intolerable itching at the neck of the bladder and contiguous parts are often very troublesome to others. . . . Women are sometimes affected with low spirits and melancholy."

Turning Point: From Midwives to Physicians

In colonial America, most medical care for women was provided by women in the home. Women were also prominent as lay practitioners, midwives, and "doctoresses." Pregnant women relied on midwives, female relatives, and friends until the decline of midwifery around 1800, when the shift from midwives to male doctors started among urban middle-class women. These well-to-do women had come to accept the physicians' claims of superior skill despite some moral opposition to male physicians attending childbirth. The idea that symptoms representing emotional disturbance arose from women's reproductive crises coincided with the replacement of midwives by male physicians. That male physicians described, and sometimes invented, dangers at such crisis points may be related to the demands of the professionalization of medicine, as well as to presumed fears on the part of men of women's elaborate reproductive physiology, in particular, menstruation.

The Victorians

The Victorians used metaphor to describe the menopause. "Before the golden calm of Indian Summer come the long wearying autumnal rains that beat the latest blooming chrysanthemums into the earth and despoil the trees of their liveries of russet and purple" (Harland, 1882, p. 314). Similar florid descriptions of symptoms were the rule. Napheys (1871), a widely-read Victorian physician who wrote on women's sexual physiology, speaks of the dangers of the beginning and ending of the period of childbearing, dangers which had *not* been described by midwives and lay practitioners: "The green-sickness, chlorosis, is by no means exclusively a disease of girls. It may occur at any period of childbearing life. . . . Hardly any one has watched women closely without having observed the peculiar tint of skin, the debility, the dislike of society, the change of temper, the fitful appetite, the paleness of the eye, and the other traits that show the presence of such a condition of the nervous system in those about renouncing their powers of reproduction" (p. 296).

According to Napheys, this "change of life" causes a number of changes in the lives of women: there is a diminution of the sexual passions; soon after this period they quite disappear. Sometimes, however, the reverse takes place, and the sexual sensations increase in intensity, occasionally exceeding what they were before. Napheys suggests that this should be regarded with alarm as it is contrary to the design of nature. He implies the presence of a "deep-seated disease of the uterus or ovaries . . . or an unnatural nervous excitability." Gratification may have dangerous consequences and should be temperate, and at rare intervals, or wholly denied (p. 301). Women are also said to experience "a sense of fulness in the head, a giddiness, and a dulness of the brain, sometimes going so far as to cause an uncertainty in the step, a slowness of comprehension, and a feeling as if one might fall at any moment in some sort of a fit" (p. 297). She develops an "inward nervousness," she becomes confused, imagines that "she is watched with suspicious and unkind eyes . . . every ache and pain is magnified." She becomes a hypochondriac and fears she will die (p. 297).

Napheys noted not only changes in sexual desire, cognitive and psychomotor deficits, but depression as well: "Vibrating between a distressing excitement and a gloomy depression, her temper gives way . . . She becomes fretful, and yet full of remorse for yielding to her peevishness; she seeks for sympathy without being able to give reasons for needing it; she annoys those around her by groundless fears; and is angered when they show their annoyance. In *fine*, she is utterly wretched, without any obvious cause of wretchedness."

Napheys was only one of the many male Victorian physicians who contributed to the construction of the link between menopause and depression. This view soon became the prevalent one in the medical literature as well as in popular books written by male physicians. Popular magazines, on the other hand, entirely omitted references to women's reproductive life, in line with custom: "A women would not complain about any ailment occurring between her neck and her knees" (Kunciov, 1971, p. 152).

According to Showalter (1981), who examined insanity during Victorian times, the old notion that madness was a disease of the blood maintained itself into modern times. It was believed that menstrual blood predisposed women to insanity, in that an abnormality of the flow might affect the brain. "Suppressed" menstruation was forcefully treated with medicines, purgatives, or leeches applied to the thighs.

The menopausal form of insanity (later to be named "involutional melancholia") accounted for 196 out of 228 cases in the Royal Edinburgh Asylum, between 1874 and 1882, and the diagnosis seems to have been a convenient label for all older women patients. Treatment was cruel, especially if the woman patient exhibited signs of unconventional erotic behavior. Smith (1848, in Showalter, 1981) recommended injections of ice water into the rectum, ice into the vagina and leeching the labia and the cervix. Clitorectomies were performed for many conditions including masturbation, disobedience, digestive troubles, and the operation was believed to be the treatment of choice for both nymphomania and insanity. In the United States in particular, the removal of the ovaries—oophorectomy—was used as a treatment for insanity during the latter part of the 19th century, especially on institutionalized women (Showalter, 1981).

Thus, the medicalization of women's reproductive crises led to crippling operations and other painful treatments, in total ignorance of the nature of women's physiology, and without regard for their wellbeing.

The medicalization and pathologization of puberty and menopause by male physicians were influenced by sociohistorical factors that also influenced the consciousness of the larger society. We must therefore consider changes in the perception of women, specifically the idealization of the maternal role, a 19th century development associated with the rise of the middle class.

The Idealization of Motherhood (1800–1860)

With the rise of the middle class a new type of family life emerged. It was characterized as "women's sphere" and linked women together in domesticity and child rearing. Female character was redefined: the home was idealized as "a bastion of feminine values, of piety and morality, affection and self-sacrifice" (Woloch, 1984, p. 116). Concomitant with the increasing importance of the home, the family was becoming smaller. While the average family in 1800 had seven children, by 1900 the average was between three and four children. And as the size of the family began to shrink, the value of motherhood rose. Child-raising became the family's central focus. Nationally distributed magazines (*Ladies Magazine, Godey's Lady's Book*) featured sentimental scenes of mothers at home, surrounded by children. Motherhood was celebrated as the ultimate opportunity for self-sacrifice and as the major role for women (Woloch, 1984, p. 118).

The emphasis on, and the idealization of motherhood and feminine qualities influenced the construction of women's identity. If motherhood was woman's main role and function, it was presumed that the end of her reproductive capacity was cause for unhappiness. But the descriptions of the symptoms accompanying the end of woman's reproductive functioning were written by male doctors, and women were not consulted. Since not all menopausal women consult physicians today, we may assume that those without complaints were also unknown to physicians during the 19th century. Physicians' assumptions that all women who had reached the menopause were ill were based on faulty generalizations and misogynist perceptions. That physicians' prescriptions for the treatment of women's ailments included prohibitions in regard to their pursuit of higher education or suffrage further suggests a political agenda.

Thus, it appears that the sufferings of the menopause were socially constructed and projected onto women, many of whom probably innocently cooperated by reporting the symptoms expected by their physicians.

DISCREPANT MEANINGS OF THE MENOPAUSE

There was and still is a discrepancy between the views of physicians and the actual experience of menopausal women. Contributing to this discrepancy is limited communication between physician and patient, particularly a hesitancy on the part of the male physician to inquire into the intricacies of women's reproductive experiences. With the advent of women physicians in the late 1800s, one assumes that communication improved. Nevertheless in 1913, physicians were still advised to be "delicate" in taking a case history: "Having inquired regarding the regularity of the bowels, one may ask if the patient is "regular in her own health," or "regular in her unwell times." Further questions were directed to facts: length of menstrual period, intervals between periods, whether it has stopped altogether, how much blood is lost, whether pain is present, the age at which menstruation began, and the occurrence or not of intermenstrual leucorrhea ("white discharge") (Hutchinson & Rainy, 1913, p. 6). Since these questions refer to objective and statistical events only, it is no wonder physicians knew little of actual menstrual or menopausal experience. And knowing little probably served to perpetuate earlier myths as well as aiding the construction of pathological conditions which either had no reality (e.g., chlorosis) or which were usually benign (e.g., leucorrhea).

Yet menopause had positive meanings for individual women who longed for a limitation of their reproductive powers.

"I am forty-four years of age and the mother of fourteen living children," a letter to Margaret Sanger (1928) begins. "My baby is five months old. I am anxious to know what you can tell me. Please send me the information (on birth control) at once for I am still thinking that my age won't interfere with me continuing to become a mother yet awhile" (p. 206). According to Mrs.

A.M. Longshore-Potts (1895), one of the new female physicians, "many pass on until ten, twelve, or even fifteen children have been born, with an accumulation of troubles to correspond. . . . But after these years have passed, and the climax of her womanhood has been reached, when there are no more children to be born, no more teeth to come, no more measles or whooping-cough, and no more babies' deaths to break her heart . . . Now they have leisure to read, think, and talk on subjects congenial to their age and development, now is the time for them to lay aside the more worldly cares, and to let the intellect have opportunity to grasp what may be learned in social life, or from public lectures" (p. 102). Social reformer and suffrage advocate Eliza Farnham believed that menopause could become "woman's golden age" and the post-menopausal years the period of woman's "super-exaltation" (see Smith-Rosenberg, 1985).

Thus, by the end of the nineteenth-century, menopause had two different meanings depending upon whether a male physician or a female physician, social reformer, or menopausal woman, especially one with many children, was consulted: for most men, it represented the beginning of a woman's decline of physical, emotional and cognitive functioning. But for most women, it was a golden age, a time at which pregnancies were no longer dreaded.

Divergent meanings of menopause appear to exist today as well, as shown in a study by Cowdan, Warren, and Young (1985) who asked 35 physicians, 43 nurses and 35 menopausal or postmenopausal women to rate the frequency, severity and causality of 15 menopausal symptoms. Results suggested that medical persons saw the menopausal symptoms as more pathological than the menopausal women did.

There has been, however, an increasing awareness within the nursing profession of the discrepancies in views between physicians and women, particularly those nurses concerned with women's health. MacPherson (1981), expressing views similar to those in the present chapter, contrasts the "health and illness" approach, in a paper entitled "Menopause as Disease: The Social Construction of a Metaphor." MacPherson goes beyond a description, however, and calls for the dismantling of the metaphor by the nursing profession.

INVOLUTIONAL MELANCHOLIA

Out of earlier collections of emotional symptoms suggestive of insanity and depression, Kraepelin (1909), an influential German psychiatrist, reformulated "involutional psychoses"—depressive episodes of major proportions occurring for the first time in the involutional ages without a prior history of depressive illness.[1] According to Kraepelin, involutional psychoses constituted one-third of all functional psychoses, the other two being dementia praecox and manic-depressive psychosis. Involutional melancholia had a gradual onset during the climacterium, was marked by hypochondriasis, pessimism, and irritability, and led to a full-blown depressive syndrome. The most prominent features, according to Kraepelin, were agitation, restlessness, anxiety and apprehension, occasionally bizarre delusions or paranoid ideation, insomnia, anorexia, and feelings of guilt and worthlessness.

Recently the concept of involutional depression became controversial, however, and while it was present in DSM II, it was omitted as an entry to DSM III.

PSYCHOANALYTIC FORMULATIONS

In the presence of taboos and the absence of precise information, old myths rarely fade away. Rather, they are sometimes given new life through reinterpretation. Deutsch (1924) retained 19th-century pejorative medical myths about the menopause but used Freud's account of psychosexual development to explain its significance. The myths Deutsch retained include the following: 1. The similarity between the course of puberty and menopause. 2. The correlation between the ending of menstruation and the ending of women's sexuality, together with inappropriate sexual desires. 3. The presence of multiple symptoms, especially depression, ascribed to menopause. 4. Woman's presumed yearning for a continuation of her ability to reproduce.

The menopause, according to Deutsch, "woman's last traumatic experience as a sexual being . . . is under the aegis of an incurable narcissistic wound." Parallel to the physical process, the menopause represents a psychosexual regression towards earlier, infantile libidinal positions, a "dethroning" of libido. At puberty, Deutsch states, "the narcissistic wound of the final renunciation of masculinity is wiped out by the appearance of secondary sexual characteristics and a new feminine physical attractiveness" (p. 56). At the menopause, what was granted at puberty is now taken back, at the same time that the woman's attractiveness is lost.

Deutsch speaks of typical behavioral changes during menopause, similar to those attending puberty. "She feels like a young girl, believes herself

---

[1]"Involutional" is used in biology to denote a retrograde or degenerative change (Webster's New 20th Century Dictionary, 1970).

able to make a fresh start in life. . . . feels ready for any passion, etc. She starts keeping a diary as she did when she was a girl, develops enthusiasm for some abstract idea as she did then, changes her behavior to her family as she did before, leaves home for the same psychical reasons as girls do at puberty, etc. . . . many women who are frigid during the reproductive period now become sexually sensitive, and others become frigid for the first time. . . . Others who have hitherto put up well with frigidity now begin to demonstrate all its typical concomitant phenomena; changes of mood, unbalanced behavior and irritability set in and make life a torment for the woman herself and those about her" (p. 58).

Symptoms of depression abound, resemble those of puberty and express the irritability of the unsatisfied, their anxiety, giddiness, palpitations, high pulse rates, headaches, neuralgia, vasomotor disturbances, heart sensations, and digestive troubles. Although Deutsch later, in 1945, revised some of her views, she continued to interpret the meaning of the menopause according to the stages of psychosexual development. Yet she differed with Freud who had considered libido as masculine, and referred to "the unappreciated female libido." Deutsch stressed the need for a psychology of women, one deserving equal importance to that of men, but her views of the menopause had a most negative influence on women and on their therapists.

Benedek's (1947) view of the menopausal woman is more benign than that of Deutsch. She criticized Deutsch's account of the menopausal woman as more descriptive of an infantile personality than of a normal woman.

According to Benedek, the climacterium is a "developmental phase." Benedek observed "women of all ages [who] were working productively in industry and in the professions in various capacities. Many of them were of climacteric age or beyond. . . . They went to work in what I felt was a womanly manner; they did it because they were needed. . . . I had to wonder, what were the psychological processes that made such a release of constructive energy possible at this stage of life?" She then defined the "normal climacterium as a progressive psychologic adaptation to a regressive biologic process" (p. 322).

Benedek suggests that, parallel with declining hormone production, menopause desexualizes emotional needs; thus sublimatory energies are freed which further the integration of the personality. Depression, if it appears, may not be directly related to the physiology of the menopause but rather motivated by a woman's psychosexual history. In addition, cultural patterns exert an influence on women's expectations of the menopause.

Analogous to 19th century medical opinion and to Helene Deutsch,

Benedek also believed that certain psychological aspects of the menopause represent a repetition of the affect, behavior and perception of self which was typical of the woman's puberty. The 19th century view that the course of puberty presages the course of the menopause for the individual woman was reformulated by Benedek in light of new knowledge about hormones: "The rebellion of puberty appears to be repeated when the internal frustration of the declining hormonal function activates aggressive, hostile and regressive behavior" (p. 333). Benedek described women who become anxious and overactive instead of, or before the development of depression. Some climacteric women feel that they did not achieve the goal of femininity, and may be seized by fear of aging, or fear of losing their sexual attractiveness.

A more recent psychoanalytic view, one influenced by object relations and psychoanalytic developmental theory, is exemplified by Lax (1982). She has suggested that a woman's climacteric response will be determined by the severity of her physiological symptoms, the nature of her past experiences, her internalized object relations, her psychic structure, her libidinal investments, the width of her conflict-free ego sphere, her ego interests, her healthy narcissism, her current object relations, and the nature of her familial and social setting—in other words, both internal and external reality are capable of exerting an influence on a woman's response during this period. Moreover, Lax argues that the changes attending the climacteric "make it more difficult and sometimes even impossible for the menopausal woman to achieve those goals of her wishful self-image which she had previously taken for granted. This whole constellation of factors accounts for the development of the expectable depressive climacteric reaction" (p. 163).

Lax suggests that depression is an affect integral to psychic life which occurs when a loss is experienced, and refers to the "depressive mood of little girls confronted with their lack of a penis, the sadness of rapprochement children recognizing their limitations, and adolescent depression, as well as the expectable climacteric reaction" (p. 163). This reaction "manifests itself in sadness, in a sense of loss, and in mourning for the youthful self of one's past" (p. 164). The expectable climacteric reaction may last for a few years and vary in intensity. While it may lead to upheavals in all aspects of psychic functioning, it has an adaptive function: successful mourning allows a woman to renounce the no longer attainable goals and ideals of her youthful self-image, and to develop an identification with an idealized matriarchal model whose generativity, generosity, and compassion become her own goals.

While empirical studies tend to find primarily vasomotor symptoms among menopausal women, psychoanalytic investigations have focused on depressive reactions. It is therefore of interest that recent life-event studies measuring stress (see below) have similarly documented the presence of a vulnerability to depression among menopausal women, but only in certain cultures with particular sensitivities to loss.

FLASHBACK TO THE 1920S: THE DISCOVERY AND MARKETING OF ESTROGENS

When Butenandt, a Nobel prize winner in chemistry isolated a hormone from the urine of pregnant women in 1929, the physiology of the menopause began to be understood. Despite this important discovery, however, the myths and stereotypes of menopausal women remained unchanged. Moreover, the 1960s saw a recurrence of the exaggeration of women's hormonal deficiency, this time motivated by the greed of pharmaceutical manufacturers and members of the medical profession supported by them. According to writers such as Wilson and Wilson, women were said to show a stiffness of muscles and ligaments, the "dowager's hump," and a "negativistic expression." "Some exhibit signs and symptoms similar to those in the early stages of Parkinson's disease. They exist rather than live." The Wilsons describe "unfortunate women abounding in the streets walking stiffly in twos and threes, seeing little and observing less. The world appears [to them] as through a grey veil, and they live as docile, harmless creatures missing most of life's values . . . in a vapid cow-like negative state" (cited by Fausto-Sterling, 1985). Wilson defined the menopause as an estrogen deficiency disease and, in his book *Feminine Forever* (1966), he offered women estrogen replacement therapy. Although the book was excerpted in *Look* and in *Vogue* and sold 100,000 copies in the first seven months after publication, Wilson was dismissed as a quack by his more responsible colleagues. What Wilson had promised was relief from 26 symptoms of estrogen deficiency which included anxiety, hot flashes, joint pains, melancholia, crying spells, headache, loss of memory, indigestion, itching, backache, neurosis, a tendency to take alcohol and sleeping pills, and even to contemplate suicide. In 1964, the Wilson Research Foundation, headed by Dr. Wilson, received $17,000 from the Searle Foundation, $8,700 from Ayerst Laboratories and $5,600 from the Upjohn Company, according to the *Washington Post* (Seaman & Seaman, 1977). Ayerst also supported the Information Center on the Mature Woman, a public relations firm that promoted estrogen replacement therapy. Estrogen in the form of Premarin® (Ayerst) was prescribed for long-term use for six million women and became the fourth or fifth most popular drug in the United States. The drug rapidly lost its popularity when, in 1975, a report was published which indicated a correlation between estrogen replacement therapy and uterine cancer. Today, estrogens are again prescribed, sometimes in combination with progesterone. Research now suggests that estrogens may be useful in the prevention of osteoporosis. Although estrogens might have many uses, the exaggerated claims that they will confer eternal youth are no longer credible.

Thus, the social construction of the link between menopause and physical and psychological symptoms maintained itself and helped to increase profits for the pharmaceutical industry. What negative effects the advertising of Premarin® had on menopausal women has not been researched. There can be no doubt, however, that women must have cringed, and perhaps felt depressed when they read that "no woman can be sure of escaping the horror of this living decay" (Wilson, 1966, p. 43).

MENOPAUSAL SYMPTOMS

On the basis of empirical findings, Kraepelin's diagnosis of "involutional melancholia" is now considered untenable as a specific condition which has its first onset during the climacteric. When menopausal or postmenopausal women are depressed, it is usually possible to discover episodes of depression at earlier times in their lives.

A study by Weissman (1979), for example, found no support for the presence of involutional melancholia. She examined a group of 422 women patients with a diagnosis of major depression at the Yale University Depression Research Unit. The women were divided according to age: premenopausal (younger than 45 years), menopausal (46 to 55 years), and postmenopausal (over 56 years). The symptom patterns of patients in these groups were compared and no differences were found. Nor did the three groups differ in regard to a history of depressive illness. Weissman concluded that there was no support for the validity of involutional melancholia as a distinct diagnostic entity. Although age itself may predispose to depression in both women and men, the present-day modal age for depression in women is well below middle age.

Many other studies carried out over the last 25 years have concluded that no specific involutional depression could be documented. Greene (1984) lists 14 nonclinical population surveys of symptoms among menopausal women. The only symptoms closely related to the menopause are vasomotor ones. Hot flushes peak during the menopause, reported to go from 18% before the menopause to 75% during the perimenopause. The rates for depression, when reported at all, show a less dramatic increase, going from 39% to 55% during the same time period. Thus increases in the symptoms of depression among women parallel those found among men during the same time period. Among men, such symptoms are referred to as constituting a "mid-life" depression and are believed to derive from psychosocial stressors. Such stressors affect women as well.

In contrast to the confusion between symptoms due to estrogen depletion and those due to the process of aging, the present consensus is that the menopause is a normal event which occurs during the climacteric, and is one of the consequences of hormonal changes. Estrogen depletion causes vasomotor instability (hot flushes, perspiration) and atrophic vaginitis. It is estimated that approximately 75% of menopausal women experience flushes but that their intensity, duration and number of years they are experienced vary tremendously from woman to woman.

The nonspecific symptoms due to aging need to be separated from the symptoms of estrogen deficiency. In addition, the effects of women's social status, their education, social and family problems, and their identification with earlier societal views of women's deficiency need exploration. The construction of the link between menopause and depression, i.e., the ascribing of pathological symptoms such as cognitive impairments, memory loss, hypochondriasis, etc., to the menopause, had a generally disparaging effect on women's feelings about themselves (Formanek, 1986). For this reason, one must search for the *meaning* of potential symptoms to the woman rather than record their presence or absence.

Research on menopausal symptoms has been poor and sparse. In addition to some studies of hot flashes (Voda, 1982), information is now available on nonspecific symptoms, such as sleep disturbances believed to be a sign of depression. Ballinger (1976), for example, compared menopausal with premenopausal women in regard to sleep disturbances. She suggests that sleep disturbance may be a reflection of increasing age rather than be directly related to menopause. That increasing age may account for many nonspecific "menopausal" symptoms is the conclusion of many empirical studies.

INFLUENCE OF LIFE EVENTS ON SYMPTOMS

The climacterium is a developmental phase and, as such, has its specific characteristics. It exerts a particular effect on women, based partly on its meaning to the individual and partly on cultural expectations. Epidemiological researchers (e.g., Paykel et al., 1971; Brown, 1981; Brown & Harris, 1978; Greene, 1984; Cooke & Greene, 1981) have focused on measuring life events as contributing to stress for the individual. They have proposed sophisticated models which consider "vulnerabilities" in individuals as following "provoking events."

Life stress peaks during the early climacteric period, but being menopausal did not contribute to increased vulnerability to life stress. However, when *types* of life events of urban Scottish women were investigated (Greene & Cooke, 1981), the life event which differentiated older from younger women was "exits." The "exits" included children leaving the home, separations, and the loss due to deaths of close friends or family members. Greene (1984) concludes that the increase in symptoms among his Scottish sample is associated with the degree of current life stress women are exposed to. Moreover, different symptoms were influenced by different life events in complex ways. Psychological symptoms seemed to be related to stress arising from financial, legal, work, housing conditions, illness in the family, etc., but such stressful events did not increase among the climacteric women. Yet some climacteric women showed a vulnerability to common difficulties, which manifested itself in the form of psychological complaints. Somatic symptoms were also reported more frequently by climacteric women who were experiencing high levels of stress. But *only* if the women had also experienced a recent bereavement.

Brown and Prudo (1981) report that bereavement appeared to provoke psychiatric disorders among 48% of first-onset depressive cases in the Hebrides, but only in 16% of London women. Chronicity of psychiatric condition showed a similar pattern: the loss of a member of the woman's primary family preceded chronicity of psychiatric condition in 77% of Hebrides women, but in only 16% in London. The authors consider the greater sensitivity of Hebrides women to death—a cultural factor—to add to their vulnerability. What makes climacteric and probably older women even more vulnerable is that the death of a close person deprives the woman of social support.

SOCIOCULTURAL DIFFERENCES

Negative attitudes toward the menopause in our society are usually based on stereotypes, and found to be stronger in younger than in older women. Women who are actually experiencing the menopause show a decline in negative attitudes. In addition to younger women, those of lower socioeconomic status, income, and less education also show more negative attitudes toward the menopause. In general, as age, education, and information increase, so do more positive attitudes (see Neugarten & Kraines, 1965; Notman, 1979).

In regard to individual women, the more a woman has valued her reproductive role the more negative her attitude towards the menopause is likely to be. However, this appears to be subject to cultural influences, as the social consequences of the menopause in a particular society affect a woman's role and status, and thus her attitudes (see Kaufert, 1985).

Datan et al. (1985) studied 1148 women from five Israeli subcultures, ranging along a continuum from the more to the less highly developed: immigrant Jews from Central Europe, Turkey, Persia, and North Africa, and Israeli-born Muslim Arabs. The researchers conclude that cultural patterns produced greater stress in the more highly developed culture, manifested at the extreme as depression, and that there are different modes of stress expression: Persian and North African women tended to have more psychosomatic complaints, while Europeans voiced more psychological distress. The most important finding of the research was that clinical depression was rare but appeared in approximately equal rates across cultures. Datan et al. (1985) conclude that "the response to middle age and to the climacterium is shaped by ethnic origin, that the balance of gains and losses is specific to each subculture, that there is no linear relationship between psychological well-being and the degree of modernity, and finally, that the cessation of fertility is welcomed by women in all cultures" (p. 179).

These empirical studies seem at variance with earlier notions of the meaning of the menopause, as well as with some psychoanalytic views of the "expectable depression" as a reaction to the menopause. It does seem likely, however, that the menopause, especially if it occurs very early, might produce a depression in those who wanted children but now know that it will never be. What both common sense, personal experience, and empirical research agree on is the lack of general statements that can be confirmed for all menopausal women regardless of age, number of children, socioeconomic status, education, culture, and many other factors. The idiosyncratic responses to the menopause have in the past been muted, not talked about, considered taboo. As a result, strong statements from medical and psychiatric sources have been accepted as they offered to define the darkness.

While this chapter offers no social-activist program (as MacPherson does) for the eradication of the socially constructed view of menopause as a time of impending depression, if not insanity, it has tried to document the evolution of such negative attitudes. It has examined the historical development of pejorative views of the menopause, the meaning of menopause to different societies and time periods and the contribution of such views to maintaining women in a denigrated position during the 19th and 20th century. Psychoanalytic views of the menopause were summarized.

The last 25 years have seen efforts to research women's functioning during the climacteric by means of both clinical and population surveys. Early but firmly held assumptoms based on myth rather than reality about the pathology of women's being "unwell," as well as the cessation of their being "unwell," have crumbled or are about to crumble. The deletion of the diagnostic category "involutional melancholia" in DSM III was neither a trivial action nor does it suggest temporary predilections in classifying patients. "Involutional melancholia" was an iatrogenic construction: a link between a normal physiological marker—menopause—and ancient views relating to menstruation. The 19th century medicalization of this view, which connected menstrual blood to insanity, inseparably linked menopause to depression.

But more research needs to be done. Stressors due to negative life events must be further examined as they interact with personality types, life experience, life style, relationships, culture, etc. The almost total absence of the understanding of the subjective experience of the menopause must be replaced with first-hand accounts, psychoanalytical and other explorations, structured interviews, and information from women's physicians.

REFERENCES

Ballinger, C.B. (1976). Subjective sleep disturbance at the menopause. *Journal of Psychosomatic Research, 20,* 599–613.

Benedek, T. (1947/1973). Climacterium: a developmental phase. In *Psychoanalytic investigations. Selected papers.* New York: Quadrangle.

Brown, G.W. (1981). Life events, psychiatric disorder and physical illness. *Journal of Psychosomatic Research, 25,* 461–473.

Brown, G.W., & Harris, T. (1978). *Social origins of depression.* New York: Free Press.

Brown, G.W., & Prudo, R. (1981) Psychiatric disorder in a rural and an urban population: 1. Aetiology and depression. *Psychological Medicine, 11,* 581–599.

Cooke, D.J., & Greene, J.G. (1981). Types of life events in relation to symptoms of the climacterium. *Journal of Psychosomatic Research, 25,* 5–11.

Cowdan, G., Warren, L.W., & Young, J.L. (1985). Medical perceptions of menopausal symptoms. *Psychology of Women Quarterly, 9,* 3–14.

Datan, N., & Antonovsky, N. (1985). Tradition, modernity, and transitions in five Israeli subcultures. In J.K. Browne & V. Kerns (Eds.), *In her prime: A new view of the middle-aged woman.* South Hadley, MA: Bergin and Garvey.

Deutsch, H. (1924/1984). The menopause. *International Journal of Psychoanalysis, 65,* 55–62.

Formanek, R. (1986). Learning the lines: women's aging and self esteem. In J. Alpert (Ed.), *Women and Psychoanalysis.* Hillsdale, NJ: Analytic Press.

Freind, J. (1729). *Emmenologia.* London: T. Cox.

Greene, J.B. (1984). *The social and psychological origins of the climacteric syndrome.* Brookfield, VT: Gower.

Harland, M. (1882). *Eve's daughters; or, common sense for maid, wife, and mother.* New York: Anderson and Allen.

Hutchinson, R., & Rainy, H. (1913). *Clinical Methods,* (5th ed.). New York: Funk and Wagnalls.

Kaufert, P. (1985). Midlife in the Midwest, Canadian women in Manitoba. In J.K. Brown & V. Kerns (Eds.), *In her prime: A new view of the middle-aged woman.* South Hadley, MA: Bergin and Garvey.

Kraepelin E. (1909). *Psychiatrie. 8th edition.* Leipsic: J.A. Barth.

Lax, R. (1982). The expectable depressive climacteric reaction. *Bulletin of the Menninger Clinic, 46,* 151–167.

Longshore-Potts, A.M. (1895). *Discourses to women on medical subjects.* Published by the author. National City, San Diego, CA.

MacPherson, K.I. (1981). Menopause as disease: The social construction of a metaphor. *Advances in Nursing Science, 3,* 95–113.

Napheys, G.H. (1871). *The physical life of a woman: Advice to the maiden, wife, and mother.* Philadelphia: Maclean.

Neugarten, B., & Kraines, R.J. (1965). Menopausal symptoms in women at various ages. *Psychosomatic Medicine, 27,* 266–273.

Notman, M. (1979). Midlife concerns of women: Implications of the menopause. *American Journal of Psychiatry, 1,* 1270–1274.

Paykel, E.S. (1971). Scaling of life events. *Archives of General Psychiatry, 25,* 240–347.

Sanger, M. (1928). *Motherhood in bondage.* New York: Brentano's.

Seaman, B., & Seaman, G. (1977). *Women and the crisis in sex hormones.* New York: Rawson Associates.

Smith, W.T. (1848). The climacteric disease in women. *London Medical Journal, 1,* 601.

Smith-Rosenberg, C. (1985). Puberty to menopause: The cycle of femininity in nineteenth century America. In C. Smith-Rosenberg (Ed.), *Disorderly conduct.* New York: Oxford University Press.

Utian, W. (1980). *Menopause in modern perspective.* New York: Appleton-Century.

Utian, W.H., & Serr, D. (1976). Report on workshop: The climacteric syndrome. In P.A. van Keep, R.B. Greenblatt, & M. Albeaux-Fernet (Eds.), *Consensus on Menopause Research.* Lancaster, PA: MTP Press.

Voda, A.M. (1982). Menopausal hot flash. In A.M. Voda, M. Dinnerstein, & S.R. O'Donnell (Eds.), *Changing perspectives on menopause.* Austin, TX: University of Texas Press.

Weissman, M.M. (1979). Sex differences and the epidemiology of depression. *Archives of General Psychiatry, 34,* 98–111.

Wilson, R.A. (1966). *Feminine forever.* New York: Mayflower-Dell.

Wilson & Wilson, cited by Fausto-Sterling, A. (1985). *Myths of gender.* New York: Basic Books.

Woloch, N. (1984). *Women and the American experience.* New York: Knopf.

■ 17
Depression and the Older Woman

RUTH FORMANEK, Ph.D.

Similar to childhood and adolescence, old age is a social construction. The time period regarded as "old age" varies with culture and historical period. When the lifespan was short, "old age" probably referred to those now considered in "middle age." In the United States today, markers of old age include retirement, social security, and Medicare eligibility. For the purpose of this discussion, we are defining old age as beginning with 65 years.

A discussion of depression in older women must begin by comparing several groups: (1) older women and older men and (2) younger and older women. The literature on older women is superficial, narrow in scope and small in quantity, and reflects investigators' neglect of gender differences at this age period. Moreover, old people, in both popular and scientific literature are homogenized as to age and one gets the impression that, once you are over 65, you might as well be over 90. And similar to the literature on infancy, childhood, and adolescent depression, gender differences are rarely analyzed.

Thus, information on depression in older women is submerged in the literature on depression in older people as well as in the general literature on older women. Attention to the intersect between depression among older people and the problems of older women should illuminate the issue of the depressed older woman.

This paper includes ideas contributed by Margot Tallmer, Ph.D. Claude Brunell was the researcher who also contributed some of the conceptualizations.

PREVALENCE OF DEPRESSION

The prevalence of depression in older women is variously estimated as less than two to more than 50%. Complicating the varying estimates of depression among older women are varying definitions of depression, that is, whether diagnosis rests on DSM III categories or on symptoms reported on depression check lists. Whether depression is primary or reactive to life stress, such as widowhood, or as a side effect of medication prescribed for physical illness, is usually not distinguished. Moreover, depression check lists are weighted on symptoms that may be produced, in the absence of depression, by physical illness so often present in the older adult. Blazer and Williams (1980) found a prevalence of 14.7% "depressive state" although only 1.8% in their sample had a "primary depression." Thus, physical symptoms frequently mimic depression.

In contrast to clinical studies, community surveys reach multitudes of people who never come for treatment. In the United States, such surveys have consistently found that more women than men are depressed, but that the group of younger women shows a higher proportion of depression than the group of older women. Weissman and Myers (1979), in a sample of over 2,000 respondents, found 7.1% of 18- to 29-year-old women, and 8.4% of 30- to 44-year-old women to be depressed. Among those of 75 years of age and older, only 1.2% of women and 0.6% of the men were classified as depressed. Radloff and Rae (1981) also found higher proportions of younger people to be depressed.

Clinical studies have suggested a significant association between lateness of onset (60 years or older) and the presence of delusions. Alexopoulous (1985) found elderly patients with organic brain syndrome to show more depressive symptoms than same-age cognitively intact patients. Again, one suspects the confounding of illness with depression! Findings differ when individuals who are in the hospital or nursing home are compared to those not so confined.

Many studies do not distinguish those with a lifetime of depressive episodes from those reporting a first-onset episode late in life. According to Haug, Ford, and Sheafor (1985), of 23 older subjects meeting criteria for depression, only five reported onset after the age of 65.

Prevalence rates may furthermore be influenced by the transient nature of symptoms, or the confusion of depressive symptoms with expected signs of aging (Jarvik & Perl, 1981), the presence of memory problems, and older people's unwillingness to acknowledge depression in favor of physical complaints. Moreover, few clinicians are familiar with developments in old age, have contact with older supervisors, or have experienced old age themselves. This is true for men and women alike.

OLDER VS. YOUNGER DEPRESSED WOMEN

Depression in older women may be similar to depression in younger women, but it is doubtful whether a similar clinical picture will necessarily have similar causes. While this reasoning usually holds true for physical illness, in psychological illness a given clinical picture may result from any one of several unrelated causes.

Haug et al. (1985) point to the low incidence of first-onset depression after the age of 65. Most likely, many of those experiencing depression at a younger age continue to experience depression later in life although evidence is so far lacking.

DEPRESSED OLDER WOMEN VS. DEPRESSED OLDER MEN

A comparison of older women with older men in regard to depression includes the following findings:

1. Older men report symptom patterns different from those of older women: women report higher levels of anxiety and interpersonal sensitivity and a lower level of paranoid ideation as compared to men. Level of depression, however, does not differ according to gender (Hale & Cochran, 1983).

2. Miller (1979), who summarized 19 articles on geriatric suicide, has questioned the observed plurality of male suicides when rates of depression are about the same for older men as they are for older women.

3. Utilization rates for depressive disorder at three types of mental health facilities indicate a decline in utilization for women after certain ages. For example, state, county and private inpatient facilities show a peak for women at ages 45 to 64, and a decline after age 64, and outpatient services show a peak for ages 25 to 44. The rate of utilization for men and women converges at older ages (Belle, 1982).

4. Radloff and Rae (1981) found that scores on a depression scale decrease with age for both men and women.

5. According to Brown and Harris (1978), pure depressive illness is of later onset for males than for females. Older women with first onset of depression are more likely to have psychotic types of depressions.

6. A recent community study (Lewinson et al., 1986) investigated the relation of age at onset to the duration of episodes in depression. The main findings were that (1) the duration of depressive episodes did not increase with age of onset, and (2) *women did not have longer lasting episodes than did men* (authors' italics).

RETIREMENT AND WIDOWHOOD AND THEIR
CONTRIBUTION TO DEPRESSION

A. Retirement

Retirement, an age-related and predictable phase of the life cycle today, is a development of recent times only. In the United States, retirement became a stage of life following the Great Depression. The era of the New Deal, a period of dramatic social innovations which included social security, made life without work feasible after age 65. But few older women have role models of retirement available and reactions to retirement are largely unfamiliar, uncharted ground.

In the first half of this century, women were exhorted to direct their energies toward a strong, inner, intuitive life if they would be feminine. Striving for competitive, assertive work roles was discouraged. Performance in such "masculine" roles was seen as compensatory at best. These views buttressed long-standing social norms which customarily dictated marriage and mothering as the most acceptable female goals. Any woman who chose to delay or completely abstain from traversing the societally approved routes had to be highly motivated and intensely determined. The greater the barriers to the pursuit of achievement, the greater was the required commitment. We must infer then that women who chose to work throughout their lives, married or unmarried, professional or nonprofessional, must have transcended the popular beliefs of their times, possibly by compromise measures—that is, they may have chosen careers that would tolerate interruptions, or elected part-time employment. They may have felt (or been) isolated, lacking the peer support available today.

Today women's participation in the labor force is accepted. Increasing numbers of women work, a trend noted particularly among middle-aged women. In 1978, 53.8% of all women aged 54 to 59 years of age, and 31.7% of all women aged 60 to 64 years of age worked outside of the home.

Common sense suggests that the effects of retirement will vary according to several variables: health, socioeconomic status, age, attitude toward work, gender, reason for retirement and preretirement planning. Women generally retire at an earlier age than men, with lower pensions and less money available to them, analogous to their lesser earning power when compared to men at any age.

The contributions of women's retirement to depression are unknown. Women's retirement in general is a relatively unexplored topic due to the still prevalent view that men retire and women remain housewives. Most investigations of retirement in the United States as well as in other countries have relied almost entirely on male subjects. Work, many researchers believe, has more salience to the lives of men than to the lives of women. Moreover, women are believed to have discontinuous work histories and a lesser commitment to work. As a result, women are not expected to experience loss of the role of worker as a significant life event. Rather, women are believed to react less negatively to retirement, and to experience less stress than men because their major life interests are believed to center around their roles as mother and housewife.

Empirical research, however, contradicts most of these notions. That working is the norm rather than the exception is reflected in women's perceptions of themselves. According to a recent Harris report, for example, the majority of women aged 65 and over who were questioned considered themselves retirees (50%) rather than housewives (30%) (Szinovacz, 1983).

Despite unsupported views to the contrary, women do not enjoy retirement as much as men and take longer to adapt to the retirement transition (Atchley, 1976; Streib & Schneider, 1971). Moreover, women who approach retirement with a negative attitude seem unable to adjust to it even after a long period of time, feeling useless and lonely, missing social contacts and the satisfactions derived from work. In general, women worry more about their financial state after retirement, and are more anxious about retirement than men. On the other hand, according to a study by Sheldon et al. (1975), women adjusted better and more quickly to retirement. A clear relationship exists between retirement attitudes and post-retirement morale (Levy, 1980), in both men and women, but negative attitudes seem to have more lasting effects on women.

It has further been assumed that retiring women will resume their household roles and that the division of tasks between spouses will follow stereotypical sex roles. Research evidence suggests that this is only rarely the case, and many women have complained that it is particularly difficult for them to settle down to household tasks after retirement (Szinovacz, 1978, 1980).

Retirement is a major marker of old age in our society and a crisis point for many. It is inadequately researched for women but may be a time of major upheaval. Research has suggested that nonworking women who emphasized their roles as homemakers and mothers are more likely to become depressed and to suffer from more physical symptoms than women who had worked. Yet women who retire often go through a difficult transition period whose length is unknown. One can conclude that homemakers and mothers, as well as working women who retire are vulnerable to depression.

B. Widowhood

Role loss has been viewed as an important causal factor in predicting changes in both health and social functioning (Ferraro, 1984). Being widowed resembles retiring in that both involve the loss of a role.

Women appear to react strongly to the loss of significant others and, with age, such losses accumulate. Older women are more likely to have experienced past losses than younger women. Loss of the mother before age 11 has been found to be one important factor contributing to the possibility of depression at any time (Brown & Harris, 1978). But the vulnerability stemming from early experiences of loss does not directly lead to depression; rather it requires interaction with current adversity before depression is experienced. In the absence of current adversity, depression may not occur (Brown, Harris, & Bifulco, 1986).

Widowhood is a fairly predictable event for a woman in view of her longer lifespan and the fact that she is usually younger than her husband. Since a woman may anticipate widowhood, it may be easier to accept, especially when she vicariously participated in the adjustment of other widows. It is therefore not surprising that mortality rates for widowers are considerably higher than for widows (Berardo, 1970). Widows seem to have an easier time adjusting to their status. It may be that they are often able to continue in their household functions, in their relationships to children, grandchildren, other relatives and friends, and that they establish a role and function for themselves in their own communities. A woman is more likely to have had continued relationships with her own family throughout her marriage, and kinships continue as before widowhood.

Does widowhood precipitate depression? Clayton (1983) found that 35% of recent widows and widowers met the criteria for depression at one month, 35% at four months, and 17% at one year after the loss of the spouse. However, few of the subjects regarded their depressions as abnormal and fewer sought psychiatric care. Clinical experience suggests that some women blame themselves for the deaths of their husbands, i.e., experience survivor guilt, and become depressed. Their previously disavowed rage and ambivalence toward their husbands may account for depression although, for most widows, the normal mourning process is time-limited.

Although the data on retirement and widowhood are inconclusive, they suggest a possible explanation for depression in some older women. The experience of one event may render the woman vulnerable to the effects of the second. Exactly what these effects will be depends on many factors, especially on the ego strength and internalized object relations of the individual woman.

INTERNAL FACTORS

In regard to psychological functioning, researchers' approach toward old people differs from that taken towards the young. Investigators of old people keep their distance from them, focusing mostly on external and superficial issues, such as SES, the prevalence of disease, the number of relatives or friends visited, or whether the old person is married, divorced, or widowed.

Those studying infants, on the other hand, search for signs of intelligent life, for evidence of inner processes, for responses to sounds, sights, interpersonal sensitivity, or the capacity to learn. That older persons react to their experiences depending on factors other than obvious, external and easily measurable ones seems to astonish some researchers. The focus on external events is probably due to the absence of information on internal ones. It is rare for the elderly to enter therapy and/or to make public their inner worlds in other ways. Aside from reactions of the elderly to loss, few studies have considered inner processes.

Psychoanalysis has viewed depression in developmental terms, that is, depression is expected to attend developmental crises, and must be worked through with each crisis. A. Sandler (1984), for example, has called attention to a group of elderly patients who come to the analyst because they need assistance in coping with the developmental tasks of aging.

The type of transitional depression as well as its intensity, which attends each developmental crisis, varies idiosyncratically. It is, however, not confirmed that all developmental transitions are attended by either the experience of crisis or by depression and needs further research. Moreover, one may assume that particular social constructions evoke or do not evoke a crisis. The age of 30 appears to be a recently constructed marker in the United States, while in Sweden, for example, the fiftieth year has been of major significance. Crisis is not a purely intrapsychic phenomenon but depends to some degree on one's sensitivity to socially-constructed markers and expectations.

Increasingly more researchers refer to the existence of inner processes or to the influence of personality variables:

1. While actual social relations are important predictors of happiness, *perceived* companionship is the best predictor of continued health (Baldassare et al., 1983).
2. In Henderson's (1983) longitudinal study, the overriding dominance of constitutional or personality attributes was documented. In the face of adversity these are more powerful than the lack of supportive relationships. Vulnerabiltiy to depression more likely resides within

the individual than with the individual's social environment. Henderson suggests that his results were contrary to hypotheses and that, "more important than the social environment is how individuals construe it."

3. Lieberman and Tobin (1983) found that, for all life stages and for all cultural groups, personality charateristics were more robustly associated with successful adaptation than were social characteristics. The authors suggest that, in order to maintain a coherent, consistent self, an inner task more critical than the interactional task of maintaining an accepted self, it is essential that action at this stage of life be viewed as internal—not transactional and not interactional.

4. Gutmann (1985) has focused on gender differences. He has collected data on the psychological growth and patterns of change in older women, in cross-cultural perspective. He lists several such patterns and suggests that, across a wide range of societies, the older woman moves aggressively towards a position of matriarchy and the assumption of power. Gutmann argues that the virility of the older woman is released when she emerges from the adult period of chronic emergency—from parenting. When her children can maintain their own emotional security, the "postparental" woman can reclaim the aggression that, earlier, might have put her children at risk. Such eruptive energies may lead to rivalry with men, and the power crisis may lead to psychiatric symptoms. Such women, according to Gutmann, sometimes come to psychiatric treatment for the first time in the postparental years and are often misdiagnosed as "depressed."

5. Self-in-relation theorists also focus on gender differences. They point to the socialization of girls as future mothers, with stress on the *internalization* of maternal attributes. Women derive strength from their ability to care for others and, for this reason, the loss of a relationship equals the loss of their ability to continue such care. Thus, according to self-in-relation theorists, the loss of a relationship represents the loss of confirmation of self for women. Not only do women suffer over the loss of a loved one but they experience the loss of intimacy as a failure of the self—they feel responsible for failed relationships. With loss, women tend to feel inadequate and experience a lowering of self esteem. Thus the ideals of female socialization may predispose women to depression, especially with aging and the accumulation of losses.

CONCLUSION

Depression is clearly a risk for women at younger ages. At older ages, some factors both predispose to, as well as militate against, a first-onset depression. Diagnostically, an artifact may exist in that older women (and men) may be viewed as depressed when "depression" is a secondary reaction to medicines taken for physical illness or to the illness itself. Surveys suggest that older women are more vulnerable to the experience of loss, and that the loss of relatives or friends also represents the loss of a support system. Thus more older women than men may be expected to be depressed. Aspects of socialization, i.e., the internalization of female ego ideals, differential self esteem deriving from a socialization which emphasizes the maternal, the caring, the social context, renders women more vulnerable to depression. But the same factors may aid women in resisting depression as well. Women's continuity in their close relationships to family and friends over time lends a consistency to their lives and may prevent depression. Moreover, some women's apparent ascendency in their "postparental" years, together with their physical zest also render them less vulnerable to depression.

Research on old age, especially on older women has been sparse and tied to concrete concerns. While far from consensus, many investigators have pointed to the need to examine internal rather than external factors. It is not the reality of our physical health, our personal circumstances or social world. Rather it is our *perception* of our lives which determines our satisfaction or dissatisfaction. Not only in old age, but at any time.

REFERENCES

Alexopoulous, Q.S., Young, R.C., Haycox, J., Blass, J.P., Lieberman, K.W., & Shamoian, C.A. (1985). Biological Studies in depression with reversible dementia. In C.A. Shamoian (Ed.), *Treatment of Affective Disorders in the Elderly.* Progress in Psychiatry series. Washington, DC: American Psychiatric Association.

Atchley, R.C. (1976). *The sociology of retirement.* New York: Halstead Press.

Baldassare, M., Rosenfield, S., & Rook, K.S. (1984). The types of social relations predicting elderly well-being. *Research on Aging, 6,* 549–559.

Belle, D. (1982). *Lives in stress: Women and depression.* Beverly Hills, CA: Sage Publications.

Berardo, F. (1970). Survivorship and social isolation: The case of the aged widower. *The family coordinator, 19,* 58–61.

Blazer, D., & Williams, C.D. (1980). Epidemiology of dysphoria and depression in an elderly population. *American Journal of Psychiatry, 137,* 439–444.

Brown, G., & Harris, T. (1978). *Social origins of depression.* New York: The Free Press.

Brown, G.W., Harris, T.O., & Bifulco, A. (1986). In M. Rutter (Ed.), *Depression and Young People*. New York: Guilford.

Clayton, P.J. (1983). Gender and depression. In J. Angst (Ed.), *The origins of depression*. Berlin: Springer-Verlag.

Ferraro, K.F. (1984). Widowhood and social participation in later life: Isolation or compensation? *Research on Aging, 6,* 451–468.

Freedman, N., Bucci, W., & Elkowitz, E. (1982). Depression in a family practice elderly population. *American Geriatrics Society Journal, 30,* 372–377.

Gutmann, D. (1985). Beyond nurture: Developmental perspectives on the vital older woman. In J.K. Brown & V. Kerns (Eds.), *Her prime: A new view of middle-aged women*. South Hadley, MA: Bergin and Garvin.

Hale, W.D., & Cochran, C.D. (1983). Sex differences in patterns of self-reported psychopathology in the married elderly. *Journal of Clinical Psychology, 39,* 647–650.

Haug, M.R., Ford, A.B., & Sheafor, M. (Eds.). (1985). *The physical and mental health of aged women*. New York: Springer Publishing Co.

Henderson, A.S. (1983). Vulnerability to depression. In J. Angst (Ed.), *The Dahlem workshop on the origins of depression*. Berlin: Springer-Verlag.

Jarvik, L.F., & Perl, M. (1981). Overview of physiologic dysfunctions related to psychiatric problems in the elderly. In A.J. Levenson & R.C.W. Hall (Eds.), *Aging, Vol. 14*. New York: Raven Press.

Levy, S.M. (1980). The adjustment of the older woman: Effects of chronic ill health and attitudes toward retirement. *International Journal of Aging and Human Development, 12,* 93–110.

Lewinsohn, P.M., Fenn, D.S., Stanton, A.K., & Franklin, J. (1986). Relation of age at onset to duration of episode in unipolar depression. *Psychology and Aging, 1,* 63–68.

Lieberman, M.A., & Tobin, S.S. (1983). *The experience of old age*. New York: Basic Books.

Miller, M. (1979). A review of the research on geriatric suicide. *Death Education, 3,* 283–296.

Radloff, L.S., & Rae, D.S. (1981). Components of the sex difference in depression. In R.G. Simmons (Eds.), *Research in community and mental health, Vol. 2* (pp. 111–137). Greenwich, CT: JAI Press.

Sandler, A. (1984). Problems of development and adaptation in an elderly patient. *The Psychoanalytic Study of the Child, 39,* 471–489.

Sheldon, A. (1975). *Retirement, patterns and predictions* (DHEW No. ADM 74-79). Washington, DC: NIMH.

Streib, G.F., & Schneider, S.J. (1971). *Retirement in American society*. Ithaca, NY: Cornell University Press.

Szinovacz, M.E. (1983). Beyond the hearth: Older women and retirement. In E.W. Markson (Ed.), *Older women: Issues and prospects*. Lexington, MA: Lexington Books.

Weissman, M.M., & Myers, J.K. (1979). Depression in the elderly: Research directions in psychopathology, epidemiology, and treatment. *Journal of Geriatric Psychiatry, 12,* 187–202.

■ 18
"Old Wives' Tales": Retrospective Views of Elderly Women

LISA R. GREENBERG, Ph.D.

The focus of this investigation is the subjective experiences of older women. Specifically, to what extent do women in their 70s feel fulfilled and satisfied, as opposed to empty and depressed, and what do they report feeling at other times in their lives, in their mid-20s (young adulthood), and at age 50 (middle age)? Two groups of women were studied; one group was retired, having had a substantial work experience outside their homes, whereas the other group spent their adult lives as homemakers.

Some of the questions this study was intended to clarify include:

- Do elderly women report feeling more satisfied or dissatisfied with their lives?
- What are their sources of satisfaction and dissatisfaction? Are these sources in the present, e.g., having friends and a nice apartment, or in the past, e.g., having had a successful career?
- What relationship exists between a woman's reported experience of earlier times in her life and her reported experience of the present?
- Are there people who report always having been either basically content or depressed, or do people tend to report periods of both contentment and depression?
- Are these women basically content with the choices they made in their lives, or do they regret not having lived differently?
- Are retirees and homemakers equally content with their choices? If not, what differences exist?

In addition, I wanted to examine these findings in light of Erikson's (1963) theoretical formulation of "ego integrity vs. despair" as the final stage of the human life cycle.

Researchers (e.g., Palmore & Kivett, 1977; Palmore & Luikart, 1972), have begun to ask similar questions about the elderly. However, much of their research suffers from a lack of emphasis on the reported experiences of old people themselves. For example, in order to study "life satisfaction," the most logical first step would be to simply ask people about what in their life does and does not satisfy them. Many researchers, however, instead hand their subjects lengthy questionnaires, and thereby often end up with results that miss the forest and find only certain trees. One of the goals of this study was to avoid using old people only to confirm prematurely formulated theories about them, but instead to listen as they themselves describe how depressed or content they feel, and to what they attribute these feelings.

PROCEDURE

The subjects for this study consisted of 60 white, Jewish women between the ages of 70 and 79, of whom 30 were retired women and 30 were homemakers. To serve as a subject, a woman had to have been married for a minimum of five years at some point in her life, and had to report that she believed herself to be in good health and to have adequate financial resources. These questions were included to control for differences in the subjects' perceived health and income, which have accounted for much of the variance in many studies of the elderly (e.g., Jaslow, 1976; Palmore & Kivett, 1977).

Subjects were recruited through a large activity center for senior citizens in Brooklyn, New York, in 1981. The participation of all subjects was voluntary. Each subject was interviewed to gather data on age, work, and marital history. A structured interview and the Osgood Semantic Differential (Osgood, Suci, & Tanenbaum, 1957) were then administered. The Semantic Differential was administered four times, differentiating the concepts, "Work," "Self at Present," "Self at Age 25," and "Self at Age 50."

In the structured interview, the subject was asked to describe her present life, focusing on how satisfied she felt, how busy she was, how much contact she had with others, and how satisfying she found this contact to be. She was also asked to identify sources of satisfaction and dissatisfaction in her current life. She was then asked to describe her life in her mid-20s and to compare her feelings at that time with her present feelings, and to do the same for age 50. Finally, she was asked to identify the most satisfying decade of her life, and to discuss what, if anything, she would do differently, focusing on changes she would have made in her work life and in her personal life.

RESULTS

Many of the subjects in the study were immigrants to this country from various eastern European countries. Of the 30 retirees, almost all had been employed in either clerical or sales positions. The subjects had been married for between five and 58 years, with a mean of 39 years. The number of children the subjects had ranged from zero to three. Of the 42 subjects who were unmarried at the time the data were collected, almost all were widows. An average of almost 10 years had passed since the unmarried subjects had last been married. The retirees had worked an average of 31 years each, the homemakers, less than three. It had been over seven years on average since the retirees had been involved in paid employment.

Levels of Satisfaction

On the most general level, the results of this study indicate that the subjects were *not* a very depressed group. For the total sample, in the present as well as at ages 25 and 50, the subjects' mean satisfaction scores fell between "fairly satisfied" and "neutral" on the rating scale used. In fact, over 50 of the 60 subjects scored one of these two ratings, indicating that for a subject to feel either extremely satisfied or extremely dissatisfied was highly unusual.

It is possible that the high morale identified might have been an artifact of the selection process, which mitigated against the selection of very depressed subjects, and of the fact that the data are based on the subjects' recollections of a time as much as fifty years in the past. On the other hand, the congruence of these findings with those of other investigators (e.g., Cameron, 1967; Lieberman, 1970) counters the idea that this level of satisfaction is unusual.

Ambivalence and Denial

It should, however, be noted that scoring was done on the basis of the manifest content of the interview only, and this fact boosted satisfaction ratings somewhat, as it seemed clear that some subjects were more depressed than they felt comfortable admitting. In filling out the Semantic Differential, for example, a few subjects, when choosing between "painful" and "pleasurable" to describe themselves at present, made such comments as, "Well, it would be a shame to say 'painful,' so I'll say 'pleasurable'," reflecting an unwillingness to accept or acknowledge feelings that were less than positive. This difficulty in admitting to feelings of dissatisfaction seemed in some cases to be primarily intrapsychic, in that the subject could not admit her dissatisfaction to herself, and in other cases interpersonal, in that the subject was reluctant to admit her dissatisfaction to the interviewer.

The fact that this was a population of women essentially without choices also seems relevant to their difficulty in acknowledging depression and dissatisfaction. Home, husband, and particularly children had clearly been their major focus for nearly their entire adult lives. This was the case for those classified as retirees, as well as for the homemakers. In fact, subjects seldom spontaneously mentioned work at all, though when the experimenter raised the topic with women who had worked, their comments were generally positive.

Clearly homemaking was more gratifying for some women than for others, but, gratifying or not, almost none of these women saw any other possible way of life, particularly in their earlier years. As one subject, describing her mid-20s, phrased it, "You didn't know from anything, how could you be unhappy? Like a caveman, he was happy in his cave, everybody believed the same." There was, in short, massive social support for this home-and-hearth emphasis, and any dissatisfaction or underlying depression seems to have been ignored as much as possible.

This is in marked contrast to the current social climate, in which women frequently expect to have a wide range of options open to them, to choose a life that they find satisfying, and to verbalize their feelings of both satisfaction and dissatisfaction. The women in this study, however, particularly when they were young adults, simply assumed that they would uncomplainingly fulfill the roles set out for them, and, by and large, they did so. It was further assumed that these roles were basically satisfying ones, but, if they were not satisfying to a particular woman, this seems to have been viewed as unimportant. One can surmise that there were casualties—women who became severely depressed, alcoholic, or disturbed—but there were no indications that this was the case for any of the women in this study.

Even in their 70s, with their years as wives and mothers largely behind them, many of the subjects were unable to acknowledge ambivalence about this type of life. Many found it very difficult to acknowledge any negative feelings at all about their experiences, and husbands in particular were widely idealized. A few subjects were clearly struggling with guilt over feeling relieved by a husband's death. Others did talk about difficulties with their traditional lifestyle, often focusing on the burden of caring for young children. A very few said explicitly that they regretted having had children; one said children "aren't bad, but you give your whole life to them."

One reflection of the difficulty for these women in acknowledging ambivalence about their lives is that only about half the subjects freely acknowledged any regrets at all, while approximately 23% were uncertain and 20% denied any regrets. Some of those who denied any regrets idealized their experience, e.g., "everything was beautiful in my life," or seemed to feel helpless about their lives, e.g., "I couldn't have done it any differently." One woman said that, given the chance, she "wouldn't want to do it over again." Others who denied regrets did so more in the context of feeling generally pleased with how they had lived, and regretted nothing of major importance.

Of the regrets that were expressed, most related to the desire to have been better educated and more work-oriented, hinting perhaps that the wife and mother role was not as all-satisfying as was sometimes indicated, but also perhaps reflecting the current social climate in which working women have come to be more highly valued. The regrets varied in intensity and importance to the woman. One of the more bitter and depressed women said, "I should have been somebody, I really should have been somebody, if I had the chance, I didn't have the chance, let's face it."

Homemakers and Retirees: Differing Perceptions

There were a very few exceptions to this general tendency among the women to view work as unimportant. A small number of them spontaneously mentioned their work as satisfying and important; not surprisingly, these were women who were either unmarried or in stormy marriages at the points in their lives at which they came to value their work.

One of these unusual subjects, for example, described her 50s as the best time in her life because she had ended an unhappy marriage by divorce, her children were doing well, and her work as a dressmaker was satisfying. As she put it, "I had it my own way." Another subject described being very satisfied as a housewife for 20 years and feeling terrified about having to work after her husband's death. She ended up finding work very exciting and spoke of having proved that "I had a brain" and "I had the ability to do whatever I had to do."

This study did find differences between the retirees and the home-makers, despite the general lack of importance of work for this sample. Though the groups were equally content overall with how they had chosen to live their lives, they did not report equal levels of satisfaction at each stage of life. It was hypothesized that the homemaking subjects might be more likely to face a personal crisis in middle age around the "empty nest" issue, while the workers might avoid this but face a later crisis at retire-ment. However, an interaction effect, concerning degree of satisfaction, demonstrated just the opposite: the homemakers felt more content than the workers at age 50, and less content at present.

The main reason for this seems to be that middle age was experienced as a positive time for subjects in terms of their families. The fact of children leaving home did not indicate to these women that they were giving up the mothering role and was frequently viewed positively. Many subjects spoke of pleasure in planning weddings and graduations; they relished retaining the role of mother and staying highly involved with their children's lives, while at the same time not having a great deal of day-to-day responsibility for them. Being able to be more involved with one's husband again was seen as another advantage of this time.

On the other hand, at age 50 some of the retirees had either recently lost husbands and returned to work, or had already spent a good many years working in low-paying jobs, and may have been feeling particularly frus-trated at this point in their working lives. The retired women seem to feel proud in the present of having worked in the past, but did not much enjoy work at the time they were engaged in it.

In general, then, and contrary to predictions, age 50 was experienced positively by those highly involved with families, but less positively by those involved in work. In the present, however, the workers, who were dissatisfied at 50, can enjoy their retirement, whereas the homemakers feel deprived by the less intense involvement with their families. The home-makers may also find other pursuits less satisfying, either because the pleasures of leisure time have worn thin, or because they are less experi-enced in finding gratification in other than traditional roles.

This finding, that retirees in their 70s are more satisified than home-makers in their 70s, indicates that there may actually be psychosocial benefits of working that carry over into old age, as was reported by Jaslow (1976) in his study of retired women.

In addition to their pride in having worked, and their pleasure in their new-found leisure time, work may have provided the retirees with par-ticular assets that have helped them cope with old age, and which the homemakers have never had the opportunity to develop. These might in-clude, for example, skills in developing relationships with new people or in coping with unfamiliar situations. The retirees also had greater exposure to roles other than those of housewife and mother, and this may be helpful in old age, when the housewife-mother role becomes less consuming.

Sources of Satisfaction at Different Ages

Homemakers and retirees did not differ in which aspects of their lives they identified as satisfying or dissatisfying, either in the present or at the previous ages. Sources of satisfaction and dissatisfaction did, however, change somewhat from stage to stage.

With regard to satisfaction, there was found to be a greater emphasis on health issues in the present than at ages 25 and 50. Indicators of financial security, such as "having a nice apartment," were mentioned as satisfying about the same percentage of times across the three stages, as were issues concerning family and children, though in this case the content varied somewhat. When describing age 25, subjects tended to speak of the joys of the day-by-day experience of marriage and of having small children, whereas by 50, the accomplishments of one's children, often including marriages and graduations, were reported as important. The pleasure of being alone again with one's husband was also mentioned in describing age 50. In describing the present, the accomplishments of one's children continued to be important. These women often spoke of their children and grandchildren, either implicitly or explicitly, as important both because of present relationships with them, and as a source of pride.

At age 25, the day-to-day pleasures of home life were often mentioned, as in this quote: "I guess I was just an old housewife that people object to very strongly today, this was my time, and this was what I loved to do." The combination of working, dating, and being involved with friends was also mentioned, as were positive experiences with one's family of origin. A sense of a high level of activity was often implicit in these responses.

At age 50, a few subjects mentioned work as satisfying. Relationships with friends, and various social activities, such as card games and travel, were brought up more often.

In discussing the present, friends and social activities were again mentioned, with "The Center" clearly an important focus for many subjects. Volunteer work, and the corresponding sense of being helpful, were important to some subjects. Some subjects also expressed a sense of satisfaction that they had "reached this point in life," one saying, "If I am the way I am with all I went through, then I am good." Another was proud of "having come up in the world." A prominent lifestyle theme at this age concerned the sense of freedom, the feeling that "I do what I feel like doing."

Sources of Dissatisfaction at Different Ages

Sources of dissatisfaction at different ages differed more than did the sources of satisfaction. Again, health issues were mentioned significantly more often in the present than at other ages. Generally, these were either concerns about future health problems, or complaints about a particular current problem, such as arthritis or a visual impairment. Whereas health problems were of minimal concern at age 25, by age 50, a substantial minority of subjects cited health as a source of dissatisfaction. These references tended to be to either hysterectomies or mastectomies.

Financial issues were of concern to many more subjects at age 25 than at any other point. It will be recalled that this population was selected in part on the basis of financial security in the present. The greater financial problems at age 25 were clearly related to the Great Depression, which affected most subjects just as they were marrying and beginning their families.

Children were cited as a source of dissatisfaction most often when subjects discussed the present. At times the concern centered around family conflicts, but more often the subject reported worrying about a particular child or grandchild, such as a son who was getting divorced or a sick daughter. The extent to which most subjects were involved with the activities of their middle-aged children was striking, and is reminiscent of the finding of Lowenthal, Thurner, Chiriboga, et al. (1975). Their female subjects were much more likely than their male subjects to perceive an event involving someone else as either a positive or a negative stress. Also related is the work of Gilligan (1982), who described the tendency of women, in contrast to men, to focus their lives around relationships with others. One or two subjects explicitly wished to be closer to their children, and it seemed likely that this was the unspoken wish of many others who seemed highly focused on what was happening in their children's lives.

In discussing age 50, subjects also spoke of worries abut their children, and there seemed to be particular concern about their children not "making good" in the adult world. These concerns probably related to ambivalence about the possibility of their children remaining dependent on them, as well as fears about what it would reflect about their parenting if their children failed to succeed. Dissatisfactions voiced about children when discussing age 25 were usually about the restrictions imposed by having small children.

At 25, and for a smaller group of subjects at 50, there was dissatisfaction about living life at a very hectic pace. There were other, less frequent, sources of dissatisfaction at these ages, including disagreements with parents about a potential husband, a husband's bad temper, and an ill mother. A very small number of subjects complained about unsatisfying jobs.

Complaints about one's general style of living were discussed most frequently in the subjects' present lives, and probably provide the clearest window into sources of depression for these women.

Loneliness was one theme: the lack of a spouse, or of any relationship with a man, was mentioned frequently. One subject went so far as to say, "The Indians are smart to kill wives when their husbands die, especially at this age." Some subjects spoke more generally of the pain of not feeling close to anybody; this often seemed to be the flip side of the positive sense of freedom experienced at this time. Several subjects felt that it was harder to develop new friendships at the present time than it had been at other points in their lives. Boredom, and the inability to do things one used to enjoy were mentioned. Fears about crime and health problems leading to greater dependency in the future were also raised as sources of concern. One subject spoke eloquently about feeling that she, as an old person, was "looked down on" because she was no longer "in the mainstream."

None of the subjects mentioned religion as a source of satisfaction. With the exception of one subject, who reported that sex had still been a source of satisfaction at age 50, and another, who described an illegal abortion as a crisis in her mid-20s, almost no mention was made of any topic related to sex. Death was another topic seldom mentioned. One subject said "the only thing I have to look forward to is to die." A very small number of subjects mentioned not feeling concerned about death, saying that they were content with their lives and realized that they might die at any time.

Past vs. Present Orientation

One question raised in this study concerned whether the sources of satisfaction and dissatisfaction in the present lives of elderly women relate more to past or to present experiences.

The answer is that the subjects studied clearly reported more sources of both satisfaction and dissatisfaction in the present than in the past, and were generally oriented to experiences in their present. The only exception was in the relationships of the subjects with their children, which can be viewed as rooted in both past and present. The relatively few sources from the past that were mentioned usually dealt with feeling proud of something one had accomplished. A few subjects reported something from the past as a source of dissatisfaction, e.g., "a rejection I suffered a couple of years ago." In general, these women seemed strongly oriented to the present.

Consistency of Level of Satisfaction Over Time

While these data indicate that, on average, the present, young adulthood, and middle age were experienced as equally satisfying, these figures do not show how a particular subject's level of satisfaction may have varied throughout her life.

There seem to be roughly three patterns regarding consistency of level of satisfaction among individual subjects. Some women reported a relatively constant, fairly high level of satisfaction throughout their lives, broken occasionally by a particular event—most often a loss, such as the death of a spouse or child. Most of these women described themselves as recovering fairly quickly from these traumas, and some spoke with pride about their resiliency. One woman said, for example, "I'm a happy-go-lucky . . . the hardest times we had, I took it easy."

Other women had longer positive and negative periods, related to their general life situation rather than to a particular incident. This group includes a subject who had difficulty relating to others in her 20s and was clearly quite depressed, but who then felt happier as she grew older, and a subject who had been satisfied throughout her life, but experienced old age as very difficult. Some women combined these two patterns. This group includes a subject who was generally satisfied for most of her life, except for a painful period around a loss at age 50, from which she recovered, but who then experienced a more general, longer-lasting sense of dissatisfaction in old age.

There were also a few subjects who demonstrated a different pattern, mostly those who failed to recover successfully from a particularly difficult event, and who seemed to remain chronically depressed following this event. A clear example of this type was a woman who had never been able to return to her prior level of functioning following the death of a daughter over 20 years before.

What Contributes to Satisfaction?

Looking at all the data gathered for this study makes it possible to come to some conclusions about what contributes to a sense of contentment, rather than depression, in old age.

The first critical fact is that these women, including almost all those classified as retired workers, identified themselves primarily as wives and mothers.

It must then be noted that, as these women aged, their life situations gradually changed, until, by the time they were interviewed in their 70s, their children had left home, and, in most cases, their husbands had died.

Caring for a small apartment was most of what remained of what they had regarded as their life's work.

Their task, then, was to refocus on, and to learn to value, aspects of life other than those which had always provided them with an identity. More precisely, the task was to decrease the amount of gratification expected from others, in particular children, and to increase the amount of gratification received from oneself.

This task could be accomplished in a number of ways. Some subjects placed new emphasis on aspects of their lives that had always existed, but which had been less salient in the past. The increased attention to physical health may be explained in this way, as can some subjects' expressions of satisfaction from reflecting on their past achievements, or their increased involvement in hobbies and activities that had been of minor interest in the past.

Other subjects developed and focused on new attitudes, values and activities, while some developed their refocused lives around a combination of both old and new experiences.

Not surprisingly, some subjects seemed to have made a transition from focus-on-other to focus-on-self more successfully than others. Some subjects seemed to be in the midst of trying to make the transition to a new focus on themselves. One recently widowed subject said, "I'm not really happy, I'm just trying to be a person." One could surmise that she was trying to learn to be a different kind of person than she had been in the past. Still other subjects spoke of "trying to make the best of things," but seemed unable to learn to do this successfully.

Viewing the data in this light helps to clarify the somewhat surprising finding that, though the subjects reported themselves to have been equally satisfied throughout their lives, their responses to the Semantic Differential indicate that they view themselves now as less active, less powerful, and less good than at earlier ages.

The explanation seems to be that at present, these women are less active and powerful in their dealings with the world, and even, in terms of fulfilling the homemaker-wife-mother roles they had always valued, less good, but—to the extent that they have learned to value other aspects of themselves and their lives—they may be equally well satisfied.

Along the same lines, while an equal number of subjects reported being satisfied with their levels of activity and contact across the three ages studied, fewer subjects have very high levels of activity and contact in the present than at other times, and more subjects have lower levels. In other words, they are more satisfied with a lower level of activty and contact now than they might have been in the past. This may well indicate a redirection of one's focus to different aspects of life, involving, for some, less activity and contact, but providing the same degree of satisfaction.

It is worth asking what factors correlate with the ability to refocus one-self in order to age successfully. The fact that the retirees are somewhat more satisfied than the homemakers in old age indicates that having worked may be of some value, possibly in that it gave these women a chance to experience a role other than that of homemaker-wife-mother. Even if this role never became very salient, or very satisfying, the retirees did have greater experience in finding at least some gratification in a wider range of activities than did the homemakers.

Other factors may be involved. Perhaps the women who found the homemaker-wife-mother roles less satisfying were the ones more able to embrace the opportunity presented to them in old age to find other sourc-es of satisfaction.

One can also hypothesize that even for those women for whom tra-ditional roles were basically satisfying, the ability to acknowledge am-bivalence about these roles might have made a subject more comfortable shifting the focus of her satisfactions in old age. The subjects in this study varied considerably in their ability to acknowledge this ambivalence, rang-ing from those who clearly and explicitly wished for very different lives, to those who idealized long-dead husbands and the lifestyles they repre-sented.

The conclusion of Lowenthal et al. (1975) is generally in agreement with the views expressed here. Their oldest women subjects were in their "preretirement" years, and the authors report that, as these women aged and were freed from the obligations of their traditional roles, they came to derive their sense of self less from their relationships with others and more from their own abilities and feelings. These authors believe that, with age, the quality rather than the scope of personal relationships becomes in-creasingly important, and furthermore, that removing unwanted tasks and relationships from one's life to establish a successful old age may be a major developmental task. They suggest a decline in "emotional complexity," though not in happiness, across the life course. Lowenthal (1980), in an up-date on the subjects reported on in 1975, also selected as one group of peo-ple likely to be satisfied with their ways of life, those who "reordered their commitments."

However, the current study shows that, to a large extent at least, willingly relinquishing tasks, relationships and roles as one ages is not the issue. On the contrary, these tend to drop away of their own accord, when one's spouse and other family and friends die, and children grow up and move on. The developmental task instead is to come to a successful means of dealing with these changes that are essentially out of one's control.

Sucessfully dealing with these changes involves focusing oneself on new aspects of self and world, generally on one's own abilities and feelings, rather than on other people. This increased focus on the self and decreased focus on others may look like decreased "emotional complexity," but the relationship with oneself may be more complex than at other times. Several subjects, in describing why their present was better than other times of their lives, made comments along the lines of these: "I have more understanding about life . . . can analyze life more." "I would say I feel much more relaxed and secure now . . . I'm more in with myself." The pleasures of having time to reflect, rather than being caught up in a flood of activities, were also mentioned.

This is not to imply, however, that successfully refocusing on oneself in old age requires a less physically active, more contemplative lifestyle. Some subjects spoke enthusiastically about being involved in dance groups every day, and had clearly found a satisfying, new, active lifestyle.

The relationship of the findings of this study and the ideas discussed here to Erikson's (1963) formulation of old age is worth considering. Erikson's formulation suggests that different experiences in the past, in the form of different degrees of involvement in paid employment, would lead the subjects studied to characterize their essentially similar present lives as different.

A difference between the two groups' present experience was indeed found, in terms of their levels of satisfaction. While this could be interpreted, in line with Erikson's theory, to indicate that the groups differ in their current levels of satisfaction because they look back on their pasts with varying amounts of satisfaction, it seems more reasonable to suggest that differences in present levels of satisfaction are instead the result of the fact that different life experiences prepared subjects in different degrees to cope with the stresses of aging, enabling them to manage their similar present lives with varying degrees of success.

In terms of these sources of satisfaction, a limited degree of support can be found for Erikson's views. Though this study did not reveal the increased interest in religion and ethics with age found by some investigators, some subjects did mention pride and satisfaction from helping others and pride in their accomplishments. One subject seemed to be speaking very much in Erikson's terms when she said of her present, "I'm more at peace, I really don't worry, there's nothing to be afraid of."

This paper does support Erikson theory that there is an important intrapsychic achievement which occurs for some people in old age. Erikson labels this achievement "ego integrity" and views it both as a transcendence and as a valuing of one's entire life.

The current study describes a key transition from focus-on-other to focus-on-self. This construct is similar to ego integrity in that it involves an increased valuing of oneself and one's life, but seems, at least for many people, to lack the quality of transcendence, which tends to take older people out of the mainstream of life. Although having achieved ego integrity in Erikson's terms would seem to imply a withdrawal of psychic energy from the world and a readiness for death, a refocusing on oneself can easily be manifested by a lifestyle full of active involvement in a wide range of activities. It seems that the determinants of genuine life satisfaction are more internal than external, particularly for healthy people with adequate incomes. This study demonstrates that many people can feel satisfied in many different kinds of lives, provided they have learned to value their own choices.

REFERENCES

Cameron, P. (1967). Ego strength and happiness of the aged. *Journal of Gerontology, 22,* 199–202.

Erikson, E.H. (1963). *Childhood and society.* New York: W.W. Norton & Co.

Gilligan, C. (1982). *In a different voice.* Cambridge, MA: Harvard University Press.

Jaslow, P. (1976). Employment, retirement and morale among older women. *Journal of Gerontology, 31*(2), 212–218.

Lieberman, L.R. (1970). Life satisfaction in the young and the old. *Psychological Reports, 27,* 75–79.

Lowenthal, M.F. (1980). Changing hierarchies of commitments in adulthood. In N.J. Smelser & E.H. Erikson (Eds.), *Themes of work and love in adulthood.* Cambridge, MA: Harvard University Press.

Lowenthal, M.F., Thurnher, M., Chiriboga, D., et al. (1975). *Four stages of life. A comparative study of men and women facing transitions.* Washington: Jossey-Bass.

Osgood, C.E., Suci, G.E., & Tannenbaum, P.H. (1957). *The measurement of meaning.* Chicago: University of Illinois Press.

Palmore, E., & Kivett, V. (1977). Change in life satisfaction: A longitudinal study of persons aged 46–70. *Journal of Gerontology, 32*(3), 311–316.

Palmore, E., & Luikart, C. (1972). Health and social factors related to life satisfaction. *Journal of Health and Social Behavior, 13,* 68–80.

Index

Index